# SAT 2400

# 2400

## in JUST 7 STEPS

*Shaan Patel*

New York  Chicago  San Francisco  Lisbon  London  Madrid  Mexico City
Milan  New Delhi  San Juan  Seoul  Singapore  Sydney  Toronto

**The McGraw·Hill** Companies

Copyright © 2012 by The McGraw-Hill Companies, Inc. All rights reserved. Printed
in the United States of America. Except as permitted under the United States Copyright
Act of 1976, no part of this publication may be reproduced or distributed in any form
or by any means, or stored in a database or retrieval system, without the prior written
permission of the publisher.

1  2  3  4  5  6  7  8  9  10  11  12  13  14  15    QFR/QFR    1  9  8  7  6  5  4  3  2

ISBN      978-0-07-178099-5
MHID        0-07-178099-8

e-ISBN   978-0-07-178100-8
e-MHID     0-07-178100-5

Library of Congress Control Number 2012931067

SAT is a registered trademark of the College Entrance Examination Board, which was
not involved in the production of, and does not endorse, this product.

McGraw-Hill products are available at special quantity discounts to use as premiums
and sales promotions or for use in corporate training programs. To contact a
representative, please e-mail us at bulksales@mcgraw-hill.com.

This book is printed on acid-free paper.

# Contents

# Master WYPAD and other keys to success on SAT Reading   133

# Use unconventional methods to score high on SAT Math  285

# Practice with a simulated SAT test  361

## Use 2400 Strategies to analyze your answers   427

## Do's and don'ts for test day   453

# Acknowledgments

I kindly thank everyone who has helped bring this project to fruition:

- My parents, Bharat and Gita, for their unparalleled love and support
- My brother and sister, Sunny and Jetoon, for their unlimited goodwill
- My literary agent, Grace Freedson, for making my dream a reality
- My editors Chuck Wall, Daniel Franklin, and Terry Yokota, for their contributions to the editorial and production quality of this book
- My family and friends, for their encouragement and optimism

# Learn how to study for the SAT

Dear SAT Test Taker,

**Welcome!** You have just picked up the only full-length SAT preparation manual written by a student who achieved a perfect 2400 score in high school. *SAT 2400 in Just 7 Steps* offers an innovative, practical, unparalleled approach to SAT preparation. If you follow the methods I used to achieve a perfect 2400, you will surely be successful.

**Who am I?** Well, on paper I'm a student who scored a perfect 2400 on his SAT, was admitted to prestigious universities, won over $230,000 in college scholarships, and was awarded honors such as National Merit Finalist, *USA Today*'s All-USA High School Academic Team Honorable Mention, Presidential Scholar, and even Homecoming King.

**But who am I *really*?** Well, I am just like you. Although I now have some impressive honors, I once had no clue. As a teenager, I spent a lot of time playing sports, procrastinating on homework, text messaging, devouring fast food, checking Facebook—and knowing hardly anything about the SAT. I attended various urban public schools and lived in a small, inner-city motel that my family owned. My parents emigrated from India to America in the late 1980s and never attended college in the U.S.

Before I began uncovering the strategies, methods, and approaches necessary to do well on the SAT, I was no genius at taking standardized tests. In fact, on the first practice SAT I ever took, I only scored 1760. That's when I began to scour every SAT prep book I could find, read loads of college-prep information, and pester high-scoring SAT students for their test-taking secrets. Eventually, I became a self-taught SAT expert myself. Luckily, I've done all the hard work for you: I've put everything you need to know about how to succeed on the SAT in this simple, easy-to-read book.

**So who am I *now*?** I'm your personal SAT 2400 tutor. Of the 2,000 or so SAT "experts" who have achieved a perfect 2400, few have shared their wisdom. But I will teach you every SAT rule and strategy I used so that you too can conquer this difficult test.

SAT preparation is not easy, and it takes a substantial amount of time. I had to balance AP courses, sports, and after-school activities with SAT preparation. It wasn't fun. But I promise that your effort will be rewarded with major score improvements. Best of all, I will be with you every step of the way on your journey to ace the SAT.

Sincerely,

*Shaan Patel*

SAT 2400 test taker, regular everyday student, and your personal SAT tutor

# Four key principles

Four key principles are essential to successful SAT preparation. You must follow these four key principles in order to advance from *ordinary* SAT prep to *perfect* SAT prep!

**Step 1**
Learn how
to study
for the SAT

2

## Principle 1 • *Learn 2400 Strategies*

*2400 Strategies* are methods and approaches to tackle different question types on the SAT. I developed the strategies in two ways: (1) I pulled strategies directly from the SAT notebook I kept in high school. (2) I reworked every SAT question type, but this time I recorded my subtle thought processes as I solved each problem. *2400 Strategies* will allow you to literally peek at the notes of a perfect 2400 SAT student!

## Principle 2 • *Study 2400 Examples*

*2400 Examples* clarify SAT concepts. You will learn by seeing concrete examples of SAT strategies in action. *2400 Examples* show how to use *2400 Strategies* on actual SAT problems.

## Principle 3 • *Complete 2400 Practice Problem Sets*

So that you can practice what you have learned, SAT problem types are typically followed by *2400 Practice Problem Sets*. The best way to improve your SAT score is to practice the strategies you learn. Complete each *2400 Practice Problem Set* to get a sense of how to use *2400 Strategies* on real SAT questions.

## Principle 4 • *Concentrate on 2400 Review*

This principle is often overlooked in SAT preparation. Working practice problems is fine, but if you practice without taking the time to figure out why you are making certain mistakes, you will have a difficult time improving. How can you identify your weak areas? The answer is *2400 Review*: the regular reexamination of the *2400 Strategies*, *2400 Examples*, and *2400 Practice Problem Sets* that you have already studied. You will learn more about this principle in **Work together: 2400 Practice and 2400 Review** (page 11).

# The SAT: the basics

Every student should know a few essential facts before taking the SAT.

## What is the SAT?

The SAT is a college entrance test that is produced by the College Board and required by most U.S. universities. The test consists of three subjects: Writing, Reading, and Mathematics. Each section is worth 800 points, for a total possible score of 2400.

## What is the format of the SAT?

The SAT contains 10 sections.

- ◄ 3 Writing sections
- ◄ 3 Reading sections
- ◄ 3 Math sections
- ◄ 1 variable section

The variable section, which can be Writing, Reading, or Math, doesn't count toward your score; it is used for diagnostic test purposes only. You will encounter four sections of one subject on the SAT. Because there is no way to determine which of the four sections is the variable section, you must complete all 10 sections of the test.

## How many questions are on the SAT?

The SAT requires that you write one essay and answer 170 questions.

- ◄ Writing (800 points)
  - 1 essay
  - 49 multiple-choice questions
- ◄ Reading (800 points)
  - 67 multiple-choice questions
- ◄ Math (800 points)
  - 44 multiple-choice questions
  - 10 student-produced response questions

## How is your raw score determined?

To determine your raw score, you add one point for every question you answer correctly, subtract ¼ point for every question you answer incorrectly, and add 0 points for every question you leave blank.

Let's say, of the 67 multiple-choice Reading questions, you answered 50 questions correctly, 14 incorrectly, and left three questions blank. Your raw score would be calculated as follows:

### SAT Reading raw score

| | | | |
|---|---|---|---|
| 50 correct | × (+1) | = | +50 |
| 14 incorrect | × (−¼) | = | − 3.5 |
| 3 blank | × (+0) | = | + 0 |
| | | | +46.5 |

The SAT is generous and rounds up, so your raw score is actually +47!

NOTE You aren't penalized ¼ point for incorrect answers on the student-produced response section of SAT Math.

# How is your scaled score determined?

Once your SAT raw score is known, the College Board uses a statistical method known as "equating" to calculate your SAT scaled score. The equated scale varies from one test to another in order to account for differences in the tests' difficulty. For example, an SAT Reading raw score of +47 may be equivalent to a scaled score of 590 on the October SAT, but may be equivalent to a score of 610 on the June SAT. A sample conversion table for SAT raw and scaled scores is shown below. The conversion table for your SAT will be slightly different.

## Conversion table for SAT raw and scaled scores (example)

| Reading | | Math | | Writing multiple-choice* | |
|---|---|---|---|---|---|
| RAW | SCALED | RAW | SCALED | RAW | SCALED |
| 67 | 800 | 54 | 800 | 49 | 80 |
| 66 | 800 | 53 | 790 | 48 | 78 |
| 65 | 800 | 52 | 760 | 47 | 75 |
| 64 | 790 | 51 | 740 | 46 | 73 |
| 63 | 770 | 50 | 720 | 45 | 71 |
| 62 | 760 | 49 | 710 | 44 | 70 |
| 61 | 740 | 48 | 700 | 43 | 68 |
| 60 | 730 | 47 | 690 | 42 | 67 |
| 59 | 720 | 46 | 680 | 41 | 66 |
| 58 | 700 | 45 | 670 | 40 | 64 |
| 57 | 690 | 44 | 660 | 39 | 63 |
| 56 | 680 | 43 | 650 | 38 | 62 |
| 55 | 680 | 42 | 640 | 37 | 61 |
| 54 | 670 | 41 | 640 | 36 | 60 |
| 53 | 660 | 40 | 630 | 35 | 59 |
| 52 | 650 | 39 | 620 | 34 | 58 |
| 51 | 640 | 38 | 610 | 33 | 57 |
| 50 | 630 | 37 | 600 | 32 | 56 |
| 49 | 620 | 36 | 600 | 31 | 55 |
| 48 | 620 | 35 | 590 | 30 | 54 |
| 47 | 610 | 34 | 580 | 29 | 53 |
| 46 | 600 | 33 | 570 | 28 | 52 |
| 45 | 600 | 32 | 560 | 27 | 51 |
| 44 | 590 | 31 | 550 | 26 | 50 |
| 43 | 580 | 30 | 540 | 25 | 49 |
| 42 | 570 | 29 | 540 | 24 | 48 |
| 41 | 570 | 28 | 530 | 23 | 47 |
| 40 | 560 | 27 | 520 | 22 | 46 |
| 39 | 550 | 26 | 510 | 21 | 45 |
| 38 | 550 | 25 | 500 | 20 | 44 |
| 37 | 540 | 24 | 490 | 19 | 43 |
| 36 | 530 | 23 | 480 | 18 | 42 |
| 35 | 530 | 22 | 480 | 17 | 41 |
| 34 | 520 | 21 | 470 | 16 | 40 |

*Your final Writing score is determined by factoring 70% of your Writing multiple-choice scaled score and 30% of your Essay score.

## How often is the SAT administered?

The SAT is offered seven times a year, usually during the following months: October, November, December, January, March, May, and June.

## How much time does the SAT take?

The SAT takes a total of 3 hours and 45 minutes to complete. You will probably spend more than four hours at the testing center, however, because of intro-

| Reading | | Math | | Writing multiple-choice* | |
|---|---|---|---|---|---|
| RAW | SCALED | RAW | SCALED | RAW | SCALED |
| 33 | 520 | 20 | 460 | 15 | 39 |
| 32 | 510 | 19 | 450 | 14 | 38 |
| 31 | 500 | 18 | 440 | 13 | 38 |
| 30 | 500 | 17 | 430 | 12 | 37 |
| 29 | 490 | 16 | 420 | 11 | 36 |
| 28 | 480 | 15 | 420 | 10 | 35 |
| 27 | 480 | 14 | 410 | 9 | 34 |
| 26 | 470 | 13 | 400 | 8 | 33 |
| 25 | 460 | 12 | 390 | 7 | 32 |
| 24 | 460 | 11 | 380 | 6 | 31 |
| 23 | 450 | 10 | 370 | 5 | 30 |
| 22 | 440 | 9 | 360 | 4 | 29 |
| 21 | 440 | 8 | 350 | 3 | 27 |
| 20 | 430 | 7 | 330 | 2 | 26 |
| 19 | 420 | 6 | 320 | 1 | 24 |
| 18 | 410 | 5 | 310 | 0 | 22 |
| 17 | 410 | 4 | 290 | −1 | 20 |
| 16 | 400 | 3 | 280 | −2 | 20 |
| 15 | 390 | 2 | 260 | −3 | 20 |
| 14 | 380 | 1 | 240 | −4 | 20 |
| 13 | 380 | 0 | 220 | −5 | 20 |
| 12 | 370 | −1 | 200 | −6 | 20 |
| 11 | 360 | −2 | 200 | | |
| 10 | 350 | −3 | 200 | | |
| 9 | 340 | −4 | 200 | | |
| 8 | 330 | −5 | 200 | | |
| 7 | 320 | −6 | 200 | | |
| 6 | 310 | | | | |
| 5 | 300 | | | | |
| 4 | 290 | | | | |
| 3 | 270 | | | | |
| 2 | 260 | | | | |
| 1 | 240 | | | | |
| 0 | 220 | | | | |

ductory test instructions and procedures, as well as short breaks between sections. The amount of time varies from section to section, as follows:

One 25-minute Essay section
One 25-minute Writing section
Two 25-minute Reading sections
Two 25-minute Math sections
One 20-minute Reading section
One 20-minute Math section
One 10-minute Writing section
One 25-minute variable section (Writing, Reading, or Math)

The order of sections differs from test to test.

## How important is the SAT?

College admissions officers use SAT scores as one of many important factors when determining which students are accepted into their institution. Other factors include high-school grade point average, class rank/standing, difficulty of course load, extracurricular activities, community service, recommendation letters, essays, and scores from other standardized tests, such as the SAT subject tests.

The importance of a solid SAT score should not be minimized. Every year, college admissions becomes more and more competitive. As a result, the SAT—one of the few standard measures colleges have to rely on—is crucial to the admissions process. A good SAT score can also open doors to private, state, and university scholarships, as it did for me.

Ultimately, the importance of the SAT depends on your goals. Are you aiming to attend an Ivy League school? Do you need a certain score to obtain an athletic scholarship? Whatever your situation is, it is important to take the SAT seriously.

## How many times should you take the SAT?

Technically, you can take the SAT every time it's offered. However, how many times you *should* take the SAT is controversial. Before 2008, students had to send all their SAT scores when applying to a college, which meant that college admissions officers may have frowned on students taking the SAT "too many" times. In 2008, however, the College Board launched an initiative known as Score Choice. This allows a student to pick which SAT score he or she wants to send to a college. (Note, however, that some colleges do not accept Score Choice.) Personally, I advise students not to take the SAT more than four times. Taking the test five or more times causes unnecessary stress and takes time away from other aspects of the college application process that you should be focusing on.

### What is the Question-and-Answer Service?

If you take the SAT in October, January, or May, you may order the actual test you took from the College Board's Question-and-Answer Service (QAS). I highly recommend ordering this service: If you plan to retake the SAT, this detailed score report will help you target areas for improvement.

QAS should not be confused with the SAS (Student Answer Service), which provides a list of question numbers that you answered correctly or incorrectly. Since the SAS doesn't include the actual questions of the SAT you took, ordering it is pointless.

# The big myth

I have one serious issue with the College Board. The company claims that your performance on the SAT is directly related to your readiness for college: If you do well on the SAT, then you are academically prepared for college. In my view, and in the opinion of many others who have studied the test, this claim is false.

Your performance on the SAT only measures how well you take the SAT. That's it! Your SAT score is not an indication of how smart you are. If your current SAT score is low, don't be discouraged. The SAT tests very specific subject matter, most of which you are not explicitly taught in high school anyway. Nevertheless, the College Board maintains that the SAT is an excellent indicator of what you have learned in high school. They say, "[The SAT] tests your skills in reading, writing, and mathematics—the same subjects you're learning in high school," "[The SAT] measures what you already know," and "If you take rigorous, challenging courses in high school, you'll be ready for the test." Nothing could be further from the truth.

A tough high school course load does not guarantee a good score on the SAT. The truth is, you can diligently train for the SAT, and you will find that most of what I will teach you in this book has not been taught to you in high school.

# Essential materials

You will need the following materials before you start preparing for the SAT.

- ◄ **This book** *SAT 2400 in Just 7 Steps* will be your source of no-nonsense strategies, methods, and approaches for SAT preparation.

- ◄ **A 2400 Review notebook** Purchase a notebook with at least 150 sheets, divided into five sections. As you prepare for the SAT, you will use this notebook to take notes on questions/areas you have trouble with, to list vocabulary words you need to memorize, to prepare your essay ahead of

time, to create your own personalized test methods, and more. Label the five sections as follows:

1. SAT essay
2. Writing multiple-choice
3. Sentence completion/vocabulary
4. Passage-based reading
5. Math

Alternatively, you can buy five small notebooks, but it will probably be more helpful if you have all of your SAT notes in one notebook.

◄ **Practice SAT tests** Practice makes perfect. But you need something to practice on before you can become perfect: practice SAT questions. This book provides hundreds of practice SAT questions to hone your SAT skills, but you will need more! Buy a book that has several SAT practice tests, or locate free online tests. You will need at least 10 practice SAT tests.

◄ **The College Board's Official SAT Question of the Day** Every day, the College Board releases an SAT question through its website, and it's free! The question is not some throwaway problem, but is an authentic SAT question. You can also subscribe to the Official SAT Question of the Day sent via e-mail. By subscribing, you can create a bank of real SAT questions for reference. If you mark down in your *SAT 2400 Review Notebook* that you had trouble with an SAT Question of the Day on a certain date, you can find that question in your e-mail folder—but not on the College Board's website. You can find a direct link to the College Board's SAT Question of the Day at www.2400expert.com. I post occasional comments about the SAT Question of the Day via *2400 Expert's* Twitter and Facebook Fan Page.

◄ **Pencils, eraser, wristwatch, and calculator** Since you will have these items with you on test day, you should also have them when you are prepping. A wristwatch gives you a sense of whether you are going too fast, too slow, or at the right pace when you are completing practice sections. You can't use a cell phone to time yourself on test day, so you shouldn't use a cell phone to time yourself when you practice. You don't need a graphing calculator for the SAT, but it doesn't hurt to have one.

◄ **Self-motivation (absolutely essential, and it's free)** This is by far the most important tool you will need to prepare for the SAT. No one can magically raise your SAT score; you must put in the effort. You will have

to learn hundreds of vocabulary words, learn strategies that may not be easy to grasp, and perform hours and hours of trial-and-error practice. *SAT 2400 in Just 7 Steps* can provide you with the tools necessary to succeed on the SAT, but it is up to you to use those tools.

You will need something to keep you going. That something is *self-motivation*. What drives you to study for the SAT? Your motivation should come from within, rather than from an external source (for example, your parents). It's great if your parents want you to do well, but when you want to do well yourself, preparing for the SAT becomes less painful.

Look at the road ahead. Are you taking the SAT to get into a good college, to be eligible for college athletics, to become more competitive for scholarships? When I was preparing for the SAT, I wanted to get into a dual-degree medical program that offered admission to medical school from high school so that I wouldn't have to worry about applying again in college. (That way, I could do other things during my undergraduate years, like write this book!) However, I knew that these programs were ultracompetitive and a score under 2200 probably wouldn't be enough. I always kept my ultimate goal in mind. You should too.

Write your SAT motivations on the first page of your 2400 notebook. Another goal of mine was to score high on the SAT like some of the upperclassmen at my school that I admired. Before I began my SAT preparation journey, I wrote the following on the first page of my notebook:

| | |
|---|---|
| Henry | 2400 |
| Vina | 2390 |
| Bill | 2330 |
| Joanna | 2290 |
| Shaan | ? |

After many hours of preparation and never losing motivation, I was able to pencil in "2400" next to my name.

The sky is the limit. I never thought that I would score above 2200. If you really apply yourself, you too will surpass your own expectations. When I secluded myself in a library study room four days a week during a hot summer, did I ever think that my effort would lead me to a 2400; admission to schools like Brown, Johns Hopkins, and UC Berkeley; more than $230,000 in college scholarships; and the opportunity to write a book about all of it one day? Not even in my dreams. So when there seems to be no sparkle in the sky, remember that your preparation is not futile. Keep your eye on the prize and stay self-motivated. Your effort will pay large dividends!

# General SAT preparation

*Please do not skip this section.* When people see the word "general," they assume the information will be generic and not very helpful. In the next few pages, however, I will share key insights into how I prepared for the SAT in high school.

Most SAT prep books tell you *what* to study for the SAT (and this one is no exception), but this section also tells you *how* to study for the SAT. This is very important. There is a plethora of information available to help you prepare for the SAT. Ask yourself: If two students have exactly the same information to study for the SAT, why does one student score significantly higher than the other? The difference lies in how each student *applies* that information. I will explain the many factors that account for that difference.

Furthermore, this section will give you a concrete sense of how to study. Most students begin learning how to study properly in high school. Studying is a vital life skill that requires practice. You must practice studying in order to get good at it, just as you must practice a sport in order to get good at playing that sport. In this section, I will reveal the approaches I used to study for the SAT. My advice is not the only way to prepare for the SAT; other students have scored high on the SAT without doing everything I did. But the approaches I used definitely work, and they work for the "average" person—like you and me. If you follow my suggestions, you too will get a not-so-average SAT score.

## Take a diagnostic test

If you have not already done so, take at least one full-length SAT practice test before you begin your SAT preparation. This test will help you identify areas you need to work on. To simulate real testing conditions, be sure you time each section. After you take your diagnostic SAT, fill in the chart below:

**Number of questions incorrect/Total number of questions**

| | |
|---|---|
| SAT essay | _____ (Refer to the SAT Essay section for scoring information.) |
| Improving sentences | _____ /25 |
| Identifying sentence errors | _____ /18 |
| Improving paragraphs | _____ /6 |
| Sentence completion | _____ /19 |
| Passage-based reading | _____ /48 |
| Multiple-choice math | _____ /44 |
| Student-produced response math | _____ /10 |

If you are unsure what a particular problem type in the chart above looks like, refer to its corresponding section in this book. Your goal should be to significantly decrease your "Number of questions incorrect." Once you identify areas

that you need to focus on, you can spend your time and energy more efficiently when preparing for the SAT.

## Work together: 2400 Practice and 2400 Review

The keys to SAT preparation are practice and review. The seven steps below outline exactly how *2400 Practice* and *2400 Review* work together.

---

1 · Learn 2400 Strategies
2 · Complete an SAT practice section
3 · Score your SAT practice section
4 · Check questions you answered correctly
5 · Check questions you answered incorrectly
6 · Complete your 2400 Review
7 · Repeat steps 1–6

---

### Step 1 ⁄ *Learn 2400 Strategies*

Study this book's strategies for an SAT subject area that gives you trouble.

### Step 2 ⁄ *Complete an SAT practice section*

Practice on a section that contains questions related to the weak area.

### Step 3 ⁄ *Score your SAT practice section*

Score the section to determine how you did.

### Step 4 ⁄ *Check questions you answered correctly*

Check that you understand the concept/strategy behind each question you answered correctly. Be sure that you can repeat the problem-solving process if presented with a similar question later. This process should not take more than 10 to 20 seconds per question. If you realize that your correct answer was just a lucky guess, enter the problem under a "Problems to Review" heading in the appropriate section of your 2400 notebook.

### Step 5 ⁄ *Check questions you answered incorrectly*

Enter the problem under "Problems to Review" in the appropriate section of your 2400 notebook. For future reference, note the test, section, page, and question number of the problem. Write the main part of the question, as well as the key to solving the problem that you missed earlier. If you are not sure why you got the question wrong, mark it for later review.

NOTE You don't need to create an entry for every question you answer incorrectly—just ones that you have a lot of trouble with. Make no more than seven entries per practice section.

Here are examples from my 2400 notebook:

**Math problem for review**

<u>Reference</u>:  Test 1, Section 6, Question 17

<u>Question</u>:  Graph of $x = y^2 - 9$ intersects line at $(0,m)$ and $(7,n)$. Greatest possible slope?

<u>Answer</u>:

| | |
|---|---|
| Step 1: Plug in points | When $x = 0$ ... $m = +/-3$ |
| | When $x = 7$ ... $n = +/-4$ |
| Step 2: Identify points | $(0,3); (0,-3); (7,4); (7,-4)$ |
| Step 3: Identify steepest slope | $[4 - (-3)]/[7 - 0] = 1$ |
| <u>Key</u>:  Remember Step 1 | Always plug in what you can! |

**Writing problem for review**

<u>Reference</u>:  Test 7, Section 3, Question 27

<u>Question</u>:  "were <u>inconsistent to</u> those"

<u>Answer</u>:  Should be "inconsistent with"

<u>Key</u>:  Be more cautious of IDIOM ERRORS!

**Reading problem for review**

<u>Reference</u>:  Test 8, Section 4, Question 11

<u>Question</u>:  What's the purpose of the first paragraph?

<u>Answer</u>:  Clearly, the first paragraph is concerned with deformities of frogs—this must be clear in the answer!

<u>Key</u>:  Look for summaries of what is found in the passage.

## Step 6 ⚡ *Complete your 2400 Review*

Review your Writing, Reading, and Math "Problems to Review" once a week. This will maintain your familiarity with the problems that are the most difficult for you. If there are questions you are unable to solve on your own, seek help from a friend.

## Step 7 ⚡ *Repeat steps 1–6*

Repeat this process for another SAT subject area that gives you trouble. Although it isn't necessary to constantly review *2400 Strategies*, you should review the same set of strategies two or three times so that you really understand them. In addition, take all of the sections in one SAT practice test before tackling practice sections in another practice test. By completing entire practice tests, you can fill in the following charts to track your progress.

## Test 1

### Number of questions incorrect/Total number of questions

SAT essay ................................ _____ (*Refer to the SAT Essay section for scoring information.*)

Improving sentences ...................... _____ /25
Identifying sentence errors .............. _____ /18
Improving paragraphs ..................... _____ /6
Sentence completion ...................... _____ /19
Passage-based reading .................... _____ /48
Multiple-choice math ..................... _____ /44
Student-produced response math ........... _____ /10

## Test 2

### Number of questions incorrect/Total number of questions

SAT essay ................................ _____ (*Refer to the SAT Essay section for scoring information.*)

Improving sentences ...................... _____ /25
Identifying sentence errors .............. _____ /18
Improving paragraphs ..................... _____ /6
Sentence completion ...................... _____ /19
Passage-based reading .................... _____ /48
Multiple-choice math ..................... _____ /44
Student-produced response math ........... _____ /10

## Test 3

### Number of questions incorrect/Total number of questions

SAT essay ................................ _____ (*Refer to the SAT Essay section for scoring information.*)

Improving sentences ...................... _____ /25
Identifying sentence errors .............. _____ /18
Improving paragraphs ..................... _____ /6
Sentence completion ...................... _____ /19
Passage-based reading .................... _____ /48
Multiple-choice math ..................... _____ /44
Student-produced response math ........... _____ /10

## Test 4

### Number of questions incorrect/Total number of questions

SAT essay           _____ (*Refer to the SAT Essay section for scoring information.*)

Improving sentences       _____ /25
Identifying sentence errors       _____ /18
Improving paragraphs       _____ /6
Sentence completion       _____ /19
Passage-based reading       _____ /48
Multiple-choice math       _____ /44
Student-produced response math       _____ /10

## Test 5

### Number of questions incorrect/Total number of questions

SAT essay           _____ (*Refer to the SAT Essay section for scoring information.*)

Improving sentences       _____ /25
Identifying sentence errors       _____ /18
Improving paragraphs       _____ /6
Sentence completion       _____ /19
Passage-based reading       _____ /48
Multiple-choice math       _____ /44
Student-produced response math       _____ /10

## Test 6

### Number of questions incorrect/Total number of questions

SAT essay           _____ (*Refer to the SAT Essay section for scoring information.*)

Improving sentences       _____ /25
Identifying sentence errors       _____ /18
Improving paragraphs       _____ /6
Sentence completion       _____ /19
Passage-based reading       _____ /48
Multiple-choice math       _____ /44
Student-produced response math       _____ /10

## Test 7

### Number of questions incorrect/Total number of questions

SAT essay                             _____ (*Refer to the SAT Essay section
                                        for scoring information.*)

Improving sentences                   _____ /25
Identifying sentence errors           _____ /18
Improving paragraphs                  _____ /6
Sentence completion                   _____ /19
Passage-based reading                 _____ /48
Multiple-choice math                  _____ /44
Student-produced response math        _____ /10

## Test 8

### Number of questions incorrect/Total number of questions

SAT essay                             _____ (*Refer to the SAT Essay section
                                        for scoring information.*)

Improving sentences                   _____ /25
Identifying sentence errors           _____ /18
Improving paragraphs                  _____ /6
Sentence completion                   _____ /19
Passage-based reading                 _____ /48
Multiple-choice math                  _____ /44
Student-produced response math        _____ /10

## Test 9

### Number of questions incorrect/Total number of questions

SAT essay                             _____ (*Refer to the SAT Essay section
                                        for scoring information.*)

Improving sentences                   _____ /25
Identifying sentence errors           _____ /18
Improving paragraphs                  _____ /6
Sentence completion                   _____ /19
Passage-based reading                 _____ /48
Multiple-choice math                  _____ /44
Student-produced response math        _____ /10

**Test 10**

**Number of questions incorrect/Total number of questions**

| | |
|---|---|
| SAT essay | _____ (*Refer to the SAT Essay section for scoring information.*) |
| Improving sentences | _____ /25 |
| Identifying sentence errors | _____ /18 |
| Improving paragraphs | _____ /6 |
| Sentence completion | _____ /19 |
| Passage-based reading | _____ /48 |
| Multiple-choice math | _____ /44 |
| Student-produced response math | _____ /10 |

The goal of this seven-step plan is to take full-length SATs in manageable blocks of time (usually 20 to 30 minutes). Each time you practice, you will gain valuable test-taking experience to solve difficult SAT questions. The problem-solving keys you develop will serve as custom test strategies that no book could furnish.

This is not a quick process: Working through steps 1 to 6 could take a couple of hours. But you don't have to do steps 1 to 6 in one sitting—you can do each step in a separate 20- to 30-minute interval.

## When to prepare

It isn't easy to find time for all this practice and review. Like many students, you are probably already overwhelmed with schoolwork, sports, orchestra, band, after-school clubs, student council, and part-time jobs. The truth is, you will have to add SAT prep to your already long list of activities. SAT preparation should be a top priority; it should be in your planner day in and day out. You can't prepare for the SAT only when you "feel like it." Making SAT prep a necessary task rather than an optional undertaking will add consistency and regularity to your test preparation.

**During the school year**  Finding time during the school year to prepare for the SAT was one of the most difficult tasks I've ever done. Here's how you should approach it:

◂ Prepare for the SAT a total of 4 to 10 hours a week.
◂ Prepare for the SAT at least 4 days a week.
◂ An SAT prep session should last no less than 30 minutes and no more than 3 hours.

**During the summer** Finding time during the summer to prepare for the SAT is usually much easier. To avoid wasting precious time, however, you need to be even more disciplined about SAT preparation in the summer:

- ◄ Prepare for the SAT a total of 8 to 15 hours a week.
- ◄ Prepare for the SAT at least 5 days a week.
- ◄ An SAT prep session should last no less than 30 minutes and no more than 3 hours.

**Baby steps** In addition to regular SAT prep sessions, you can turn your spare time into big SAT gains. Do you have five minutes before class begins? How about 10 minutes while you wait for the student council meeting to start? Fifteen minutes while you are waiting to pick up your little brother from school? All of this time adds up, and if you use it wisely, it can result in big SAT score improvements! Here are a few baby steps you can squeeze into your ultrabusy day:

- ◄ Memorize two or more words from *Vocabulary 2400*.
- ◄ Do the College Board's Official SAT Question of the Day.
- ◄ Complete as much of an SAT practice section as you can.

Yes, this advice requires you to carry this book around with you and to practice SAT tests, but it's a sacrifice that a successful SAT student should be willing to make.

### The 2400 six-phase schedule

Use this schedule to plan your SAT preparation. It is flexible, because it is divided into six *phases*—rather than into weeks or months.

No matter how much time you have before you take the SAT, this schedule will work for you. For example, if you have four months (120 days) before the SAT, you should complete each phase in 20 days. If you have six weeks (42 days) before the SAT, you should complete each phase in seven days.

Using this six-phase schedule, you will study all the steps in this book, complete the *2400 Practice Test,* complete 10 additional SAT practice tests, and memorize all 500 vocabulary words in this book! You won't be overwhelmed if you perform one phase at a time and stick to the schedule.

### Phase 1

☐ Complete the diagnostic *2400 Practice Test* (page 361) in a single, timed sitting.

☐ Study **General SAT preparation** (page 10), **The SAT essay** (page 30), **SAT sentence completion** (page 135), and **SAT vocabulary** (page 257).

☐ Complete each section of SAT practice test 1.

☐ Review each question in the *SAT 2400 Practice Test* and in SAT practice test 1. (Write problems for review, questions, and keys in your 2400 notebook.)

☐ Memorize *Vocabulary 2400* Sets 1–4 (page 270).

☐ Review your 2400 notebook.

In Phase 1, you don't read the chapters of this book in order, because you first need to review **SAT sentence completion** (page 135) and the **SAT vocabulary** introduction (page 257), which explains the method I used to memorize hundreds of vocabulary words. This approach helps you memorize the 80 vocabulary words in Phase I so that you don't forget them.

## Phase 2

☐ Complete SAT practice test 2 in a single, timed sitting.

☐ Study **Improving sentences and identifying sentence errors** (page 50), **Improving paragraphs** (page 118), and **SAT passage-based reading** (page 161).

☐ Complete each section of SAT practice test 3.

☐ Review SAT practice tests 2 and 3.

☐ Memorize *Vocabulary 2400* Sets 5–8 (page 272).

☐ Review your 2400 notebook.

☐ Review all previous *Vocabulary 2400* words.

## Phase 3

☐ Complete SAT practice test 4 in a single, timed sitting.

☐ Study the math chapter of this book (page 285).

☐ Complete each section of SAT practice test 5.

☐ Review SAT practice tests 4 and 5.

☐ Memorize *Vocabulary 2400* Sets 9–12 (page 274).

☐ Review your 2400 notebook.

☐ Review all previous *Vocabulary 2400* words.

## Phase 4

☐ Complete SAT practice test 6 in a single, timed sitting.

☐ Study **The SAT essay, Improving sentences and identifying sentence errors, Improving paragraphs**, and **SAT passage-based reading** again.

☐ Complete each section of SAT practice test 7.

☐ Review SAT practice tests 6 and 7.

- ☐ Memorize *Vocabulary 2400* Sets 13–16 (page 276).
- ☐ Review your 2400 notebook.
- ☐ Review all previous *Vocabulary 2400* words.

## Phase 5

- ☐ Complete SAT practice test 8 in a single, timed sitting.
- ☐ Study **SAT sentence completion** and the math chapter of this book again.
- ☐ Complete each section of SAT practice test 9.
- ☐ Review SAT practice tests 8 and 9.
- ☐ Memorize *Vocabulary 2400* Sets 17–21 (page 278).
- ☐ Review your 2400 notebook.
- ☐ Review all previous *Vocabulary 2400* words.

## Phase 6

- ☐ Complete each section of SAT practice test 10.
- ☐ Review SAT practice test 10.
- ☐ Memorize *Vocabulary 2400* Sets 22–25 (page 281).
- ☐ Review your 2400 notebook.
- ☐ Review all previous *Vocabulary 2400* words.

You don't learn any new concepts in Phase 6. The concepts that you have difficulty with are already in your 2400 notebook; focus on these instead of trying to learn last-minute SAT rules, which will only make you tense. Don't worry about material you "missed." The light preparation will keep your mind fresh immediately before you take the real SAT.

Let's say that you have completed the six-phase schedule and taken the SAT, but are unsatisfied with your score. You need to repeat the schedule and retake the SAT—just find new SAT practice tests and vocabulary words!

Notice two key themes in the six-phase schedule: *repetition* and *review*. You *repeat* each chapter of this book twice. You constantly *review* questions you've already practiced, problems you had trouble with, and your 2400 notebook, which is full of SAT insights. From Phase 2 on, you *review* vocabulary words from previous phases. Although repetition and review sound boring, these two principles change how you take the test so that your score will change too.

NOTE Don't let repetition and review get in the way of efficiency. If you really understand a section, don't waste your time reviewing it. For example, if you are a math genius consistently scoring 750+ on SAT Math, you should only focus on math concepts that give you trouble. Review quickly—or not at all. Save time! Of course, if you are even slightly unsure of certain problem types, by all means review them.

## A consistent schedule

Successful SAT prep requires a regular schedule. The six-phase schedule outlined above gives you specific goals within set phases. However, you need to set aside a particular time and day for SAT preparation to reach those goals. Otherwise, the SAT will be like that English research paper you had three months to write . . . which, because of the disease known as procrastination, you now have only three days to write! You can't treat the SAT the same way. You need to chip away at SAT preparation on a regular basis. Gradual preparation every week is the only way to accomplish the goals set in the six-phase schedule.

## Where to prepare

Where you prepare for the SAT is almost as important as when you prepare. SAT prep requires a great deal of concentration, which means that the school lunchroom is not the best study location.

When I prepared for the SAT, I completed my concentrated SAT preparation *exclusively* at my local public library. I spent several hours per week in a small study room there, preparing for the SAT. Sure, it was boring and quiet—but that's exactly the type of place you want to prepare for the SAT. Let's face it: It's not fun to study for the SAT. To do so in a noisy, social atmosphere is almost certain to doom your efforts to score high.

If you have never studied at a library before, your initial experience may be uncomfortable. But I challenge you: Complete two hours of SAT prep at home, complete two hours of SAT prep at the library, and compare what you accomplished at the two locations. You will be amazed at how much more efficient you are at the library.

If a library is not easily accessible, try to find another location with these features:

- ◄ **Quiet** When you are trying to memorize new vocabulary words or learn a difficult SAT concept, you don't want a noisy environment.

- ◄ **Plenty of work space** Every time you prepare for the SAT, you will need this book, your 2400 notebook, and several practice SAT tests. A large desk area gives you room to spread out all of your SAT materials.

- ◄ **Away from home** The doorbell rings, your mom asks you to do a load of laundry, the TV is on in the next room, your little sister is yelling, or you decide to take a five-minute break—which turns into a 45-minute nap. These are just some of the many distractions at home that can deter you from focusing.

- ◄ **Away from friends** Sorry, but preparing for the SAT is a process best done alone. You might think that studying with a buddy would be more productive, but friends only cause you to become distracted, lose focus, and waste precious time.

◄ **Away from technology** With the advent of Facebook and Twitter, the presence of technology during study is the equivalent of chatting with a friend while you are trying to prepare for the SAT. When you are studying, stay away from your computer, laptop, smartphone, iPad—all Internet access—unless you are using the technology to prepare for the SAT. If you are a textaholic, set your cell phone to silent and put it in your backpack, or turn it off completely. You can take periodic breaks for texting, Facebook, and snacks.

I also recommend that you don't listen to music while you prepare for the SAT. Some people claim that they can tune the music out, but the SAT requires a high level of concentration that is difficult to achieve when Kanye West is playing in the background.

## What to memorize

These general SAT preparation rules may seem overwhelming. You need to study for a certain number of hours each week . . . at set times . . . in a boring study area . . . and so forth. I have some good news for you, however: The amount of material you need to memorize for the SAT is surprisingly small—vocabulary words, and that's it.

For the SAT, you should keep memorization (robotic, mindless retention of information) to a minimum. Concentrate, instead, on the strategies and concepts in this book. With practice, you will learn to apply *2400 Strategies* to every Reading, Writing multiple-choice, and Math question on the SAT. Except for vocabulary words, no memorization is required!

## Exercise and eat healthy

You may have a confused look on your face. This is a test prep guide, not a fitness book. Well, yes. But I can't overemphasize the importance of a healthy lifestyle when it comes to preparing for the SAT. When I was preparing for the October SAT during the summer of 2006, I was getting into the best shape of my life. I was doing cardio workouts, lifting weights, and eating a healthy vegetarian diet. When you improve your physical well-being, you improve your mental well-being too. Your mind needs physical activity and stimulation for peak performance.

I'm not saying that Mr. Universe would do spectacularly well on the SAT. But a significant amount of scientific research supports the idea that exercise and a healthy diet improve the effectiveness of studying. Google this if you don't believe me! A recent study by clinical psychologist Charles Emery of Ohio State University found that exercising with music enhances mental performance even more. So if you've been cooped up studying at your desk for hours, leave the sedentary lifestyle behind. Lace up your running shoes, cue up your favorite iTunes playlist, and get moving!

# General 2400 Strategies

Throughout this book, you will encounter *2400 Strategies* that serve as the building blocks for success on the SAT. Normally these strategies are associated with specific subjects. But the five *General 2400 Strategies* that follow are used in all aspects of SAT preparation.

**Step 1**
Learn how
to study
for the SAT

22

1 · Practice what I preach
2 · Write everything down
3 · Bubble page by page
4 · Skip and return
5 · When you can eliminate at least two answer choices, guess

## General 2400 Strategy 1 ⁄ *Practice what I preach*

Follow every SAT method and approach in this book exactly. No deviations! This strategy helps combat the biggest mistake students make when preparing for the SAT: They don't change *how* they take the test. Students often listen to a strategy I teach, but don't use that strategy when they take the SAT. Instead, they will revert to their usual test-taking methods when they practice, believing that they will somehow be able to use my proven strategies on the actual SAT.

Don't wait until game day to practice what I preach in this book. To change your SAT score, you need to change the way you take the test. To change the way you take the SAT, you need to *practice* every strategy I teach you. Don't choose some strategies to use on certain SAT sections, then stick to your old strategies on other sections. You need to use and practice everything I teach you. Change is difficult, so be sure to practice, practice, and practice changing your natural test-taking habits to my proven test-taking skills.

## General 2400 Strategy 2 ⁄ *Write everything down*

Write everything down in your test booklet. When I say "everything," I mean *everything*.

Does this describe your approach to taking the SAT? You read the question without underlining key information, look over the answer choices, trying to remember which ones could be wrong and which ones could be correct, then go straight to the answer sheet to bubble in the choice you think is correct. If this is your approach, you're making a big mistake.

As you read the question, circle key information. Cross out the letter of every incorrect answer choice. Circle the letter of the correct answer choice. Then, and only then, are you ready to bubble in your answer.

Although writing everything down takes more time, your accuracy will improve tremendously. With more and more practice, you will learn how to

write everything down within the 10 to 25 minutes you are allowed to complete a test section. After you finish an entire SAT test, your test booklet should be covered with underlines, circles, notes, scribbles, doodles, and squiggles.

Once you have mastered this strategy, your SAT score will improve. By marking your test booklet, you are actually freeing your mind to think more. No longer will you have to remember the key information in the question, what the question is asking, which answer choices are most likely incorrect, or which could be correct. You have physically marked down all of that information with your pencil. The less your brain has to remember, the more it is free to solve the problem.

Not writing in your SAT test booklet is a bad habit, and you must break it immediately! You probably developed the habit from years of school, when you weren't allowed to write in a test booklet because the teacher planned to reuse it. This is not a high school English exam. You need to write all over your SAT test booklet. If you don't, the test will overwhelm you.

The SAT contains a lot of information to process. If you try to keep everything in your head, you will suffer information overload. Your brain can handle only so much information before it begins to flounder.

## General 2400 Strategy 3 ⋰ *Bubble page by page*

Writing everything down takes more time, but you can save time by using this strategy. Most students take a test this way: They read a question, pick an answer choice, bubble in the answer choice, then proceed to the next question. This is not the most efficient way to take the SAT.

Instead, circle your answer selections for all questions on the same page of the test booklet—before you even look at the answer sheet. Once you have circled all your selections on a page, go to the answer sheet and bubble in your selections for the whole page at one time.

This strategy may not seem important, but it has many benefits. First, you save time, because you aren't flipping back and forth between your test booklet and answer sheet. Constantly keeping your place in the test booklet and on the answer sheet wastes time. Second, this strategy helps you stay focused on a series of questions, which is especially helpful for passage-based reading questions. Third, you gain a sense of completion and confidence, knowing that you have just answered an entire page of SAT questions to the best of your ability. Confidence is crucial when you're taking the SAT.

## General 2400 Strategy 4 ⋰ *Skip and return*

When you are stumped by a question on the SAT, circle the question number, step away from the problem, and tackle the next question. That's the *skip* part. When you have completed the entire section, go back to the questions you circled and skipped, and try to solve them. That's the *return* part.

Most students, when they come to a difficult question, wrack their brains for an answer. They read and reread the question, try several strategies to solve the problem, or stare blankly at the question in hopes that the answer will "come" to them. Not only are these students wasting precious time, they're frustrating themselves to the point that they will have difficulty answering other questions. Instead, you should skip the question completely.

You will very likely have time after you complete the section to return to questions that previously confused you; after all, you spent almost no time on these questions during your first pass. This strategy not only saves you time, but—like writing everything down—it will keep your mind fresh during the test. *Skip and return* also helps you avoid frustration, and when you're not frustrated, you can think more clearly.

Many students have difficulty skipping a question. This test-taking skill must be thoroughly practiced. You should skip a question immediately

- ◄ when you have no idea what the question is asking.
- ◄ when the question confuses you.
- ◄ when you cannot eliminate more than one answer choice.

Skipping a question prematurely is scary—what if you could have answered it correctly? Don't worry—the benefit of this strategy appears in the second stage: *Return*.

If you have the willpower and discipline to immediately skip questions you have difficulty with, you've done the hard part. You will find that when you return to questions that previously stumped you, you can solve some of them almost immediately! This is especially true of math questions.

Why does skipping and returning allow you to answer questions correctly that previously bamboozled you? Perhaps your brain wasn't focusing clearly on a particular concept in a question, and you just need to give the gears some time to mesh. Perhaps you gained a sense of completion and confidence from answering all the other questions in the section. Perhaps your brain has more thinking power because you weren't frustrated by the difficult question during the first pass. Perhaps a similar question in the section has reminded you of a way to solve the question. Or perhaps your subconscious was "thinking" about the question you skipped while you were consciously solving other questions.

Whatever the reason for this strategy's excellent results, it's quite a remarkable phenomenon and you will be amazed at its usefulness. Of course, the strategy isn't foolproof: There may be some questions that you simply can't figure out. The more you practice this strategy, however, the better you will become at solving questions that you initially thought were impossible. Just remember: The hardest part is to discipline yourself to *immediately* skip a difficult question.

## General 2400 Strategy 5 ⌁ *When you can eliminate at least two answer choices, guess*

Have you been told—by a friend, parent, or teacher—that it's better to leave questions blank on the SAT than to guess, or that leaving questions blank doesn't hurt your SAT score? If so, your advisor is oversimplifying the benefits of leaving questions blank on the SAT.

Let's recall how the SAT is scored. The SAT raw score is calculated by

- ◂ adding one point for each correct answer.
- ◂ subtracting ¼ point for an incorrect answer.
- ◂ neither adding nor subtracting for an answer left blank.

If your goal is to rack up as many raw score points as possible, it's better to not answer a question than to answer it incorrectly. Intuitively, you may think that you are better off leaving the answer blank because you are likely to answer a question incorrectly if you guess. This is the basis of the advice from your friend, parent, or teacher. But there is more to the story.

Big test-prep companies think they know the rest of the story. Many of them offer a method that they claim "beats" the SAT scoring system.

- ◂ **Big company guessing strategy**  If you can eliminate at least one of the five possible answer choices, you should *randomly* guess from the remaining four answer choices. If you can't eliminate a single answer choice, you should leave the question blank.
- ◂ **The reasoning**  Let's say Student A eliminates one incorrect answer choice on each of 12 SAT questions. He's not confident enough, however, to guess by eliminating just one answer choice, so he decides to leave all 12 questions blank. His net raw score for those 12 questions would be $+0$.

  Now, let's say Student B also eliminates one incorrect answer choice on each of 12 SAT questions. However, she uses the big company theory of *randomly* guessing from the remaining four choices. Probability predicts that if she *randomly* guesses from four answer choices, she has a one-in-four chance (25%) of guessing correctly. Therefore, of the 12 questions, she would guess three correctly and nine incorrectly. Her net raw score for the 12 questions would be $3(+1) - 9(¼) = +¾$.

The big test-prep company strategy that Student B used is more effective, in theory. Although both Student A and Student B could only eliminate one answer choice on 12 SAT questions, Student B would be able to achieve a higher raw score because she used the big company guessing strategy.

There is a serious flaw in this strategy, however: The method assumes that you are guessing *randomly*. Randomness is a difficult concept to grasp. What

exactly is "random guessing" when it comes to the SAT? Random guessing means that if you are presented with four answer choices, you will pick one answer choice without any prejudice, partiality, or predisposition. That isn't how any student "guesses" on the SAT, unfortunately.

Your guess is always biased in some way, because you have an inclination to one answer choice and an aversion to others. What makes matters even worse is that the College Board is really, really, *really* good at making wrong answer choices look appealing to unsure students, especially on difficult SAT questions. If you remove randomness from the equation, your chance of guessing the correct answer actually becomes less than 25%.

◄ **My guessing method** If you can eliminate at least two answer choices on a question, you should guess with as little bias as possible from the remaining answer choices. If you cannot eliminate at least two incorrect answer choices, you should leave the question blank.

◄ **The reasoning** Let's say that Student C eliminates two incorrect answers on each of 12 SAT questions. He then attempts to guess, with as little prejudice as possible, from the remaining three answer choices on each question. Probability predicts that if he *randomly* guesses from the three answer choices on each of the 12 questions, he would get four correct and eight incorrect. But because eliminating bias completely from guessing is impossible, let's say Student C answers only three correctly and nine incorrectly. His net raw score for the 12 questions would be $3(+1) - 9(¼)$ $= +¾$.

Notice that Student C's net raw score is the same as Student B's. But Student B's guessing strategy is impossible, because there is no such thing as random guessing. To be sure, Student C has to eliminate *two* incorrect answer choices on each of the 12 questions, not just one.

Eliminate bias from guessing as much as you can. If you think that the answer to a particular question cannot be (B) because you have filled in (B) for the last three questions, you are not eliminating bias. If you think that the answer to a particular math question is (C) because it is easily derivable from the numbers in the question, you are not eliminating bias. To try to eliminate bias, let your pencil land on a random letter and choose that answer.

NOTE For the student-produced response Math questions, there is no penalty for guessing. You should answer every question in this section of the test.

## Bonus General 2400 tips

◄ Don't allow the letter you filled in on previous questions to influence your decision on what letter to fill in on the current question. If you have filled in four E's in a row, don't think that the answer to the next question cannot be E.

◄ Take breaks and eat snacks when studying. Your brain needs to relax every hour or so, and it needs food for energy.

◄ Don't get down on yourself if you don't accomplish much while studying for the SAT on some days. Efficiency fluctuates: You will feel very productive during some SAT prep sessions and feel like you just can't concentrate during other sessions. Recover your focus the next day.

◄ Don't bubble in answer choices too hard or worry about bubbling them in perfectly. Focus on the SAT questions, not on the art of filling in the answer sheet.

◄ Don't bother erasing anything you write in your test booklet. The booklet is just scratch paper, so there's no reason to make it look "presentable."

# Forget your English classes and prepare for SAT Writing

Which of the following statements describes you best?

- ◄ You are an excellent writer who aces every English writing assignment.
- ◄ You are an average writer who would rather do math problems.
- ◄ You are a poor writer who cringes at the very idea of an essay.

No matter which category you fall into, I have good news: You are just as ready to score unbelievably high on SAT Writing as anyone else! Why? Because SAT Writing is different from high school writing. In high school, English teachers reward you for creativity, deep insights, and outstanding stylistic approaches. These qualities don't matter on SAT Writing, which is very methodical and systematic.

Like SAT Math, SAT Writing sections are clear and to the point. But unlike SAT Math, SAT Writing covers less material and has fewer types of questions. Because of this, SAT Writing is probably the easiest section to prepare for. No matter how good or bad you think you are at high school writing, you have a very good shot at succeeding in SAT Writing.

SAT Writing has two major components:

- ◄ The SAT essay (30% of your Writing score)
- ◄ 49 multiple-choice questions (70% of your Writing score)
      25 IMPROVING SENTENCES questions
      18 IDENTIFYING SENTENCE ERRORS questions
       6 IMPROVING PARAGRAPHS questions

Don't worry if you have struggled in the past with high school English classes. I didn't learn any of the *Writing 2400 Strategies* in my high school English classes. Instead, my mastery of SAT Writing came from specifically preparing for the SAT.

If English isn't your first language, you may have more difficulty with SAT Writing than others. Of course, you can consult a grammar guide to get a good sense of English grammar, but I suggest that you work through this chapter at least once before you seek outside assistance.

# The SAT essay

Imagine that you are calmly sitting in English class. The bell rings at the beginning of the period, and your teacher unexpectedly proclaims:

"Today, class, we are going to have an impromptu in-class essay!"

Suddenly your stomach hurts, your heart races, and you are overcome by a feeling of anxiety. As your teacher hands out the essay booklets, you realize that you have never seen the long-winded two-paragraph topic before. The instructions say that you have only 25 minutes to complete the essay. To make matters worse, the booklet contains two blank pages. *How does your teacher expect you to write two pages when it takes you five minutes just to read the topic?*

You hastily begin to write down a few thoughts, but midway through the third sentence, you get writer's block. You begin to rely on personal experiences that barely relate to the topic. Before long, you notice that there are two minutes left on the clock, so you tack a vague one-sentence conclusion onto the single paragraph you've managed to complete. Finally, you turn in a disorganized, ¾-page essay that is surely doomed.

This happens to many students who take the SAT.

When I was in high school, there was nothing I feared more than an in-class essay. For me, it was like being thrown into the deep end of a pool without being able to swim. I share the fear that most students have for the composition portion of the SAT.

The essay is the first section of every SAT. Although it accounts for only 30% of your SAT Writing score, you still want to approach this section as the most important. How well you do on the SAT essay sets the tone for how well you do on the rest of the test. If your heart is racing and your mind is frantic during the essay section, you will be anxious for the rest of the test. On the other hand, if you are positive that you have written an articulate, well-reasoned essay, you will be confident for the rest of the test.

The strategies in this chapter will help you be positive and confident. It doesn't matter if you would rather do a thousand math problems than write an essay or if you think you're the next J. K. Rowling; following these strategies will help you succeed on the SAT essay. I was once a poor writer without a plan, but with key strategies and practice, I trained myself to ace the SAT essay. And you can too!

## Essay 2400 Strategies

1 · Don't read the instructions
2 · Build a five-paragraph SAT essay
3 · Use big words
4 · Write a lot
5 · Brainstorm an outline
6 · Relate topic sentences to your thesis
7 · Use the active voice
8 · Employ transitions
9 · Don't get personal
10 · Build essay templates

## Essay 2400 Strategy 1 *Don't read the instructions*

Here is a typical SAT essay question:

The essay provides an opportunity for you to show how effectively you can develop and express ideas. As you write, make certain that you develop your point of view, present your ideas logically and clearly, and use language precisely.

Write your essay on the lines provided on your answer sheet—you will receive no other paper on which to write. Write on every line, avoid wide margins, and keep your handwriting to a reasonable size. Remember that your essay will be read by people who are not familiar with your handwriting. Try to write or print as clearly as possible.

You have twenty-five minutes to write an essay on the topic assigned below. DO NOT WRITE ON ANOTHER TOPIC. AN OFF-TOPIC ESSAY WILL RECEIVE A SCORE OF ZERO.

> Read the excerpt below. Think about the issue presented in the excerpt and respond to the assignment that follows.
>
> > The important thing is not to stop questioning. Curiosity has its own reason for existing. One cannot help but be in awe when he contemplates the mysteries of eternity, of life, of the marvelous structure of reality. It is enough if one tries merely to comprehend a little of this mystery every day. Never lose a holy curiosity.
> >
> > —Albert Einstein
>
> **Assignment: Does curiosity benefit us?** Plan and write an essay in which you develop your point of view on this issue. Support your position with reasoning and examples taken from your reading, studies, experiences, or observations.

Wow, that was wordy! If you read all of that, kudos. Now make sure you never do it again. There is nothing useful in the SAT essay instructions other than the advice that you should stay on topic.

Ignore everything on the directions page of the SAT essay except what immediately follows "Assignment"—in the directions above, the question "Does curiosity benefit us?" This is all you need to consider when composing your essay.

Now that you have a question to focus on, your job becomes easy. Just pick a position. Either agree or disagree with the question presented, then support your viewpoint with evidence. The SAT essay is a *persuasive* essay, so you need to persuade the graders that your position is the right one by presenting strong and convincing evidence. But first, you must know how to organize a persuasive essay.

## Essay 2400 Strategy 2 ⁄ *Build a five-paragraph SAT essay*

Confronted with two blank pages at the beginning of the test, students are often unsure how to begin their SAT essay. How many paragraphs should you write? What should each paragraph be about? Should you even use paragraphs—what about one long, continuous composition?

High school English teachers may cringe when they hear this, but the SAT essay should be written using the standard five-paragraph format. No creativity is required.

Your essay should include the following parts:

- **The introduction** contains your *thesis,* a sentence or two of generalities, and your plan of procedure.
- **Body paragraph 1** contains your first example in support of the thesis. Include your strongest example here.
- **Body paragraph 2** contains your second example in support of the thesis.
- **Body paragraph 3** contains your third example in support of the thesis.
- **The conclusion** is the shortest paragraph of your essay—only two or three sentences. Restate your thesis in different words.

### What is a thesis?

Your thesis is the sentence in your introduction that you will prove. Although most English instructors teach that the thesis should be the last sentence of your introduction, I advocate making it the first sentence of your essay.

- On the SAT, this sentence usually tells whether you agree or disagree with the topic.

## ⊡ Essay topics

SAT essay topics are *general*. You don't need to have a lot of specific knowledge in order to answer the essay question. The SAT won't ask you about the Protestant Reformation in the sixteenth century or about selected poems of Robert Frost. The following are representative of SAT essay topics:

- ◄ Can triumph be devastating?
- ◄ Is innovation lacking in the world?
- ◄ Is attempting to prove others wrong a path to success?
- ◄ Does challenging those in power create a better civilization?
- ◄ Is privacy essential for society?

As you can see, SAT essay questions are very *broad* and give you a lot of room to choose the direction of your response.

◄ If you are unsure whether you are asserting an opinion (a *thesis*) or just making a statement (not a thesis), insert your sentence in the following thesis test:

"In this essay, I will prove that ＿＿＿＿＿＿＿."

If the sentence makes sense, you have a thesis. If the sentence doesn't make sense, you are probably stating a fact instead of asserting an opinion.

Here are examples of theses I used to start some of my high school practice SAT essays:

*The notion that people should make an effort to be more private is absolutely false.*

*The presupposition that challenging authority only makes a society stronger is a categorical truth.*

*The notion that there is hope and opportunity through hardships is an absolute truth.*

*The presupposition that an attempt to please everyone will breed success is categorically false.*

Notice that you can tell exactly what the essay questions were asking simply by reading my theses. Always restate the topic in your thesis as I did, then pick a position on the topic by claiming, as I did, that the idea is "false" or "a truth." You can check that my theses are real theses by putting them to the thesis test above.

## What is a plan of procedure (POP)?

Your plan of procedure is an ordered list of examples that you will use in body paragraphs to support your thesis. The POP is the last sentence of your introduction.

Here are examples of POPs I used on practice SAT essays:

*Three classic archetypes that show how privacy can be a vice are Nathaniel Hawthorne's The Scarlet Letter, the tragic Holocaust, and the current state of North Korea.*

*Three prominent archetypes that exemplify how defying power enriches a society are Thomas Paine's Common Sense, the communist state of North Korea, and George Orwell's 1984.*

*Three prominent paradigms that display society's genius can be found in the Normandy invasion of World War II, the engendering of more efficient energy sources, and Frederick Douglass's amazing struggle to learn how to read.*

As you can see, POPs are pretty straightforward: Simply state what is to come. The first example refers to the first body paragraph, the second to the second body paragraph, and the third to the third body paragraph. Follow these guidelines, and your SAT essay format will never need to change.

## Impress your graders!
### Essay 2400 Strategy 3 ⚹ *Use big words*

If your high school English teachers are like mine were, this strategy goes against everything they ever preached. I remember my English teacher lecturing about the importance of quality ideas rather than big vocabulary words in essays. This is not the case for the SAT. If you were an SAT essay grader, what would be one solid way to tell if a student is knowledgeable or not? That's right: vocabulary.

This *2400 Strategy* is especially important in your essay's introduction, where you should include two to four big words. The graders will develop an impression of you as a writer within seconds of reading your introduction. After the first paragraph, they will have an almost unchangeable impression of your writing ability and will read the rest of your essay looking to reaffirm their initial judgment. If you give them a good first impression, you will have immediately boosted your essay score!

What are "big words"? I'm not necessarily referring to long words. Instead, I'm talking about academic words that are not often used in everyday high school work, but that you would encounter in a scholarly article. Don't worry:

You don't have to read a dozen articles to figure out which words to use. Most words from *Vocabulary 2400* will do.

In high school, I had a list of words that I would try to incorporate into my SAT essay. You should prepare a similar list. To do this, think of ordinary words that you would often use in your essay, then find big-word equivalents in a thesaurus.

# ⮑ Scoring the essay

Understanding how your essay is scored is important for appreciation of the *Essay 2400 Strategies* that follow. Two separate graders will grade your SAT essay. Each grader will give your essay a score between 1 and 6, based on a number of criteria. Here is what the graders will be looking for:

1. A logical and compelling argument
2. Strong evidence to support claims
3. Proper organization of ideas
4. Proficient use of prose
5. Few grammatical errors

The two graders' scores are then added together, so the range of the SAT essay's raw score is 2 to 12. If the two scores differ by more than one point (for example, one grader gives your essay a score of 4 and another gives it a score of 6), a third, senior grader will assign the final score. The SAT essay's raw score out of 12 will then be scaled to account for approximately 30% of your scaled SAT Writing score.

It is essential that you understand the conditions under which your essay is graded. The College Board hires professionals with backgrounds in writing and teaching (often, high school English teachers) to score SAT essays. These teachers receive "reader training" to ensure accuracy and consistency in grading. However, unlike high school essays that English teachers can spend hours examining for brilliant subtleties and original insights, your SAT essay receives only a hasty read-through, perhaps only two or three minutes. The graders have to score dozens of essays every day and don't have much time to grade each essay. Remember, too, that the graders have no idea who you are, how smart you are, or how well you normally write if given more time.

Being aware of this key information, you need to give the graders quick clues to help them identify you as an intelligent high school student. *Essay 2400 Strategies* 3 and 4 show you how to convey this idea.

Here are examples from my list of words:

**Step 2**
Forget your
English classes
and prepare for
SAT Writing
....................
**36**

| INSTEAD OF | USE |
|------------|-----|
| idea | notion, presupposition, premise |
| example | archetype, paradigm, paragon |
| statement | assertion |
| bad thing | vice, depravity |
| good thing | virtue |
| narrow view | dogmatic view, provincial view |
| to create | to engender, to breed |
| harmful | deleterious |
| absolute | categorical |
| idealistic | romantic |
| poor | impoverished, destitute |
| generous | philanthropic, altruistic |

Obviously, I didn't use all of these words in a single essay. Instead, I knew I could sound smart by using a few of these words in any essay! Make a list of 10 to 15 words in the SAT essay section of your 2400 notebook. Review the list once a week, and try to use them in your high school writing and in everyday speech (as nerdy as that sounds).

## Essay 2400 Strategy 4 ⸱ *Write a lot*

This strategy also runs counter to the dictates of high school English teachers across the country. But on the SAT, it's about quantity more than quality: You need to fill up both blank pages for the SAT essay. Graders may not know you personally, but they do know that smarter students usually have more to say. A grader will almost always score two pages of writing higher than one page. In fact, an MIT study found that longer SAT essays are typically awarded higher scores. Filling two full pages in 25 minutes is no easy task, so be sure that your pencil is constantly moving!

These two *2400 Strategies*, using big words and writing a lot, will account for the biggest score gains on your SAT essay.

## Amaze your graders!

Now that you understand the two major ways to impress your graders, you are ready to take your writing skills to the next level.

## Essay 2400 Strategy 5 ⸱ *Brainstorm an outline*

After you have read the SAT essay topic question, take two or three minutes to brainstorm an outline for your essay. This *2400 Strategy* goes hand in hand with the previous one (Write a lot). To fill both pages of the essay booklet, you must avoid getting stuck. And to avoid getting stuck under the pressure of the SAT, you need a road map to serve as a guide so you don't get writer's block.

Your brainstorm consists of your position (thesis), your examples, and a few words about how each example relates to your thesis. Here is my outline for a practice essay on the topic of whether privacy is good or not:

Position: No.

Ex. 1 World War II—concentration camps, Holocaust, closed-door policy should have been lifted, few gov. officials knew of atrocities taking place.

Ex. 2 North Korea—Kim Jung Il, insurgents with video cameras need to get information of mayhem onto internet but gov. doesn't allow

Ex. 3 Scarlet Letter—Dimmesdale destroys his well-being, secretiveness eats him alive, goes crazy, hallucinates, vs. Hester who confessed and is living well even though confined

Don't worry if this brainstorm doesn't make sense to you. The only person who needed to make sense of it was me, because it was *my* road map. Notice how I jotted down incomplete thoughts in a few words instead of using full sentences. Each phrase could be expanded into a sentence or two to serve as the material for my body paragraphs. Notice, too, that each phrase described how my example related to my thesis that privacy is not good. For example, "closed-door policy should have been lifted" prompted me to write the following paragraph in my essay:

During World War II, America had a "closed door policy," which meant that only a select few immigrants, excluding those from Mexico, were allowed to come into the United States. This policy indirectly caused the murder of millions of people in the Holocaust. If only American officials knew of the atrocities taking place in concentration camps in Germany, they would have lifted this anti-immigration policy.

Notice how a simple phrase in my outline allowed me to start a train of thought, elaborate on ideas, and fill in details. If you forget particulars as you write your essay, phrases in your outline should trigger those details in your mind. Keep your ideas and facts on paper, not in your head.

## Essay 2400 Strategy 6 — *Relate topic sentences to your thesis*

The topic sentence of each body paragraph needs to introduce your example and relate it to your thesis. Many students make the mistake of starting a body paragraph by summarizing the example. When I began to practice for the SAT essay, that's what I did. Here is an example of a topic sentence that summarizes:

The Scarlet Letter is a book by Nathaniel Hawthorne about the consequences that two characters, Hester and Dimmesdale, face after committing adultery in a Puritan village.

What's wrong with this topic sentence? Nothing on the surface. But the example isn't related to the student's thesis; it merely describes what the literary work is about. Instead, topic sentences need to immediately connect your example to your thesis. Here are the three topic sentences I used in my essay on privacy:

> *Dimmesdale's lack of confession and secretiveness drive him to insanity and show how privacy is a vice in The Scarlet Letter.*

> *Another paradigm that prominently displays the detrimental effects of privacy is the lack of knowledge America had about the Holocaust while it was taking place.*

> *A situation that parallels that of World War II and shows the negative effects of privacy is the current condition of North Korea.*

Notice how I used different words in the topic sentences to restate the same basic thesis: "Privacy is bad." I also stated that each example proves my point. Assume that the grader is familiar with your examples. Even if your example is obscure, you should spend less time explaining what the example is about—and more time explaining how the example supports your thesis.

Restating your thesis in different words is not redundant. Connecting examples to your thesis actually makes your SAT essay coherent. You should also refer to the thesis one more time in each body paragraph (usually as a wrap-up in the last sentence).

## Essay 2400 Strategy 7 ⚹ *Use the active voice*
### What is the active voice?
SAT test writers prefer sentences in the active voice, where the subject performs the action and the object receives the action. The active voice often takes the following form:

SUBJECT (doing the verb)    VERB (done by the subject)    OBJECT

### Examples of the active voice

| SUBJECT | VERB | OBJECT | |
|---|---|---|---|
| John | caught | the ball. | |
| The dog | scared | the baby. | |
| The note | reminded | me | of my appointment. |
| The politicians | have agreed on | the policy. | |

### What is the passive voice?
SAT test writers don't like sentences in the passive voice, where the subject receives the action and the object performs the action. The passive voice often takes the following form:

SUBJECT    VERB (done by the object)    OBJECT (doing the verb)

**Examples of the passive voice**

| SUBJECT | VERB | OBJECT |
|---------|------|--------|
| The ball | was caught | by John. |
| The baby | was scared | by the dog. |
| I | was reminded of my appointment | by the note. |
| The policy | has been agreed on | by the politicians. |

Most passive voice sentences contain "by" and a form of "to be" (for example, "was," "been," or "is").

## Essay 2400 Strategy 8 ⟋ *Employ transitions*

Transitions improve the logic and flow of your essay. You should incorporate at least four transitions in your SAT essay. Not only will they assist you in developing your thoughts, but they will also help the grader quickly comprehend where you are going in your essay. Here are some personal examples of transitions I would often use in my practice SAT essays in high school:

**TRANSITIONS TO FURTHER EXPLAIN**

furthermore
moreover
additionally
therefore

**TRANSITIONS TO INTRODUCE EXAMPLES**

for example
another paradigm
for instance

**TRANSITIONS TO COMPARE SIMILAR IDEAS**

similarly
accordingly

**TRANSITIONS TO CONTRAST DISSIMILAR IDEAS**

nevertheless
although
on the other hand
conversely
however

**TRANSITIONS TO CONCLUDE**

in conclusion
in summation
finally
consequently

Transitions can also help you get unstuck. If you get writer's block while writing your essay, think of a few of the above transitions. Ideas should immediately spring to mind about where to take your essay next.

## Essay 2400 Strategy 9 · *Don't get personal*

Don't use any of the following words in your SAT essay: "I," "me," "you," "we," "us," "our," "myself," "yourself," "ourselves." Even if the essay question asks "Should we follow leaders?" you should not use "we" in your essay. Instead, write about "society" or "civilization."

## Essay material

You now have all of the *Essay 2400 Strategies* necessary to impress and amaze your graders, but you're not done yet! You still need to figure out what you're going to write about.

What examples should you use in your SAT essay to support your thesis?

Ideally, you would use one example from a literary work (a book, poem, or short story), one example from history (an event or character), and one example from a current event. However, you may use two literary works and one historical event, two current events and one literary work, or mix and match if you cannot think of a solid example of each type. What is important, though, is that you have a total of three examples from these categories.

You may be apprehensive, because you know that there is no way you can think of such varied examples in less than 25 minutes. Don't worry: You won't have to think of any examples during the test. You will have your examples ready before you arrive at the SAT test center!

To make this happen, you need to prepare a list of four to seven literary works, four to seven historical events or characters, and four to seven current events to write in the SAT essay section of your 2400 notebook. The list should consist of examples that you have thorough knowledge of. Many of the literary works can come from your English class. Have you read a novel, short story, or poem recently in class? If so, put it on your list. (It doesn't matter if the work is well known or not.) If you are currently taking a history class, you can use events, anecdotes, and characters you have recently studied as examples. If you don't already read the news, check out the headlines every week and choose stories that interest you to add to your list. You don't need to complete your list in one sitting; depending on how much time you have, you can add two or three examples to your list every day, week, or even month!

Once you have a list of 15 to 20 examples, you should be able to apply at least three of those examples to any SAT essay prompt. This works, because SAT essay topics are so general that you can easily find a connection between several of the examples you know and the topic. The key is to know each of your examples in enough detail so that you can apply it to any topic.

This process eliminates the need to spontaneously think of examples during the test! Not only will you have a wide array of intelligent examples, but you will also be able to cite specific details such as authors, characters, settings, plots, and time frames—which will impress your graders.

NOTE Don't use a personal experience as an example for your essay. Graders almost always grade an essay with convincing literary, historical, and current event evidence higher than an essay that uses stories from the test taker's experience.

## My material

To provide a better idea of exactly what kind of examples are excellent candidates for your list, here is a list of all of my SAT essay examples:

### Literature

"To Build a Fire" by Jack London
*Lord of the Flies* by William Golding
*Scarlet Letter* by Nathaniel Hawthorne
*1984* by George Orwell
*Heart of Darkness* by Joseph Conrad
"Araby" by James Joyce
*Brave New World* by Aldous Huxley
*The Odyssey* by Homer
*The Great Gatsby* by F. Scott Fitzgerald
"Mending Wall" by Robert Frost
*Night* by Elie Wiesel
*The Crucible* by Arthur Miller

### History

Thomas Jefferson
Alexander Hamilton vs. Aaron Burr
Andrew Jackson
Benedict Arnold and General Braddock
Eli Whitney's cotton gin
American neutrality and Woodrow Wilson

### Current events (circa 2006)

North Korea, Kim Jung Il
Bird flu
Hurricane Katrina
Gay marriage in Spain
Creation of more efficient energy sources

Many of these examples are from my English and U.S. History classes; you may not be familiar with them—which is perfectly okay. I had many more literary examples than historical or current events. If you are a history whiz, you may have more historical events. If you are addicted to the news, you may have more current events. The exact numbers don't matter as much as having solid examples in each category.

For each example on your list, you need to make an entry in your 2400 notebook that includes details about the example. Here's how I constructed my notebook entries:

LITERATURE

Title:  The Great Gatsby

Author:  F. Scott Fitzgerald

Time period:  Early part of the twentieth century

Setting:  Long Island

Main characters:  Nick Carraway, Jay Gatsby, & Daisy Buchanan

Key facts:

- Gatsby built a fortune by bootlegging alcohol
- Gatsby's goal: to court Daisy
- Gatsby throws lavish parties for the upper social class, but doesn't even know many of the guests
- Gatsby is fooled into thinking he is popular
- His attempt to please everyone is futile and he ends up a sad & lonely man

HISTORY

Event/character:  American neutrality & Woodrow Wilson

Time period:  WWI/early part of the twentieth century

Key facts:

- Many criticized America for staying neutral during the majority of WWI.
- Woodrow Wilson stuck to the tenet established by George Washington in the War of 1812 that America should stay out of foreign wars.
- Wilson made a "Proclamation of Neutrality" in what was called "the war to end all wars."
- Many activists protested Wilson's proclamation and he was criticized harshly.
- Woodrow Wilson stood his ground and did not concern himself with trivial opponents, and in the end was successful . . . because Germany and Allies bought supplies from us.

CURRENT EVENTS

<u>Event</u>: Creation of more efficient energy sources in the resource-expending society we live in today

<u>Key facts</u>:

- Beyond Petroleum (BP) is creating photovoltaic cells that will change the way society is run.
- World's petroleum supply is estimated to run out in 40 yrs.
- However, with hydrogen and solar-powered machinery, we may be able to save some of that petroleum for longer.
- Brazil, one of the most populous countries in the world, is beginning to run cars on ethanol, an extract from corn.
- Reusable energy benefits the environment and preserves petroleum supplies.
- Britain is another country that is beginning to have cars that run on ethanol + gas.

The more details you include about each example, the better. Once you have completed your entries, review them occasionally so that you stay familiar with the examples you are going to use on your SAT essay.

## Write the essay before you see the topic!

You may be skeptical. How could you possibly write your essay before you know what the topic is? The truth is, you can probably write 70% of your essay before you ever set foot in the SAT test center!

## Essay 2400 Strategy 10 — *Build essay templates*

The essay template serves as the skeleton of your essay, no matter what the SAT essay topic is. For certain parts of the essay, you can build an essay template: the introduction, the topic sentence of each body paragraph, and the conclusion. After I had written several practice SAT essays, I discovered that I could build templates that were identical from essay to essay. I realized that I could begin and end any SAT essay in the same way—and save lots of time.

The essay template remains the same every time you take a practice SAT, as well as when you take the real test, because the grader has never read your essay before. No creativity is required.

Here are examples of essay templates that I used:

### Introduction template

The presupposition that __TOPIC__ is false / a categorical

truth. Although some advocates of __SIDE YOU ARE AGAINST__

would argue that __WHAT OPPONENTS WOULD SAY__, these

romantic critics are too dogmatic in their provincial ideology.

___ADD A GENERAL SENTENCE REGARDING THE TOPIC HERE___ Three prominent archetypes that exemplify how ___SIDE YOU BELIEVE IN___ are ___EXAMPLE 1___, ___EXAMPLE 2___, and ___EXAMPLE 3___.

### The introduction template in action (topic: challenging authority)

The presupposition that _challenging authority only makes a society stronger_ is a categorical truth. Although some advocates of _a powerful, central government_ would argue that _a strong authority is what maintains a stable society_, these romantic critics are too dogmatic in their provincial ideology. _When a civilization is repressed, denizens have no choice but to rebel against authority._ Three prominent archetypes that exemplify how _defying power enriches a society_ are _Thomas Paine's Common Sense_, _the communist state of North Korea_, and _George Orwell's 1984_.

## Topic sentence templates

Set in the early/middle/late part of the ___th century, ___ EXAMPLE ___ illustrates how ___ RESTATEMENT OF THESIS ___.

Another paradigm that prominently displays ___ RESTATEMENT OF THESIS ___ is ___ EXAMPLE ___.

Yet another archetype of ___ RESTATEMENT OF THESIS ___ is established in ___ EXAMPLE ___.

### The topic sentence templates in action (various topics)

Set in the early part of the _20_ th century, _F. Scott Fitzgerald's The Great Gatsby_ illustrates how _the accumulation of wealth actually engenders distress rather than happiness_.

Another paradigm that prominently displays _the detrimental effects of privacy_ is _the lack of knowledge America had about the Holocaust while it was taking place_.

Yet another archetype of _when challenging authority only fortifies a society_ is established in _George Orwell's dystopian society of 1984_.

## Conclusion template

In summation, the notion that __ SIDE YOU ARE AGAINST __ is a fallacy that will often end in failure. It is only by __ RESTATEMENT OF THESIS __ that one/society can achieve success/happiness.

### The conclusion template in action (topic: success and happiness)

In summation, the notion that _the pursuit of success will result in jubilation and triumph_ is a fallacy that will often end in failure. It is only by _naturally pursuing one's passion_ that one can achieve happiness.

Now it's *your* turn! Build your own essay templates that will lead to SAT essay success! Keep these key aspects of my essay templates in mind as you build yours:

- ◄ The first sentence in my introduction is my thesis.
- ◄ My thesis is straightforward so that my position is clear to the grader.
- ◄ My introduction includes several SAT "intelligent" words, such as "presupposition," "romantic," "dogmatic," "provincial," and "ideology."
- ◄ I include the opposite point of view in my introduction and then disparage it. SAT graders like it when you can counter the other side's opinion, because it shows depth of thought.
- ◄ The conclusion is short and to the point.

Don't worry if, at first, you have trouble finding the inspiration necessary to build an essay template. It will come to you as you practice more SAT essays. In addition, you can use aspects of my essay templates. Doing so will not hurt your essay score, since the SAT is a standardized test. Essays written now must be graded the same as essays written years ago. Remember: Creativity is not a criterion for grading.

Essay templates will save you 5 to 10 minutes—time that other students waste thinking of an introduction, topic sentences, and a conclusion. This gives you more time to stuff your body paragraphs with clever insights and facts so you can fill up those two pages!

## My SAT essay

Now that you have the resources you need to ace the SAT essay, let me show you how I incorporated all of the *Essay 2400 Strategies* in my SAT essay written in October 2006. The essay received a raw score of 12, and I scored 2400 on the test. Here is what I wrote on the topic of questioning those in authority:

> The presupposition that it is necessary and important to challenge the tenets of those with authority is an absolute truth. Although some naive critics would argue that those in power are impeccable, they are

too dogmatic in their provincial ideology. Three classic archetypes that show why questioning power is important are Vincent Bugliosi's The Betrayal of America, George Orwell's 1984, and the current state of conditions in North Korea.

In The Betrayal of America, Bugliosi engenders a compelling argument which justifies how challenging authority, in this case The Supreme Court, is not only important but also necessary. He questions the basis of the Bush v. Gore Ruling on December 11, 2000 which ruled that a recount in Florida violated the equal protection clause of the 14th amendment rendering all undervotes in Florida impotent. This inevitably handed the election to George Bush. Bugliosi makes point after point on how this decision was politically motivated by the far right wing and clearly absurd. For example, the five conservative justices would have never stopped a recount if it would have favored Gore, and they most certainly do not favor the equal protection clause unless it is to shoot down affirmative action plans. Not to mention they included a clause that made Bush v. Gore the only Supreme Court case to ever not be referenced again. Even in a society as judicial as our own and a matter as large as the presidency, Bugliosi proves that those in authority must be challenged due to their sometimes ludicrous and self-interested decisions.

Another paradigm which exemplifies the significance of impeaching authority can be seen in the protagonist Winston in 1984. Although Winston is a member of the Outer Party, he still rebels silently by writing his journal in his room against the Inner Party. He is unable to quite comprehend the injustices and machinations inflicted upon him because of his lack of memory. Nevertheless, he knows that there were better times before and rebels against the authority of the Inner Party. He tries to join the underground society dedicated to undermining the party by contacting "leader" O'Brien, he makes love, and even visits an antique store where the proles live for privacy! His actions, although unknown to him, are important because they gradually pick at the Inner Party's authority even though he fails at the end.

A modern day 1984 with plenty of rebels taking action can be found in North Korea. The proletariat of North Korea is left desolate and isolated from the globe. They are unable to use cell phones, have no connection through the internet to the outside world, and the media is controlled by the government to keep them ignorant. However, this ignorance of utter depravity where people lie pallid and dead on the sidewalk will soon be vindicated by rebels who videotape these atrocities. Hopefully their significant challenge to authority will be successful.

Ultimately, the impeachment of authority is always necessary and proper to fight against tyranny. However, even if not successful, challenging innate injustices imbedded in society is nevertheless important.

Notice that my essay is far from perfect. I have many grammatical mistakes, I use the passive voice in several sentences, and I even use "our" at one point! Don't worry: The SAT graders understand that this is not a final copy of an essay and are considerate enough to overlook minor errors. Also, if my use of "big words" scared you because you think you are not capable of using such diction, have no fear. I was able to use so many big words because I had just memorized hundreds of vocabulary words in preparing for the SAT—and you will too! Also, notice that under the pressure of the 25-minute limit, I strayed from my essay template in certain areas. Nevertheless, my SAT essay turned out just fine, and yours will too.

## Extra 2400 essay tips

- ◄ The *Writing 2400 Strategies* for the multiple-choice section (see below) contain principles that can improve your own writing (for example, using parallelism, avoiding unidentified pronouns, and transitioning correctly). Include these principles in your SAT essay.
- ◄ When citing literary works, put the author's name before the title of the work. Write "Nathaniel Hawthorne's *The Scarlet Letter*"—not "*The Scarlet Letter* by Nathaniel Hawthorne."
- ◄ When referring to time periods, cite the century. Write "in the late nineteenth century"—not "in the 1880s."
- ◄ Don't skip lines between paragraphs. The grader will immediately suspect that you are just trying to fill space.
- ◄ Don't erase. Just cross out a word or sentence. Your SAT essay does not need to look like a final draft.

## Practice problem set

Congratulations! You now have all the tools necessary to succeed on the SAT essay, and you've seen how I used the tools in my own 2400 essay. Now, it's your turn to practice. Here is a list of *Essay 2400 Practice* prompts for you to rehearse what you have just learned:

- ◄ Is innovation lacking in the world?
- ◄ Is attempting to prove others wrong a path to success?
- ◄ Can happiness be achieved without peace?
- ◄ Is creativity necessary in a society?
- ◄ Should people worry about others' activities?
- ◄ Can one achieve success without struggle?
- ◄ Is it always better to do what others agree with?
- ◄ Should one focus on personal motives instead of societal goals?
- ◄ Is technology hindering creativity?
- ◄ Can humility work to your disadvantage?

Complete one prompt every week or month, depending on how much time you have before test day. When you practice for the SAT essay, you need to limit

yourself to 25 minutes; use the same wristwatch you will wear during the actual test. This will get you in the habit of building an outline and writing quickly in order to fill two pages. Have a notebook sheet in front of you, and try to fill both sides when you practice. Don't worry if you have trouble filling both pages at first—so did I. With more practice, you will learn how far into your essay you need to be when 5, 10, and 20 minutes have elapsed on your wristwatch.

# ⊡ Scoring your own essay

## Essay score of 6

- ◂ Is 1.5–2 pages long
- ◂ Presents a logical and compelling argument
- ◂ Offers substantial, strong, academic evidence to support claims
- ◂ Has superbly organized ideas
- ◂ Displays a mastery of prose
- ◂ Contains few grammatical errors

## Essay score of 5

- ◂ Is 1.5–2 pages long
- ◂ Presents a logical and persuasive argument
- ◂ Offers strong, academic evidence to support claims
- ◂ Has well-organized ideas
- ◂ Displays a proficient use of prose
- ◂ Contains few grammatical errors

## Essay score of 4

- ◂ Is 1–2 pages long
- ◂ Presents a logical argument
- ◂ Offers academic evidence to support claims
- ◂ Has well-organized ideas
- ◂ Displays a capable use of prose
- ◂ Contains some grammatical errors

Be sure that you have practiced all 10 SAT essay prompts before test day. The most important aspect of practicing for the SAT essay is weekly *2400 Review* of the essays you have written. Evaluate how well you are following *Essay 2400 Strategies* and identify areas where you can improve.

Once you have practiced the SAT essay enough, you might even find yourself excited the next time your English teacher says the words that most students dread: "In-class essay!"

## Essay score of 3

- ◄ Is 1–2 pages long
- ◄ Presents an argument
- ◄ Offers general or personal evidence to support claims
- ◄ Has satisfactorily organized ideas
- ◄ Displays a capable use of prose
- ◄ Contains some grammatical errors

## Essay score of 2

- ◄ Is 0–1 pages long
- ◄ Lacks a sufficient argument
- ◄ Offers general or personal evidence to support claims
- ◄ Has poorly organized ideas
- ◄ Displays a mediocre use of prose
- ◄ Contains many grammatical errors

## Essay score of 1

- ◄ Is 0–1 pages long
- ◄ Lacks an argument
- ◄ Hardly supports claims
- ◄ Has no organization of ideas
- ◄ Displays a poor use of prose
- ◄ Contains many grammatical errors

To obtain your SAT essay raw score of 2 to 12, double your self-assigned essay score. If you can't decide between two scores, double the average of the scores.

# Improving sentences and identifying sentence errors

SAT Writing consists of two major types of multiple-choice questions:

◀ IMPROVING SENTENCES          25 questions
◀ IDENTIFYING SENTENCE ERRORS  18 questions

**Step 2**

Forget your
English classes
and prepare for
SAT Writing
....................

**50**

The goal of these two types of questions is to determine if you can spot writing errors in sentences. The same set of *Writing 2400 Strategies* can be used to solve both types.

## Improving sentences

The sample below shows how the SAT presents directions for IMPROVING SENTENCES questions.

---

**Directions:** Each question in this section has five answer choices labeled (A), (B), (C), (D), and (E). For each question, select the best answer from among the choices given and fill in the corresponding circle on the answer sheet.

---

The following sentences test correctness and effectiveness of expression. Part of each sentence or the entire sentence is underlined. Beneath each sentence are five ways of phrasing the underlined part. Choice (A) repeats the original phrasing. The other four choices are different. If you think the original phrasing is best, select choice (A). If not, select one of the other choices.

As you make your selection, follow the requirements of standard written English, paying attention to grammar, word choice, sentence construction, and punctuation. The correct choice should result in the most effective sentence—clear and precise, without awkwardness or ambiguity.

**Example**
The speaker praised the charitable organization but stressed that <u>more funding is needed if the group is to continue its excellent work in the community</u>.

(A) more funding is needed if the group is to continue its excellent work in the community
(B) more funding is needed for the group's continuing its excellent work in the community
(C) there is a need for more funding so the group continues its excellent work in the community
(D) a need for more funding for the group to continue its excellent work in the community
(E) they need more funding to continue its excellent work in the community

Correct answer: (A)

**Analysis** Choose the correct choice from (A) to (E) to replace the underlined portion of the original sentence. Although more than one choice may "sound" correct, only one choice is grammatically correct; you must identify the grammar error(s) to determine which is the only acceptable answer choice. Don't bother reading answer choice (A)—it only repeats the original sentence. If you believe there is nothing wrong with the sentence as it is originally written, choose answer choice (A).

## Identifying sentence errors

The sample below shows how the SAT presents directions for IDENTIFYING SENTENCE ERRORS questions.

---

The following sentences test your ability to recognize errors in grammar and usage. Each sentence contains either a single error or no error at all. The error, if there is one, is underlined and lettered. If the sentence contains an error, select the one underlined part that must be changed to make the sentence correct. If the sentence is correct as written, select choice E. As you choose your answers, follow the requirements of standard written English. No sentence contains more than one error.

**Example**

Geologists <u>study</u> data on recent earthquakes <u>around the world</u> as
      A                                 B

a means <u>to predict</u> when the next big quake <u>might hit</u>. <u>No error</u>
        C                              D     E

Correct answer: C

---

**Analysis** Choose the answer choice from (A) to (D) that contains a writing error. Sometimes, an answer choice may "sound" incorrect, but that doesn't mean it's wrong. If none of the choices (A) to (D) contains a writing error, select (E). Of the 18 questions of this type on the SAT, three to five typically contain no error.

## Writing 2400 Strategies

The following 15 *Writing 2400 Strategies* provide the means for tackling almost any IMPROVING SENTENCES or IDENTIFYING SENTENCE ERRORS question. If you haven't studied for SAT Writing multiple-choice before, be prepared for major score improvements!

---

### ✎ Writing 2400 Strategies ✎

1 · Ignore prepositional phrases
2 · Check for incorrect pronouns
3 · Catch unidentified pronouns
4 · Check for verb tense agreement
5 · Get parallel
6 · Check for subject-verb agreement
7 · Identify misplaced modifiers
8 · Recognize redundancy
9 · Know your idioms
10 · Conjunct correctly
11 · Spot faulty transitions
12 · Compare apples to apples
13 · Don't swap adjectives and adverbs
14 · Avoid the passive voice
15 · Avoid awkward phrases

---

## Writing 2400 Strategy 1 ✎ *Ignore prepositional phrases*

This is the most important of the *Writing 2400 Strategies*. Prepositional phrases almost never contain writing errors. And because your goal is to spot writing errors, you can ignore prepositional phrases altogether! Once you master this skill, you will find yourself spotting writing errors much more easily.

### What is a prepositional phrase?

A prepositional phrase is a group of words consisting of a preposition, its object, and any modifiers of the object. The phrase indicates a relationship, often spatial, of one word to another.

Think of a preposition as a means of characterizing a relationship between squirrels and logs. Squirrels can go *above, across, against, around, behind, beneath, beside, between, by, in, inside, into, near, on, onto, out of, outside, over, through, toward,* and *under* logs.

Other common prepositions include "about," "at," "for," "of," and "with."

There are two techniques you can use to ignore prepositional phrases on the SAT. Try both techniques, then use the one that is most comfortable for you.

1. Cross out the prepositional phrase completely.
2. Put the prepositional phrase in parentheses and pretend it isn't there.

I personally used parentheses to block out prepositional phrases on SAT Writing questions just in case an error did occur in a prepositional phrase.

Here are four examples of ignoring prepositional phrases:

| ORIGINAL SENTENCE 1 | The toddler walked around the sofa with the help of his mother but then began crying. |
| IGNORE PREPOSITIONAL PHRASE(S) | The toddler walked ~~around the sofa with the help of his mother~~ but then began crying. |
| SIMPLIFIED SENTENCE | The toddler walked but then began crying. |
| | |
| ORIGINAL SENTENCE 2 | Over the hill, the road runs beside the river. |
| IGNORE PREPOSITIONAL PHRASE(S) | (Over the hill,) the road runs (beside the river.) |
| SIMPLIFIED SENTENCE | The road runs. |
| | |
| ORIGINAL SENTENCE 3 | The cake had so much frosting on top no one could eat it. |
| IGNORE PREPOSITIONAL PHRASE(S) | The cake had so much frosting (on top) no one could eat it. |
| SIMPLIFIED SENTENCE | The cake had so much frosting no one could eat it. |
| | |
| ORIGINAL SENTENCE 4 | John is glued to his laptop for hours on end. |
| IGNORE PREPOSITIONAL PHRASE(S) | John is glued to his laptop ~~for hours on end~~. |
| SIMPLIFIED SENTENCE | John is glued to his laptop. |

"To his laptop" in the last sentence is technically a prepositional phrase, but I decided not to ignore it. Here's why: In addition to its function as a preposition, "to" can introduce the infinitive form of a verb (for example, "to jump")—these are not prepositional phrases. To avoid accidentally ignoring infinitives on the SAT, I suggest that you not ignore "to" even when it appears to be used as a preposition.

A sentence becomes simplified when you ignore its prepositional phrases. Simplification is one of your main goals in SAT Writing and on the SAT in general. The College Board uses prepositional phrases to make questions seem more complex. SAT Writing is much easier when you ignore these phrases.

**Step 1**  *Read the question*

The main purpose of the research experiment by Professor Balkin in the organic chemistry department is to discover more efficient energy sources and to develop cost-effective production methods.

(A) The main purpose of the research experiment by Professor Balkin
     in the organic chemistry department is

(B) The main purposes of the research experiment by Professor Balkin
     in the organic chemistry department is

(C) The main purpose of the research experiment by Professor Balkin
     in the organic chemistry department is that they will be able

(D) The main purposes of the research experiment by Professor Balkin
     in the organic chemistry department are

(E) The main purpose of the research experiment by Professor Balkin
     in the organic chemistry department are

**Step 2**
Forget your
English classes
and prepare for
SAT Writing

54

**Step 2**  *Ignore prepositional phrases*

The main purpose ~~of the research experiment~~ ~~by Professor Balkin~~ ~~in the organic chemistry department~~ is to discover more efficient energy sources and to develop cost-effective production methods.

# ⮌ Fixing errors

To solve IMPROVING SENTENCES questions, figure out how a specific error should be fixed before looking at possible answer choices. In this way, you can focus on small differences in answer choices rather than having to read each choice completely. In addition, you will save time by already knowing the answer you are looking for. In the example above, you know that you are seeking an answer choice that includes both "purposes" and "are."

SAT test writers attempt to confuse you by offering so many different, but similar, answer choices. If you know the correct answer, you can avoid the uncertainty that other students have. In this example, you only have to read one word—"purpose"—in answer choices (A), (C), and (E) in order to eliminate them. In answer choice (B), you see that "purposes" is correct, but you know that this choice can be eliminated when you read the second word of interest—"is."

Understanding how to fix errors is a skill that comes with practice. If you are unable to figure out how the underlined portion of an IMPROVING SENTENCES question should be adjusted, you should at least identify an error (if one is present). Only then should you read each possible answer choice and decide which one not only eliminates the original error, but also avoids introducing new errors.

**Step 3** _Examine the simplified sentence for errors_

> The main purpose <u>is</u> to discover more efficient energy sources **and** to develop cost-effective production methods.

The use of "and" indicates that the experiment has more than one purpose.

**Step 4** _Think of the correct adjustment_

The sentence should read "The main purposes are" instead.

(A) Uses "purpose"
(B) Pairs "purposes" with singular verb "is"
(C) Uses "purpose"
(D)
(E) Uses "purpose"

Get in the habit of physically crossing out incorrect answer choices and circling correct ones. Remember: The more you write down in the test booklet, the better you will do on the test.

## Writing 2400 Example    _Ignoring prepositional phrases_

**Step 1** _Read the question_

> Disappointed by <u>our actions</u>, mom and dad scolded <u>John and I</u> vehemently
>           A                               B
>
> <u>at the theme park</u> so that we would not run off <u>by ourselves</u> again.
>     C                                          D
>
> <u>No error</u>
>   E

**Step 2** _Ignore prepositional phrases_

> Disappointed (by <u>our actions,</u>) mom and dad scolded <u>John and I</u> vehemently
>                   A                            B
>
> (<u>at the theme park</u>) so that we would not run off (<u>by ourselves</u>) again.
>       C                                      D
>
> <u>No error</u>
>   E

**Step 3** _Examine the simplified sentence for errors_

> Disappointed, mom and dad scolded <u>John and **I**</u> vehemently
>                                       B
>
> so that we would not run off again. <u>No error</u>
>                                      E

The sentence incorrectly uses the subject pronoun "I." You will learn about this error in _Writing 2400 Strategy 2._

**Step 4** ⚊ *Think of the correct adjustment*

The sentence should read "mom and dad scolded John and me." Select (B) as your answer choice.

By ignoring prepositional phrases, you didn't have to examine answer choices (A), (C), or (D) at all. But this doesn't mean you can avoid examining prepositional phrases for errors altogether. You should first check to see if an error is in an answer choice that doesn't contain a prepositional phrase. If not, you need to go back and examine the answer choices with prepositional phrases for errors. If answer choice (B) in the example above didn't contain an error, then you would *not* immediately mark (E). Instead, you would examine answers (A), (C), and (D) (choices that contain prepositional phrases) for errors before you would choose (E). Sometimes, there are writing errors in answer choices with prepositional phrases!

Notice that Step 4 (Think of the correct adjustment) isn't as important for IDENTIFYING SENTENCE ERRORS questions as it is for IMPROVING SENTENCES questions. This step allows you to save lots of time and confusion on IMPROVING SENTENCES questions. But on IDENTIFYING SENTENCE ERRORS questions, simply knowing that an answer choice contains an error is enough.

Still, I encourage you to do Step 4 in IDENTIFYING SENTENCE ERRORS questions. If you know how to adjust an error, there is a greater likelihood that there actually is an error. You may sometimes think that a certain answer choice contains an error, but don't know how to correct it. If you know how to change an answer choice to make it correct, you have a much higher probability of answering the question correctly, because you have pinpointed a specific element in the question that you know how to fix.

The *Writing 2400 Strategy* of ignoring prepositional phrases can also be applied to nonessential modifiers (that is, appositives). A nonessential modifier is a phrase that describes an adjacent noun. On the SAT, modifiers can appear at the beginning, in the middle, or at the end of a sentence. You should only ignore nonessential modifiers enclosed by two commas that appear in the middle of a sentence.

### Writing 2400 Example    *Ignore nonessential modifiers*

**Step 1** ⚊ *Read the question*

A filibuster, a drawn-out speech used by politicians to prevent bills
    A        B

from passing, often delay the political process. No error
    C            D       E

**Step 2** ⚊ *Ignore nonessential modifiers*

The prepositional phrases "by politicians" and "from passing" are both contained in the nonessential modifier. You should just ignore the entire nonessential modifier.

A filibuster, ~~a drawn-out speech used by politicians to prevent bills~~
   A               B

~~from passing~~, often <u>delay</u> the political process. <u>No error</u>
   C                    D          E

### Step 3   *Examine the simplified sentence for errors*

<u>A filibuster</u> often **delay** the political process. <u>No error</u>
   A                       D         E

The sentence incorrectly pairs the plural verb "delay" with the singular noun "filibuster." You will learn about this error in *Writing 2400 Strategy 6*.

### Step 4   *Think of the correct adjustment*

"Filibuster" is a singular noun that requires the singular verb "delays." The sentence should read "A filibuster often delays." Select (D) as your answer choice.

Always check all of the choices before you select an answer. You may think that answer choice (A) has an error, but are not sure what it is. If you mark (A) and move on before examining the other choices, you will often get the question wrong. If you check the other answers, you will frequently discover that another answer choice clearly has a writing error—and that choice (A) doesn't have an error after all.

Even though ignoring prepositional phrases is the most valuable test-taking tool in SAT Writing, it is also time-consuming. You will be more accurate if you ignore prepositional phrases, but you will also work more slowly. You must find a balance between accuracy and speed. The more you practice, the better you will become at ignoring large numbers of prepositional phrases and still finishing SAT Writing sections on time.

### Practice problem set   *Ignore prepositional phrases*

The answer key for this problem set is on page 131.

### Questions 1–2

> The following sentences test correctness and effectiveness of expression. Part of each sentence or the entire sentence is underlined. Beneath each sentence are five ways of phrasing the underlined part. Choice (A) repeats the original phrasing. The other four choices are different. If you think the original phrasing is best, select choice (A). If not, select one of the other choices.
>
> As you make your selection, follow the requirements of standard written English, paying attention to grammar, word choice, sentence construction, and punctuation. The correct choice should result in the most effective sentence—clear and precise, without awkwardness or ambiguity.

1. By the middle of World War I, wartime technology had improved so much that it was no longer feasible to fight on horseback, <u>and they soon were replaced by</u> tanks and armored vehicles.

   (A) and they soon were replaced by
   (B) so the replacement was soon with
   (C) with them soon being replaced by
   (D) and horses were soon replaced by
   (E) thus they soon found a replacement in

2. Not one of the children who participated in the practical joke <u>have apologized for disrupting</u> the classroom.

   (A) have apologized for disrupting
   (B) have apologized for the disruption of
   (C) has apologized for the disruption of
   (D) have been apologizing for disrupting
   (E) has apologized for disrupting

## Questions 3–4

> The following sentences test your ability to recognize errors in grammar and usage. Each sentence contains either a single error or no error at all. The error, if there is one, is underlined and lettered. If the sentence contains an error, select the one underlined part that must be changed to make the sentence correct. If the sentence is correct as written, select choice E. As you choose your answers, follow the requirements of standard written English. No sentence contains more than one error.

3. The skeletal structure <u>of a dolphin's</u> flippers <u>are eerily</u> similar to
   　　　　　　　　　　　　A　　　　　　　　　B

   <u>that of</u> a human hand, with five digits that look <u>very much</u> like our
   　　C　　　　　　　　　　　　　　　　　　　　　　　D

   fingers. <u>No error</u>
   　　　　　　E

4. In some <u>drought-stricken</u> cities, municipal governments
   　　　　　　　A

   <u>have implemented</u> restrictions <u>on</u> the number of times per week
   　　　　B　　　　　　　　　　　C

   <u>that people</u> may water their lawns. <u>No error</u>
   　　　D　　　　　　　　　　　　　　E

## Writing 2400 Strategy 2 — *Check for incorrect pronouns*

SAT test writers often use an incorrect pronoun in place of a correct pronoun.

## What is a pronoun?

A pronoun is a word that substitutes for a noun, usually a person.

**COMMON PRONOUNS ON THE SAT**

| | | |
|---|---|---|
| I | his | anyone |
| me | she | everyone |
| we | her | none |
| us | it | each |
| he | they | this |
| him | them | that |

## Types of incorrect pronouns

There are four types of incorrect pronouns on the SAT.

### Singular vs. plural pronouns

SAT test writers sometimes use a singular pronoun where a plural pronoun is needed, and vice versa. Here is an example:

| | |
|---|---|
| ORIGINAL SENTENCE | When the toddler slipped on the wet pavement, they immediately began to cry. |
| CHECK FOR INCORRECT PRONOUNS | When the toddler slipped on the wet pavement, **they** immediately began to cry. |
| CORRECT SENTENCE | When the toddler slipped on the wet pavement, **he** (or **she**) immediately began to cry. |

### Subject vs. object pronouns

SAT test writers sometimes use a subject pronoun where an object pronoun is needed, and vice versa.

What is a subject pronoun? A subject pronoun performs the action of a verb. Here's a memory trick: A subject pronoun is any pronoun that can "use a computer."

| | |
|---|---|
| **I** can use a computer. | I = subject pronoun |
| **He** can use a computer. | He = subject pronoun |
| **She** can use a computer. | She = subject pronoun |
| **We** can use a computer. | We = subject pronoun |
| BUT | |
| **Him** *cannot* use a computer. | Him = object pronoun |

What is an object pronoun? An object pronoun "receives" the action of a verb or preposition. Here's a memory trick: An object pronoun is any pronoun that "a computer can be used by."

| | |
|---|---|
| A computer can be used by **me**. | me = object pronoun |
| A computer can be used by **him**. | him = object pronoun |
| A computer can be used by **her**. | her = object pronoun |
| A computer can be used by **us**. | us = object pronoun |
| BUT | |
| A computer *cannot* be used by **he**. | he = subject pronoun |

Here is an example of a subject pronoun being used incorrectly in place of an object pronoun:

| | |
|---|---|
| ORIGINAL SENTENCE | After the game, the coach told John and I that we played well. |
| CHECK FOR INCORRECT PRONOUNS | After the game, the coach told John and **I** that we played well. |
| CORRECT SENTENCE | After the game, the coach told John and **me** that we played well. |

### Person vs. "thing" pronouns

SAT test writers sometimes use a person pronoun where a "thing" pronoun is needed, and vice versa. Here is an example:

| | |
|---|---|
| ORIGINAL SENTENCE | Scientists have broadened its outlook on evolution. |
| CHECK FOR INCORRECT PRONOUNS | Scientists have broadened **its** outlook on evolution. |
| CORRECT SENTENCE | Scientists have broadened **their** outlook on evolution. |

### Pronouns used in specific contexts

Certain pronouns can only be used in specific contexts. SAT test writers often use these pronouns in an incorrect context.

### The 4 W's + 1 (*who, whom, where, when, one*)

*who*

| | |
|---|---|
| CONTEXT | Can only refer to a person |
| EXAMPLE | J. K. Rowling is the author **who** wrote *Harry Potter*. |
| NOTE | Use "who" if you can replace it in the sentence with a subject pronoun such as "she." |

*whom*

| | |
|---|---|
| CONTEXT | Can only refer to a person |
| EXAMPLE | Jerry was in love with a girl **whom** he had never even talked to. |
| NOTE | Use "whom" if you can replace it in the sentence with an object pronoun such as "her." |

*where*

CONTEXT    Can only refer to a geographical location

EXAMPLE    Technology has allowed humans to live in deserts
        **where** people would not normally be able to survive.

*when*

CONTEXT    Can only refer to time

EXAMPLE    The Great Depression, **when** even wealthy Americans
        were starving, was a sad period in American history.

*one*

CONTEXT    Can only be used if "one" is used throughout the entire
        sentence (and not pronouns such as "you," "we," and "he")

EXAMPLE    **One** would think that **one** cannot study for the SAT,
        but that isn't true.

### Writing 2400 Example    *Check for incorrect pronouns*

**Step 1** ⟋ *Read the question*

The golfers who participated in the tournament believed that the very
   A                                      B

windy day threw off his game. No error
  C           D     E

**Step 2** ⟋ *Ignore prepositional phrases*

The golfers who participated ~~in the tournament~~ believed that the very
   A                                        B

windy day threw off his game. No error
  C           D     E

**Step 3** ⟋ *Examine the simplified sentence for errors*

The golfers who participated believed that the very windy day
   A                   B              C

threw off **his** game. No error
        D     E

**Step 4** ⟋ *Think of the correct adjustment*

Because "golfers" is a plural noun that requires a plural pronoun, the sentence should use the pronoun "their" instead of "his." Select (D) as your answer choice.

Step 2

Forget your
English classes
and prepare for
SAT Writing
. . . . . . . . . . . . . . . . . . .

62

**Writing 2400 Example**   *Check for incorrect pronouns*

### Step 1 ⁓ *Read the question*

More than anything else, <u>John and me wanted a new computer with
a bigger hard drive from our parents</u>.

(A)  John and me wanted a new computer with a bigger hard drive from
      our parents

(B)  John and I wanted a new computer with a bigger hard drive from
      their parents

(C)  John and I wanted a new computer with a bigger hard drive from
      our parents

(D)  John and I wanted a new computer with a bigger hard drive from
      our parents above all else

(E)  me and John wanted a new computer with a bigger hard drive from
      our parents

### Step 2 ⁓ *Ignore prepositional phrases*

More than anything else, <u>John and me wanted a new computer</u> ~~with
a bigger hard drive from our parents~~.

### Step 3 ⁓ *Examine the simplified sentence for errors*

More than anything else, <u>John and **me** wanted a new computer</u>.

### Step 4 ⁓ *Think of the correct adjustment*

The sentence should read "John and I wanted" instead.

(A̶)̶ Uses "me"

(B̶)̶ Introduces incorrect pronoun "their"

Ⓒ

(D̶)̶ Introduces redundancy by adding the phrase "above all else" at the end of
the sentence when "more than anything else" is already stated at the beginning. You will learn about redundancy in *Writing 2400 Strategy 8.*

(E̶)̶ Uses "me"

**Writing 2400 Example**   *Check for incorrect pronouns*

### Step 1 ⁓ *Read the question*

The dance teacher <u>did not appreciate</u> Jerry's fooling around,
A

so <u>she</u> made sure <u>it did not misbehave again</u> by making him dance
　B　　　　　　　　　　C

in front of the entire class. No error
　　　　D　　　　　　　E

**Step 2** ⟋ *Ignore prepositional phrases*

> The dance teacher <u>did not appreciate</u> Jerry's fooling around,
>          A
>
> so she made sure <u>it did not misbehave again</u> (by making him dance)
>  B                    C
>
> (in front of the entire class.) <u>No error</u>
>          D                              E

**Step 3** ⟋ *Examine the simplified sentence for errors*

> The dance teacher <u>did not appreciate</u> Jerry's fooling around,
>          A
>
> so she made sure **it** <u>did not misbehave again.</u> <u>No error</u>
>  B                              C                              E

**Step 4** ⟋ *Think of the correct adjustment*

Because "Jerry" requires a person pronoun, the sentence should use the pronoun "he" instead of "it." Select (C) as your answer choice.

**Writing 2400 Example**   *Check for incorrect pronouns*

**Step 1** ⟋ *Read the question*

> Political advocates of the new policy rallied outside the office
> of the governor in an attempt to change one's opinion.
> (A) of the governor in an attempt to change one's opinion
> (B) of the governor's in an attempt to change one's opinion
> (C) of the governor's in an attempt to change his opinion
> (D) of the governor in an attempt to change his opinion
> (E) of the governor in an attempt to change your opinion

**Step 2** ⟋ *Ignore prepositional phrases*

> Political advocates (of the new policy) rallied (outside the office)
> (of the governor) (in an attempt) to change one's opinion.

**Step 3** ⟋ *Examine the simplified sentence for errors*

> Political advocates rallied <u>to change **one's** opinion.</u>

**Step 4** ⟋ *Think of the correct adjustment*

The sentence should read "to change his opinion" instead.

(A̶) Uses "one's"
(B̶) Uses "one's"
(C̶) Introduces redundancy by using "the office of the governor's"
(D̶)
(E̶) Uses wrong pronoun "your"

The answer key for this problem set is on page 131.

**Questions 1–4**

**Step 2**
Forget your
English classes
and prepare for
SAT Writing
........................
**64**

> The following sentences test correctness and effectiveness of expression. Part of each sentence or the entire sentence is underlined. Beneath each sentence are five ways of phrasing the underlined part. Choice (A) repeats the original phrasing. The other four choices are different. If you think the original phrasing is best, select choice (A). If not, select one of the other choices.
>
> As you make your selection, follow the requirements of standard written English, paying attention to grammar, word choice, sentence construction, and punctuation. The correct choice should result in the most effective sentence—clear and precise, without awkwardness or ambiguity.

1. The goji berry or Asian wolfberry is becoming more and more popular in Western countries <u>because of their potential health benefits</u>, including possible anti-cancer properties.

   (A) because of their potential health benefits
   (B) because they potentially have health benefits
   (C) because of its potential health benefits
   (D) due to their potential health benefits
   (E) due to the potential for health benefits

2. Our bodies contain four different types of tissue, <u>each with its own unique characteristics</u>.

   (A) each with its own unique characteristics
   (B) each having their own characteristics that are unique
   (C) with each having their own unique characteristics
   (D) each has its own characteristics that are unique
   (E) each uniquely having its own characteristics

3. <u>A tenant farmer is when a person lives on and farms</u> land that is owned by someone else.

   (A) A tenant farmer is when a person lives on and farms
   (B) A tenant farmer, who is a person that lives on and farms
   (C) A tenant farmer is a person who lives on and farms
   (D) A tenant farmer, a person who lives on and farms
   (E) A tenant farmer, being a person who lives on and farms

4. Participating in mock trial or debate clubs <u>can help students become a stronger applicant</u> to many law schools around the country.

   (A) can help students become a stronger applicant
   (B) can help students becoming a stronger applicant
   (C) can help students become stronger applicants
   (D) is helping students become stronger applicants
   (E) is helping students become a stronger applicant

> The following sentences test your ability to recognize errors in grammar and usage. Each sentence contains either a single error or no error at all. The error, if there is one, is underlined and lettered. If the sentence contains an error, select the one underlined part that must be changed to make the sentence correct. If the sentence is correct as written, select choice E. As you choose your answers, follow the requirements of standard written English. No sentence contains more than one error.

**5.** As we begin to shop online with more and more frequency,
                     A

it is important to be mindful of how your credit card or bank details
                     B              C

are being stored. No error
     D              E

**6.** If you want to make yourself more desirable to potential employers,
                     A

one strategy we can take is to create several different resumes,
              B           C

each one tailored to a different type of job. No error
         D                                    E

**7.** Previously regarded as a place to just get your morning coffee and go,
                         A          B

many coffeehouses are now offering comfortable couches and free
                   C

Internet to entice patrons to stay. No error
          D                         E

**8.** To understand the debate between the presidential candidates,
     A

we must have a basic knowledge of their platforms, whether one
B            C

agrees with them or not. No error
D                        E

**9.** Biographers must thoroughly research nearly all facets
                       A

of their subjects' lives, including the relationships between they
     B                       C                              D

and their family members. No error
                          E

**10.** The Olympic Games <u>have been held</u> continuously since 1896

                       A

except for three instances when <u>it was cancelled</u> <u>due to</u> World Wars

      B                           C        D

I and II. <u>No error</u>

           E

# Writing 2400 Strategy 3 ⁄ *Catch unidentified pronouns*

SAT test writers sometimes use a pronoun that doesn't refer to any noun in the sentence; such pronouns are called "unidentified pronouns." These anonymous troublemakers attempt to fool you into thinking they are legitimate placeholders.

## Types of unidentified pronouns

**A pronoun at the end of a sentence or clause**  This pronoun should clearly refer to only one noun earlier in the sentence. Here is an example:

INCORRECT    The judges were not sure whether Jim or John had performed better, but **he** certainly seemed more nervous.

CORRECT    The judges were not sure whether Jim or John had performed better, but John certainly seemed more nervous.

In the first sentence, it is unclear whether "he" refers to "Jim" or "John." The second sentence removes this ambiguity.

**"It"—a red flag**  Always be wary of the pronoun "it" in a sentence. "It" is the most frequent unidentified pronoun on the SAT. If you see "it" in a Writing multiple-choice question, make sure that there is only one noun in the sentence to which the "it" could logically refer.

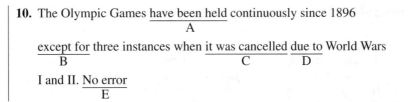

## Writing 2400 Example    *Catch unidentified pronouns*

### Step 1 ⁄ *Read the question*

Dr. Johnson told Sally that <u>she can no longer</u> swim in the summer heat

        A                          B

<u>due to sensitive skin</u>. <u>No error</u>

 C       D       E

### Step 2 ⁄ *Ignore prepositional phrases*

Dr. Johnson told Sally that <u>she can no longer</u> swim ~~in the summer heat~~

        A                          B

~~due to sensitive skin~~. <u>No error</u>

 C       D       E

**Step 3** ⌁ *Examine the simplified sentence for errors*

> Dr. Johnson told Sally that **she** can no longer swim. No error
>    A                           B               E

**Step 4** ⌁ *Think of the correct adjustment*

The sentence should identify whether "Dr. Johnson" or "Sally" can no longer swim. Select (B) as your answer choice.

In everyday language, this sentence makes complete sense. You would assume that Dr. Johnson is instructing Sally not to "swim in the summer heat." But make no assumptions on the SAT. What if Dr. Johnson is a woman telling her friend Sally that she herself (Dr. Johnson) can't swim? If you learn to read literally and insist on clarity, you will succeed on the SAT.

> **Writing 2400 Example**   *Catch unidentified pronouns*

**Step 1** ⌁ *Read the question*

> The downtown building has been in the city for longer than <u>it, but certainly looks classier than the shopping center.</u>
> (A) it, but certainly looks classier than the shopping center
> (B) the shopping center, but certainly looks classier than it
> (C) the shopping center, but certainly looks classier
> (D) it, but certainly looks classier than it
> (E) it, but certainly looks classier

**Step 2** ⌁ *Ignore prepositional phrases*

> The downtown building has been (in the city) (for longer than <u>it,</u>) but certainly looks classier than the shopping center.

**Step 3** ⌁ *Examine the simplified sentence for errors*

Incorporate "for longer than it" back into the sentence, because eliminating this particular prepositional phrase removes "it," which is a key part of the sentence. You may sometimes not know that a prepositional phrase is important until you realize that the sentence has no errors without it.

> The downtown building has been for longer than **it,** but certainly looks classier than the shopping center.

**Step 4** ⌁ *Think of the correct adjustment*

The sentence should read "for longer than the shopping center" instead.

(A) Uses "it"

(B) Introduces an unnecessary "it" at the end of the sentence

(C)

(D) Uses "it"

(E) Uses "it"

"It" is unidentified. In everyday language, we would assume that "it" refers to "the shopping center." But make no assumptions on the SAT. What if "it" is referring to a restaurant that isn't mentioned in the sentence?

**Practice problem set**  *Catch unidentified pronouns*

The answer key for this problem set is on page 131.

**Questions 1–4**

> The following sentences test correctness and effectiveness of expression. Part of each sentence or the entire sentence is underlined. Beneath each sentence are five ways of phrasing the underlined part. Choice (A) repeats the original phrasing. The other four choices are different. If you think the original phrasing is best, select choice (A). If not, select one of the other choices.
>
> As you make your selection, follow the requirements of standard written English, paying attention to grammar, word choice, sentence construction, and punctuation. The correct choice should result in the most effective sentence—clear and precise, without awkwardness or ambiguity.

1. In *To Kill a Mockingbird*, the main character discovers that one's first impressions of a person may cause you to judge them unfairly.

   (A) cause you to judge them unfairly
   (B) cause you to judge that person unfairly
   (C) be causing one to judge them unfairly
   (D) cause one to judge that person unfairly
   (E) cause one to judge them unfairly

2. The sport of BASE jumping, which involves a free-fall jump off of a fixed object, is one of the most dangerous activities in the world: they estimate that one out of every sixty participants actually dies each year.

   (A) they estimate that one out of every sixty participants
   (B) they have estimated that out of every sixty participants, one
   (C) it has been estimated that out of every sixty participants, there is one that
   (D) it is estimated that there is one participant out of every sixty that
   (E) experts estimate that one out of every sixty participants

**3.** The author's latest book, describing the ancient cultures of South America, is an inspiring and beautiful read.

(A) The author's latest book, describing the ancient cultures of South America, is

(B) The author's latest book through its description of the ancient cultures of South America is

(C) Because the author's latest book describing the ancient cultures of South America, it is

(D) With the author's latest book that describes the ancient cultures of South America, it is

(E) Describing the ancient cultures of South America, the author's latest book, it is

**4.** Although the teacher promised both to return graded exams promptly and never give a pop quiz, she failed to keep either of them as the semester progressed.

(A) Although the teacher promised both to return graded exams promptly and never give a pop quiz, she

(B) The teacher, having promised both to return graded exams promptly and never give a pop quiz,

(C) Although the teacher made promises both to return graded exams promptly and to never give a pop quiz, she

(D) Having promised firstly, to return graded exams promptly, and secondly, to never give a pop quiz, the teacher

(E) The teacher's promises included both returning graded exams promptly and never giving a pop quiz

## Questions 5–6

The following sentences test your ability to recognize errors in grammar and usage. Each sentence contains either a single error or no error at all. The error, if there is one, is underlined and lettered. If the sentence contains an error, select the one underlined part that must be changed to make the sentence correct. If the sentence is correct as written, select choice E. As you choose your answers, follow the requirements of standard written English. No sentence contains more than one error.

**5.** The renovations <u>greatly</u> modernized and <u>improved</u> the look and feel
　　　　　　　　　　 A　　　　　　　　　　　 B

of the kitchen, but <u>it</u> required <u>a lot of</u> time and money. <u>No error</u>
　　　　　　　　　　 C　　　　　　 D　　　　　　　　　　　 E

**6.** Medical school students <u>know</u> that <u>one</u> should make long-term plans
　　　　　　　　　　　　　 A　　　　 B

<u>rather than</u> short-term ones because <u>becoming</u> an established doctor
　 C　　　　　　　　　　　　　　　　　　 D

can take many years. <u>No error</u>
　　　　　　　　　　 E

## Writing 2400 Strategy 4 — *Check for verb tense agreement*

SAT test writers often attempt to switch verb tenses in a single sentence. For the purposes of the test, the verbs in a sentence usually are of the same tense. If one verb is in the present tense, a verb in the past tense is out of place. If one verb is in the past tense, a verb in the present tense is out of place.

### The six major tenses on the SAT

Don't worry about memorizing the names of the grammatical terms used below. Simply know that tenses must be consistent throughout a sentence.

**Present tense**  This tense is used to state facts and to describe habitual actions.

> He surfs all day.
> They surf all day.

**Past tense**  This tense is used to describe an action that happened earlier.

> He surfed all day.
> They surfed all day.

**Future tense**  This tense is used to describe an action that has not yet occurred.

> He will surf all day.
> They will surf all day.

**Progressive tenses**  There are three simple progressive tenses; they are used to describe an action that is ongoing. The main verb ends in "-ing."

| | |
|---|---|
| PRESENT PROGRESSIVE | He is surfing all day.<br>They are surfing all day. |
| PAST PROGRESSIVE | He was surfing all day.<br>They were surfing all day. |
| FUTURE PROGRESSIVE | He will be surfing all day.<br>They will be surfing all day. |

**Perfect tenses**  There are three perfect tenses; all are formed with the past participle of the main verb.

| | |
|---|---|
| PRESENT PERFECT | He has surfed all day.<br>They have surfed all day. |
| PAST PERFECT | He had surfed all day.<br>They had surfed all day. |
| FUTURE PERFECT | He will have surfed all day.<br>They will have surfed all day. |

The present perfect tense ("has/have" + past participle) is used to describe an action that began in the past and has continued to the present time. It can be used in a sentence with the basic present tense.

The past perfect tense ("had" + past participle) is used to describe a past action that was completed before another past action happened. It can be used in a sentence with the basic past tense.

The future perfect tense ("will have" + past participle) is used to describe a future action that will be completed before another future action happens. It can be used in a sentence with the basic future tense.

**Perfect progressive tenses**  There are three perfect progressive tenses. The main verb ends in "-ing."

| PRESENT PERFECT PROGRESSIVE | He has been surfing all day. |
| | They have been surfing all day. |
| PAST PERFECT PROGRESSIVE | He had been surfing all day. |
| | They had been surfing all day. |
| FUTURE PERFECT PROGRESSIVE | He will have been surfing all day. |
| | They will have been surfing all day. |

## The infinitive

The infinitive typically has the form "to [VERB]." Since an infinitive is not an actual tense, it may appear in a sentence with any verb tense.

to jump    to grow    to drive    to study

**Writing 2400 Example**  *Check for verb tense agreement*

**Step 1**  *Read the question*

Jane Austen, author of *Persuasion*, completed the book in August of 1816 after she finished *Emma* and just before she dies at the age of 41.

(A)  after she finished *Emma* and just before she dies at the age of 41
(B)  after she finished *Emma* and just before she died at the age of 41
(C)  after she finishes *Emma* and just before she died at the age of 41
(D)  after she finishes *Emma* and just before she dies at the age of 41
(E)  after she had finished *Emma* and just before she dies at the age of 41

**Step 2**  *Ignore prepositional phrases and nonessential modifiers*

Jane Austen, ~~author of Persuasion~~, completed the book ~~in August of 1816~~ after she finished *Emma* and just before she dies ~~at the age of 41~~.

### Step 3 ⟋ *Examine the simplified sentence for errors*

Jane Austen completed the book <u>after she finished *Emma* and just before</u> she **dies**.

### Step 4 ⟋ *Think of the correct adjustment*

The sentence should read "just before she died" instead.

(A) Uses "dies"

(B)

(C) Introduces the incorrect present tense verb "finishes"

(D) Uses "dies"

(E) Uses "dies"

---

**Writing 2400 Example**    *Check for verb tense agreement*

### Step 1 ⟋ *Read the question*

The children <u>had finished</u> their game of catch <u>just before</u> the sky
          A                                           B
turned <u>dark</u> and thunder <u>rumbles</u> in the distance. <u>No error</u>
          C                        D                              E

### Step 2 ⟋ *Ignore prepositional phrases*

The children <u>had finished</u> their game (of catch) <u>just before</u> the sky
          A                                              B
turned <u>dark</u> and thunder <u>rumbles</u> (in the distance.) <u>No error</u>
          C                        D                                E

### Step 3 ⟋ *Examine simplified sentence for errors*

The children <u>had finished</u> their game <u>just before</u> the sky
          A                                    B
turned <u>dark</u> and thunder **rumbles**. <u>No error</u>
          C                        D            E

Note that a past perfect verb ("had finished") is technically consistent with a basic past tense verb, so answer choice (A) is acceptable.

### Step 4 ⟋ *Think of the correct adjustment*

The sentence should read "thunder rumbled," because a past tense verb is required. Select (D) as your answer choice.

## When does verb tense change?

Verb tense can sometimes shift in a sentence if there is a compelling reason. On the SAT, the compelling reason—a cue that signals a verb tense shift—should be fairly logical. Here are two such cues:

1. A transition

> **While travelling** through India, George Harrison **developed** an intense interest in South Asian culture.

> **Although** scientists **have discovered** a link between nicotine and weight loss, there **is** no reason to start smoking in order to drop a few pounds.

2. A phrase indicating a different time period

> **Having graduated** from college at the **age of 15**, Charles **is** undoubtedly a child prodigy.

> The farmers, who **at one time were** upset that developers **built** an amusement park on the countryside, **are** now happy that tourists **buy** fruits from local growers.

You should be able to recognize a logical change in verb tense. Make an entry in the review section of your 2400 notebook for each SAT practice problem in which the verb tense changes, and explain why the shift is appropriate there.

**Practice problem set** *Check for verb tense agreement*

The answer key for this problem set is on page 131.

### Question 1

> The following sentence tests correctness and effectiveness of expression. Part of the sentence is underlined. Beneath the sentence are five ways of phrasing the underlined part. Choice (A) repeats the original phrasing. The other four choices are different. If you think the original phrasing is best, select choice (A). If not, select one of the other choices.
>
> As you make your selection, follow the requirements of standard written English, paying attention to grammar, word choice, sentence construction, and punctuation. The correct choice should result in the most effective sentence—clear and precise, without awkwardness or ambiguity.

1. The process of preparing a large meal <u>begins with drawing up a shopping list and culminates</u> in the clean-up of the food preparation workspace.

   (A) begins with drawing up a shopping list and culminates
   (B) that begin with drawing up a shopping list and culminates
   (C) have begun with drawing up a shopping list and culminates
   (D) have begun with drawing up a shopping list and culminating
   (E) began with drawing up a shopping list and culminating

## Questions 2–4

> The following sentences test your ability to recognize errors in grammar and usage. Each sentence contains either a single error or no error at all. The error, if there is one, is underlined and lettered. If the sentence contains an error, select the one underlined part that must be changed to make the sentence correct. If the sentence is correct as written, select choice E. As you choose your answers, follow the requirements of standard written English. No sentence contains more than one error.

2. During the past twenty years, we <u>come</u> to rely on e-mail <u>for nearly</u>
   $\phantom{During}$ A $\phantom{years, we}$ B $\phantom{rely on e-mail}$ C

   all facets of <u>our daily lives</u>, both personal and professional. <u>No error</u>
   $\phantom{all facets of}$ D $\phantom{both personal and professional.}$ E

3. Experts <u>believe</u> that by the end <u>of this decade</u>, our mobile phones
   $\phantom{Experts}$ A $\phantom{that by the end}$ B

   are powerful enough to be thought of <u>as</u> small computers. <u>No error</u>
   <u>C</u> $\phantom{are powerful enough to be thought of}$ D $\phantom{small computers.}$ E

4. Ever since Alyssa learned <u>about</u> the horrors of human trafficking,
   $\phantom{Ever since Alyssa learned}$ A

   she <u>works</u> <u>tirelessly</u> to educate others about the problem and <u>its</u>
   $\phantom{she}$ B $\phantom{works}$ C $\phantom{to educate others about the problem and}$ D

   possible solutions. <u>No error</u>
   $\phantom{possible solutions.}$ E

## Writing 2400 Strategy 5 ⟋ *Get parallel*

You probably learned about parallelism in a math class. If you don't know much about parallelism as it relates to SAT Math, your score probably won't suffer. But if you don't learn exactly how parallelism relates to SAT Writing, your score will definitely suffer.

### What is parallelism?

Parallelism requires that two or more phrases or clauses have the same structure. Parallelism has two forms.

**Parallelism in lists**  Parallelism appears in its simplest form in a list of items.

INCORRECT    John enjoys **reading**, **writing**, and **to draw**.

CORRECT      John enjoys reading, writing, and **drawing**.

**Parallelism before and after conjunctions**  Parallelism requires that items have the same form before and after conjunctions, especially the conjunction "and."

INCORRECT    John likes **reading** and **to write**.

CORRECT      John likes reading and **writing**.

CORRECT      John likes **to read** and to write.

## Writing 2400 Example    *Get parallel*

**Step 1**  *Read the question*

The pirates had stolen a treasure chest that <u>contained copper coins, silver dollars, and watches that were gold</u>.
(A) contained copper coins, silver dollars, and watches that were gold
(B) contained coins that were copper in appearance, silver dollars, and gold watches
(C) containing copper coins, silver dollars, and watches that were gold
(D) containing copper coins, silver dollars, and gold watches
(E) contained copper coins, silver dollars, and gold watches

**Step 2**  *Ignore prepositional phrases*

The pirates had stolen a treasure chest that <u>contained copper coins, silver dollars, and watches that were gold</u>.

**Step 3**  *Examine the simplified sentence for errors*

The pirates had stolen a treasure chest that <u>contained copper coins, silver dollars, and **watches that were gold**</u>.

**Step 4**  *Think of the correct adjustment*

In order to keep the items in the list parallel, the sentence should read "gold watches" instead of "watches that were gold."

(A) Uses "watches that were gold"
(B) Uses "were copper in appearance"
(C) Uses "watches that were gold"
(D) Turns sentence into a fragment by using "containing"
(E)

## Writing 2400 Example  *Get parallel*

### Step 1  *Read the question*

> The economic expert predicted that fewer people would now choose
>         A                                         B
>
> to settle down in New Orleans after Hurricane Katrina and starting a new
>             C                                            D
>
> life. No error
>       E

**Step 2**
Forget your English classes and prepare for SAT Writing

76

### Step 2  *Ignore prepositional phrases*

> The economic expert predicted that fewer people would now choose
>         A                                         B
>
> to settle down ~~in New Orleans~~ ~~after Hurricane Katrina~~ and starting a new
>             C                                            D
>
> life. No error
>       E

### Step 3  *Examine the simplified sentence for errors*

> The economic expert predicted that fewer people would now choose
>         A                                         B
>
> to settle down and **starting a new** life. No error
>        C            D            E

### Step 4  *Think of the correct adjustment*

The sentence should use "start a new" instead of "starting a new." The conjunction "and" cues you to check that items on both sides are parallel. Because the first item, "choose to settle," isn't underlined, it must have the appropriate form. Select (D) as your answer choice.

### Practice problem set  *Get parallel*

The answer key for this problem set is on page 131.

### Questions 1–4

> The following sentences test correctness and effectiveness of expression. Part of each sentence or the entire sentence is underlined. Beneath each sentence are five ways of phrasing the underlined part. Choice (A) repeats the original phrasing. The other four choices are different. If you think the original phrasing is best, select choice (A). If not, select one of the other choices.

As you make your selection, follow the requirements of standard written English, paying attention to grammar, word choice, sentence construction, and punctuation. The correct choice should result in the most effective sentence—clear and precise, without awkwardness or ambiguity.

1. Inside the luxurious Versailles Palace are hallways lined with golden mirrors, large ballrooms accented by enormous fireplaces, and <u>there are high ceilings decorated with elaborate murals</u>.

   (A) there are high ceilings decorated with elaborate murals
   (B) high ceilings decorated with elaborate murals
   (C) decorated with elaborate murals were the high ceilings
   (D) the high ceilings were decorated with elaborate murals
   (E) elaborate murals decorating ceilings that are high

2. Sharks are often caught in Japan because they are considered a <u>delicacy there, but there isn't much consumption of them in other parts of the world</u>.

   (A) delicacy there, but there isn't much consumption of them in other parts of the world
   (B) delicacy there, but consumption isn't done much in other parts of the world
   (C) delicacy there, but they are rarely eaten in other parts of the world
   (D) delicacy there but eating them is rare in other parts of the world
   (E) delicacy there but in other parts of the world there isn't much consumption

3. After completing the mandatory safety course, we felt equally confident in operating the machinery and <u>the instruction to others on how to use it</u>.

   (A) the instruction to others on how to use it
   (B) in instructing others on how to use it
   (C) to instruct others on how to use it
   (D) the instruction on how to use it to others
   (E) in instructing to others its use

4. The scientists who are attending the conference on quantum physics expect both to learn more about recent developments in the field <u>and meeting the physicists</u> responsible for the latest discoveries.

   (A) and meeting the physicists
   (B) and to meet the physicists
   (C) and they meet the physicists
   (D) and also meeting the physicists
   (E) and a meeting with the physicists

The following sentences test your ability to recognize errors in grammar and usage. Each sentence contains either a single error or no error at all. The error, if there is one, is underlined and lettered. If the sentence contains an error, select the one underlined part that must be changed to make the sentence correct. If the sentence is correct as written, select choice E. As you choose your answers, follow the requirements of standard written English. No sentence contains more than one error.

5. Encouraging people to replace their old appliances with
                         A

    energy-efficient models is not only good for the environment
                        B

    but also saving people money on utility bills. No error
              C                    D                    E

6. Scientists Watson and Crick gained fame after discovering the
                               A

    double helix structure of DNA and by winning the 1962 Nobel Prize
                     B                    C

    for their work. No error
         D              E

7. Her passion for animal conservation has led her to volunteer at
                  A                        B

    a sanctuary for endangered species and even a job as a government
                                              C

    lobbyist for conservation efforts. No error
            D                            E

8. Most endurance athletes find that regular training is essential
                           A

    to improve race times, but athletic talent also plays a big role
           B                                    C

    in determining how fast an athlete will be on race day. No error
         D                                              E

## Writing 2400 Strategy 6 ⟋ *Check for subject-verb agreement*

SAT test writers commonly pair a plural verb with a singular noun subject, or a singular verb with a plural noun subject.

### What is a noun?

A noun is a word that refers to a person, place, or thing.

**Singular nouns** Singular nouns refer to only one person, place, or thing.

| | |
|---|---|
| SIMPLE SINGULAR NOUNS | I, you, he, she, me, John, Sally, school, library, computer, sneaker |
| COMPLEX SINGULAR NOUNS | anybody, anyone, anything, each, either, everybody, everyone, everything, much, neither, no one, nobody, nothing, one, other, somebody, someone, something |
| | ANY COUNTRY |
| | (for example, "the United States") |
| | TWO SINGULAR NOUNS SEPARATED BY "or" |
| | (for example, "Jim or John") |

**Plural nouns** Plural nouns refer to more than one person, place, or thing.

| | |
|---|---|
| SIMPLE PLURAL NOUNS | we, they, the Crawfords, rivers, states, teammates, dogs, cars, computers, sneakers |
| COMPLEX PLURAL NOUNS | both, few, many, others, several |
| | TWO NOUNS SEPARATED BY "and" |
| | (for example, "Jim and John") |

## What is a verb?

A verb is a word that describes a noun's action.

**Singular verbs** Singular verbs typically end in "-s" in the present tense if the subject is a singular noun (for example, "Sally walks").

| | | |
|---|---|---|
| runs | reads | expects |
| talks | swims | struggles |
| writes | plays | thinks |

If you are unsure if a verb is singular, ask yourself this question: "Would I say 'He __VERB__'?" For example, if you are not sure whether the verb "confiscate" is singular or plural, ask yourself, "Would I say 'He **confiscate**'?" No—you would say "He **confiscates**." Therefore, "confiscate" is not a singular verb.

Singular verbs must be paired with singular nouns.

| | |
|---|---|
| INCORRECT | **Jim enjoy** reading. |
| CORRECT | **Jim enjoys** reading. |

**Plural verbs** Plural verbs typically don't end in "-s" in the present tense (for example, "The stars shine").

| | | |
|---|---|---|
| run | read | expect |
| talk | swim | struggle |
| write | play | think |

If you are unsure if a verb is plural, ask yourself this question: "Would I say 'They __VERB__'?" For example, if you are not sure whether the verb "confiscates" is singular or plural, ask yourself, "Would I say 'They **confiscates**'?" No—you would say "They **confiscate**." Therefore, "confiscates" is not a plural verb.

Plural verbs must be paired with plural nouns.

**Step 2**
Forget your
English classes
and prepare for
SAT Writing
..............................
**80**

| INCORRECT | **Jim and John enjoys** reading. |
| CORRECT | **Jim and John enjoy** reading. |

## Tips on recognizing subject-verb disagreement

◄ It is much easier to spot subject-verb disagreement if you ignore prepositional phrases (*Writing 2400 Strategy 1*).

◄ Subject-verb disagreement often appears at least once at the beginning of an IDENTIFYING SENTENCE ERRORS section.

◄ At the end of an IDENTIFYING SENTENCE ERRORS section, there is sometimes a question in which a singular verb comes before its plural noun subject.

| INCORRECT | Celebrated by the fans **was** the rock star's new album and tour after a ten-year hiatus. |
| CORRECT | Celebrated by the fans **were** the rock star's new album and tour after a ten-year hiatus. |

In the first sentence, the subject-verb disagreement is difficult to spot, because the singular verb ("was") appears before the plural noun subject ("new album and tour"), whose first item is singular. Ask yourself the following question: "Would I say 'The rock star's new album and tour **was** celebrated by fans'?" No—you would use "were."

| Writing 2400 Example | *Check for subject-verb agreement* |

### Step 1 ⚊ *Read the question*

The insightful documentary about social upheavals in African countries in the 1960s show disturbing imagery and violent anecdotes that many people find difficult to watch.

(A) about social upheavals in African countries in the 1960s show disturbing imagery and violent anecdotes

(B) about social upheavals in African countries in the 1960s showed disturbing imagery and violent anecdotes

(C) being about social upheavals in African countries in the 1960s shows disturbing imagery and violent anecdotes

(D) about social upheavals in African countries in the 1960s shows disturbing imagery and violent anecdotes

(E) was about social upheavals in African countries in the 1960s show disturbing imagery and violent anecdotes

**Step 2**  *Ignore prepositional phrases*

The insightful documentary (about social upheavals) (in African countries) (in the 1960s) show disturbing imagery and violent anecdotes that many people find difficult to watch.

**Step 3**  *Examine the simplified sentence for errors*

The insightful documentary **show** disturbing imagery and violent anecdotes that many people find difficult to watch.

The singular noun was separated from its verb by a series of prepositional phrases that end in plural nouns: "about social upheavals," "in African countries," and "in the 1960s." SAT test writers commonly use prepositional phrases to hide subject-verb disagreement.

**Step 4**  *Think of the correct adjustment*

The sentence should read "shows" instead of "show."

(A) Uses plural verb "show"
(B) Incorrectly changes to past tense ("showed")
(C) "being" is almost always incorrect in SAT Writing
(D)
(E) Uses plural verb "show"

---

> **Writing 2400 Example**   *Check for subject-verb agreement*

**Step 1**  *Read the question*

The loans given out by the banks reduces the debt
         A                    B
of students graduating from college by avoiding large interest rates.
              C                                        D
No error
  E

**Step 2**  *Ignore prepositional phrases*

The loans given out ~~by the banks~~ reduces the debt
         A                        B
~~of students graduating from college~~ ~~by avoiding large interest rates~~.
              C                                        D
No error
  E

**Step 3**  *Examine the simplified sentence for errors*

The loans given out **reduces** the debt. No error
         A           B                    E

**Step 4**  *Think of the correct adjustment*

The sentence should use the plural verb "reduce" instead of the singular verb "reduces." Select (B) as your answer choice.

The answer key for this problem set is on page 131.

### Questions 1–2

**Step 2**
Forget your
English classes
and prepare for
SAT Writing

82

> The following sentences test correctness and effectiveness of
> expression. Part of each sentence or the entire sentence is underlined.
> Beneath each sentence are five ways of phrasing the underlined part.
> Choice (A) repeats the original phrasing. The other four choices are
> different. If you think the original phrasing is best, select choice (A).
> If not, select one of the other choices.
>
> As you make your selection, follow the requirements of standard
> written English, paying attention to grammar, word choice, sentence
> construction, and punctuation. The correct choice should result in the
> most effective sentence—clear and precise, without awkwardness or
> ambiguity.

1. The Native American artwork for sale at the roadside gas station, like
   most indigenous artwork for sale in regions far from the reservations,
   <u>are not likely to be very authentic.</u>

   (A) are not likely to be very authentic
   (B) they are not likely to be very authentic
   (C) is not likely to be very authentic
   (D) its authenticity is in question
   (E) it is not likely to be very authentic

2. One of the best aspects of owning a home <u>is that it is an investment,
   so you do not feel as though you are</u> throwing away money on rent
   every month.

   (A) is that it is an investment, so you do not feel as though you are
   (B) are that it is an investment, so you do not feel like
   (C) is that it is an investment, so you do not feel like
   (D) are that it is an investment, so you do not feel as though you are
   (E) is the fact that it is an investment, you do not feel as though you are

### Questions 3–6

> The following sentences test your ability to recognize errors in
> grammar and usage. Each sentence contains either a single error or
> no error at all. The error, if there is one, is underlined and lettered.
> If the sentence contains an error, select the one underlined part that
> must be changed to make the sentence correct. If the sentence is correct
> as written, select choice E. As you choose your answers, follow the
> requirements of standard written English. No sentence contains more
> than one error.

**3.** The determination of the <u>young</u> immigrants to work <u>hard</u> and
                               A                                     B

    <u>make</u> something of their lives <u>serve</u> as an inspiring and poignant story.
     C                                D

    <u>No error</u>
      E

**4.** Most experts believe that <u>maintaining a healthy</u> <u>work-life balance</u>
                                A                      B

    or keeping up with regular exercise <u>are the key</u> to reducing stress
                                          C

    <u>in one's life.</u> <u>No error</u>
        D       E

**5.** Some people <u>believe</u> that natural gas could be <u>an excellent source</u>
                   A                            B

    of alternative energy, but <u>there is</u> certain environmental factors
                              C

    to consider <u>because</u> natural gas can pollute the atmosphere. <u>No error</u>
              D                                       E

**6.** The crowd of protesters <u>demonstrating</u> against the new energy policy
                              A

    <u>were</u> asked <u>to lay down</u> their signs and instead <u>come to</u> a city council
      B           C                          D

    meeting to discuss the new policy. <u>No error</u>
                           E

## Writing 2400 Strategy 7 — *Identify misplaced modifiers*

### What is a modifier?

For SAT purposes, a modifier is a phrase or clause that describes or qualifies a noun.

### What is a misplaced modifier?

A misplaced modifier doesn't describe the correct noun. On the SAT, an improper modifier typically appears at the beginning or end of a sentence.

    INCORRECT    Carrying his suitcase, the hotel looked great to John.

"The hotel" wasn't carrying his suitcase!

    CORRECT    Carrying his suitcase, John thought the hotel looked great.

"John" is the person who carried his suitcase. The modifying phrase must be placed next to the noun it modifies.

**Step 2**
Forget your
English classes
and prepare for
SAT Writing
.....................
84

**Writing 2400 Example**   *Identify misplaced modifiers*

### Step 1 ⌐ *Read the question*

Ari Emanuel's life is the basis for the television show *Entourage,*
a powerful Hollywood agent who does not care to be courteous.

(A) Ari Emanuel's life is the basis for the television show *Entourage,*
(B) Ari Emanuel is the basis for the television show *Entourage,*
(C) The television show *Entourage* is based on the life of Ari Emanuel,
(D) The television show *Entourage* is based on Ari Emanuel's life,
(E) The life of Ari Emanuel is the basis for the television show *Entourage,*

### Step 2 ⌐ *Ignore prepositional phrases*

Ari Emanuel's life is the basis (for the television show *Entourage,*)
a powerful Hollywood agent who does not care to be courteous.

You can't completely ignore this prepositional phrase, because it is next to the modifier at the end of the sentence: "a powerful Hollywood agent who doesn't care to be courteous." You need to scrutinize the word next to the comma—in this case, "*Entourage*"—and since "*Entourage*" is part of the prepositional phrase, you cannot eliminate it.

### Step 3 ⌐ *Examine the simplified sentence for errors*

Ari Emanuel's life is the basis for the television show **Entourage,**
a powerful Hollywood agent who does not care to be courteous.

### Step 4 ⌐ *Think of the correct adjustment*

(A̶) Places "*Entourage*" next to modifier describing Ari Emanuel
(B̶) Places "*Entourage*" next to modifier describing Ari Emanuel
Ⓒ
(D̶) Places "Ari Emmanuel's life" next to modifier describing Ari Emanuel
(E̶) Places "*Entourage*" next to modifier describing Ari Emanuel

**Writing 2400 Example**   *Identify misplaced modifiers*

### Step 1 ⌐ *Read the question*

Working for hours in the heat in the middle of July, the toughness
     A              B               C
of construction workers is certainly admirable. No error
          D                              E

### Step 2 ⌐ *Ignore prepositional phrases*

Working ~~for hours~~ ~~in the heat~~ ~~in the middle~~ ~~of July,~~ the toughness
     A              B               C
~~of construction workers~~ is certainly admirable. No error
          D                              E

**Step 3** Examine the simplified sentence for errors

> Working, **the toughness** is certainly admirable. No error
>   A        C   D                  E

**Step 4** Think of the correct adjustment

The modifying phrase that begins with "working" should be placed next to "construction workers" rather than next to "the toughness." Select (C) as your answer choice.

**Practice problem set** *Identify misplaced modifiers*

The answer key for this problem set is on page 131.

**Questions 1–2**

> The following sentences test correctness and effectiveness of expression. Part of each sentence or the entire sentence is underlined. Beneath each sentence are five ways of phrasing the underlined part. Choice (A) repeats the original phrasing. The other four choices are different. If you think the original phrasing is best, select choice (A). If not, select one of the other choices.
>
> As you make your selection, follow the requirements of standard written English, paying attention to grammar, word choice, sentence construction, and punctuation. The correct choice should result in the most effective sentence—clear and precise, without awkwardness or ambiguity.

1. Set free after thirty years in a federal prison, <u>a normal life with friends and family was what the former political dissidents wanted and nothing more.</u>

   (A) a normal life with friends and family was what the former political dissidents wanted and nothing more
   (B) spending a normal life with friends and family was what the former political dissidents wanted, nothing more
   (C) to spend a normal life with friends and family was wanted by the former political dissidents and nothing more
   (D) the former political dissidents wanted nothing more than to spend a normal life with friends and family
   (E) a normal life with friends and family, nothing more, was wanted by the former political dissidents

2. <u>Costing too much, most experts agree</u> that a high-speed rail line between the two cities will have to wait until the economy is better.

   (A) Costing too much, most experts agree
   (B) Because of costing too much, most experts agree
   (C) Due to high cost, the agreement of experts is that
   (D) Because it costs too much, most experts agree
   (E) Due to costing too much, the agreement of experts is

## Writing 2400 Strategy 8 — *Recognize redundancy*

According to Merriam-Webster's online dictionary, a redundancy is "the part of a message that can be eliminated without loss of essential information." When taking the SAT, you should avoid sentences that have words or phrases that express the same idea more than once. Redundancy is also associated with wordiness. If two answer choices both avoid writing errors and express the same idea, select the answer choice that expresses the idea most succinctly.

**Step 2**
Forget your
English classes
and prepare for
SAT Writing

REDUNDANT    Like what happened with other jobs in the area, a career in coal mining is no longer possible.

"Like" expresses the same idea as "what happened with"; they both express the idea of similarity. This error would be difficult to spot unless you realized how the sentence could be written correctly (as shown below). This is why redundancy errors most often appear in IMPROVING SENTENCES questions rather than IDENTIFYING SENTENCE ERRORS questions.

CORRECT    Like other jobs in the area, a career in coal mining is no longer possible.

### Writing 2400 Example    *Recognize redundancy*

#### Step 1 — *Read the question*

Unlike the case like most superheroes, Hancock is a troubled and disliked fighter of crime who is homeless, but he still manages to save the day for the citizens of Los Angeles.

(A) Unlike the case like most superheroes
(B) Unlike the situation with most superheroes
(C) Dissimilar to that of most superheroes
(D) Far different than that of most superheroes
(E) Unlike most superheroes

#### Step 2 — *Ignore prepositional phrases*

Unlike the case like most superheroes, Hancock is a troubled and disliked fighter ~~of crime~~ who is homeless, but he still manages to save the day ~~for the citizens of Los Angeles~~.

#### Step 3 — *Examine the simplified sentence for errors*

**Unlike the case like most superheroes**, Hancock is a troubled and disliked fighter who is homeless, but he still manages to save the day.

**Step 4** ⌐ *Think of the correct adjustment*

(A) "the case like" is unnecessary
(B) "the situation with" is unnecessary
(C) "that" is unnecessary
(D) "that" is unnecessary
(E)

Notice that this example could also qualify as a misplaced modifier, because every answer choice except (E) compares "Hancock" to something other than "superheroes."

## Writing 2400 Example   *Recognize redundancy*

**Step 1** ⌐ *Read the question*

We were surprised to see that John was no longer the skinny, weak kid
       A                                B

we once knew; instead, he was now more tougher than any of our friends.
           C                     D

No error
  E

**Step 2** ⌐ *Ignore prepositional phrases*

We were surprised to see that John was no longer the skinny, weak kid
       A                                B

we once knew; instead, he was now more tougher than any (of our friends.)
           C                     D

No error
  E

**Step 3** ⌐ *Examine the simplified sentence for errors*

We were surprised to see that John was no longer the skinny, weak kid
       A                                B

we once knew; instead, he was now **more tougher** than any. No error
           C                     D                E

**Step 4** ⌐ *Think of the correct adjustment*

The sentence should use "tougher than" rather than "more tougher than." Select (D) as your answer choice.

The answer key for this problem set is on page 131.

### Question 1

> The following sentence tests correctness and effectiveness of expression. Part of the sentence is underlined. Beneath the sentence are five ways of phrasing the underlined part. Choice (A) repeats the original phrasing. The other four choices are different. If you think the original phrasing is best, select choice (A). If not, select one of the other choices.
>
> As you make your selection, follow the requirements of standard written English, paying attention to grammar, word choice, sentence construction, and punctuation. The correct choice should result in the most effective sentence—clear and precise, without awkwardness or ambiguity.

1. At the time at which gas prices reach a certain point and driving a car becomes unaffordable for most middle-class Americans, it is likely that public transport use will skyrocket.

   (A) At the time at which gas prices reach
   (B) When gas prices reach
   (C) With gas prices reaching
   (D) At the time for gas prices reaching
   (E) As gas prices reaching

### Question 2

> The following sentence tests your ability to recognize errors in grammar and usage. The sentence contains either a single error or no error at all. The error, if there is one, is underlined and lettered. If the sentence contains an error, select the one underlined part that must be changed to make the sentence correct. If the sentence is correct as written, select choice E. As you choose your answer, follow the requirements of standard written English. No sentence contains more than one error.

2. After the city's pet overpopulation crisis became more widelier
                                                  A              B

   publicized, many people began adopting needy animals
                                C

   from the municipal shelter. No error
              D                      E

# Writing 2400 Strategy 9 — *Know your idioms*

Improper idiom usage in SAT Writing is often overlooked by test takers. Idiom errors are especially difficult to spot if English isn't your first language.

## What is an idiom?

An idiom is a set expression of commonly associated words in everyday English. Here are several examples:

| | |
|---|---|
| INCORRECT | John is **capable to** lifting 250 pounds. |
| CORRECT | John is **capable of** lifting 250 pounds. |
| INCORRECT | The child's bad behavior was **attributed as to** his parents. |
| CORRECT | The child's bad behavior was **attributed to** his parents. |
| INCORRECT | Superman has the **ability of** fly. |
| CORRECT | Superman has the **ability to** fly. |
| INCORRECT | The group of friends **agreed for** celebrate their achievement. |
| CORRECT | The group of friends **agreed to** celebrate their achievement. |

If you are unsure if an idiom is correct on the SAT, use the idiom in a different context. For example, ask yourself whether you would say "John is **capable to** doing well on the SAT" or "John is **capable of** doing well on the SAT."

Idiom errors in SAT Writing are not as easy to spot as those in the examples above. The SAT tends to use lengthy sentences, but idiom errors usually involve words that are only two or three characters in length, such as "to," "of," and "for." At least one idiom error appears at the end of an IDENTIFYING SENTENCE ERRORS section.

Idiom errors are also difficult to spot, because many of them use prepositions. For this reason, ignoring prepositional phrases may cause you to miss idiom errors in your first pass. You must go back and check prepositional phrases for errors before concluding that a sentence contains no error.

### Step 1  *Read the question*

Al Capone, a notorious gangster who has been thoroughly portrayed in a wide range of movies, is most well known in bootlegging alcohol in the early part of the twentieth century.

(A) is most well known in bootlegging alcohol in the early part of the twentieth century.

(B) is most well known for bootlegging alcohol in the early part of the twentieth century.

(C) is most well known to bootlegging alcohol in the early part of the twentieth century.

(D) is most well known for bootlegging alcohol to the early part of the twentieth century.

(E) is most well known for bootlegging alcohol in the early part in the twentieth century.

**Step 2**
Forget your
English classes
and prepare for
SAT Writing

**90**

### Step 2  *Ignore prepositional phrases and nonessential modifiers*

Al Capone, ~~a notorious gangster who has been thoroughly portrayed in a wide range of movies~~, is most well known ~~in bootlegging alcohol in the early part~~ of the twentieth century.

### Step 3  *Examine the simplified sentence for errors*

Al Capone is most well known.

Since there is no error in the above sentence, you should check to see if there are any errors in the prepositional phrases and nonessential modifier that you have ignored.

### Step 4  *Think of the correct adjustment*

(A) "well known in" is idiomatically incorrect

(B)

(C) "well known to" is idiomatically incorrect

(D) "to the early part" is idiomatically incorrect

(E) "part in the twentieth century" is idiomatically incorrect

## Writing 2400 Example  *Know your idioms*

### Step 1  *Read the question*

At the press conference, the baseball player attributed his home runs,
         A                                              B

making sure to avoid questions of athletic enhancement drug usage,
         C

as hard work and training. No error
         D                    E

## Step 2 ✎ *Ignore prepositional phrases and nonessential modifiers*

~~At the press conference~~, the baseball player <u>attributed his home runs</u>,
         A                                              B

~~making sure to avoid questions of athletic enhancement drug usage~~,
                C

<u>as hard work</u> and training. <u>No error</u>
     D                        E

## Step 3 ✎ *Examine the simplified sentence for errors*

The baseball player <u>attributed his home runs</u> **as** <u>hard work</u> and
                                  B                  D

training. <u>No error</u>
         E

The incorrect idiom here is "attributed . . . as"; the correct expression is "attributed . . . to." Ignoring the nonessential modifier between "attributed" and "as" highlights the idiom error. SAT test writers often place prepositions, modifiers, and other phrases between one word (here, "attributed") and the short word (here, "as") of an idiomatic expression.

## Step 4 ✎ *Think of the correct adjustment*

The sentence should read "to hard work and training," because "attributed to" is an idiomatically correct expression. Select (D) as your answer choice.

### Practice problem set    *Know your idioms*

The answer key for this problem set is on page 131.

### Question 1

> The following sentence tests correctness and effectiveness of expression. Part of the sentence is underlined. Beneath the sentence are five ways of phrasing the underlined part. Choice (A) repeats the original phrasing. The other four choices are different. If you think the original phrasing is best, select choice (A). If not, select one of the other choices.
>
> As you make your selection, follow the requirements of standard written English, paying attention to grammar, word choice, sentence construction, and punctuation. The correct choice should result in the most effective sentence—clear and precise, without awkwardness or ambiguity.

1. <u>Being more diligent and thorough compared with</u> the other employees, John was awarded the title of "Employee of the Month."

(A) Being more diligent and thorough compared with
(B) Both more diligent and thorough compared to
(C) More diligent and thorough than
(D) By being more diligent and thorough compared with
(E) More diligent as well as thorough, unlike

## Questions 2–3

The following sentences test your ability to recognize errors in grammar and usage. Each sentence contains either a single error or no error at all. The error, if there is one, is underlined and lettered. If the sentence contains an error, select the one underlined part that must be changed to make the sentence correct. If the sentence is correct as written, select choice E. As you choose your answers, follow the requirements of standard written English. No sentence contains more than one error.

2. In team sports <u>as to</u> individual sports, the <u>best way</u> to <u>improve</u>
               A                            B        C

   <u>is always</u> regular and dedicated practice. <u>No error</u>
      D                                  E

3. In the Victorian era, straitjackets were often used to prevent

   <u>prisoners or patients</u> <u>who were</u> mentally ill <u>to move</u> their arms;
           A                 B                   C

   with such restricted movement, they were unable to harm

   <u>themselves or others</u>. <u>No error</u>
         D               E

## Writing 2400 Strategy 10 ⁄ Conjunct correctly

Although you can connect ideas and sentences in a variety of ways in everyday language, SAT test writers have specific ways of connecting ideas with one another. It's their way—or the wrong way!

### Three major types of SAT conjunctions

**Conjunctions that connect like ideas** This group includes conjunctions such as "and" and "therefore."

John likes basketball **and** tennis.

**Conjunctions that connect opposing ideas** This group includes conjunctions such as "but," "however," "although," and "despite."

John likes basketball **but** not swimming.

**Conjunctions that work in pairs**  This group includes conjunction pairs such as "both . . . and," "either . . . or," "neither . . . nor," "not only . . . but also," and "as . . . as."

| | |
|---|---|
| INCORRECT | **Both** John **or** Jim like basketball. |
| CORRECT | **Both** John **and** Jim like basketball. |
| INCORRECT | **Either** John likes basketball **nor** he likes tennis. |
| CORRECT | **Either** John likes basketball **or** he likes tennis. |
| INCORRECT | John likes **neither** basketball **or** tennis. |
| CORRECT | John likes **neither** basketball **nor** tennis. |
| INCORRECT | **Not only** does John like basketball **but** he likes tennis. |
| CORRECT | **Not only** does John like basketball, **but** he **also** likes tennis. |
| INCORRECT | John likes basketball **as** much **like** tennis. |
| CORRECT | John likes basketball **as** much **as** tennis. |

## Punctuation of conjunctions (and a pronoun)

You also should be familiar with how conjunctions are punctuated on the SAT. Certain conjunctions almost always have very specific punctuation.

**"Therefore," "however," and "consequently"**  These conjunctions are usually followed by a comma, especially at the beginning of a sentence.

> **Therefore,** John likes basketball and tennis.
> **However,** John doesn't like swimming.
> **Consequently,** John never swims.

In the middle of a sentence, these conjunctions are usually preceded by a semicolon.

> John likes to run**; therefore,** he participates in marathons.
> Jim likes to run**; however,** he does not participate in marathons.
> Jim does not like to run**; consequently,** he does not participate
>    in marathons.

**"Because" and "although"**  When placed at the beginning of a sentence, these conjunctions have the structure "Because [SUBJECT VERB], [SUBJECT VERB]." There shouldn't be another conjunction after the comma.

| | |
|---|---|
| INCORRECT | **Because** John likes to run, **and** he also participates in marathons. |
| CORRECT | **Because** John likes to run, he also participates in marathons. |

**"Which"**  This is actually a pronoun; it is often preceded by a comma.

| | |
|---|---|
| INCORRECT | John likes to run **which** inspired him to run a marathon. |
| CORRECT | John likes to run, **which** inspired him to run a marathon. |

## Writing 2400 Example    *Conjunct correctly*

### Step 1 ⌐ *Read the question*

Scientists, working at a research lab in the United States, have discovered a new technique to deliver vaccines and other medications to <u>patients and that involves splitting human cells open with a laser for a split second.</u>

(A) patients and that involves splitting human cells open with a laser for a split second
(B) patients that involving splitting human cells open with a laser for a split second
(C) patients with involving splitting human cells open with a laser for a split second
(D) patients which involves splitting human cells open with a laser for a split second
(E) patients, which involves splitting human cells open with a laser for a split second

### Step 2 ⌐ *Ignore prepositional phrases and nonessential modifiers*

Scientists, (working at a research lab in the United States,) have discovered a new technique to deliver vaccines and other medications (<u>to patients</u>) and that involves splitting human cells open (with a laser) (for a split second.)

### Step 3 ⌐ *Examine the simplified sentence for errors*

Scientists have discovered a new technique to deliver vaccines and other medications **and that** involves splitting human cells open.

### Step 4 ⌐ *Think of the correct adjustment*

(A̶) "and that" introduces a nonparallel construction
(B̶) "involving" doesn't belong
(C̶) "involving" doesn't belong
(D̶) "which" isn't preceded by a comma
(E)

## Writing 2400 Example    *Conjunct correctly*

### Step 1 ⌐ *Read the question*

<u>Not only did</u> the Florida farm grow oranges, <u>perhaps the fruits</u>
    A                                                                    B

it is most well known for, <u>but vegetables</u> such as corn, carrots,
                                                  C

squash, and <u>cabbages.</u> <u>No error</u>
                        D              E

**Step 2** ✓ *Ignore nonessential modifiers*

<u>Not only</u> did the Florida farm grow oranges, ~~perhaps the fruits~~
    A                                                        B

~~it is most well known for~~, but <u>vegetables</u> such as corn, carrots,
                                 C

squash, and <u>cabbages</u>. <u>No error</u>
          D      E

**Step 3** ✓ *Examine the simplified sentence for errors*

**Not only** did the Florida farm grow oranges, **but** vegetables
  A                                            C

such as corn, carrots, squash, and <u>cabbages</u>. <u>No error</u>
                                 D       E

**Step 4** ✓ *Think of the correct adjustment*

The sentence should read "but also vegetables," because the phrase "not only" must always be paired with "but also" on the SAT. Select (C) as your answer choice.

**Practice problem set**  *Conjunct correctly*

The answer key for this problem set is on page 132.

**Questions 1–8**

> The following sentences test correctness and effectiveness of expression. Part of each sentence or the entire sentence is underlined. Beneath each sentence are five ways of phrasing the underlined part. Choice (A) repeats the original phrasing. The other four choices are different. If you think the original phrasing is best, select choice (A). If not, select one of the other choices.
>
> As you make your selection, follow the requirements of standard written English, paying attention to grammar, word choice, sentence construction, and punctuation. The correct choice should result in the most effective sentence—clear and precise, without awkwardness or ambiguity.

1. Elizabeth Blackwell was not only the first female doctor in the United States, but <u>she has also been the first woman to have</u> her name added to the registry of doctors in the United Kingdom.

   (A) she has also been the first woman to have
   (B) she also been the first woman to have
   (C) also the first woman having
   (D) also the first woman to have
   (E) also having been the first woman to have

2. The doctor placed my x-rays on the screen, he proceeded to show me
exactly where I had broken my leg.

(A) The doctor placed my x-rays on the screen, he
(B) The doctor, placing my x-rays on the screen, he
(C) The x-rays, which were placed on the screen by the doctor,
(D) After placing my x-rays on the screen, the doctor
(E) The doctor, having placed my x-rays on the screen, he

3. The speakers at the technology conference lectured on topics diverse as
the use of personal computers in developing countries, the future of
superconductors, and the need for more research into nanotechnology.

(A) topics diverse as
(B) topics that are diverse like
(C) topics being diverse like
(D) topics as diverse as
(E) topics of such diversity as

4. After a long winter in Alaska, the grizzly bears and the wildlife
photographers emerge from their warm, cozy homes, and the bears
would look for food and the wildlife photographers would look
for bears.

(A) and the bears would look for food and the wildlife photographers
would look
(B) and the bears looking for food while the wildlife photographers
looking
(C) the bears look for food and the wildlife photographers are looking
(D) the bears looking for food while wildlife photographers would look
(E) the bears to look for food and the wildlife photographers to look

5. During the month of April, thousands of people visit Quebec
to experience the Maple Festival, which celebrates the importance
of maple syrup to the economy of that region.

(A) During the month of April, thousands of people visit Quebec
to experience the Maple Festival, which celebrates the importance
of maple syrup to the economy of that region.
(B) Celebrating the importance of maple syrup to the economy of that
region, thousands of people visit Quebec during the month of April
to experience the Maple Festival.
(C) Thousands of people visit Quebec to experience the Maple Festival
during the month of April, which celebrates the importance of
maple syrup to the economy of that region.
(D) Thousands of people had visited Quebec during the month of April
to experience the Maple Festival and celebrated the importance
of maple syrup to the economy of that region.
(E) During the month of April, celebrating the importance of maple
syrup to the economy of that region, thousands of people visit
Quebec to experience the Maple Festival.

**6.** Lion cubs learn the basics of hunting <u>although observing</u> their mothers and other lionesses on the hunt for wildebeest and gazelles.

(A) although observing
(B) while observing
(C) in spite of observing
(D) due to their observing
(E) in the course of which they observe

**7.** The talented sculptor was invited to display his artwork at the opening of the new <u>gallery, his work having been recently praised</u> as innovative and inspirational.

(A) gallery, his work having been recently praised
(B) gallery with his work being recently praised as
(C) gallery, due to his work having recently been praised
(D) gallery, for his work has recently been praised
(E) gallery with his work having been recently praised as

**8.** The strongest earthquake ever recorded was the 1960 Great Chilean <u>earthquake, it killed an estimated 6,000 people and triggering</u> a number of other natural disasters, including a flood, multiple landslides, a volcanic eruption, and a deadly tsunami that raced across the Pacific Ocean to Hilo, Hawaii.

(A) earthquake, it killed an estimated 6,000 people and triggering
(B) earthquake, killing an estimated 6,000 people and triggered
(C) earthquake that killed an estimated 6,000 people and triggering
(D) earthquake; killing an estimated 6,000 people and triggering
(E) earthquake, which killed an estimated 6,000 people and triggered

## Questions 9–10

> The following sentences test your ability to recognize errors in grammar and usage. Each sentence contains either a single error or no error at all. The error, if there is one, is underlined and lettered. If the sentence contains an error, select the one underlined part that must be changed to make the sentence correct. If the sentence is correct as written, select choice E. As you choose your answers, follow the requirements of standard written English. No sentence contains more than one error.

**9.** Both the effort <u>to reduce</u> needless spending <u>plus</u> a more useful
             A                        B

re-allocation of existing resources <u>have allowed</u> the company
                                     C

<u>to become</u> more prosperous. <u>No error</u>
   D                     E

**10.** Because the giant panda <u>eats</u> a diet of bamboo <u>plus being</u> too large
　　　　　　　　　A　　　　　　　　B　　　　　　　　C

to move long distances, <u>it</u> is greatly threatened by the destruction
　　　　　　　　　　　　D

of its natural habitat. <u>No error</u>
　　　　　　　　　　　　E

## Writing 2400 Strategy 11 ⸻ *Spot faulty transitions*

This *2400 Strategy* goes hand in hand with the previous one. Transition errors are very similar to conjunction errors.

### What is a transition?

For SAT purposes, a transition is the way two different clauses are connected. A conjunction can be a type of transition.

### Types of transitions

**Same-subject transitions**  If two adjacent clauses have the same subject, they are often connected by transition words such as "and," "but," "because," and "which."

> John likes the zoo **because** he likes biology.

**Different-subject transitions**  If two adjacent clauses have different subjects, they are often connected in one of the following ways.

A conjunction at the beginning of the sentence + a comma

> **Because** John likes to watch football**,** Julie watches along with him.

A semicolon (used almost exactly like a period)

> John likes to watch football**;** Julie prefers to watch tennis.

A colon (used to introduce a list or phrase)

> John likes to watch three sports on TV**:** football, basketball, and baseball.

A period (rare on the SAT)

> John likes to watch football**.** Julie doesn't like to watch football.

### Fragments

A fragment is an incomplete sentence. A complete sentence includes a subject, a verb, and a predicate. SAT test writers frequently create fragments by switching the verb to an "-ing" form.

| | |
|---|---|
| INCORRECT | John **running** a three-mile route around his neighborhood every day. |
| CORRECT | John **runs** a three-mile route around his neighborhood every day. |

## Run-ons

A run-on is a sentence that incorrectly combines two sentences into one. SAT test writers often create a run-on by separating two complete sentences with only a comma.

| | |
|---|---|
| INCORRECT | John likes to watch football**,** Julie doesn't like to watch football. |
| CORRECT | **Although** John likes to watch football, Julie doesn't like to watch football. |
| CORRECT | John likes to watch football**;** Julie doesn't like to watch football. |
| CORRECT | John likes to watch football**.** Julie doesn't like to watch football. |

> **Writing 2400 Example**  *Spot faulty transitions*

### Step 1 ⌐ *Read the question*

Although John and Sally didn't experience much traffic <u>for most of the way, their road trip from Los Angeles to San Francisco still took unusually long</u> because of John's overly cautious, slow driving.

(A) for most of the way, their road trip from Los Angeles to San Francisco still took unusually long

(B) for most of the way, and their road trip from Los Angeles to San Francisco still took unusually long

(C) for most of the way, so their road trip from Los Angeles to San Francisco still took unusually long

(D) for most of the way; their road trip from Los Angeles to San Francisco still took unusually long

(E) for most of the way, which their road trip from Los Angeles to San Francisco still took unusually long

### Step 2 ⌐ *Ignore prepositional phrases*

Although John and Sally didn't experience much traffic ~~for most of the way~~, their road trip ~~from Los Angeles to San Francisco~~ <u>still took unusually long</u> ~~because of John's overly cautious, slow driving~~.

### Step 3 ⟋ *Examine the simplified sentence for errors*

Although John and Sally didn't experience much traffic, <u>their road trip still took unusually long</u>.

### Step 4 ⟋ *Think of the correct adjustment*

(Ⓐ)
(B̶) Unnecessarily uses two transitions: "Although" and "and"
(C̶) Unnecessarily uses two transitions: "Although" and "so"
(D̶) Unnecessarily uses two transitions: "Although" and ";"
(E̶) Unnecessarily uses two transitions: "Although" and "which"

**Step 2**
Forget your English classes and prepare for SAT Writing

**100**

> ## Writing 2400 Example    *Spot faulty transitions*

### Step 1 ⟋ *Read the question*

Johnny got just what he wanted for graduation from his <u>grandparents, and so they gave him a brand new laptop</u> for college.
(A) grandparents, and so they gave him a brand new laptop
(B) grandparents; being that they gave him a brand new laptop
(C) grandparents: a brand new laptop
(D) grandparents; which they gave him a brand new laptop
(E) grandparents, they ended up giving him a brand new laptop

### Step 2 ⟋ *Ignore prepositional phrases*

Johnny got just what he wanted (for graduation) (from his <u>grandparents,)</u> <u>and so they gave him a brand new laptop</u> (for college.)

### Step 3 ⟋ *Examine the simplified sentence for errors*

Johnny got just what he wanted, **and so** they gave him a brand new laptop.

### Step 4 ⟋ *Think of the correct adjustment*

(A̶) Unnecessarily uses two transitions: "and" and "so"
(B̶) "being" is almost always incorrect on the SAT
(Ⓒ)
(D̶) Incorrectly pairs a semicolon with "which"
(E̶) Creates a run-on sentence by transitioning with only a comma

The answer key for this problem set is on page 132.

### Questions 1–5

Improving
sentences and
identifying
sentence errors
. . . . . . . . . . . . . . . . . .
**101**

> The following sentences test correctness and effectiveness of expression. Part of each sentence or the entire sentence is underlined. Beneath each sentence are five ways of phrasing the underlined part. Choice (A) repeats the original phrasing. The other four choices are different. If you think the original phrasing is best, select choice (A). If not, select one of the other choices.
>
> As you make your selection, follow the requirements of standard written English, paying attention to grammar, word choice, sentence construction, and punctuation. The correct choice should result in the most effective sentence—clear and precise, without awkwardness or ambiguity.

1. Many people with emotional issues don't want to see a <u>psychologist, it is because they don't want anyone to judge them or think they are crazy</u>.

   (A) psychologist, it is because they don't want anyone to judge them or think they are crazy
   (B) psychologist because they are not wanting anyone judging them or thinking they are crazy
   (C) psychologist for the reason that they don't want anyone to judge them or thinking they are crazy
   (D) psychologist because they don't want anyone to judge them or think they are crazy
   (E) psychologist, their reason being that they don't want anyone to judge them or think them crazy

2. <u>Julia believes she is the best pastry chef in the whole city; and she</u> has the rave reviews to prove it.

   (A) Julia believes she is the best pastry chef in the whole city; and she
   (B) Julia believes she is the best pastry chef in the whole city, and she
   (C) Julia believes she is the best pastry chef in the whole city, consequently she
   (D) To believe that she is the best pastry chef in the whole city, Julia
   (E) Not only believing that she is the best pastry chef in the whole city, Julia

**Step 2**

Forget your
English classes
and prepare for
SAT Writing

· · · · · · · · · · · · · · · · · · ·

**102**

3. Sacajawea, a Native American woman, whose ability to translate between indigenous languages and English was extremely helpful to the explorers Lewis and Clark on their expedition to the Pacific Ocean.

(A) Sacajawea, a Native American woman, whose ability
(B) Sacajawea, who was a Native American woman and whose ability
(C) A Native American woman with an ability
(D) Sacajawea was a Native American woman whose ability
(E) A Native American woman, Sacajawea, whose ability

4. The student researchers discovered that the fieldwork on the archaeological dig was far more boring than they first expected, having discovered nothing for months except for an old coin that was not very valuable.

(A) expected, having discovered nothing
(B) expected; when they discovered nothing
(C) expected: they discovered nothing
(D) expected, there was nothing discovered
(E) expected, and so they discovered nothing

5. In an effort to do better in school, Marcus hired a tutor, the result was his grades improved.

(A) a tutor, the result was his grades improved
(B) a tutor, the result was an improvement in his grades
(C) a tutor, and his grades improved as a result
(D) a tutor, with the result being an improvement in his grades
(E) a tutor, resulting in improving his grades

## Question 6

The following sentence tests your ability to recognize errors in grammar and usage. The sentence contains either a single error or no error at all. The error, if there is one, is underlined and lettered. If the sentence contains an error, select the one underlined part that must be changed to make the sentence correct. If the sentence is correct as written, select choice E. As you choose your answer, follow the requirements of standard written English. No sentence contains more than one error.

6. A chain of nine volcanic islands in the middle of the Atlantic Ocean,
     A                       B

the Azores located over a thousand miles from anything else. No error
        C                            D     E

# Writing 2400 Strategy 12 — *Compare apples to apples*

## Apples to oranges

Don't compare apples to oranges on the SAT.

| | |
|---|---|
| INCORRECT | Jim's painting was more intricate than John. |
| CORRECT | Jim's painting was more intricate than John's painting. |
| CORRECT | Jim's painting was more intricate than John's. |

You cannot compare "Jim's painting" (an apple) to "Jim" (an orange). You can only compare "Jim's painting" (an apple) to "John's painting" (an apple) or "John's" (an apple).

| | |
|---|---|
| INCORRECT | The plane was able to accommodate more passengers than the travelers of any other airplane ever made. |
| CORRECT | The plane was able to accommodate more passengers than any other airplane ever made. |

You cannot compare "plane" (an apple) to "travelers" (an orange). You can only compare "plane" (an apple) to "airplane" (an apple).

## Comparison trigger words

Several common words signal that a comparison is being made.

### "Than"

| | |
|---|---|
| INCORRECT | The automobile was slower **than** the motorcycle's speed. |
| CORRECT | The automobile's speed was slower **than** the motorcycle's speed. |
| CORRECT | The automobile was much slower **than** the motorcycle. |

You cannot compare "automobile" (an apple) to "motorcycle's speed" (an orange). You can compare "automobile's speed" (an orange) to "motorcycle's speed" (an orange), or "automobile" (an apple) to "motorcycle" (an apple).

### "As"

| | |
|---|---|
| INCORRECT | Just **as** John's experiment had won the science fair last year, Jim was determined to take home the prize this year. |
| CORRECT | Just **as** John had won the science fair last year, Jim was determined to take home the prize this year. |

You cannot compare "John's experiment" (an apple) to "Jim" (an orange). You can only compare "John" (an orange) to "Jim" (an orange).

### "Like" and "unlike"

INCORRECT    **Like** the economy of the United States, Great Britain also suffered immensely during the Great Depression.

CORRECT    **Like** the economy of the United States, Great Britain's economy also suffered immensely during the Great Depression.

**Step 2**
Forget your
English classes
and prepare for
SAT Writing

**104**

You cannot compare "economy" (an apple) to "Great Britain" (an orange). You can only compare "economy" (an apple) to "economy" (an apple).

### "-er" and "-est"

Adjectives ending in "-er" are used to compare two items. Adjectives ending in "-est" are used to compare three or more items.

INCORRECT    John runs **faster** than Jim and Tom.

CORRECT    John runs **faster** than Jim.

CORRECT    Although Jim and Tom are quick, John runs the **fastest**.

### Writing 2400 Example   *Compare apples to apples*

#### Step 1   *Read the question*

The sun, which in many cultures has long been believed to have mystic powers, <u>produces more power and heat than the energy of a million steam engines.</u>

(A) produces more power and heat than the energy of a million steam engines.

(B) produces more power and heat than the force of a million steam engines.

(C) produce more power and heat than a million steam engines.

(D) produces more power and heat than a million steam engines.

(E) which produces more power and heat than a million steam engines.

#### Step 2   *Ignore prepositional phrases and nonessential modifiers*

The sun, ~~which in many cultures has long been believed to have mystic powers~~, <u>produces more power and heat than the energy ~~of a million steam engines~~.</u>

#### Step 3   *Examine the simplified sentence for errors*

The sun <u>produces more power and heat **than the energy**</u>.

You cannot compare "the sun" (an apple) to "energy" (an orange). The sun produces energy, so it must be compared to something else that produces energy, not to energy itself.

**Step 4** ✐ *Think of the correct adjustment*

(A) Compares "sun" to "energy"
(B) Compares "sun" to "force"
(C) Pairs the singular noun "sun" with the plural verb "produce"
(D)
(E) Unnecessarily uses two transitions: "which" and "which"

**Writing 2400 Example** *Compare apples to apples*

**Step 1** ✐ *Read the question*

Unlike <u>the tiger's existence</u>, which is now <u>rare in the region</u>, the lion
             A                                      B
continues <u>to rule</u> supreme over <u>the vast plains</u> despite the intrusion
              C                     D
of humans. <u>No error</u>
            E

**Step 2** ✐ *Ignore prepositional phrases and nonessential modifiers*

Unlike <u>the tiger's existence</u>, (which is now <u>rare in the region</u>,) the lion
             A                            B
continues <u>to rule</u> supreme (over <u>the vast plains</u>) (despite the intrusion)
              C                     D
(of humans.) <u>No error</u>
             E

**Step 3** ✐ *Examine the simplified sentence for errors*

Unlike the **tiger's existence**, the lion continues <u>to rule</u> supreme.
             A                            C
<u>No error</u>
  E

**Step 4** ✐ *Think of the correct adjustment*

The sentence should compare "tiger" to "lion" rather than "tiger's existence" to "lion." Select (A) as your answer choice.

The answer key for this problem set is on page 132.

### Questions 1–4

**Step 2**

Forget your
English classes
and prepare for
SAT Writing
.....................

**106**

The following sentences test correctness and effectiveness of expression. Part of each sentence or the entire sentence is underlined. Beneath each sentence are five ways of phrasing the underlined part. Choice (A) repeats the original phrasing. The other four choices are different. If you think the original phrasing is best, select choice (A). If not, select one of the other choices.

As you make your selection, follow the requirements of standard written English, paying attention to grammar, word choice, sentence construction, and punctuation. The correct choice should result in the most effective sentence—clear and precise, without awkwardness or ambiguity.

1. <u>Only slightly different from the Americans are the Canadian accents, which</u> may easily be confused by someone who has never been to North America.

   (A) Only slightly different from the Americans are the Canadian accents, which
   (B) The Canadian accent is only slightly different from the American accent, and they
   (C) Differing only slightly from American accents, the Canadian accent
   (D) The American accent differs only slightly from the Canadian accent, they
   (E) The American accents differ from the Canadian accents only slightly, they

2. In some Hindi-speaking communities in the United States, the stars of Bollywood movies are often more idolized than <u>American movies</u>.

   (A) American movies
   (B) in American movies
   (C) those of American movies
   (D) the movies in America
   (E) the American movies' plots

3. Some experts believe that giving birth puts as much stress on a woman's body <u>than if you ran</u> a marathon.

   (A) than if you ran
   (B) than to run
   (C) as running
   (D) as if one runs
   (E) as it does when running

4. The inspiring words of Dr. Martin Luther King, Jr., are taught in many schools around the <u>world, including China</u>.

    (A) world, including China
    (B) world, including those in China
    (C) world, this includes China
    (D) world and in China as well
    (E) world, and China is included

## Questions 5–7

The following sentences test your ability to recognize errors in grammar and usage. Each sentence contains either a single error or no error at all. The error, if there is one, is underlined and lettered. If the sentence contains an error, select the one underlined part that must be changed to make the sentence correct. If the sentence is correct as written, select choice E. As you choose your answers, follow the requirements of standard written English. No sentence contains more than one error.

5. <u>Like her</u> previous novel, in her new book the author <u>does</u> an excellent
       A                                       B

   job <u>of blending</u> vivid imagery <u>with</u> straightforward, realistic dialogue.
          C                  D

   <u>No error</u>
     E

6. <u>Of all</u> the threatened animal species in the world, the Amur leopard
    A

   <u>may be</u> the <u>more critically</u> endangered, with <u>fewer</u> than 35 individuals
    B          C                 D
   left in the wild. <u>No error</u>
             E

7. The notes of an oboe, compared to <u>a clarinet</u>, <u>are</u> often <u>said</u> to sound
                          A     B       C

   reedier and <u>more melancholy</u>. <u>No error</u>
             D       E

# Writing 2400 Strategy 13  *Don't swap adjectives and adverbs*

SAT test writers often use an adjective where an adverb is needed, and vice versa.

## What is an adjective?

An adjective is a word that describes a noun. Here are several examples:

Although many people believe that diet drugs are **safe**, there is no scientific research that supports this general observation.

"Safe" is an adjective that describes the noun "drugs."

> The modern, spherical house was designed by perhaps the most **skillful** architect of our time.

"Skillful" is an adjective that describes the noun "architect."

> Doctors and scientists have yet to agree on what treatment is most **effective** to treat the disease.

"Effective" is an adjective that describes the noun "treatment."

**Step 2**
Forget your
English classes
and prepare for
SAT Writing

**108**

## What is an adverb?

An adverb is a word that describes an adjective, verb, or another adverb. On the SAT, adverbs almost always end in "-ly." Here are several examples:

> During our car wash for charity, the temperature seemed to continue to get **increasingly** hot throughout the day.

"Increasingly" is an adverb that describes "hot," and "hot" is an adjective that describes the noun "temperature."

> The blacksmith can **skillfully** weld the hot silica into a beautiful glass horse in a matter of minutes.

"Skillfully" is an adverb that describes "weld," and "weld" is a verb that describes the action of the noun "blacksmith."

> The school's new tardy policy, which locks students out of the building if they are more than ten minutes late to class, **very** effectively solved the problem of teenagers arriving late to school.

"Very" is an adverb that describes the adverb "effectively," and "effectively" is an adverb that describes the verb "solved."

## Adjective/adverb swapping

SAT test writers often use an adjective where an adverb is needed, and vice versa.

> INCORRECT    During our car wash for charity, the temperature seemed to continue to get **increasing** hot throughout the day.

"Increasing" is an adjective and cannot modify another adjective such as "hot."

> INCORRECT    The modern, spherical house was designed by perhaps the most **skillfully** architect of our time.

"Skillfully" is an adverb and cannot modify a noun such as "architect."

Improving
sentences and
identifying
sentence errors
...................

109

INCORRECT    The school's new tardy policy, which locks students out
of the building if they are more than ten minutes late
to class, solved the problem of teenagers arriving late
to school **effective**.

"Effective" is an adjective and cannot modify a verb such as "solved."

## Writing 2400 Example    *Don't swap adjectives and adverbs*

### Step 1 ⌐ *Read the question*

> Many animal activists, who are especially empathetic, oppose keeping
> creatures in zoos because the protesters believe that such confined
> environments prevent <u>animals from moving free in the wild where
> animals should be</u>.
>
> (A)  animals from moving free in the wild where animals should be
> (B)  them from moving freely in the wild where animals should be
> (C)  animals from moving freely in the wild where animals should be
> (D)  animals from moving free in the wild where they should be
> (E)  animals from moving freely in the wild where they should be

### Step 2 ⌐ *Ignore prepositional phrases and nonessential modifiers*

> Many animal activists, ~~who are especially empathetic~~, oppose keeping
> creatures ~~in zoos~~ because the protesters believe that such confined
> environments prevent <u>animals from moving free ~~in the wild~~ where
> animals should be</u>.

### Step 3 ⌐ *Examine the simplified sentence for errors*

> Many animal activists oppose keeping creatures because the protesters
> believe that such confined environments prevent <u>animals from moving **free**
> where animals should be</u>.

Although there is a lot going on in this sentence, you should be able to spot the
adjective/adverb swap. The adjective "free" cannot describe the verb "moving."

### Step 4 ⌐ *Think of the correct adjustment*

(A̶)  An adjective ("free") cannot describe a verb ("moving")
(B̶)  Includes the unidentified pronoun "them"
(C̲)
(D̶)  An adjective ("free") cannot describe a verb ("moving")
(E̶)  Includes the unidentified pronoun "they"

## Writing 2400 Example   *Don't swap adjectives and adverbs*

### Step 1 ⟋ *Read the question*

Certainly, <u>the doctoral student's dissertation</u> <u>elucidated the repercussions</u>
                    A                                            B

of the Cold War <u>on the world</u> we live in today <u>as brilliant</u> as any critique
                      C                                    D

the committee had ever seen. <u>No error</u>
                                    E

**Step 2**
Forget your
English classes
and prepare for
SAT Writing

**110**

### Step 2 ⟋ *Ignore prepositional phrases*

Certainly, <u>the doctoral student's dissertation</u> <u>elucidated the repercussions</u>
                    A                                            B

~~of the Cold War~~ <u>~~on the world we live in today~~</u> as brilliant as any critique
                              C                                    D

the committee had ever seen. <u>No error</u>
                                    E

### Step 3 ⟋ *Examine the simplified sentence for errors*

Certainly, <u>the doctoral student's</u> dissertation <u>elucidated the repercussions</u>
                    A                                            B

as **brilliant** as any critique the committee had ever seen. <u>No error</u>
        D                                                          E

### Step 4 ⟋ *Think of the correct adjustment*

The sentence should use the adverb "brilliantly," not the adjective "brilliant,"
to describe the verb "elucidated." Select (D) as your answer choice.

### Practice problem set   *Don't swap adjectives and adverbs*

The answer key for this problem set is on page 132.

### Questions 1–2

> The following sentences test your ability to recognize errors in
> grammar and usage. Each sentence contains either a single error or
> no error at all. The error, if there is one, is underlined and lettered.
> If the sentence contains an error, select the one underlined part that
> must be changed to make the sentence correct. If the sentence is correct
> as written, select choice E. As you choose your answers, follow the
> requirements of standard written English. No sentence contains more
> than one error.

1. The new luxury cruise ships were said to be able to cross the Atlantic
                                        ‾‾‾A‾‾      ‾B‾
   much more rapid than other ships, despite their massive size. No error
             ‾‾C‾‾                    ‾‾D‾‾‾                      ‾‾E‾‾

2. The ambitiously fashion designer surprised everyone by launching a
       ‾‾‾A‾‾‾‾                      ‾‾B‾‾‾          ‾‾‾C‾‾‾
   very successful clothing line in spite of her lack of industry experience.
                                  ‾‾‾‾D‾‾‾‾

   No error
   ‾‾E‾‾

## Writing 2400 Strategy 14 ⁄ *Avoid the passive voice*

Use of the passive voice is a stylistic issue, not a grammar error. For this reason, passive voice "errors" are found almost exclusively in IMPROVING SENTENCES questions. Use of the passive voice is typically not the principal error in an IMPROVING SENTENCES question; the principal error is usually one of the errors previously discussed, such as an unidentified pronoun, a transition error, or a comparison error. Use of the passive voice makes one answer choice worse than another if both choices have solved the principal error. Think of passive voice errors as secondary errors.

The passive voice was discussed in connection with *Essay 2400 Strategy 7*; the discussion is repeated here.

### What is the active voice?

The SAT prefers sentences in the active voice, where the subject performs the action and the object receives the action. The active voice often takes the following form:

SUBJECT (doing the verb)   VERB (done by the subject)   OBJECT

### Examples of the active voice

| SUBJECT | VERB | OBJECT | |
|---|---|---|---|
| John | caught | the ball. | |
| The dog | scared | the baby. | |
| The note | reminded | me | of my appointment. |
| The politicians | have agreed on | the policy. | |

### What is the passive voice?

The SAT doesn't like sentences in the passive voice, where the subject receives the action and the object performs the action. The passive voice often takes the following form:

SUBJECT   VERB (done by the object)   OBJECT (doing the verb)

## Examples of the passive voice

| SUBJECT | VERB | OBJECT |
|---------|------|--------|
| The ball | was caught | by John. |
| The baby | was scared | by the dog. |
| I | was reminded of my appointment | by the note. |
| The policy | has been agreed on | by the politicians. |

Most passive voice sentences contain "by" and a form of "to be" (for example, "was," "been," or "is.")

Step 2

Forget your
English classes
and prepare for
SAT Writing

112

### Writing 2400 Example  *Avoid the passive voice*

#### Step 1 ⚊ *Read the question*

Since the side effects of the treatment are still unknown, <u>the medication that might improve the blood sugar levels of diabetes patients are not prescribed by most doctors.</u>

(A) the medication that might improve the blood sugar levels of diabetes patients are not prescribed by most doctors.

(B) the medication, that might improve the blood sugar levels of diabetes patients isn't prescribed by most doctors.

(C) most doctors don't prescribe the medication that might improve the blood sugar levels of diabetes patients.

(D) most doctors have yet to prescribe the medications which might improve the blood sugar levels of diabetes patients.

(E) the medication that might improve the blood sugar levels of diabetes patients isn't prescribed by most doctors.

#### Step 2 ⚊ *Ignore prepositional phrases*

Since the side effects (of the treatment) are still unknown, <u>the medication that might improve the blood sugar levels (of diabetes patients) are not prescribed (by most doctors).</u>

#### Step 3 ⚊ *Examine the simplified sentence for errors*

Since the side effects are still unknown, <u>the medication that might improve the blood sugar levels **are** not prescribed.</u>

#### Step 4 ⚊ *Think of the correct adjustment*

(A) Subject-verb disagreement plus passive voice

(B) Unnecessary comma plus passive voice

(C)

(D) Tense error plus no comma preceding "which"

(E) Passive voice

## Step 1 ⚊ *Read the question*

> To make sure that the hiking trail is safe during all times of the year, an inspection of the path is done every two months by park rangers to ensure that visitors are never in any immediate danger.
>
> (A) an inspection of the path is done every two months by park rangers to ensure that visitors are never in any immediate danger.
> (B) the park ranger do an inspection of the path every two months to ensure that visitors are never in any immediate danger.
> (C) the park rangers do an inspection of the path every two months to ensure that visitors are never in any immediate danger.
> (D) an inspection of the path is done every two months by park rangers so that visitors are never in any immediate danger.
> (E) the park rangers does an inspection of the path every two months to ensure that visitors are never in any immediate danger.

Improving
sentences and
identifying
sentence errors
........................

**113**

## Step 2 ⚊ *Ignore prepositional phrases*

> To make sure that the hiking trail is safe ~~during all times of the year~~, an inspection ~~of the path~~ is done every two months ~~by park rangers~~ to ensure that visitors are never ~~in any immediate danger~~.

## Step 3 ⚊ *Examine the simplified sentence for errors*

> To make sure that the hiking trail is safe, an inspection **is done** every two months to ensure that visitors are never.

Because the prepositional phrase "by park rangers" was ignored in the sentence above, the passive voice may be difficult to spot.

## Step 4 ⚊ *Think of the correct adjustment*

(A̶) Passive voice
(B̶) Subject-verb disagreement
Ⓒ
(D̶) Passive voice
(E̶) Subject-verb disagreement

**Step 2**
Forget your
English classes
and prepare for
SAT Writing

114

**Practice problem set** *Avoid the passive voice*

The answer key for this problem set is on page 132.

**Questions 1–3**

> The following sentences test correctness and effectiveness of expression. Part of each sentence or the entire sentence is underlined. Beneath each sentence are five ways of phrasing the underlined part. Choice (A) repeats the original phrasing. The other four choices are different. If you think the original phrasing is best, select choice (A). If not, select one of the other choices.
>
> As you make your selection, follow the requirements of standard written English, paying attention to grammar, word choice, sentence construction, and punctuation. The correct choice should result in the most effective sentence—clear and precise, without awkwardness or ambiguity.

1. When the imagery in poems is interpreted too rigidly by scholars, they risk missing the deeper meaning of the work as a whole.

   (A) When the imagery in poems is interpreted too rigidly by scholars, they risk missing the deeper meaning of the work as a whole.
   (B) When the imagery in poems is interpreted too rigidly by scholars, it risks missing the deeper meaning of the work as a whole.
   (C) Imagery in poems, if interpreted too rigidly, risks missing the deeper meaning of the work as a whole.
   (D) If you interpret imagery in poems too rigidly, it risks missing the deeper meaning of the work as a whole.
   (E) When scholars interpret the imagery in poems too rigidly, they risk missing the deeper meaning of the work as a whole.

2. Politicians cannot expect to make false promises without notice by someone.

   (A) without notice by someone
   (B) and have no one notice
   (C) without someone noticing
   (D) without no one noticing
   (E) without having no one notice

3. Louisa was not surprised that she made several spelling and punctuation mistakes on her essay, since work was not started on it until very late at night, when she was already tired.

   (A) essay, since work was not started on it until very late at night
   (B) essay since work was not starting on it until very late at night
   (C) essay, being that it was very late at night that she started working on it
   (D) essay; it was very late at night when working started on it
   (E) essay: she didn't start working on it until very late at night

## Writing 2400 Strategy 15 ⁄ *Avoid awkward phrases*

Like passive voice "errors," awkward phrases generally appear as secondary errors on the SAT. Awkward phrasing makes one answer choice worse than another in IMPROVING SENTENCES questions.

**"Being"**  "Being" is almost always wrong on the SAT.

Improving
sentences and
identifying
sentence errors
. . . . . . . . . . . . . . . . . .
115

| | |
|---|---|
| INCORRECT | **Being** a former long distance runner, the older senior at the gym looked much younger than his age. |
| INCORRECT | The author lost much of his readership **being** that his comments in the media were politically controversial. |

**"Is why," "is because," and "is the reason"**  These phrases are almost always wrong on the SAT.

| | |
|---|---|
| INCORRECT | The clown **is why** kids had fun at the party. |
| INCORRECT | The reason the young mother reprimanded her child **is because** he almost ran out onto a busy street filled with cars. |
| INCORRECT | The recent scandal **is the reason** wealthy individuals are hesitant to entrust their money to any third party now. |

---

### Writing 2400 Example   *Avoid awkward phrases*

#### Step 1 ⁄ *Read the question*

> Ernest Hemingway, being that he spent much time in Spain during the early twentieth century, had decided to use that particular country as the setting for his novel *The Sun Also Rises.*
>
> (A) Hemingway, being that he spent much time in Spain during the early twentieth century, had decided to use that particular country as the setting for his novel *The Sun Also Rises.*
> (B) Hemingway decided to use Spain as the setting for his novel *The Sun Also Rises* because he spent much time there during the early twentieth century.
> (C) Hemingway, he spent much time in Spain during the early twentieth century, had decided to use that particular country as the setting for his novel *The Sun Also Rises.*
> (D) Hemingway had decided to use Spain as the setting for his novel *The Sun Also Rises,* being that he spent much time in that particular country during the early twentieth century.
> (E) Hemingway spent much time in Spain during the early twentieth century so then he had decided to use that particular country as the setting for his novel *The Sun Also Rises.*

#### Step 2 ⁄ *Ignore prepositional phrases and nonessential modifiers*

> Ernest Hemingway, ~~being that he spent much time in Spain during the early twentieth century~~, had decided to use that particular country as the setting ~~for his novel The Sun Also Rises~~.

### Step 3 — *Examine the simplified sentence for errors*

Ernest <u>Hemingway</u> had decided to use that particular country as the <u>setting.</u>

### Step 4 — *Think of the correct adjustment*

(A) Awkward phrase "being"

(B)

(C) Redundancy (adding "he" immediately after "Hemingway")

(D) Awkward phrase "being"

(E) "so then" is an incorrect double conjunction

**Step 2**
Forget your
English classes
and prepare for
SAT Writing

116

## Writing 2400 Example   *Avoid awkward phrases*

### Step 1 — *Read the question*

In the past, correspondence between readers and journalists was inefficient due to slow delivery of postal mail, <u>until the advent of the internet, and now allows them to quickly send e-mails to writers.</u>

(A) until the advent of the internet, and now allows them to quickly send e-mails to writers.

(B) until the advent of the internet being that it allows readers to quickly send e-mails to writers.

(C) until the advent of the internet, which now allows readers to quickly send e-mails to writers.

(D) being until the advent of the internet, which now allows them to quickly send e-mails to writers.

(E) until the advent of the internet, which now allows them to quickly send e-mails to them.

### Step 2 — *Ignore prepositional phrases*

(In the past,) correspondence (between readers and journalists) was inefficient due to slow delivery (of postal mail,) (until the advent) (of the internet,) and now allows them to quickly send e-mails (to writers.)

### Step 3 — *Examine the simplified sentence for errors*

Correspondence was inefficient due to slow delivery, **and** now allows **them** to quickly send e-mails.

### Step 4 — *Think of the correct adjustment*

(A) Incorrect conjunction "and" plus unidentified pronoun "them"

(B) Awkward phrase "being"

(C)

(D) Awkward phrase "being"

(E) Two unidentified pronouns ("them")

**Practice problem set**  *Avoid awkward phrases*

The answer key for this problem set is on page 132.

### Questions 1–5

The following sentences test correctness and effectiveness of expression. Part of each sentence or the entire sentence is underlined. Beneath each sentence are five ways of phrasing the underlined part. Choice (A) repeats the original phrasing. The other four choices are different. If you think the original phrasing is best, select choice (A). If not, select one of the other choices.

As you make your selection, follow the requirements of standard written English, paying attention to grammar, word choice, sentence construction, and punctuation. The correct choice should result in the most effective sentence—clear and precise, without awkwardness or ambiguity.

1. The bookshelves were poorly constructed, without enough time being devoted to building it by anybody.

   (A) constructed, without enough time being devoted to building it by anybody
   (B) constructed, without enough time being devoted to building them by anybody
   (C) constructed because nobody had devoted enough time to building it
   (D) constructed, nobody devoting time to building it
   (E) constructed because nobody had devoted enough time to building them

2. Neither of the viral samples were dangerous enough to warrant being stored in the secure area for highly infectious diseases.

   (A) were dangerous enough to warrant being stored
   (B) was dangerous enough to warrant the storage of them
   (C) was dangerous enough to warrant storing them
   (D) were dangerous enough to warrant their being stored
   (E) was dangerous enough to warrant the storing of them

3. Many experts believe that in regions near the North Pole, people's not being exposed to the sun during the long winter, this can cause a Vitamin D deficiency.

   (A) people's not being exposed to the sun during the long winter, this
   (B) people's not being exposed to the sun during the long winter
   (C) for people to not be exposed to the sun during the long winter, it
   (D) the lack of being exposed to the sun during the long winter
   (E) the lack of exposure to the sun during the long winter

**Step 2**

Forget your
English classes
and prepare for
SAT Writing

...................

**118**

4. Seventeenth-century artist Jan van Almeloveen, <u>being that he spent most of his life in rural Holland</u>, drew Dutch villages and rivers in nearly all of his engravings and paintings.

(A) being that he spent most of his life in rural Holland
(B) who spent most of his life in rural Holland
(C) while he spent most of his life in rural Holland
(D) since he was spending most of his life in rural Holland
(E) because of him spending most of his life in rural Holland

5. Venezuela's Angel <u>Falls, being more than 3,200 feet high, and</u> the world's tallest waterfall.

(A) Falls, being more than 3,200 feet high, and
(B) Falls, more than 3,200 feet high, it is
(C) Falls, which is more than 3,200 feet high, being
(D) Falls, more than 3,200 feet high, is
(E) Falls, more than 3,200 feet high; it is

# Improving paragraphs

The six IMPROVING PARAGRAPHS questions are probably the most logic-based questions on the SAT. They are essentially a combination of the IMPROVING SENTENCES, IDENTIFYING SENTENCE ERRORS, and PASSAGE-BASED READING questions. Once you have mastered the *2400 Strategies* for those questions, you should have no difficulty with the IMPROVING PARAGRAPHS section. Nevertheless, a few *Paragraph 2400 Strategies* are useful in answering IMPROVING PARAGRAPHS questions in particular.

The IMPROVING PARAGRAPHS section presents a short essay written by a student. The SAT then asks a series of questions about how to improve the grammatical correctness, clarity, coherence, and structure of the essay. A sample of IMPROVING PARAGRAPHS directions follows. Become familiar with the directions now so you don't waste time struggling to understand them on the actual SAT.

---

**Directions:** The following passage is an early draft of an essay. Some parts of the passage need to be rewritten to correct errors in grammar and word choice or to improve the organization and structure of the essay.

Read the passage and select the best answers for the questions that follow. Some questions are about particular sentences or parts of sentences. Other questions ask you to consider organization and development of the essay as a whole. In choosing answers, follow the requirements of standard written English.

---

---

### ⚊ Paragraph 2400 Strategies ⚊
1 · Write down the main idea
2 · Be critical and ensure continuity
3 · Use correct grammar
4 · Check sentence and paragraph function
5 · Revise the underlined portion

---

## Paragraph 2400 Strategy 1 ⚊ *Write down the main idea*

Before you tackle IMPROVING PARAGRAPHS questions, read the first paragraph or two of the essay so that you understand what the essay is about. Write down the main idea. If you can't jot down a concrete topic in a few words, you don't understand the essay and should read further until you can.

The essay below will serve as the *2400 Example* on which you will practice the five *Paragraph 2400 Strategies*. First, read through sentence 5 and write down the main idea.

> **(1)** Marriage was once a religious institution authorized only by sacred establishments. **(2)** In contemporary times the concept of marriage has become more of a state convention and less of a holy bond. **(3)** Most have accepted such social customs as divorce and remarriage. **(4)** Gay marriage is another one. **(5)** Many important sociological consequences with this secular attribution of marriage including the evaluation of individual happiness in marriage.
>
> **(6)** One permissive aspect of the contemporary marriage that affects happiness is the effect of cohabitation prior to marriage. **(7)** Living in the same household with another prior to marrying that individual is rare in conventional, religious-based marriages. **(8)** Researchers found that many aspects of relationship quality including interaction, fairness, conflict management, and most importantly happiness decreased if a couple had previously cohabited. **(9)** Researchers have also found that those who had cohabited prior to marriage experienced a lower level of relationship instability and disagreements over time. **(10)** These studies indicate that previous cohabitation may have some benefits including a more stable marriage, but does nevertheless decrease happiness in marriage.
>
> **(11)** Marriage is the most profound institution when they come to pursuing happiness in both the traditional and contemporary form. **(12)** Nevertheless, the constantly changing and dynamic form of the modern marriage will continue to play an important role regarding the nature of the happiness we pursue.

Write down the main idea on the lines below.

_____

_____

Here is what I jotted down as the main idea:

*Marriage isn't as religious as it once was, which affects happiness.*

Notice that I wrote a concrete summary in about 10 words. Your summary doesn't need to be lengthy, but it does need to contain enough detail to demonstrate that you really understand the main idea. Don't tackle the questions until you comprehend the main topic of the essay. This step is crucial, because the main idea is the key thread underlying the six questions you have to answer about the passage.

**Step 2**
Forget your
English classes
and prepare for
SAT Writing
..................
**120**

### Paragraph 2400 Example    *Write down the main idea*

Which of the following, if inserted prior to sentence 1, would make a good introduction to the passage?

(A) Many spouses are unhappy because marriage is no longer religious.
(B) The government will one day control marriage.
(C) Happiness in marriage depends on the willingness of spouses to openly communicate.
(D) The changing and dynamic nature of marriage has had significant repercussions.
(E) To avoid issues in one's marriage, one should attempt to focus on the bright side.

### *Write down the main idea*

Before looking at the answer choices, write down the main idea of the essay: "Marriage isn't as religious as it once was, which affects happiness." Once you have written down the main idea, examine the answer choices.

(A) Main idea doesn't mention spouses
(B) Main idea doesn't mention government
(C) Main idea doesn't mention spouses
(D) Main idea mentions that marriage is changing and describes a repercussion of that
(E) Main idea doesn't mention issues in one's marriage

## Paragraph 2400 Strategy 2  *Be critical and ensure continuity*

Unlike the academic passages in the SAT Reading sections, which are polished selections written by professionals, the essay in the IMPROVING PARAGRAPHS section is intended to be the first draft of an essay written by a student. Therefore, you need to *be critical* of every sentence. As you read the essay, ask yourself questions like the following:

◄ Does this sentence really belong here?
◄ Does this sentence transition correctly?
◄ How could this paragraph flow better?
◄ What sentence could be deleted from this paragraph?

You also need to *ensure continuity* throughout the essay. Many of the errors in the IMPROVING PARAGRAPHS section result from a lack of continuity. For example, the amateur writer may have expressed a simple idea in a convoluted manner, communicated fragmented thoughts, or placed an idea in the wrong part of the paragraph or essay. Be extremely critical, and think about how you could improve the continuity of the composition.

The first five sentences of the essay are reproduced below.

> (**1**) Marriage was once a religious institution authorized only by sacred establishments. (**2**) In contemporary times the concept of marriage has become more of a state convention and less of a holy bond. (**3**) Most have accepted such social customs as divorce and remarriage. (**4**) Gay marriage is another one. (**5**) Many important sociological consequences with this secular attribution of marriage including the evaluation of individual happiness in marriage.

Here are some questions I asked myself as I was reading these sentences:

- Shouldn't there be a transition between sentence (1) and sentence (2), because the passage is contrasting the perception of marriage between the past and "contemporary times"?
- Why isn't "gay marriage" in sentence (4) simply placed in the list in sentence (3), along with "divorce" and "remarriage"?
- Why is there no verb in sentence (5)?

Just a few sentences into the essay, I already had several important questions on my mind. Notice that I was critically looking for gaps in continuity with my questions. You don't need to write your questions down as you did for the main idea, but you should formulate these questions in your head, because there will likely be a question or two related to these "errors." And if you have already been contemplating an error, you will have a good sense about how to correct it. Don't give the SAT a chance to confuse you with enticing (but wrong) answer choices.

My first question addresses continuity between sentences. My SAT-focused mind-set had me wondering why there wasn't an appropriate contrasting transition between two sentences that clearly have contrasting ideas. My second question also addresses continuity. My SAT-focused mind-set recognized that sentence (4) was a continuation of sentence (3), but the two sentences were separated. Although I didn't consciously look for continuity errors, the questions themselves related to continuity anyway. A lack of continuity is the principal issue of many IMPROVING PARAGRAPHS questions. In other words, if you are *critical* as you read, you will inevitably find several *continuity* errors.

Step 2
Forget your
English classes
and prepare for
SAT Writing

122

## Paragraph 2400 Example   *Be critical and ensure continuity*

In context, which of the following is the best way to combine sentences 1 and 2 (reproduced below)?

*Marriage was once a sacred religious institution authorized only by sacred establishments. In contemporary times the concept of marriage has become more of a state convention and less of a holy bond.*

(A) Marriage was once a religious institution authorized only by sacred establishments, in contemporary times the concept of marriage has become more of a state convention and less of a holy bond.

(B) Marriage was once a religious institution authorized only by sacred establishments and in contemporary times the concept of marriage has become more of a state convention and less of a holy bond.

(C) Marriage was once a religious institution authorized only by sacred establishments; however, in contemporary times the concept of marriage has become more of a state convention and less of a holy bond.

(D) Marriage was once a religious institution authorized only by sacred establishments, now in contemporary times the concept of marriage has become more of a state convention and less of a holy bond.

(E) Marriage was once a religious institution authorized only by sacred establishments; therefore, in contemporary times the concept of marriage has become more of a state convention and less of a holy bond.

### Be critical and ensure continuity

Because you were already critical of the continuity between sentences 1 and 2, you can anticipate that the correct answer choice will include a transition that indicates contrast.

(A) Two complete sentences separated only by a comma form a run-on sentence (see *Writing 2400 Strategy 11*)

(B) "and" doesn't indicate contrast

(C)

(D) "now" doesn't indicate contrast

(E) "therefore" doesn't indicate contrast

## Paragraph 2400 Strategy 3 ⚬ *Use correct grammar*

This third strategy groups the 15 *Writing 2400 Strategies* you already know into one category. You don't need to learn new material for this particular *Paragraph 2400 Strategy*. But you do need to watch out for a variety of grammar errors in IMPROVING PARAGRAPHS sentences—the errors you learned about in **Improving sentences and identifying sentence errors**. Continue to be critical of the grammatical correctness of sentences.

What must be done to sentence 5 (reproduced below)?

*Many important sociological consequences with this secular attribution of marriage including the evaluation of individual happiness in marriage.*

(A) Combine it with sentence (4) by placing a comma after "one".
(B) Begin it with the words "It still has".
(C) Insert the words "have come along" after "consequences".
(D) Insert a colon after "including".
(E) Delete "secular attribution of".

## Use correct grammar

Because you were critical as you were reading the paragraph earlier, you have already asked yourself the question "Why is there no verb in sentence (5)?" This means that the sentence is a fragment (see *Writing 2400 Strategy 11*) and that the correct answer choice solves this error by including a verb in sentence 5.

(A) Doesn't logically transition sentences 4 and 5
(B) Unidentified pronoun "it"
(C)
(D) Doesn't insert a verb
(E) Doesn't insert a verb

## Paragraph 2400 Strategy 4 — *Check sentence and paragraph function*

Being critical and ensuring continuity powerfully enhances this *Paragraph 2400 Strategy*. Instead of criticizing the grammatical correctness of a sentence, this strategy requires that you criticize the *function* of a particular sentence or paragraph in the essay. Function—the intended purpose of part of an essay— is often related to continuity. The organization of a sentence within a paragraph or of a paragraph within an essay is often incorrect. This is not only an error in *function*, but also an error in *continuity*.

You can usually understand the idea that the essay writer is trying to convey; however, the essayist could have written the sentence or paragraph more clearly. Here are some questions that you should ask yourself as you read these unpolished essays:

- Does the sentence/paragraph reaffirm or contradict what comes before it?
- Does the sentence/paragraph reaffirm or contradict what comes after it?
- Does the sentence/paragraph serve as a transition?
- Could the sentence/paragraph be better placed somewhere else?
- Could the sentence/paragraph be deleted altogether?

Critical questioning is crucial in the IMPROVING PARAGRAPHS section; it becomes much easier once you become skeptical of the grammatical and functional correctness of the essay. Here are typical SAT questions related to functional clarity:

- What must be done to sentence/paragraph X?
- What is the purpose of sentence/paragraph X?
- Which of the following is the best revision to sentence X?
- Which sentence/paragraph could be deleted?
- By adding which of the following sentences could paragraph X be improved?
- Which of the following best combines sentence X and sentence Y into a single sentence?

**Step 2**
Forget your
English classes
and prepare for
SAT Writing
..........................
**124**

### Paragraph 2400 Example    *Check sentence and paragraph function*

What must be done to sentence 9 (reproduced below)?

*Researchers have also found that those who had cohabited prior to marriage experienced a lower level of relationship instability and disagreements over time.*

(A) Insert "However," at the beginning of sentence 9.
(B) Combine sentence 9 with sentence 10 by changing the period after "time" to a comma.
(C) Place sentence 9 before sentence 8.
(D) Insert "Furthermore," at the beginning of sentence 9.
(E) Change "who" to "whom".

### Check sentence and paragraph function

One clue that this sentence deals with function rather than grammar is that the answer choices mention sentences 8 and 10, which come before and after sentence 9. This means that you cannot answer this question by reading only sentence 9; you must also read at least the sentences before and after it.

**(8)** Researchers found that many aspects of relationship quality including interaction, fairness, conflict management, and most importantly happiness decreased if a couple had previously cohabited. **(9)** Researchers have also found that those who had cohabited prior to marriage experienced a lower level of relationship instability and disagreements over time. **(10)** These studies indicate that previous cohabitation may have some benefits including a more stable marriage, but does nevertheless decrease happiness in marriage.

Once again, be critical and ensure continuity as you read sentences 8 through 10. There is clearly no contrasting transition between sentence 8 and sentence 9, which express contrasting ideas. The correct answer choice should fix this functional issue.

(A)
(B) Doesn't contrast sentences 8 and 9
(C) Doesn't contrast sentences 8 and 9
(D) Doesn't contrast sentences 8 and 9
(E) "who" is correct because it can be replaced by "he" ("he had cohabited")

## Paragraph 2400 Strategy 5 ⚓ *Revise the underlined portion*

This *Paragraph 2400 Strategy* is intended to solve revision questions. These questions underline a portion of a sentence and ask how that portion can be improved. If the question asks how to revise an entire sentence (as in the previous *Paragraph 2400 Example*) in which no portion is underlined, the sentence usually has a functional issue. However, if only a portion of the sentence is underlined, you should apply this strategy. Revision questions in the IMPROVING PARAGRAPHS section may have one of two issues.

**Grammar issue** The underlined portion is typically long and contains a linguistic error. Treat these questions as you would an IMPROVING SENTENCES question. Use *Paragraph 2400 Strategy 3,* which refers you to the 15 *Writing 2400 Strategies.*

**Phrasing issue** The underlined portion is typically short and is expressed ineffectively. Use the following method to solve these questions.

1. Cover the answer choices with your hand.
2. Cover the underlined portion of the sentence.
3. Read the sentence, replacing the underlined portion with a blank.
4. Fill in the blank with your own phrase.
5. Lift your hand from the answer choices and decide which phrase mostly closely agrees with the phrase you filled in.

This strategy is almost identical to the method you will use to tackle SENTENCE COMPLETION questions (see Chapter 3).

## Paragraph 2400 Example   *Revise the underlined portion*

Which is the best revision of the underlined portion of sentence 11 (reproduced below)?

*Marriage is the most profound institution <u>when they come to pursuing happiness in both the traditional and contemporary form</u>.*

(A) (as it is now)

(B) in terms of pursuing happiness in both the traditional and contemporary form

(C) when they comes to pursuing happiness in both the traditional and contemporary form

(D) when it come to pursuing happiness in both the traditional form and the contemporary form

(E) having come to pursue happiness in both the traditional and contemporary form

### *Revise the underlined portion*

One clue that this sentence contains a grammar issue rather than a phrasing issue is that the underlined portion is much too long for you to substitute your own phrase. Treating the question as an IMPROVING SENTENCES question, you should realize that there is an unidentified pronoun "they" in the sentence (see *Writing 2400 Strategy 3*).

(A) Unidentified pronoun "they"

(B)

(C) Unidentified pronoun "they"

(D) "it come" introduces subject-verb disagreement

(E) "having come" introduces a verb tense error

## Paragraph 2400 Example   *Revise the underlined portion*

Which is the best revision of the underlined portion of sentence 12 (reproduced below)?

*Nevertheless, the constantly changing and dynamic form of the modern marriage will continue to <u>play an important role regarding</u> the nature of the happiness we pursue.*

(A) be established by

(B) be important to

(C) highly impact

(D) undoubtedly assume

(E) exchange

### *Revise the underlined portion*

One clue that this sentence contains a phrasing issue rather than a grammar issue is that the underlined portion is short enough for you to substitute your own phrase. After covering the answer choices and reading the sentence with a blank, I decided that the word "affect" would make sense.

(A̸) Doesn't agree with my phrase

(B̸) Doesn't agree with my phrase

(C)

(D̸) Doesn't agree with my phrase

(E̸) Doesn't agree with my phrase

**Practice problem set**  *Improving paragraphs*

The answer key for this problem set is on page 132.

> **Directions:** Each of the following passages is an early draft of an essay. Some parts of each passage need to be rewritten to correct errors in grammar and word choice or to improve the organization and structure of the essay.
>
> Read each passage and select the best answers for the questions that follow it. Some questions are about particular sentences or parts of sentences. Other questions ask you to consider organization and development of the essay as a whole. In choosing answers, follow the requirements of standard written English.

### Questions 1–6 refer to the following passage.

(1) Many people have heard of the Tasmanian devil, and they don't know why it is called that. (2) There are a number of reasons. (3) They include the Tasmanian devil's powerful bite, loud and eerie screech, and foul smell. (4) But despite these negative qualities, the devil has become the iconic symbol of Tasmania and is now in desperate need of protection. (5) Decimated by a contagious disease that causes massive facial tumors, the population of devils has been drastically reduced lately. (6) The devil is now considered an endangered species. (7) Conservationists are attempting to save the species by introducing breeding programs for devils in captivity. (8) Scientists are studying Tasmanian devils affected by the tumor-causing disease in an attempt to understand what causes it and how it might be contained. (9) So far they are completely bewildered. (10) The disease appears to be one of the few transmissible cancers ever discovered. (11) Cancers are normally not contagious. (12) So this cancer has scientists baffled. (13) It is estimated that the devil population has declined by 80% in the past twenty-five years alone. (14) Because there is no cure now or in the foreseeable future, scientists are quarantining any sick devils that they find in the wild. (15) They are doing this in hopes that this will help prevent further spread of the cancer.

**1.** What is the best way to deal with sentence 1 (reproduced below)?

*Many people have heard of the Tasmanian devil, and they don't know why it is called that.*

(A) Leave it as it is.
(B) Switch its position with that of sentence 2.
(C) Change "and" to "but".
(D) Change "that" to "such a name".
(E) Remove the comma.

**Step 2**

Forget your
English classes
and prepare for
SAT Writing

· · · · · · · · · · · · · · · · · · · · ·

**128**

**2.** In context, which of the following is the best way to revise the underlined wording in order to combine sentences 2 and 3 (reproduced below)?

*There are a number of reasons. They include the Tasmanian devil's powerful bite, loud and eerie screech, and foul smell.*

(A) number of reasons: they include the
(B) number of reasons; including the
(C) number of reasons: including the
(D) number of reasons, they include
(E) number of reasons, including the

**3.** Which of the following words or phrases is the best to insert at the beginning of sentence 8 to link it to sentence 7?

(A) However,
(B) Consequently,
(C) For this reason,
(D) In addition,
(E) Nevertheless,

**4.** In context, which of the following is the best way to revise the wording below in order to combine sentences 11 and 12 (reproduced below)?

*Cancers are normally not contagious. So this cancer has scientists baffled.*

(A) Cancers are normally not contagious: this cancer has scientists baffled.
(B) Cancers, which are normally not contagious, have scientists baffled.
(C) Cancers are normally not contagious; so this cancer has scientists baffled.
(D) This cancer, being contagious when cancers are normally not so, has scientists baffled.
(E) Cancers are normally not contagious, so this cancer has scientists baffled.

**5.** In context of the passage as a whole, where is the most logical place to put sentence 13?

(A) Where it is now
(B) After sentence 3
(C) After sentence 5
(D) After sentence 7
(E) After sentence 10

**6.** In context, which of the following is the best way to revise the underlined wording in order to combine sentences 14 and 15 (reproduced below)?

*Because there is no cure now or in the foreseeable future, scientists are quarantining any sick devils that they find in the wild. They are doing this in hopes that this will help prevent further spread of the cancer.*

(A) the wild in the hopes that
(B) the wild, done in the hopes that
(C) the wild, they hope that
(D) the wild; hoping that
(E) the wild, they hope that

## Questions 7–12 refer to the following passage.

(1) The clothing worn in ancient Rome reflected the dress code of the time. (2) Different classes wore different clothing, and the emperor wore certain styles that no one else was allowed to wear. (3) In general, however, wealthier people wore garments made of lightweight fabric and natural colors, while poorer people wore much clothing that was coarser and cheaply dyed. (4) Officials at important ceremonies would wear the *toga praetexta,* it was white with a purple border. (5) Generals celebrating a wartime victory would wear the elaborately decorated *toga picta,* which was purple with a gold border. (6) Some garments were only to be worn during religious ceremonies. (7) As an example, the *crocota* or saffron robe that was worn by women during special rites honoring Mother Earth. (8) Many different fabric materials were also used. (9) These included wool, linen, hemp, cotton, and silk. (10) Silk was not that common, as it had to be imported from China and was very expensive. (11) There was also a luxury material called "sea silk" that was derived from a mollusk and was extremely rare. (12) Wool was by far the most common material, and the Romans became quite skilled at breeding different types of sheep to produce the best types of wool. (13) Some animal skins were tanned and made into a leather that was suitable for coats that could be worn in colder climates. (14) The leather was also used for the soles of shoes, especially for soldiers being that they needed durable footwear.

**7.** Which of the following would fit logically between sentences 2 and 3?

(A) A sentence that explains the different meanings of various colors.
(B) A sentence that briefly describes the type of clothing worn by the emperor.
(C) A sentence that lists the ways in which ancient Roman fashions changed over time.
(D) A sentence that compares and contrasts the weight of certain fabrics.
(E) A sentence that cites the population of ancient Rome at important milestones in time.

**Step 2**
Forget your
English classes
and prepare for
SAT Writing
..................

**130**

**8.** Which of the following is the best way to phrase the underlined portion of sentence 4 (reproduced below)?

*Officials at important ceremonies would wear the* toga praetexta, *it was white with a purple border.*

(A) (as it is now)
(B) the *toga praetexta* since it was white
(C) the *toga praetexta,* being that it was white
(D) the white *toga praetexta,*
(E) the *toga praetexta,* which was white

**9.** Which of the following is the best way to revise and combine the underlined portion of sentences 6 and 7 (reproduced below)?

*Some garments were only to be worn during religious ceremonies. As an example, the* crocota *or saffron robe that was only worn by women during special rites honoring Mother Earth.*

(A) religious ceremonies like the *crocota* or saffron robe only worn by women
(B) religious ceremonies, this includes the *crocota* or saffron robe that only women wore
(C) religious ceremonies; for example, women only wore the *crocota* or saffron robe
(D) religious ceremonies such as the *crocota* or saffron robe, which was only worn
(E) religious ceremonies, the *crocota* or saffron robe was what women only wore

**10.** Which of the following is the best way to revise and combine the underlined portion of sentences 8 and 9 (reproduced below)?

*Many different fabric materials were also used. These included wool, linen, hemp, cotton, and silk.*

(A) being used, they include
(B) used, these include
(C) used, including
(D) had been used, including
(E) used, these included

**11.** Which of the following phrases is the best to insert at the beginning of sentence 10 to link it to the previous sentence?

(A) Thus,
(B) However,
(C) Consequently,
(D) As a result,
(E) For this reason,

**12.** Which of the following is the best way to phrase the underlined portion of sentence 14 (reproduced below)?

*The leather was also used for the soles of shoes, especially for soldiers being that they needed durable footwear.*

(A) (as it is now)
(B) soldiers because they
(C) soldiers which
(D) soldiers, they
(E) soldiers; therefore they

# Answer key for practice problem sets · *Improving sentences and identifying sentence errors*

## Ignore prepositional phrases

1. D
2. E
3. B
4. E

## Check for incorrect pronouns

1. C
2. A
3. C
4. C
5. C
6. B
7. A
8. B
9. D
10. C

## Catch unidentified pronouns

1. D
2. E
3. A
4. C
5. C
6. B

## Check for verb tense agreement

1. A
2. B
3. C
4. B

## Get parallel

1. B
2. C
3. B
4. B
5. C
6. C
7. C
8. B

## Check for subject-verb agreement

1. C
2. A
3. D
4. C
5. C
6. B

## Identify misplaced modifiers

1. D
2. D

## Recognize redundancy

1. B
2. B

## Know your idioms

1. C
2. A
3. C

Step 2
Forget your
English classes
and prepare for
SAT Writing

**132**

## Conjunct correctly

1. D
2. D
3. D
4. E
5. A
6. B
7. D
8. E
9. B
10. C

## Spot faulty transitions

1. D
2. B
3. D
4. C
5. C
6. C

## Compare apples to apples

1. B
2. C
3. C
4. B
5. A
6. C
7. A

## Don't swap adjectives and adverbs

1. C
2. A

## Avoid the passive voice

1. E
2. C
3. E

## Avoid awkward phrases

1. E
2. C
3. E
4. B
5. D

## Answer key for practice problem set · *Improving paragraphs*

1. C
2. E
3. D
4. E
5. C
6. A
7. B
8. E
9. C
10. C
11. B
12. B

# Master WYPAD and other keys to success on SAT Reading

Which of the following statements describes you best?

- ◄ You are a voracious bookworm.
- ◄ You are a speed reader.
- ◄ You read the newspaper every day.
- ◄ You know lots of difficult vocabulary words.
- ◄ You read novels for fun.
- ◄ You score well on high school English quizzes and tests.

Don't worry if none of these statements applies to you. Most high school students (and their parents) believe that only avid readers ace the SAT Reading sections. Students think they can't get high scores on SAT Reading, because they don't read much, don't read fast, don't have a large vocabulary, and don't score well on high school reading tests. Nothing could be further from the truth. In fact, when I was in high school, I would have said that none of the statements above applied to me!

SAT Reading gave me more trouble than SAT Writing and SAT Math. I had difficulty choosing among answer choices, because they all seemed so similar. I wasn't an avid reader—so the material was too dense. I wasn't a fast reader—so I had a hard time finishing the Reading sections on time. The passages and questions varied so much from test to test that there seemed to be no consistency. I blamed the SAT test writers for making the Reading sections too subjective. I scoured book after book for a "magic trick" that would unlock SAT Reading for me, but I came up empty-handed. There appeared to be no key to success for SAT Reading.

Most students attack SAT Reading as if it were a reading comprehension quiz in high school. This is the reason why so many students struggle with this section of the SAT. High school English teachers reward students for "reading into the text": recognizing subtleties, connotations, and allusions. For example, your English teacher may claim that a line in a poem alludes to a historical event or to the poet's personal struggle, but you see no such reference when you examine the line. Nothing causes more frustration in SAT Reading than "reading into the text." Even if you're an expert in analyzing poetry, you may not be prepared for SAT Reading.

If high school reading doesn't prepare you for SAT Reading, what will? You have your choice of two approaches.

### General academic reading

- ◄ Read classic novels.
- ◄ Read major national newspapers daily.
- ◄ Read journal articles related to science, politics, and history.

**Step 3**
Master
WYPAD and
other keys
to success on
SAT Reading
..................

**134**

#### Advantages

- ◄ It has long-term value. Your improved reading comprehension skills will benefit you throughout your life.
- ◄ It provides SAT essay examples. You will acquire excellent examples for the SAT essay.
- ◄ It builds sophistication. You will become more scholarly.

#### Disadvantages

- ◄ It is time-consuming. You will need at least a year to translate your newly developed comprehension skills into improved SAT scores.
- ◄ It is inefficient. You may end up reading a lot of material that isn't similar to SAT Reading passages. You may need to look up a lot of vocabulary words, most of which won't appear on the SAT.
- ◄ It lacks SAT relevance. Passive reading without answering SAT-like, analytical questions doesn't guarantee improved SAT scores.

### SAT-focused reading

- ◄ Read SAT-specific passages.
- ◄ Answer SAT passage-based questions.
- ◄ Answer SAT sentence completions.
- ◄ Memorize targeted SAT vocabulary words.

#### Advantages

- ◄ It has long-term value. You will gain considerable benefit from increasing your comprehension and critical thinking skills, especially for future tests with passage-based reading sections (for example, the GRE, GMAT, MCAT, and LSAT).
- ◄ It is efficient. You will only read literature that is related to the SAT, and you will only memorize vocabulary words that are common on the SAT.
- ◄ It has SAT relevance. You will become accustomed to the kinds of passages that appear on the SAT, as well as the types of questions that are asked.

#### Disadvantages

- ◄ It is time-consuming.

SAT Reading takes substantial time and dedication to achieve noticeable improvements, no matter which method you choose. Most busy high school students don't have time to prepare for SAT Reading via general academic read-

ing. I suggest that you prepare for SAT Reading by using the SAT-focused reading approach in order to use your time more productively.

Ideally, you would use both approaches, and if you are a sophomore or younger, this is worth trying. But you can score high on SAT Reading by following only the second approach. I did.

# SAT sentence completion

Have you seen the news clip of the poor kid who fainted on stage during a national spelling bee? When it comes to SAT SENTENCE COMPLETION questions, I am sure that many high school students feel just like that student. Although these questions don't test spelling, they do require memorization similar to that required of spelling bee participants—the kind of memorization that is robotic, repetitive, monotonous, and lonely.

When I was in high school, I despised memorizing vocabulary words more than any other aspect of SAT preparation. Having to learn hundreds of words, most of which would not appear on the test, seemed like a waste of time. But once I decided to press on and commit hundreds of SAT vocabulary words to memory, I realized the many benefits of this tedious memorization.

You *must* memorize vocabulary words for the SAT. While this chapter offers proven strategies for tackling SENTENCE COMPLETION questions, the strategies won't help if you don't build a solid vocabulary. I developed an efficient method for learning hundreds of words, including a review schedule that will keep you on track. Before you read the rest of this section, skip to **SAT vocabulary** (page 257) and commit yourself to the most boring—and most important—part of SAT preparation: vocabulary memorization.

## Question format

Read the directions for SAT SENTENCE COMPLETION questions now so that you don't waste time reading them during the actual test.

> Each sentence in this section has one or two blanks, each blank indicating that something has been omitted. Following each sentence are five words or sets of words labeled A through E. Choose the word or set of words that, when inserted in the sentence, best fits the meaning of the sentence as a whole. Mark your answer by filling in the corresponding circle on the answer sheet.

Five to eight SENTENCE COMPLETION questions appear at the beginning of each of the three SAT Reading sections. If there are four SAT Reading sections, one section is "variable" and will not count toward your score (see page 3). The SENTENCE COMPLETION questions, which are either single-blank or double-blank, are almost always one sentence long.

### Single-blank questions

This type of SENTENCE COMPLETION question has one word omitted from the sentence. The answer choices offer five different words that could fit the blank. You should select the option that is most logical.

### Example

> The professor reprimanded his research assistant for ------- the results of the experiment in the report, which could be considered fraud.
>
> (A) exchanging    (B) falsifying    (C) doing
>     (D) trading    (E) writing

Select (B) as your answer choice.

### Double-blank questions

This type of SENTENCE COMPLETION question has two words omitted from the sentence. The answer choices offer five different sets of words that could fit the blanks. You should select the option that is most logical.

### Example

> The village's ------- population of only 10,000 during its peak in 1906 is indicative of why it should not be compared to a -------.
>
> (A) small . . resident
> (B) large . . municipal
> (C) overbearing . . town
> (D) tiny . . populous
> (E) minuscule . . metropolis

Select (E) as your answer choice.

## General reading strategies

### Golden Reading 2400 Strategy ⁓ *Write your personal answer down (WYPAD)*

You can use this key *2400 Strategy* on every SAT Reading question: Write Your Personal Answer Down (WYPAD). This is the "magic trick" that I was seeking in high school to unlock SAT Reading.

WYPAD requires that you formulate your own solution to a question *before* you look at the answer choices. In this way, the SAT can't distract you with enticing, but incorrect, answer choices. SAT test writers specialize in developing answer choices that appeal to unsure students who don't know what to look for. By using WYPAD, you focus on exactly what you are looking for and ignore the rest.

You will use WYPAD on both SENTENCE COMPLETION and PASSAGE-BASED READING questions. I won't provide examples of WYPAD here; by the time you finish this chapter, you will have seen WYPAD in action on almost every type of SAT Reading question.

Don't be intimidated by WYPAD. You may think that there is no way you can come up with your own vocabulary words for SENTENCE COMPLETION questions or for scholarly solutions to PASSAGE-BASED READING questions. Don't worry: The beauty of WYPAD is that you don't need to come up with fancy answers—you can keep it simple.

## Sentence Completion 2400 Strategy ⁄ *Be aware of order of difficulty*

SENTENCE COMPLETION questions are arranged in order of difficulty, from easy to hard. In a set of five to eight questions, the first ones are easy, the next few are of medium difficulty, and the final ones are hard. Most test takers answer the easy questions correctly, about half answer medium questions correctly, and very few answer hard questions correctly. Knowing this can help you identify correct answer choices even when you don't know what every word means.

After you have narrowed the answer choices to two or three possibilities, choose easy words on early SENTENCE COMPLETION questions, and difficult words on the last few questions.

What is an easy word, and what is a difficult word? An "easy" word is recognizable and familiar, whereas a "difficult" word is strange and unfamiliar. If you can narrow the possible answer choices to two, pick the more familiar ("easy") option if the question appears early in the set. If the question appears late in the set, pick the less familiar ("hard") option.

**Example 1** If you had narrowed the answer choices for an early SENTENCE COMPLETION question to the following two options, which would you choose?

(1) obsolete
(2) unnecessary

You would choose option (2), because "unnecessary" is more familiar than "obsolete." Since this is an easy SENTENCE COMPLETION question that most test takers answer correctly, they probably would know what "unnecessary" means.

**Example 2** If you had narrowed the answer choices for a late SENTENCE COMPLETION question to the following two options, which would you choose?

(1) frustrated
(2) enfeebled

You would choose option (2), because "enfeebled" is less familiar than "frustrated." Since this is a hard SENTENCE COMPLETION question that most test takers answer incorrectly, they probably wouldn't know what "enfeebled" means.

**Step 3**
Master
WYPAD and
other keys
to success on
SAT Reading

· · · · · · · · · · · · · · ·

**138**

The *order of difficulty strategy* should be used as a general guide and not as a universal rule. Sometimes, a word that is familiar to you may be the correct answer choice on a hard SENTENCE COMPLETION question. Perhaps most test takers answer the question incorrectly because they are unfamiliar with the particular word or because there is a complex causal relationship in the sentence. In any case, you can select a familiar answer choice as long as it fits the blank.

NOTE This strategy is least effective on medium SENTENCE COMPLETION questions. Your gauge of difficulty is of little help, because "medium" words are words that appear in an average high school English class. For this reason, you will probably have a hard time selecting an answer choice based on level of difficulty.

**Example 3** If you had narrowed the answer choices for a middle-of-the-set SENTENCE COMPLETION question to the following two options, which would you choose?

(1) comprehensive
(2) designated

You cannot choose based on order of difficulty alone.

**Example 4** If you had narrowed the answer choices for a middle-of-the-set SENTENCE COMPLETION question to the following three options, which would you choose?

(1) insensitive
(2) impractical
(3) sanctimonious

You probably would not be able to definitively choose based on order of difficulty alone. But you could deduce that "sanctimonious" is likely not the correct answer, because it is too hard for a middle-of-the-set SENTENCE COMPLETION question. The *order of difficulty strategy* can often be helpful if you can narrow the answer choices to three options, even in middle-of-the-set questions.

### Practice problem set · *Order of difficulty*

The answer key for this problem set is on page 283.

**Directions** Select which answer choice you can *eliminate*, based on order of difficulty. You may choose "None" if the position of the SENTENCE COMPLETION question does not help eliminate any answer choices.

1. POSITION IN SET: Beginning    (A) calculate
                                                (B) undermine
                                                None

2. POSITION IN SET: Beginning    (A) complex
                                 (B) tranquil
                                 None

3. POSITION IN SET: Beginning    (A) obstinate
                                 (B) admirable
                                 (C) legitimate
                                 None

4. POSITION IN SET: Middle       (A) mundane
                                 (B) impartial
                                 None

5. POSITION IN SET: Middle       (A) doubtful
                                 (B) defy
                                 (C) demurral
                                 None

6. POSITION IN SET: Middle       (A) conventional
                                 (B) revolutionary
                                 None

7. POSITION IN SET: End          (A) salvo
                                 (B) encore
                                 None

8. POSITION IN SET: End          (A) repudiate
                                 (B) acrimony
                                 (C) investigate
                                 None

9. POSITION IN SET: End          (A) renounce
                                 (B) venerable
                                 None

10. POSITION IN SET: End         (A) rancor
                                 (B) enhance
                                 None

## Sentence Completion 2400 Strategies

The following strategies will help you tackle SENTENCE COMPLETION questions on the SAT. To score well on these questions, however, there is no replacement for learning vocabulary words. These strategies won't supplant a strong vocabulary, but they will supplement it. ("Supplant" = replace—see *Vocabulary 2400* Set 6, page 273.)

**Step 3**
Master
WYPAD and
other keys
to success on
SAT Reading

**140**

## ◢ Sentence Completion 2400 Strategies ◢

GOLDEN · Write your personal answer down (WYPAD)
1 · Work one at a time
2 · Fill in the exact same word
3 · Fill in the exact opposite word
4 · Fill in +/−
5 · Identify the double-blank relationship

## Sentence Completion 2400 Golden Strategy ◢ *Write your personal answer down (WYPAD)*

The key to acing the SAT SENTENCE COMPLETION sections is to Write Your Personal Answer Down (WYPAD): Fill in the blank with your own word before you look at the answer choices. This strategy will keep you from being misled by enticing, but incorrect, answers. As you learn to master WYPAD for SENTENCE COMPLETION questions, keep three things in mind.

### 1. Cover the answer choices

Cover answer choices (A) through (E) with your hand. Hiding potential answer choices from view forces you to come up with your own personal word.

### 2. Write—don't just think—your answer

Write your own word down—don't just think it. There is a reason this *2400 Strategy* is called WYPAD, and not TYPAD. Writing your own personal answer down shows that you really understand what the sentence needs, instead of merely *thinking* you understand what it needs.

### 3. Fill in any word

The word you write down doesn't have to be a single word, an SAT vocabulary word, or even a real word. Instead, you can write down a phrase, a simple word, or even a made-up word. The whole point of WYPAD is to have a concrete idea of what idea belongs in the blank, even if the idea would not be a regular answer choice.

### Sentence Completion 2400 Example   *WYPAD*

#### Step 1 ◢ *Read a medium question*

Characters can hear source music in movies whereas underscore is a melody that is ------- to them.

(A) audible     (B) mute     (C) talkative
(D) unspoken     (E) loquacious

The answer choices are grayed out as if your hand were covering them.

## Step 2 ⁄ WYPAD

> Characters can hear source music in movies whereas underscore
> is a melody that is ------- to them.

My WYPAD is *cannot listen to*. Notice that this isn't an SAT vocabulary word; it's a simple phrase that doesn't even make grammatical sense in the sentence.

## Step 3 ⁄ *Eliminate incorrect choices*

(A) audible     ≠ *cannot listen to*
(B) mute        = *cannot listen to ?*
(C) talkative   ≠ *cannot listen to*
(D) unspoken    = *cannot listen to ?*
(E) loquacious  ≠ *cannot listen to*

Selected definition

loquacious = talkative, wordy

Using the *order of difficulty strategy,* you can eliminate "loquacious": It is probably too difficult for a medium question.

## Step 4 ⁄ *Check the remaining answer choices in context*

CORRECT    Characters can hear source music in movies whereas underscore is a melody that is **mute** to them.

INCORRECT  Characters can hear source music in movies whereas underscore is a melody that is **unspoken** to them.

Select (B) as your answer choice.

### Sentence Completion 2400 Example  WYPAD

## Step 1 ⁄ *Read a hard question*

> The Dawes Act emphasized -------, or the treatment of Indians as
> individuals rather than as members of tribes, and called for the distribution
> of 160 acres of ------- land for farming.
>
> (A) communality . . reservation
> (B) individuality . . infertile
> (C) identity . . barren
> (D) severalty . . agricultural
> (E) association . . rural

**Step 3**

Master
WYPAD and
other keys
to success on
SAT Reading
................................
142

**Step 2** ⟋ *WYPAD*

> The Dawes Act emphasized -------, or the treatment of Indians as individuals rather than as members of tribes, and called for the distribution of 160 acres of ------- land for farming.

My WYPAD is *distinctiveness . . rich fertile.*

**Step 3** ⟋ *Eliminate incorrect choices*

(A) communality . . reservation ≠ *distinctiveness . . rich fertile*
(B) individuality . . infertile   ≠ *distinctiveness . . rich fertile*
(C) identity . . barren       ≠ *distinctiveness . . rich fertile*
(D) severalty . . agricultural   = *distinctiveness . . rich fertile ?*
(E) association . . rural      ≠ *distinctiveness . . rich fertile*

Selected definitions

communality = shared, collective
infertile    = unproductive, unfruitful
barren     = unproductive, unfruitful
severalty   = individuality
agricultural = relating to farming
rural      = nonurban, in the country

**Step 4** ⟋ *Check the remaining answer choices in context*

CORRECT    The Dawes Act emphasized **severalty**, or the treatment of Indians as individuals rather than as members of tribes, and called for the distribution of 160 acres of **agricultural** land for farming.

Select (D) as your answer choice.

---

**Practice problem set**   WYPAD

The answer key for this problem set is on page 283.

> Each sentence in this section has one or two blanks, each blank indicating that something has been omitted. Following each sentence are five words or sets of words labeled A through E. Choose the word or set of words that, when inserted in the sentence, best fits the meaning of the sentence as a whole.

1. The critic was notoriously -------: he could denounce a film for its overwhelming lack of realism, then later praise it for its unique and refreshing break with reality.

  (A) blatant    (B) apathetic    (C) demanding
     (D) resilient    (E) capricious

**2.** Because the giant panda's diet consists almost entirely of bamboo, ending the human encroachment on the bamboo forests of Asia is ------- to the survival of giant pandas in the wild.

(A) precarious     (B) expeditious     (C) vital
(D) insufficient     (E) adverse

**3.** At the town hall meeting, the debate about the new gun control law was highly -------: both sides held strong opinions and bickered loudly and viciously.

(A) clandestine     (B) polemical     (C) insidious
(D) complaisant     (E) repugnant

**4.** The writing in the astrophysics journal is quite -------: only a few experts in the field can decipher the scientific jargon that is prevalent throughout the journal's article.

(A) cathartic     (B) nepotistic     (C) intransigent
(D) esoteric     (E) peripatetic

**5.** The antique walnut clock in the hallway was a surprising ------- in the modern house: a throwback to centuries past, the clock was at odds with the house's sleek new contemporary furniture.

(A) anachronism     (B) dalliance     (C) evanescence
(D) ostentation     (E) perfidy

**6.** Dolphins are said to have ------- auditory senses: they can hear frequencies ten times above the upper limit of adult human hearing.

(A) acute     (B) indefinite     (C) unnatural
(D) obtuse     (E) strident

**7.** Demographers often use ------- data to help officials determine how many people may be affected by natural disasters in a certain area.

(A) marketing     (B) levy     (C) census
(D) portfolio     (E) abstract

**8.** According to environmental activists, the oil industry introduced the term "outgassing" as a euphemism for the word "pollution" in hopes that the public would not ------- the fact that the two terms were really interchangeable.

(A) distort     (B) equate     (C) belittle
(D) applaud     (E) deduce

## Sentence Completion 2400 Strategy 1 ⁀ *Work one at a time*

Have you heard the expression "Take it one step at a time"? Well, for double-blank SENTENCE COMPLETION questions, my advice is to take it one *blank* at a time. Treat each blank as its own sentence completion. In this way, you can concentrate on less information, and this will allow you to think more clearly. Remember: If one of the two words of a double-blank answer choice is wrong, the entire option is wrong.

## Sentence Completion 2400 Example   *Work one at a time*

### Step 1 — *Read an easy double-blank question*

Despite the ------- amounts of land the company had already cleared, its big executives were still not ------- and believed they had disturbed only a negligible area.

(A) large . . disgruntled
(B) vast . . satisfied
(C) small . . content
(D) insignificant . . irritated
(E) undersized . . pleased

### Step 2 — *WYPAD + Work one at a time (first blank)*

Despite the ------- amounts of land the company had already cleared . . .

My WYPAD for the first blank is *massive*.

### Step 3 — *Eliminate incorrect choices*

Keep the second word of each answer choice covered with your hand.

(A) large             = *massive* ?
(B) vast              = *massive* ?
(C) small             ≠ *massive*
(D) insignificant  ≠ *massive*
(E) undersized    ≠ *massive*

Selected definition

vast = huge, great, enormous

### Step 4 — *WYPAD + Work one at a time (second blank)*

. . . its big executives were still not ------- and believed they had disturbed only a negligible area.

My WYPAD for the second blank is *happy*.

Selected definition

negligible = insignificant, small, trivial

### Step 5 — *Eliminate incorrect choices*

(A) disgruntled  ≠ *happy*
(B) satisfied       = *happy*

Selected definition

disgruntled = dissatisfied

## Step 6 ✏ *Check the remaining answer choices in context*

CORRECT    Despite the **vast** amounts of land the company had already
cleared, its big executives were still not **satisfied** and believed
they had disturbed only a negligible area.

Select (B) as your answer choice.

### Sentence Completion 2400 Example    *Work one at a time*

## Step 1 ✏ *Read a hard double-blank question*

Many individuals once ------- believed that the world was flat; however,
Ferdinand Magellan successfully sailed around the world in the 16th
century and ------- the fact that the world is round.

(A) incorrectly . . speculated
(B) fittingly . . refuted
(C) erroneously . . verified
(D) inaccurately . . repudiated
(E) precisely . . insinuated

## Step 2 ✏ *WYPAD + Work one at a time (first blank)*

| Many individuals once ------- believed that the world was flat . . .

My WYPAD for the first blank is *incorrectly*.

## Step 3 ✏ *Eliminate incorrect choices*

Keep the second word of each answer choice covered with your hand.

(A) incorrectly    = *incorrectly* ?
(B) fittingly      ≠ *incorrectly*
(C) erroneously    = *incorrectly* ?
(D) inaccurately   = *incorrectly* ?
(E) precisely      ≠ *incorrectly*

Selected definitions

fittingly      = appropriately
erroneously = incorrectly
precisely      = exactly

## Step 4 ✏ *WYPAD + Work one at a time (second blank)*

| . . . however, Ferdinand Magellan successfully sailed around the world
in the 16th century and ------- the fact that the world is round.

My WYPAD for the second blank is *proved*.

Step 3

Master
WYPAD and
other keys
to success on
SAT Reading

146

**Step 5** ▸ *Eliminate incorrect choices*

(A) speculated ≠ proved
(C) verified    = proved ?
(D) repudiated ≠ proved

Selected definitions

speculated = guessed
repudiated = rejected, denied

**Step 6** ▸ *Check the remaining answer choices in context*

CORRECT   Many individuals once **erroneously** believed that the world was flat; however, Ferdinand Magellan successfully sailed around the world in the 16th century and **verified** the fact that the world is round.

Select (C) as your answer choice.

NOTE  At times, you may not be able to come up with an appropriate word for the first blank. In this case, work on the second blank as if the first one weren't there. After you have eliminated as many answer choices as possible based on the second blank, return to the first blank.

**Practice problem set**   *Work one at a time*

The answer key for this problem set is on page 283.

> Each sentence in this section has one or two blanks, each blank indicating that something has been omitted. Following each sentence are five words or sets of words labeled A through E. Choose the word or set of words that, when inserted in the sentence, best fits the meaning of the sentence as a whole.

1. Modern Berber carpets, which are made from densely knotted synthetic materials, are quite ------- and can last for years without showing wear; however, traditional Berber carpets, which are made from soft, natural materials, are more ------- and may get worn out more quickly.

   (A) durable . . delicate
   (B) versatile . . faded
   (C) spotless . . fickle
   (D) flexible . . authentic
   (E) unique . . comfortable

2. The audience members at the carnival were ------- by the increasingly impressive spectacle before them: each new act ------- the previous one in grandeur and excellence.

(A) humbled . . neutralized
(B) awed . . surpassed
(C) stymied . . belied
(D) dumbstruck . . reflected
(E) bemused . . ousted

3. Mid-twentieth-century actress Audrey Hepburn had a(n) ------- screen presence that ------- audiences with her enthusiasm and liveliness.

(A) effervescent . . entranced
(B) doleful . . piqued
(C) startling . . bored
(D) flat . . intrigued
(E) expansive . . confounded

4. The 18th-century lexicographer Samuel Johnson was highly influential: his ------- for words allowed him to ------- one of the most comprehensive dictionaries of the English language, an achievement that was not surpassed for another 150 years.

(A) ambivalence . . edit
(B) acuity . . criticize
(C) affinity . . craft
(D) abhorrence . . write
(E) affection . . delineate

5. Although the little girl is typically ------- in the classroom and chatters away at anyone who will listen, on the playground she acts with uncharacteristic -------.

(A) loquacious . . taciturnity
(B) querulous . . languor
(C) disaffected . . precociousness
(D) diplomatic . . decorum
(E) demure . . alacrity

6. People called Matthew a "lone wolf" because of his ------- nature; in addition, he was excessively passionate about his ideas, and such an ------- attitude would later cost him many friendships.

(A) patriotic . . altruistic
(B) maverick . . overzealous
(C) acquiescent . . obsequious
(D) abhorrent . . ingenuous
(E) clement . . obstinate

**Step 3**
Master
WYPAD and
other keys
to success on
SAT Reading

· · · · · · · · · · · · · · · · · · · · ·

**148**

**7.** After the deadly attack at the train station, the security personnel who worked at the train station were severely ------- by police investigators for ------- threats that had warned of impending violence.

(A) stymied . . proposing
(B) intimidated . . clarifying
(C) rebuked . . dismissing
(D) indicted . . developing
(E) hailed by . . responding to

## Sentence Completion 2400 Strategy 2 ⁄ *Fill in the exact same word*

Many SENTENCE COMPLETION questions contain ideas that are echoed in the blank(s). What if you can't think of your own word to fill in the blank, but you see the same concept elsewhere in the sentence? Simply write down the exact same word(s) you see. WYPAD for SENTENCE COMPLETION questions doesn't require you to be creative; you just need to have a concrete answer written down to compare the choices to.

### Sentence Completion 2400 Example  *Fill in the exact same word*

#### Step 1 ⁄ *Read a medium question*

The orations of Martin Luther King Jr. that described equality and ------- influenced the social convictions of many black Americans.

(A) liberty    (B) restriction    (C) constraint
    (D) gathering    (E) self-control

#### Step 2 ⁄ *WYPAD + Fill in the exact same word*

The orations of Martin Luther King Jr. that described equality and ------- influenced the social convictions of many black Americans.

My WYPAD is *equality*.

Selected definitions

orations    = speeches
convictions = beliefs, principles, tenets

#### Step 3 ⁄ *Eliminate incorrect choices*

(A) liberty      = equality ?
(B) restriction  ≠ equality
(C) constraint   ≠ equality
(D) gathering    ≠ equality
(E) self-control ≠ equality

Selected definitions

liberty     = freedom
constraint = limitation

### Step 4 ⁄ Check the remaining answer choices in context

CORRECT    The orations of Martin Luther King Jr. that described equality and **liberty** influenced the social convictions of many black Americans.

Select (A) as your answer choice.

## Sentence Completion 2400 Example   *Fill in the exact same word*

### Step 1 ⁄ Read a medium question

The garage sale had useless antiques, worn-out furniture, peeling ceramics, and other ------- for sale at next to nothing prices.

(A) obligations    (B) flotsam    (C) provisions
   (D) nourishment    (E) rubbish

### Step 2 ⁄ WYPAD + Fill in the exact same word

The garage sale had useless antiques, worn-out furniture, peeling ceramics, and other ------- for sale at next to nothing prices.

My WYPAD is *useless antiques.*

### Step 3 ⁄ Eliminate incorrect choices

(A) obligations    *≠ useless antiques*
(B) flotsam      *≠ useless antiques*
(C) provisions    *≠ useless antiques*
(D) nourishment *≠ useless antiques*
(E) rubbish      *= useless antiques ?*

Selected definitions

flotsam     = ship wreckage, debris
provisions = necessities, supplies
rubbish    = junk

### Step 4 ⁄ Check the remaining answer choices in context

CORRECT    The garage sale had useless antiques, worn-out furniture, peeling ceramics, and other **rubbish** for sale at next to nothing prices.

Select (E) as your answer choice.

The answer key for this problem set is on page 283.

**Step 3**

Master
WYPAD and
other keys
to success on
SAT Reading

........................

**150**

Each sentence in this section has one or two blanks, each blank indicating that something has been omitted. Following each sentence are five words or sets of words labeled A through E. Choose the word or set of words that, when inserted in the sentence, best fits the meaning of the sentence as a whole.

1. The keynote speaker was quite ------- in praising the charitable organization: he gushed for over an hour about the positive results of the organization's work in the community.

    (A) doleful     (B) spontaneous     (C) effusive
        (D) relieved     (E) succinct

2. Although the newly elected governor was adored by almost all of his constituents, skeptics warned that his election was not a ------- or cure-all for the multitude of problems that plagued the state.

    (A) ramification     (B) compromise     (C) panacea
        (D) reformation     (E) misnomer

3. Travelers to politically unstable nations are often shocked by the absolute ------- that the people feel toward their governments; such hatred is difficult to understand unless one has witnessed the people's sufferings firsthand.

    (A) haughtiness     (B) condescension     (C) rancor
        (D) deliberation     (E) mockery

4. Despite dazzling reviews by the art critics, many of whom touted the exhibit as ingenious and -------, most people found the new collection of paintings to be quite ------- and ordinary.

    (A) fortuitous . . exemplary
    (B) divergent . . profound
    (C) novel . . mediocre
    (D) relevant . . informal
    (E) brazen . . inconsistent

5. The film director is known for his charming depiction of the serene and ------- Southern life: the tranquility of the Georgia countryside and the simple kindness of its townspeople ------- the hearts of audiences that see his films.

    (A) bucolic . . gall
    (B) pastoral . . enchant
    (C) urban . . conciliate
    (D) agrarian . . disquiet
    (E) mirthless . . fortifies

**6.** Although he was ------- and even childish when he first began working on board the fishing vessel, the youth quickly gained experience and maturity as the months went by.

(A) garrulous      (B) precarious      (C) precocious
    (D) disturbed      (E) callow

## Sentence Completion 2400 Strategy 3 — Fill in the exact opposite word

Some SENTENCE COMPLETION questions contain ideas that are contradicted in the blank(s). What if you can't think of your own word to fill in the blank, but you see the opposite concept elsewhere in the sentence? Simply write down the exact opposite word you see. Just put "not" or "un-" in front of the word that needs to be opposed and use that as your WYPAD solution.

### Sentence Completion 2400 Example    *Fill in the exact opposite word*

### Step 1 — Read a hard question

John Steinbeck's high school classmates found that John had an unpredictable manner, either friendly or -------.

(A) sociable      (B) amicable      (C) gregarious
    (D) extroverted      (E) reticent

### Step 2 — WYPAD + Fill in the exact opposite word

John Steinbeck's high school classmates found that John had an unpredictable manner, either friendly or -------.

My WYPAD is *unfriendly.*

### Step 3 — Eliminate incorrect choices

(A) sociable      ≠ unfriendly
(B) amicable      ≠ unfriendly
(C) gregarious    ≠ unfriendly
(D) extroverted ≠ unfriendly
(E) reticent      = unfriendly ?

Selected definitions

amicable      = nice, kind
gregarious   = friendly, outgoing, sociable
extroverted = outgoing
reticent      = reserved, withdrawn

**Step 4** ✏ *Check the remaining answer choices in context*

CORRECT    John Steinbeck's high school classmates found that John
had an unpredictable manner, either friendly or **reticent**.

Select (E) as your answer choice.

**Step 3**

Master
WYPAD and
other keys
to success on
SAT Reading

· · · · · · · · · · · · · · · · · · · ·

**152**

> ### Sentence Completion 2400 Example    *Fill in the exact opposite word*

**Step 1** ✏ *Read a medium question*

Joey preferred living in the farming town rather than the ------- city,
which he believed was full of too many -------.

(A) rustic . . commotions
(B) metropolitan . . distractions
(C) pastoral . . disturbances
(D) bucolic . . interruptions
(E) tranquil . . riots

**Step 2** ✏ *WYPAD + Work one at a time + Fill in the exact opposite word
(first blank)*

| Joey preferred living in the farming town rather than the ------- city . . .

My WYPAD for the first blank is *nonfarming*.

**Step 3** ✏ *Eliminate incorrect choices*

Keep the second word of each answer choice covered with your hand.

(A) rustic            ≠ *nonfarming*
(B) metropolitan  = *nonfarming*  ?
(C) pastoral          ≠ *nonfarming*
(D) bucolic            ≠ *nonfarming*
(E) tranquil          = *nonfarming*  ?

Selected definitions

rustic            = rural, nonurban
metropolitan  = urban, city
pastoral          = rural, nonurban
bucolic            = rural, nonurban
tranquil          = peaceful, calm, serene

**Step 4** ✏ *WYPAD + Work one at a time + Fill in the exact opposite word
(second blank)*

| . . . which he believed was full of too many -------.

My WYPAD for the second blank is *annoyances*.

**Step 5** *Eliminate incorrect choices*

(B) distractions = annoyances ?
(E) riots ≠ annoyances

**Step 6** *Check the remaining answer choices in context*

CORRECT    Joey preferred living in the farming town rather than the **metropolitan** city, which he believed was full of too many **distractions**.

Select (B) as your answer choice.

**Practice problem set**    *Fill in the exact opposite word*

The answer key for this problem set is on page 283.

---

Each sentence in this section has one or two blanks, each blank indicating that something has been omitted. Following each sentence are five words or sets of words labeled A through E. Choose the word or set of words that, when inserted in the sentence, best fits the meaning of the sentence as a whole.

---

1. Although the latest research on alternative energy sources has largely been -------, the discovery of certain unforeseen ------- has been discouraging.

   (A) innovative . . modifications
   (B) hasty . . accidents
   (C) unexpected . . conclusions
   (D) dynamic . . procedures
   (E) promising . . drawbacks

2. The normally timid little dog surprised us all by acting quite ------- toward other dogs, nearly attacking several of them despite the fact that they were much larger animals.

   (A) nonchalant    (B) sullen    (C) hesitant
     (D) belligerent    (E) condescending

3. In the workplace, Marcus was rather -------; at social gatherings, however, he became quite forward, boldly stating his opinion on a variety of subjects.

   (A) aggressive    (B) brazen    (C) optimistic
     (D) mercurial    (E) diffident

**4.** Author M.C. Beaton's detective character, Hamish Macbeth, has a reputation for laziness, though he is often so ------- that he solves crimes quickly and then has time to give others the credit so that he can avoid being promoted.

(A) apathetic   (B) diligent   (C) vivacious
(D) inquisitive   (E) inactive

## Sentence Completion 2400 Strategy 4 ⁄ *Fill in +/−*

You may sometimes have a difficult time coming up with a word to fill in the blank of a SENTENCE COMPLETION question. Before skipping directly to the answer choices, try to decide whether the blank should be filled with a positive (+), negative (−), or neutral word. Sentences often provide enough clues to enable you to make this determination. Only as a last resort should you tackle the answer choices before you have a clue as to what the answer should look like.

### Sentence Completion 2400 Example   *Fill in +/−*

#### Step 1 ⁄ *Read a hard question*

The -------, radical sentiments underlying the postwar Red Scare and the immigration-restriction movement emerged starkly in the Massachusetts murder case.

(A) tolerant   (B) unprejudiced   (C) magnanimous
(D) broad-minded   (E) xenophobic

#### Step 2 ⁄ *Fill in +/−*

The -------, radical sentiments underlying the postwar Red Scare and the immigration-restriction movement emerged starkly in the Massachusetts murder case.

The connotation is clearly negative (−).

#### Step 3 ⁄ *Eliminate incorrect choices*

(A) tolerant        ≠ −
(B) unprejudiced    ≠ −
(C) magnanimous   ≠ −
(D) broad-minded  ≠ −
(E) xenophobic    = − ?

Selected definitions

unprejudiced  = tolerant, open-minded
magnanimous = noble, generous, giving
xenophobic   = afraid of the foreign/strange

**Step 4** ✐ *Check the remaining answer choices in context*

CORRECT The **xenophobic**, radical sentiments underlying the postwar Red Scare and the immigration-restriction movement emerged starkly in the Massachusetts murder case.

Select (E) as your answer choice.

## Sentence Completion 2400 Example   *Fill in +/−*

**Step 1** ✐ *Read a medium question*

> The ------- tone of their conversation was in contrast to the grave mood of the other guests at the reception.
>
> (A) serious   (B) ominous   (C) poignant
>     (D) jovial   (E) solemn

**Step 2** ✐ *Fill in +/−*

> The ------- tone of their conversation was in contrast to the grave mood of the other guests at the reception.

The connotation is clearly positive (+).

**Step 3** ✐ *Eliminate incorrect choices*

(A) serious   ≠ +
(B) ominous   ≠ +
(C) poignant   ≠ +
(D) jovial   = + ?
(E) solemn   ≠ +

Selected definitions

ominous  = threatening, foreboding
poignant = emotional
jovial     = happy, cheerful
solemn   = stately, grave, serious, stern

**Step 4** ✐ *Check the remaining answer choices in context*

CORRECT The **jovial** tone of their conversation was in contrast to the grave mood of the other guests at the reception.

Select (D) as your answer choice.

The answer key for this problem set is on page 283.

**Step 3**
Master
WYPAD and
other keys
to success on
SAT Reading

**156**

> Each sentence in this section has one or two blanks, each blank indicating that something has been omitted. Following each sentence are five words or sets of words labeled A through E. Choose the word or set of words that, when inserted in the sentence, <u>best</u> fits the meaning of the sentence as a whole.

1. The overthrown king decided to flee the country rather than face a life of ------- and condemnation for all of the horrendous war crimes he had committed during his reign.

   (A) impunity    (B) deference    (C) ignominy
      (D) amelioration    (E) lassitude

2. Al Capone's role in the violent St. Valentine's Day massacre of 1929 earned him long-lasting -------: decades later, we still recognize his name as one of the most vicious gangsters in American history.

   (A) notoriety    (B) reparation    (C) hostility
      (D) commendation    (E) affiliation

3. Only a few people have moved into the apartments above the fish market because the odor of seafood is so -------, spreading from room to room even when windows are closed.

   (A) luminous    (B) destructive    (C) animated
      (D) diligent    (E) pervasive

4. As one might expect, the convivial politician ------- public appearances and guest spots on the radio.

   (A) loathed    (B) preempted    (C) endorsed
      (D) dreaded    (E) relished

## Sentence Completion 2400 Strategy 5   *Identify the double-blank relationship*

On some double-blank SENTENCE COMPLETION questions, you won't be able to fill in your own words, no matter how hard you try. Why? Because SAT test writers sometimes don't offer context clues about the words that should fill the blanks. Sometimes, you need the word in the first blank before you can decide what word should go in the second blank. The test writers provide context clues about the relationship between the blanks instead. There are three categories of double-blank SENTENCE COMPLETION relationships.

### Parallel relationship

In this relationship, the two blanks should contain words that express similar ideas.

The new video game was -------: Most parents found the character and imagery to be -------.

Although you may assume two negative words should go in the blanks, two positive words could work as well.

The new video game was **satisfactory**: Most parents found the character and imagery to be **innocent**.

Note that the relationship only needs to express similar ideas; the connotations of the words may vary.

## Opposed relationship

In this relationship, the two blanks should contain words that express contrasting ideas.

Although the computer programmer was supposedly -------, his latest program showed that he was in fact -------.

Although you may assume that the first blank should contain a negative word and the second blank a positive word, the opposite could work as well.

Although the computer programmer was supposedly **skilled**, his latest program showed that he was in fact **inept**.

Note that the relationship only needs to express contrasting ideas; the connotations of the words may vary.

## Progressive relationship

In this relationship, the first blank should contain a word that is less extreme than the word that should go in the second blank.

Supervisors typically look for candidates who are ------- about the job, but not overly -------.

Supervisors typically look for candidates who are **enthusiastic** about the job, but not overly **fanatical**.

| Sentence Completion 2400 Example | *Identify the double-blank relationship* |

### Step 1 ⁄ *Read an easy question*

Despite ------- options at many fast food restaurants, most consumers in the United States prefer to eat ------- fare.

(A) healthful . . pleasant
(B) insalubrious . . noxious
(C) nutritious . . unhealthy
(D) distasteful . . natural
(E) savory . . wholesome

## Step 2 ✎ Identify the double-blank relationship

> Despite ------- options at many fast food restaurants, most consumers in the United States prefer to eat ------- fare.

The relationship is clearly opposed; "Despite" is an important clue.

Selected definition

fare = food

## Step 3 ✎ Eliminate incorrect choices

(A) healthful . . pleasant     ≠ *opposed relationship*
(B) insalubrious . . noxious  ≠ *opposed relationship*
(C) nutritious . . unhealthy  = *opposed relationship* ?
(D) distasteful . . natural      ≠ *opposed relationship*
(E) savory . . wholesome     ≠ *opposed relationship*

Because there is no WYPAD solution, you cannot apply *Sentence Completion 2400 Strategy 1* (Work one at a time). Therefore, you should determine if the two words in each answer choice contrast with one another.

Selected definitions

insalubrious  = unhealthy
noxious          = toxic, harmful
savory           = flavorful

## Step 4 ✎ Check the remaining answer choices in context

> CORRECT     Despite **nutritious** options at many fast food restaurants, most consumers in the United States prefer to eat **unhealthy** fare.

Select (C) as your answer choice.

---

**Sentence Completion 2400 Example**     *Identify the double-blank relationship*

## Step 1 ✎ Read an easy question

> Sanjay's slight ------- about the test turned to complete ------- when he finally took the exam and realized it was a lot harder than he had anticipated.
>
> (A) unease . . trepidation
> (B) anxiety . . smugness
> (C) remorse . . complacency
> (D) bewilderment . . foreboding
> (E) apprehension . . gratification

**Step 2** ✎ *Identify the double-blank relationship*

> Sanjay's slight ------- about the test turned to complete ------- when he finally took the exam and realized it was a lot harder than he had anticipated.

The relationship is clearly progressive; "slight . . . complete" is an important clue.

**Step 3** ✎ *Eliminate incorrect choices*

(A) unease . . trepidation      = *progressive relationship* **?**
(B) anxiety . . smugness      ≠ *progressive relationship*
(C) remorse . . complacency      ≠ *progressive relationship*
(D) bewilderment . . foreboding    ≠ *progressive relationship*
(E) apprehension . . gratification   ≠ *progressive relationship*

Because there is no WYPAD solution, you cannot apply *Sentence Completion 2400 Strategy 1* (Work one at a time). Therefore, you should determine if the second word in each answer choice is more extreme than the first.

Selected definitions

trepidation     = fear, apprehension
smugness       = self-satisfaction, conceit
remorse         = regret
complacency   = self-satisfaction, smugness
bewilderment = confusion
foreboding      = anxiety, worry
apprehension = anxiety, fear
gratification    = satisfaction

**Step 4** ✎ *Check the remaining answer choices in context*

CORRECT    Sanjay's slight **unease** about the test turned to complete **trepidation** when he finally took the exam and realized it was a lot harder than he had anticipated.

Select (A) as your answer choice.

**Step 3**
Master
WYPAD and
other keys
to success on
SAT Reading

**160**

**Practice problem set**  *Identify the double-blank relationship*

The answer key for this problem set is on page 283.

> Each sentence in this section has one or two blanks, each blank indicating that something has been omitted. Following each sentence are five words or sets of words labeled A through E. Choose the word or set of words that, when inserted in the sentence, best fits the meaning of the sentence as a whole.

1. Because the waterfall had seemed so ------- from a distance, the hikers were surprised and awed when they arrived at its base and saw how ------- it truly was.

   (A) minute . . vapid
   (B) diminutive . . colossal
   (C) unimportant . . tranquil
   (D) ruthless . . innocuous
   (E) exquisite . . majestic

2. The brilliant young violinist was not only ------- gifted but was also quite -------: she had a natural aptitude for music, yet still continued to practice for many hours each day.

   (A) obstinately . . resolved
   (B) effectively . . equitable
   (C) innately . . assiduous
   (D) immoderately . . ambiguous
   (E) inherently . . lethargic

3. The new roommates were initially ------- about living together because they were not sure if they would get along; however, by the end of the first month, it was easy to see that they had developed a great sense of -------.

   (A) dubious . . adversity
   (B) irritable . . acquiescence
   (C) concerned . . malevolence
   (D) skeptical . . camaraderie
   (E) surreptitious . . superiority

4. The college was gifted with a ------- research grant and was therefore able to hire three visiting lecturers that they had previously thought were ------- due to lack of funding.

   (A) prodigious . . unattainable
   (B) scholarly . . erudite
   (C) primitive . . unaffordable
   (D) influential . . workable
   (E) lackluster . . impressive

# SAT passage-based reading

Passage-based reading is perhaps the most important part of the SAT. Your ability to do well on this portion will help you on other sections of the SAT, as well as assist you on other standardized tests. In order to score high on SAT PASSAGE-BASED READING sections, you will need to develop two key skills: thinking literally and thinking critically. Learning to apply *Passage 2400 Strategies* will help you develop these skills.

## 1. Think literally

Thinking literally requires that you take passages and questions at face value and make no assumptions. Most students who score high on the SAT have the ability to think literally. It is a skill that will benefit you on other sections of the SAT, especially Writing multiple-choice sections.

## ◁ High school English is different

Although the strategies in this section will assist you on standardized tests, they won't help you on high school English tests. Standardized test writers compose *standard questions* that require that you *infer*, while English teachers compose *analysis questions* that require that you *assume*. What's the difference between an inference and an assumption? An inference is an induction based on textual evidence in a passage; an assumption is an induction *not* based on textual evidence in a passage. For SAT purposes, you should only make inferences—not assumptions.

For high school English tests, you often need to make small assumptions about literature in order to score well. But for the SAT, the less you assume, the higher you will score. Making assumptions is the worst thing you can do when answering SAT PASSAGE-BASED READING questions. I know this sounds unfair. Throughout your school career, English teachers have rewarded you for making assumptions about characters, plots, and settings. Now, the SAT will punish you for making such assumptions. I scored poorly on PASSAGE-BASED READING practice sets, partly because my high school English classes had thoroughly trained me to believe that assumptions are prized. In this section, I will show you how I tossed out my high school approach and aced SAT passage-based reading.

## 2. Think critically

Thinking critically requires that you thoroughly understand and analyze passages. Most standardized tests include sections that require you to think critically; for example, the Medical College Admission Test (MCAT) includes a verbal reasoning section similar to SAT passage-based reading. In fact, I aced MCAT Verbal Reasoning by using the same strategies I used for the SAT!

**Step 3**
Master
WYPAD and
other keys
to success on
SAT Reading

...................

**162**

## Format

There are two types of passages on the SAT. Review the directions for SAT PASSAGE-BASED READING questions so that you don't waste time reading the directions during the actual test.

1.  **Standard passages** are single passages followed by a series of questions.

> Each passage below is followed by questions based on its content. Answer the questions on the basis of what is <u>stated</u> or <u>implied</u> in the passage and in any introductory material that may be provided.

2.  **Comparison passages** are two different passages that discuss a similar topic from different viewpoints. The passages are followed by a series of questions, many of which concern the relationship between the passages.

> The passages below are followed by questions based on their content or on the relationship between the two passages. Answer the questions on the basis of what is <u>stated</u> or <u>implied</u> in the passages and in any introductory material that may be provided.

Each SAT Reading section contains 12 to 19 PASSAGE-BASED READING questions. Lengths of the passages vary, but they are usually between 100 and 800 words long. Every SAT has about the same amount of total reading.

- ◄ Two short standard passages
    - 2 questions per passage
- ◄ Two medium standard passages
    - 5–10 questions per passage
- ◄ One long standard passage
    - 11–13 questions per passage
- ◄ One set of short comparison passages
    - 4–5 questions per set
- ◄ One set of long comparison passages
    - 9–13 questions per set

Unlike SENTENCE COMPLETION questions, PASSAGE-BASED READING questions don't adhere to an order of difficulty. The first questions for a passage may be difficult, whereas the last questions may be easy.

## General reading strategies

Which of the following is the best way to approach SAT PASSAGE-BASED READING questions?

- ◄ First read the entire passage thoroughly, then answer the questions.
- ◄ First skim the entire passage, then answer the questions.
- ◄ First read the questions, then read the passage, then answer the questions.
- ◄ Don't read the passage; read only the lines cited by the questions.

Actually, none of the above is correct. SAT study guides clash on the best approach to the PASSAGE-BASED READING sections. SAT "experts" tout the methods listed above. And some of these approaches may work—for people who are already good readers. These strategies may be useful to test takers who already read the daily newspaper, are avid fiction readers, and comprehend literature with both speed and accuracy. These approaches, however, didn't work for me, because I wasn't a naturally skilled reader.

I used a different method on the Reading section of the SAT. I read each passage in chunks and answered questions as I went along. Since I read very little besides high school assignments, I found reading SAT passages in sections to be a big help. The length and complexity of the academic SAT passages often overwhelmed me when I tried other methods.

## General Reading 2400 Strategy

This strategy breaks passages into manageable segments so that you can focus more thinking power on each question. It has three parts.

### 1. Write your main idea down.

You will learn more about this step in *Passage 2400 Strategy 1.*

### 2. Answer all line-specific questions.

These questions, which refer to particular lines in the passage, generally proceed in order from start to finish. Stop to answer each line-specific question as you read through the passage. By answering all of these questions first, you will read the entire passage in chunks.

Some passages have few line-specific questions or none at all. You will learn how to tackle these questions below.

TIP  It is often helpful to read a couple of lines above and a couple of lines below the lines cited.

### 3. Answer all general questions.

General questions don't refer to particular lines in the passage. By answering these questions after you've answered the line-specific questions, you will have a solid idea of the main concepts contained in the passage.

**Step 3**
Master
WYPAD and
other keys
to success on
SAT Reading
..................

**164**

Use the *General Reading 2400 Strategy* to "read" every SAT passage you encounter. It may be difficult at first if you are used to another method of reading SAT passages. But once you master the *General Reading 2400 Strategy,* passages will no longer overwhelm you with information.

## Passage 2400 Strategies

The PASSAGE-BASED READING sections require test takers to apply a mix of *2400 Strategies* to each question. The sample text below will be used to explain the *Passage 2400 Strategies* that follow.

*The following passage was written by an American journalist in 1920.*

It is a curious thing that so many people only go into a bookshop when they happen to need some particular book. Do they never drop in for a little innocent carouse and refreshment? There are some
*Line* knightly souls who even go so far as to make their visits to bookshops
5 a kind of chivalrous errantry at large. They go in not because they need any certain volume, but because they feel that there may be some book that needs them. Some wistful, little forgotten sheaf of loveliness, long pining away on an upper shelf—why not ride up, fling her across your charger (or your charge account), and gallop
10 away. Be a little knightly, you book-lovers!

The lack of intelligence with which people use bookshops is, one supposes, no more flagrant than the lack of intelligence with which we use all the rest of the machinery of civilization. In this age, and particularly in this city, we haven't time to be intelligent.
15 A queer thing about books, if you open your heart to them, is the instant and irresistible way they follow you with their appeal. You know at once, if you are clairvoyant in these matters (libre-voyant, one might say), when you have met your book. You may dally and evade, you may go on about your affairs, but the paragraph of prose
20 your eye fell upon, or the snatch of verses, or perhaps only the spirit and flavor of the volume, more divined than reasonably noted, will follow you. A few lines glimpsed on a page may alter your whole trend of thought for the day, reverse the currents of the mind, change the profile of the city. The other evening, on a subway car, we were
25 reading Walter de la Mare's interesting little essay about Rupert Brooke. His discussion of children, their dreaming ways, their exalted simplicity and absorption, changed the whole tenor of our voyage by some magical chemistry of thought. It was no longer a wild, barbaric struggle with our fellowmen, but a venture of faith and recompense,
30 taking us home to the bedtime of a child.

GOLDEN · Write your personal answer down (WYPAD)
1 · Write your main idea down (WYMID)
2 · Read actively
3 · Make paragraph summaries
4 · Don't defend
5 · Do attack
6 · Avoid assumptions
7 · Avoid extremes
8 · Avoid plagiarism
9 · Criticize every word
10 · Choose general over specific

*Passage 2400 Strategies 1* through *5* are behind-the-scenes tactics that you should use on every passage and question you tackle. *Passage 2400 Strategies 6* through *10* are specific tactics that are applied to particular questions and answer choices.

## Passage 2400 Golden Strategy · *Write your personal answer down (WYPAD)*

The key to acing the SAT PASSAGE-BASED READING sections is to Write Your Personal Answer Down (WYPAD): Jot down your own response to questions before you look at the answer choices. This strategy will keep you from being misled by enticing, but incorrect, answers. Synthesizing your own answer is the best way to assure comprehension, which is what PASSAGE-BASED READING questions are testing. You will use this strategy on every question you tackle in these sections. As you learn to master WYPAD for PASSAGE-BASED READING questions, follow these five guidelines:

### 1. Cover the answer choices.

Cover answer choices (A) through (E) with your hand. Hiding potential answer choices forces you to come up with your own personal answer.

### 2. Write—don't just think—your answer.

Write your own answer down—don't just think it. There is a reason this *2400 Strategy* is called WYPAD, and not TYPAD. Writing your own personal answer down shows that you really understand a question, instead of merely *thinking* you understand it.

### 3. Keep it short.

Writing down a full response to every question would take far too much time. Instead, you should abbreviate and keep your answer to no more than a few words.

### 4. Keep it simple.

Your answer doesn't have to sound like an intelligent SAT answer choice. The whole point of WYPAD is to have a concrete idea of the answer, even if the idea would not be a regular answer choice.

### 5. As a last resort, peek.

Sometimes, you won't be able to come up with a *WYPAD* solution. In fact, some PASSAGE-BASED READING questions don't give you enough information to judge what kind of answer is expected. When this happens, try peeking at the answer choices for inspiration.

**Step 3**
Master
WYPAD and
other keys
to success on
SAT Reading

**166**

## Passage 2400 Strategy 1  *Write your main idea down (WYMID)*

WYMID is also the first step of the *General Reading 2400 Strategy*. Before you read any of the questions, write down the main idea of the passage. You must understand the general idea of the passage before you can answer the questions related to it. If you have a solid understanding of the main idea, you are more likely to understand the rest of the passage, as well as the questions and answer choices.

By the time you have read to the end of the first or second paragraph of a passage, you should be able to write down the main idea. If you cannot formulate the main idea of a passage in your own words, you haven't read far enough or you may be having trouble comprehending the passage. If you believe that the main idea is not expressed in the first couple of paragraphs, continue reading. If you are having trouble understanding the passage, return to the beginning and read the first two paragraphs more slowly. Take the time to understand the main idea.

Not only must you understand the main idea, you should also write it down. Your pencil shouldn't be idle while you are solving PASSAGE-BASED READING questions. WYMID follows guidelines similar to those for WYPAD.

### 1. Keep it short.

Don't get caught up in the details of a passage. Limit your main idea to a few words.

### 2. Keep it simple.

Your answer doesn't have to sound "intelligent," as long as you have a concrete understanding of the passage.

### 3. Don't plagiarize.

Avoid using phrases that are in the passage. By formulating your own summary, you demonstrate a deeper understanding of the passage. If you simply regurgitate what the passage says, you probably aren't trying to understand the main idea.

## Passage 2400 Example   *Write your main idea down*

### Step 1 ⚊ *Read the first paragraph(s) of the passage*

> It is a curious thing that so many people only go into a bookshop when they happen to need some particular book. Do they never drop in for a little innocent carouse and refreshment? There are some knightly souls who even go so far as to make their visits to bookshops a kind of chivalrous errantry at large. They go in not because they need any certain volume, but because they feel that there may be some book that needs them. Some wistful, little forgotten sheaf of loveliness, long pining away on an upper shelf—why not ride up, fling her across your charger (or your charge account), and gallop away. Be a little knightly, you book-lovers!

### Step 2 ⚊ *Write your main idea down*

*Author believes a trip to the bookstore should not be something you have to do, but something you want to do.*

Abbreviated version to write in the SAT test booklet

*Trip 2 Bstore shouldn't have 2 do, but want 2.*

## Passage 2400 Strategy 2 ⚊ *Read actively*

You understand a passage better if you're interested in it. Although the typical SAT Reading passage is notoriously boring, you must find a way to become interested in it—or at least fake your interest. If you are skimming lines just to get through a passage, you are reading *passively* and are not engaged by the material. To gain a deeper understanding of the passage, you must interact with it and read *actively*. I used three primary methods to read actively when I was faced with a dull SAT Reading passage: *Question, Comment,* and *Anticipate.*

Is there an annoying student in your class who gives his/her opinion about everything? A student who *questions* every claim, who *comments* on every statement, and who *anticipates* the teacher's next move?

For SAT Reading success, you need to be that student. *Question* every claim the passage makes. *Comment* on every statement. *Anticipate* what the passage will say next. By reading actively, you develop a curiosity about the passage. And when you're interested in the passage, you're more likely to understand it. Avid readers naturally read actively.

Of course, you don't need to write down your questions, comments, and anticipations as you read; just stay actively engaged with the reading and keep your mind interacting with the passage. Interest leads to comprehension, which leads to higher SAT Reading scores.

**Step 3**
Master
WYPAD and
other keys
to success on
SAT Reading
..........................
**168**

**Passage 2400 Example**   *Read actively*

**Step 1**  *Continue reading the passage*

> The lack of intelligence with which people use bookshops is,
> one supposes, no more flagrant than the lack of intelligence with
> which we use all the rest of the machinery of civilization. In this age,
> and particularly in this city, we haven't time to be intelligent.

**Step 2**  *Read actively*

**Question**  Does the author really think that the manner in which people use bookshops is that important?

**Comment**  I don't agree that we use all machinery with a lack of intelligence.

**Anticipate**  I bet he is going to talk about how unintelligent people are in the next paragraph.

## Passage 2400 Strategy 3  *Make paragraph summaries*

This strategy supplements *Passage 2400 Strategy 2*. One tangible way to make sure that you are reading actively is to make paragraph summaries in the margins of the test booklet. These summaries highlight key points in the passage and are especially useful when you have to read large chunks of the passage between line-specific questions or when there are no line-specific questions at all. With short paragraph summaries that recap the main points of a passage, you won't need to go back and re-read large portions. This strategy follows guidelines similar to those for WYPAD and WYMID.

### 1. Keep it short.

Don't get caught up in the details of a passage. Limit your paragraph summaries to a few words.

### 2. Keep it simple.

Your paragraph summary doesn't have to sound "intelligent," as long as you have a concrete understanding of the paragraph or section of the passage.

### 3. Don't plagiarize.

Avoid using words or phrases that are in the passage. By formulating your own summary, you demonstrate a deeper understanding of the passage. If you simply regurgitate what the paragraph or section says, you probably aren't trying to understand its point.

## Passage 2400 Example   *Make paragraph summaries*

### Step 1 ⌐ *Continue reading the passage*

A queer thing about books, if you open your heart to them, is the instant and irresistible way they follow you with their appeal. You know at once, if you are clairvoyant in these matters (libre-voyant, one might say), when you have met your book. You may dally and evade, you may go on about your affairs, but the paragraph of prose your eye fell upon, or the snatch of verses, or perhaps only the spirit and flavor of the volume, more divined than reasonably noted, will follow you. A few lines glimpsed on a page may alter your whole trend of thought for the day, reverse the currents of the mind, change the profile of the city. The other evening, on a subway car, we were reading Walter de la Mare's interesting little essay about Rupert Brooke. His discussion of children, their dreaming ways, their exalted simplicity and absorption, changed the whole tenor of our voyage by some magical chemistry of thought. It was no longer a wild, barbaric struggle with our fellowmen, but a venture of faith and recompense, taking us home to the bedtime of a child.

### Step 2 ⌐ *Make paragraph summaries*

*Know when you meet your book. Can change your day.*

Abbreviated version to write in the SAT test booklet

*Meet book. Change day.*

## Passage 2400 Strategy 4 ⌐ *Don't defend*

Don't *defend* PASSAGE-BASED READING answer choices; that is, don't look for reasons why answer choices could be correct. As you read an answer choice, avoid thinking as follows.

- ◄ Well, this answer choice *could be* correct because . . .
- ◄ I can see how the author *could be* . . .
- ◄ I suppose this answer choice *could be* logical now . . .
- ◄ The passage *could be* mentioning . . .

Such thoughts mean that you are defending the answer choices—a flawed approach to solving PASSAGE-BASED READING questions.

Step 3
Master
WYPAD and
other keys
to success on
SAT Reading

170

## Passage 2400 Example    *Don't defend*

**Step 1** ✏ *Read the question*

The primary purpose of the passage is to

(A) contrast trips to the bookstore with medieval adventures
(B) discuss the significance of books that most people don't realize
(C) characterize most people in society as ignorant and unintelligent
(D) distinguish the difference between the happiness booklovers
      experience and the sorrow non-booklovers experience
(E) provide several examples of how people have forgotten the art
      of book reading

**Step 2** ✏ *Revisit the main idea*

*Trip 2 Bstore shouldn't have 2 do, but want 2.*

**Step 3** ✏ *Don't defend*

(A) Don't have the mind set that "medieval adventures" *could be* in the
    passage.
(B) This answer choice seems okay.
(C) Don't have the mind set that characterizing people "as ignorant and intel-
    ligent" *could be* the main purpose.
(D) Don't have the mind set that "the sorrow non-booklovers experience" *could
    be* in the passage.
(E) Don't have the mind set that "several examples" *could be* in the passage.

Select (B) as your answer choice.

## Passage 2400 Strategy 5 ✏ *Do attack*

Do *attack* PASSAGE-BASED READING answer choices; that is, actively look for
reasons why answer choices are incorrect. Focus on eliminating incorrect
answer choices rather than on circling correct answer choices in these sections
of the SAT. As you read an answer choice, you should be thinking as follows.

◄ This answer choice *is incorrect* because . . .
◄ The author *is not* . . .
◄ This answer choice *is not* logical . . .
◄ The passage *does not* mention . . .

Such thoughts mean that you are attacking the answer choices—a sound
approach to solving PASSAGE-BASED READING questions.

### Passage 2400 Example   *Do attack*

**Step 1** *Read the question*

The primary purpose of the passage is to
(A) contrast trips to the bookstore with medieval adventures
(B) discuss the significance of books that most people don't realize
(C) characterize most people in society as ignorant and unintelligent
(D) distinguish the difference between the happiness booklovers experience and the sorrow non-booklovers experience
(E) provide several examples of how people have forgotten the art of book reading

**Step 2** *Revisit the main idea*

*Trip 2 Bstore shouldn't have 2 do, but want 2.*

**Step 3** *Do attack*

(A) Do have the mind set that "medieval adventures" isn't in the passage.
(B) There's nothing to attack.
(C) Do have the mind set that characterizing people "as ignorant and intelligent" isn't the main purpose.
(D) Do have the mind set that "the sorrow non-booklovers experience" isn't in the passage.
(E) Do have the mind set that "several examples" aren't in the passage.

Select (B) as your answer choice.

## Passage 2400 Strategy 6   *Avoid assumptions*

This may be the most important *Passage 2400 Strategy* to learn. Remember: An assumption is an induction that isn't based on textual evidence in a passage. Test takers often make the mistake of choosing answer choices that contain assumptions about the passage. When scrutinizing answer choices, ask yourself, "Does the passage mention this?" If the passage doesn't mention a particular phrase or idea, the answer choice contains an assumption. Every correct answer choice in the PASSAGE-BASED READING sections is based on textual evidence in the passage.

### Passage 2400 Example   *Avoid assumptions*

**Step 1** *Read the question*

The metaphor in lines 7–10 ("Some . . . book-lovers") serves to
(A) show that book reading can be just as much fun as horseback riding
(B) highlight the excitement bookstores can create
(C) direct readers to engage in an activity they may not typically choose
(D) offer insight into the reasoning behind book-lovers' philosophy
(E) compare the difference between book-lovers and casual readers

**Step 3**
Master
WYPAD and
other keys
to success on
SAT Reading

172

**Step 2** ✒ *Read the relevant lines*

> Some wistful, little forgotten sheaf
> of loveliness, long pining away on an upper shelf—why not ride up,
> fling her across your charger (or your charge account), and gallop
> away. Be a little knightly, you book-lovers!

**Step 3** ✒ *Avoid assumptions*

(A) Does the passage mention "horseback riding"?  No

(B) Does the passage mention that bookstores "create" excitement?  No

(C) Does the passage mention a suggestion "to engage in an activity" readers "may not typically choose"?  Yes

(D) Does the passage mention "the reasoning behind book-lovers' philosophy"?  No

(E) Does the passage mention a comparison "between book-lovers and casual readers"?  No

Select (C) as your answer choice.

## Passage 2400 Strategy 7 ✒ *Avoid extremes*

Avoid extreme PASSAGE-BASED READING answer choices. SAT test writers must be able to defend why certain answer choices are correct and others are incorrect, and it is much easier to defend moderate answer choices than extreme ones. Extreme answer choices often contain words or phrases like the following.

**EXTREMELY ALL-ENCOMPASSING**

all
comprehensive
every
universal

**EXTREMELY CHRONIC**

always
forever
never
throughout history/through the ages

**EXTREMELY DIFFICULT TO DO**

disprove
prove
refute

**EXTREMELY NARROW**

exclusive
only

strictly

unique

**EXTREMELY RADICAL**

absolute

complete

impossible

inevitable

unquestionably

**EXTREMELY INCORRECT TONE (OF THE PASSAGE OR THE AUTHOR'S ATTITUDE)**

apathetic

bewildered

confused

indifferent

mystified

puzzled

Sometimes, you can tell that one answer choice is more extreme than another by its diction rather than by its use of extreme words. Sometimes, too, correct answer choices contain extreme phrases. For example, a question about an assumption that the author or passage makes may have extreme phrasing in its answer choices, because assumptions are inherently extreme. In general, however, avoid extreme answer choices in PASSAGE-BASED READING sections of the SAT.

---

### Passage 2400 Example   *Avoid extremes*

**Step 1** *Read the question*

The statement in lines 18–22 ("You may . . . follow you") suggests that readers

(A) are immediately mesmerized by all books

(B) always try to do other activities rather than read

(C) are only pursued by books

(D) cannot possibly comprehend the value of what they read

(E) are relatively interested in their reading despite their activities

**Step 2** *Read the relevant lines*

You may dally and evade, you may go on about your affairs, but the paragraph of prose your eye fell upon, or the snatch of verses, or perhaps only the spirit and flavor of the volume, more divined than reasonably noted, will follow you.

**Step 3**
Master
WYPAD and
other keys
to success on
SAT Reading

174

### Step 3 ⌁ *Avoid extremes*

(A) Avoid "all."
(B) Avoid "always."
(C) Avoid "only."
(D) Avoid "cannot possibly" (= impossible).
(E) There are no extremes.

Select (E) as your answer choice.

## Passage 2400 Strategy 8 ⌁ *Avoid plagiarism*

Avoid plagiaristic PASSAGE-BASED READING answer choices, that is, choices that use exactly the same words or phrases that the passage does. Test takers who are lazy or who don't understand the passage are likely to choose answer choices that use the same diction as the passage. SAT test writers use such incorrect answer choices to bait test takers into choosing these options.

Instead, you should select the answer choice that summarizes the underlying idea of the passage. This answer choice typically captures the overall concept, but with different words or phrases than the passage itself. Note that avoiding plagiarism is not a black-and-white strategy: Correct answer choices sometimes contain the exact phrasing of the passage. Before you select such an option, however, determine that the other four choices are incorrect.

> ### Passage 2400 Example    *Avoid plagiarism*

### Step 1 ⌁ *Read the question*

Which of the following statements about children would the author of the passage most likely agree with?

(A) Children's books are more intellectually exalting than adult books.
(B) Children are likely to believe in magical thoughts.
(C) Essays about children can remind us of our childhood bedtime rituals.
(D) A child's mentality is a brilliant outlook that written works can help us experience.
(E) The dreaming ways of a child help us to understand the significance of books.

### Step 2 ⌁ *Read the relevant lines*

The other evening, on a subway car, we were reading Walter de la Mare's interesting little essay about Rupert Brooke. His discussion of children, their dreaming ways, their exalted simplicity and absorption, changed the whole tenor of our voyage by some magical chemistry of thought. It was no longer a wild, barbaric struggle with our fellowmen, but a venture of faith and recompense, taking us home to the bedtime of a child.

**Step 3** *Avoid plagiarism*

(A) "Exalting" plagiarizes "exalted simplicity" in the passage.
(B) "Magical thoughts" plagiarizes "magical chemistry of thought" in the passage.
(C) "Childhood bedtime rituals" plagiarizes "bedtime of a child" in the passage.
(D) This summarizes without plagiarism.
(E) "Dreaming ways of a child" plagiarizes "children, their dreaming ways" in the passage.

Select (D) as your answer choice.

## Passage 2400 Strategy 9 *Criticize every word*

Take every word literally in the passage, questions, and answer choices; don't cut the SAT any slack. In everyday speech, if someone says that she would like to "fly to Paris," you know that she means she would like to take an airplane flight to Paris, not to literally fly there. On the SAT, however, you should be wary of an answer choice that says a person would like to "fly to Paris," because people cannot actually fly. You need to be this critical.

Be like that annoying kid in your class. If the teacher instructs him to "pick up his water," he might respond by saying that he cannot actually lift water with his hands, but that he can "pick up his water bottle." Although you probably aren't so nitpicky in real life, it is important that you be this critical when taking the SAT. A single incorrect word can make an answer choice incorrect.

### Passage 2400 Example    *Criticize every word*

**Step 1** *Read the question*

Lines 11–14 ("The lack . . . intelligent") are particularly notable for their

(A) comical tone
(B) bright imagery
(C) pessimistic wordplay
(D) cynical language
(E) sanguine atmosphere

**Step 2** *Read the relevant lines*

The lack of intelligence with which people use bookshops is, one supposes, no more flagrant than the lack of intelligence with which we use all the rest of the machinery of civilization. In this age, and particularly in this city, we haven't time to be intelligent.

## Step 3 ~ Criticize every word

(A) "Comical tone": The tone isn't "comical."
(B) "Bright imagery": The imagery isn't "bright."
(C) "Pessimistic wordplay": There is no "wordplay."
(D) "Cynical language": The lines *do* use "cynical language."
(E) "Sanguine atmosphere": The atmosphere isn't "sanguine."

Select (D) as your answer choice.

## Passage 2400 Strategy 10 ~ *Choose general over specific*

The more detailed an answer choice is, the more likely it is wrong. Answer choices with lots of specifics offer more material to scrutinize, and the more material there is to scrutinize, the more ways there are for an answer choice to be incorrect. SAT test writers qualify words and phrases in answer choices as a way of introducing misleading and incorrect information.

Consider the progression in qualification in the following phrases.

all students
all students *in the United States*
all students *in the United States who study for the SAT*
all students *in the United States who study for the SAT using this book*

Each italicized phrase above represents a qualification in which the original phrase ("all students") is limited by a narrower condition. In PASSAGE-BASED READING answer choices, the least qualified answer choice is usually correct. General answer choices are less qualified, whereas specific answer choices are more qualified.

> ### Passage 2400 Example  *Choose general over specific*

## Step 1 ~ *Read the question*

The author mentions "charge account" in line 9 in order to
(A) illustrate that most people cannot ride horses
(B) suggest wordplay in his metaphor
(C) compare the historical significance between credit cards and horses
(D) demonstrate that medieval knights did not have the convenience of charge accounts
(E) demystify the book purchasing process

## Step 2 ~ *Read the relevant lines*

> Some wistful, little forgotten sheaf
> of loveliness, long pining away on an upper shelf—why not ride up,
> fling her across your charger (or your charge account), and gallop
> away. Be a little knightly, you book-lovers!

**Step 3** *Choose general over specific*

(A) "Most people cannot ride horses" is a specific qualification without evidence in the passage.
(B) This is a general answer choice.
(C) "Between credit cards and horses" is a specific qualification without evidence in the passage.
(D) "Medieval knights did not have the convenience of charge accounts" is a specific qualification without evidence in the passage.
(E) "Demystify" is a specific qualification without evidence in the passage.

Select (B) as your answer choice.

## Example SAT Reading passages

Each type of SAT Reading passage is represented in the examples below. By applying the *Passage 2400 Strategies,* you will learn how to solve any PASSAGE-BASED READING question—and you will learn how to think like a 2400 student. This is important for two major reasons.

1. **Operational sense** You will get a sense of how to approach PASSAGE-BASED READING sections step by step. You won't have to worry about whether you should read the passage first, the questions first, or any other method. You will know exactly how to attack SAT Reading passages.
2. **Combination sense** Until now, you've considered the *Passage 2400 Strategies* as discrete tactics used on individual questions. But on the SAT, *Passage 2400 Strategies* often overlap and work together in solving questions. You will learn how the strategies blend with each other, as well as with WYPAD and the *General Reading 2400 Strategy.*

As you work through the passages below, you may realize that some *Passage 2400 Strategies* may be applicable to questions even though they aren't specifically applied. This is perfectly okay: For individual questions, not every applicable strategy is referenced.

---

### ✒ Example SAT Reading passages ✒

1 · Short standard passages
2 · Medium standard passages
3 · Long standard passages
4 · Set of short comparison passages
5 · Set of long comparison passages

**Step 3**
Master
WYPAD and
other keys
to success on
SAT Reading
. . . . . . . . . . . . . . . . . . . .
**178**

## Example passages 1 • *Short standard passages*

### Questions 1–2 are based on the following passage.

Zion Canyon in southern Utah is one of the most beautiful sights in the United States. This majestic canyon with its spectacular cliffs and waterfalls is fifteen miles long and up *Line* to half a mile deep. Zion Canyon is part of a geologic wonder
5 known as "The Grand Staircase," a collection of rock layers that ranges from 200 million to 600 million years old and stretches from Bryce Canyon all the way down to the Grand Canyon. The rock layers consist of many different types of rock, including shale, sandstone, and limestone. All of the
10 different rock types and their varying ages create a "layer cake" of the earth, visible in the separate bands of colored rock in the many cliffs and rock formations of the Zion Canyon.

1.  It can be inferred from lines 4–8 that Zion Canyon

    (A) is located somewhere in between Bryce Canyon and the Grand Canyon
    (B) contains many rocks that are shaped like staircase steps
    (C) is longer and deeper than other parts of the Grand Staircase
    (D) displays a greater variety of rock layers than either Bryce Canyon or the Grand Canyon
    (E) is significantly older than Bryce Canyon and the Grand Canyon

2.  The words "layer cake" (lines 10–11) primarily emphasize the

    (A) spongelike texture of the rock formations in the Grand Staircase
    (B) structured physical appearance of the different rock types in Zion Canyon
    (C) effects of water erosion from the many waterfalls in Zion Canyon
    (D) blending of rock colors unique to many regions of the Grand Staircase
    (E) smooth, white appearance of limestone rocks throughout Zion Canyon

## General Reading 2400 Strategy Part 1 • *Write your main idea down*

### Step 1 ⌐ *Read the beginning of the passage*

Zion Canyon in southern Utah is one of the most beautiful sights in the United States. This majestic canyon with its spectacular cliffs and waterfalls is fifteen miles long and up to half a mile deep.

**Step 2** *WYMID*

*Zion = gorgeous*

## General Reading 2400 Strategy Part 2 • *Answer all line-specific questions*

1. It can be inferred from lines 4–8 that Zion Canyon

   (A) is located somewhere in between Bryce Canyon and the Grand Canyon
   (B) contains many rocks that are shaped like staircase steps
   (C) is longer and deeper than other parts of the Grand Staircase
   (D) displays a greater variety of rock layers than either Bryce Canyon or the Grand Canyon
   (E) is significantly older than Bryce Canyon and the Grand Canyon

**Step 1** *Read the relevant lines*

Read from where you left off, paying attention to the cited lines.

> Zion Canyon is part of a geologic wonder known as "The Grand Staircase," a collection of rock layers that ranges from 200 million to 600 million years old and stretches from Bryce Canyon all the way down to the Grand Canyon.

**Step 2** *Passage 2400 Golden Strategy: WYPAD*

*It's old & long.*

**Step 3** *Eliminate answer choices that disagree with WYPAD*

(A) ?
(B) ✗
(C) ?
(D) ✗
(E) ?

**Step 4** *Apply Passage 2400 Strategies to the remaining answer choices*

(A) *Passage 2400 Strategy 10: Choose general over specific*
   Is this a general answer choice with evidence in the passage? Yes.

(C) *Passage 2400 Strategy 6: Avoid assumptions*
   Does the passage mention "other parts of the Grand Staircase"? No.

(E) *Passage 2400 Strategy 6: Avoid assumptions*
   Does the passage mention how old "Bryce Canyon and the Grand Canyon" are? No.

**Step 5 ✒ Confirm your potential answer choice with evidence in the passage**

(A) Can you infer that "Zion Canyon is located somewhere in between Bryce Canyon and the Grand Canyon"? Yes.

> Zion Canyon is part of a geologic wonder known as "The Grand Staircase," a collection of rock layers that ranges from 200 million to 600 million years old and stretches from Bryce Canyon all the way down to the Grand Canyon.

Select (A) as your answer choice.

**Step 3**
Master WYPAD and other keys to success on SAT Reading

**180**

---

2. The words "layer cake" (lines 10–11) primarily emphasize the

   (A) spongelike texture of the rock formations in the Grand Staircase
   (B) structured physical appearance of the different rock types in Zion Canyon
   (C) effects of water erosion from the many waterfalls in Zion Canyon
   (D) blending of rock colors unique to many regions of the Grand Staircase
   (E) smooth, white appearance of limestone rocks throughout Zion Canyon

**Step 1 ✒ Read the relevant lines**

Read from where you left off, paying attention to the cited lines.

> The rock layers consist of many different types of rock, including shale, sandstone, and limestone. All of the different rock types and their varying ages create a "layer cake" of the earth, visible in the separate bands of colored rock in the many cliffs and rock formations of the Zion Canyon.

**Step 2 ✒ Passage 2400 Golden Strategy: WYPAD**

*various rock colors*

**Step 3 ✒ Eliminate answer choices that disagree with WYPAD**

(A) ✗
(B) ?
(C) ✗
(D) ?
(E) ✗

**Step 4** ⌐ *Apply Passage 2400 Strategies to the remaining answer choices*

(B) *Passage 2400 Strategy 10: Choose general over specific*
   Is this a general answer choice with evidence in the passage? Yes.

(D) *Passage 2400 Strategy 10: Choose general over specific*
   Does "unique to many regions of the Grand Staircase" (a specific qualification) have evidence in the passage? No.

**Step 5** ⌐ *Confirm your potential answer choice with evidence in the passage*

Does "layer cake" emphasize the "structured physical appearance of the different rock types in Zion Canyon"? Yes.

> create a "layer cake" of the earth, visible in the separate bands of colored rock in the many cliffs and rock formations of the Zion Canyon.

Select (B) as your answer choice.

### General Reading 2400 Strategy Part 3 ◦ *Answer all general questions*

There are no general questions.

**Practice problem set** *Short standard passages*

The answer key for this problem set is on page 284.

---

Each passage below is followed by questions based on its content. Answer the questions on the basis of what is <u>stated</u> or <u>implied</u> in the passage and in any introductory material that <u>may be</u> provided.

---

**Questions 1–2 are based on the following passage.**

The Space Race, which occurred between 1957 and 1975, began when the Soviets launched the first man-made satellite, Sputnik, into space. For the Soviet Union, Sputnik
*Line* was a tremendous technological achievement. For the United
5  States, it was an embarrassing wake-up call. The United States had previously been regarded as the forerunner in the new field of space exploration, but Sputnik proved that the Soviets were viable contenders for that role. After Sputnik was launched, the American public panicked. Many believed that if the Soviets
10  were technologically superior when it came to launching satellites, then perhaps they would also be superior when it came to developing new and terrifying weapons.

**Step 3**
Master
WYPAD and
other keys
to success on
SAT Reading

..........................

**182**

**1.** The author most likely uses the phrase "wake-up call" in line 5 in order to

(A) emphasize the bitterly competitive nature of the space race
(B) highlight the need for the United States to begin its own weapons development program
(C) imply that the Soviets did in fact contact the United States government to notify them of the launch
(D) convey the shock and humiliation the United States felt when it heard about Sputnik
(E) suggest that any American attempt to launch a satellite at that time would be doomed to fail

**2.** In line 8, "viable" most nearly means

(A) unfriendly
(B) possible
(C) dynamic
(D) living
(E) independent

**Questions 3–4 are based on the following passage.**

One of the sights upon which my eyes rest oftenest and with deepest content is a broad sweep of meadow slowly climbing the western sky until it pauses at the edge of a
*Line* noble piece of woodland. It is a playground of wind and
5 flowers and waving grasses. When the turf is fresh, all the promise of summer is in its tender green; a little later, and it is sown thick with daisies and buttercups; and as the breeze plays upon it these frolicsome flowers, which have known no human tending, seem to chase each other in
10 endless races over the whole expanse. Even as I write, I see the white and yellow heads tossing to and fro in a mood of free and buoyant being.

**3.** The author's overall tone in this passage is best described as

(A) astonished
(B) ecstatic
(C) mournful
(D) delighted
(E) restrained

**4.** It can be inferred from the passage that the "promise of summer" (line 6) most nearly means

(A) the arrival of human caretakers who will tend to the meadow
(B) the beginning of warmer, sunnier days
(C) the appearance of woodland animals
(D) the onset of stronger gusts of wind
(E) the emergence of flowers

**Questions 5–6 are based on the following passage.**

John Locke was an Enlightenment-era philosopher
from England who wrote many influential works about
human understanding and identity. He may be best known
*Line* for his "blank slate" theory, which states that we are
5 all born without innate knowledge—in other words, our
minds at birth are blank slates, and over time we "write"
to those slates as we learn and experience new things.
According to Locke, all knowledge comes from our
sensory perception—none of it is placed there at birth.
10 In addition, because we are all born with "blank slates,"
we are all born equal, independent, and morally good.
Locke's philosophical ideas, especially with regards to
basic equality and human rights, had a profound influence
on the framers of the U.S. Constitution.

5. The primary purpose of the passage is to

   (A) convey the complexity of Enlightenment-era thought
   (B) argue in favor of the "blank slate" theory
   (C) illustrate how John Locke's ideas shaped the U.S.
       Constitution
   (D) discuss the connection between sensory perception
       and learning
   (E) describe John Locke and his basic philosophical
       theories

6. According to the passage, John Locke believed that we gain
   knowledge from which of the following sources?

   (A) Our innate understanding of the world around us
   (B) Our perceptions of basic equality and human rights
   (C) Our actual experiences and observations
   (D) Our ability to discern that people are essentially
       morally good
   (E) Our awareness of individuality and uniqueness

**Questions 7–8 are based on the following passage.**

History is nothing but assisted and recorded memory. It
might almost be said to be no science at all, if memory and
faith in memory were not what science necessarily rests on.
*Line* In order to sift evidence we must rely on some witness, and
5 we must trust experience before we proceed to expand it.
The line between what is known scientifically and what has
to be assumed in order to support that knowledge is impossible
to draw. Memory itself is an internal rumour; and when to
this hearsay within the mind we add the falsified echoes that
10 reach us from others, we have but a shifting and unseizable
basis to build upon. The picture we frame of the past changes
continually and grows every day less similar to the original
experience which it purports to describe.

**Step 3**
Master
WYPAD and
other keys
to success on
SAT Reading
..........................

**184**

**7.** It can be inferred from the passage that the author would most likely agree with which of the following statements about science and memory?

(A) Our memories must be verified by scientific processes before they can be considered accurate.

(B) Many scientists have developed solid hypotheses about the way human memory works.

(C) Our memories can be flawed, just as science itself can be flawed.

(D) Very few scientists have faith in the accuracy of their own memories.

(E) Science relies on real, verifiable facts and not on memories or assumptions that might be faulty.

**8.** The primary purpose of the passage is to

(A) illustrate the damage that can be caused by inaccurate memories

(B) describe the various ways in which we recall events from the past

(C) point out that history is based on changeable memories and not on solid facts

(D) explore the connection between our memories and the memories of other people

(E) argue that people remember rumors and hearsay better than facts

**Questions 9–10 are based on the following passage.**

Cases of poisoning by articles of food may be distinguished as: (1) those caused by some injurious constituent in the food itself, and (2) those caused by a peculiar condition of the
*Line* individual consuming the food, by virtue of which essentially
5 wholesome food substances are capable of producing physiological disturbance in certain individuals. The latter group includes persons, apparently normal in other respects, who are more or less injuriously affected by some particular article of diet, such as eggs or milk, which is eaten with
10 impunity by all normal individuals. This is the so-called food sensitization or food allergy.

**9.** The author refers to eggs and milk (line 9) most nearly in order to

(A) illustrate two specific food items that people may be allergic to

(B) imply that common food items are the ones that are most dangerous

(C) suggest that dairy and protein contribute more to food allergies than fruits and vegetables

(D) insist that normal individuals cannot be harmed by eggs or milk

(E) convey the need for stricter safety regulations on chicken and dairy farms

**10.** The main point of the passage is to

    (A) suggest that most people have a food allergy that they don't know about

    (B) lament the fact that many cases of food poisoning go unsolved

    (C) make the distinction between food sensitization and food allergies

    (D) describe two potential causes of most cases of food poisoning

    (E) explain the symptoms of food poisoning to the general population

## Example passages 2 • *Medium standard passages*

**Questions 1–5 are based on the following passage.**

*This passage is from a 1919 book by an American nurse and journalist who traveled extensively throughout Asia.*

There is cholera in the land, and there is fear of cholera in
the land. Both are bad, though they are different. Those who
get cholera have no fear of it. They are simple people and
*Line* uneducated, fishermen and farmers, and little tradesmen, and
5  workers of many kinds. Those who have fear of cholera have
more intelligence, and know what it means. They have education,
and their lives are bigger lives, as it were, and they would
safeguard them. Those who are afraid are the foreigners and
the officials, yes, even the Emperor himself. He has spent many
10  weeks of this hot summer, when cholera was ravaging his country,
in his summer palace at Nikko. The cholera spread itself throughout the land, in the seaports, across the rice-fields, taking its toll
here and there, of little lives, little petty lives to the Emperor.

The foreigners are very careful as to what they eat. They avoid
15  the fruits, the ripe, rich Autumn figs, and the purple grapes, and
the hard, round, woody pears, and the sweet butter and many other
things. Oh, these days the rich foreigners are very careful, and
meal times are not as pleasant as they used to be. They discuss
their food, and worry about it, and wonder about it. What is safe?

20  And because there is cholera, rife in the seaports, the authorities
have closed the fish market of Tokyo. The people stand idly about
the empty fish market, and talk together of this fear which is
abroad, which has ruined their trade. What is this fear? They cannot understand. Only the Emperor cannot eat fish now, for
25  some reason, and their business is ruined because of his caprice.

It is very hot. All summer has this great heat continued, and it
makes one nervous. Over all the land it is like this, this heavy,
sultry heat. It is no cooler when it rains, no dryer when the
hot sun shines. A junk gets loose from its moorings, and drifts
30  down stream, stern first, on the slow current. Who cares? No one.
It will beach itself presently, on a mud flat, and can be recovered
towards evening. The great heat lies over all the land, and cholera
is in the slowly flowing water, and the fishermen and the children

**Step 3**
Master
WYPAD and
other keys
to success on
SAT Reading
..........................
**186**

live and work and play by the river bank, and they have no fear
35 of it, because they are ignorant.

They say a typhoon is coming. Word has come from Formosa
that a typhoon is rushing up from the southern seas. It will reach us
tonight. That will be better. This unnatural heat will go then,
blown from the land by the gigantic blast of the typhoon.
40 Only it did not come—the typhoon. They said it would, but it
failed. So the damp, stifling heat lingers, and the toll of cholera rolls
slowly upward day by day. Here in the hospital they lie in rows, very
quiet. Not an outcry, not a murmur.

So there is cholera in the land, and fear of cholera. Those who
45 were not afraid have cholera. With them it is a matter of a few days
only, one way or the other. But those who have fear of cholera have
something which lasts much longer, weeks and weeks. Till the heat
breaks. Till the typhoon comes.

**1.** In line 13, "petty" most nearly means

(A) childish
(B) insignificant
(C) frivolous
(D) meager
(E) miserly

**2.** According to lines 17–19 ("Oh, these . . . about it"), the
foreigners did not enjoy meal times anymore because

(A) they were concerned that the food they were eating
       might cause them to contract cholera
(B) they could no longer afford the expensive fruit and
       butter that they used to eat
(C) the food that was safe to eat did not taste as good as
       the food that was now considered unsafe
(D) their meal-time conversations focused on unpleasant
       subjects such as cholera and the heat
(E) they were not able to consume fish due to the closure
       of the port and fish market

**3.** It can be inferred from lines 23–25 that the people in the
fish market believe that the Emperor

(A) considers fish to be less safe to eat than figs, grapes,
       pears, and butter
(B) deeply resents the people for spreading cholera across
       his land
(C) believes the dirty water in the port is causing fish to
       become infected with cholera
(D) wishes to shut down the fish trade because it is no
       longer profitable
(E) has decided on a whim, for no apparent reason, to
       stop eating fish

**4.** According to lines 32–35 ("The great . . . ignorant"), the people were not afraid of living near the river because

(A) they did not realize that the cholera was in the water
(B) they thought the Emperor and the foreigners were worrying needlessly
(C) the contaminated fish were found at the seaport and not the river
(D) they were unaware that the typhoon was coming
(E) they believed cholera could only be contracted through eating fruits

**5.** At the end of the passage, the author suggests that people who are afraid of cholera

(A) have unrealistic expectations about the severity and duration of the illness
(B) may have a long and difficult wait before their fears can be alleviated
(C) should be more concerned about the oppressive heat than about the cholera
(D) are not nearly as lucky as the cholera victims, who only suffer for a few days
(E) will not get sick once the typhoon finally arrives and drives away the heat

## General Reading 2400 Strategy Part 1 • *Write your main idea down*

### Step 1 ⌐ *Read the beginning of the passage*

There is cholera in the land, and there is fear of cholera in the land. Both are bad, though they are different. Those who get cholera have no fear of it. They are simple people and uneducated, fishermen and farmers, and little tradesmen, and workers of many kinds. Those who have fear of cholera have more intelligence, and know what it means. They have education, and their lives are bigger lives, as it were, and they would safeguard them.

### Step 2 ⌐ *WYMID*

*Educated fear cholera . . . uneducated don't.*

## General Reading 2400 Strategy Part 2 • *Answer all line-specific questions*

**1.** In line 13, "petty" most nearly means

(A) childish
(B) insignificant
(C) frivolous
(D) meager
(E) miserly

## Step 1   *Read the relevant lines*

Read from where you left off, paying attention to the cited lines.

> Those who are afraid are the foreigners and the officials, yes, even the Emperor himself. He has spent many weeks of this hot summer, when cholera was ravaging his country, in his summer palace at Nikko. The cholera spread itself throughout the land, in the seaports, across the rice-fields, taking its toll here and there, of little lives, little petty lives to the Emperor.

## Step 2   *Passage 2400 Golden Strategy: WYPAD*

*unimportant*

## Step 3   *Eliminate answer choices that disagree with WYPAD*

(A) childish     ≠ *unimportant*
(B) insignificant = *unimportant* ?
(C) frivolous     ≠ *unimportant*
(D) meager     ≠ *unimportant*
(E) miserly     ≠ *unimportant*

Selected definitions

meager = insufficient
miserly = stingy

## Step 4   *Apply Passage 2400 Strategies to the remaining answer choices*

This is unnecessary: WYPAD is sufficient.

## Step 5   *Confirm your potential answer choice with evidence in the passage*

(B) Does "petty" mean "insignificant" in the passage? Yes.

> taking its toll here and there, of little lives, little **insignificant** lives to the Emperor.

Select (B) as your answer choice.

---

**2.** According to lines 17–19 ("Oh, these . . . about it"), the foreigners did not enjoy meal times anymore because

   (A) they were concerned that the food they were eating might cause them to contract cholera
   (B) they could no longer afford the expensive fruit and butter that they used to eat
   (C) the food that was safe to eat did not taste as good as the food that was now considered unsafe
   (D) their meal-time conversations focused on unpleasant subjects such as cholera and the heat
   (E) they were not able consume fish due to the closure of the port and fish market

**Step 1** ✐ *Read the relevant lines*

Read from where you left off, paying attention to the cited lines.

> The foreigners are very careful as to what they eat. They avoid the fruits, the ripe, rich Autumn figs, and the purple grapes, and the hard, round, woody pears, and the sweet butter and many other things. Oh, these days the rich foreigners are very careful, and meal times are not as pleasant as they used to be. They discuss their food, and worry about it, and wonder about it. What is safe?

**Step 2** ✐ *Passage 2400 Golden Strategy: WYPAD*

*worried if dangerous*

**Step 3** ✐ *Eliminate answer choices that disagree with WYPAD*

(A) ?
(B) ✗
(C) ?
(D) ✗
(E) ✗

**Step 4** ✐ *Apply Passage 2400 Strategies to the remaining answer choices*

(A) *Passage 2400 Strategy 6: Avoid assumptions*
There seem to be no assumptions.

(C) *Passage 2400 Strategy 6: Avoid assumptions*
Does the passage mention the "taste" of food? No.

**Step 5** ✐ *Confirm your potential answer choice with evidence in the passage*

(A) Do the foreigners not enjoy meals anymore because "they were concerned that the food they were eating might cause them to contract cholera"? Yes.

> They discuss their food, and worry about it, and wonder about it. What is safe?

Select (A) as your answer choice.

---

3. It can be inferred from lines 23–25 that the people in the fish market believe that the Emperor

   (A) considers fish to be less safe to eat than figs, grapes, pears, and butter
   (B) deeply resents the people for spreading cholera across his land
   (C) believes the dirty water in the port is causing fish to become infected with cholera
   (D) wishes to shut down the fish trade because it is no longer profitable
   (E) has decided on a whim, for no apparent reason, to stop eating fish

Step 3
Master
WYPAD and
other keys
to success on
SAT Reading

190

### Step 1 ⚬ *Read the relevant lines*

Read from where you left off, paying attention to the cited lines.

> And because there is cholera, rife in the seaports, the authorities have closed the fish market of Tokyo. The people stand idly about the empty fish market, and talk together of this fear which is abroad, which has ruined their trade. What is this fear? They cannot understand. Only the Emperor cannot eat fish now, for some reason, and their business is ruined because of his caprice.

### Step 2 ⚬ *Passage 2400 Golden Strategy: WYPAD*

*stopped eating fish for no reason*

### Step 3 ⚬ *Eliminate answer choices that disagree with WYPAD*

(A) ✗
(B) ✗
(C) ✗
(D) ✗
(E) ?

### Step 4 ⚬ *Apply Passage 2400 Strategies to the remaining answer choices*

This is unnecessary: WYPAD is sufficient.

### Step 5 ⚬ *Confirm your potential answer choice with evidence in the passage*

(A) Do the people in the fish market believe that the Emperor "has decided on a whim, for no apparent reason, to stop eating fish"? Yes.

> They cannot understand. Only the Emperor cannot eat fish now, for some reason, and their business is ruined because of his caprice.

Selected definition

caprice = whim, impulse

Select (E) as your answer choice.

---

4. According to lines 32–35 ("The great . . . ignorant"), the people were not afraid of living near the river because

   (A) they did not realize that the cholera was in the water
   (B) they thought the Emperor and the foreigners were worrying needlessly
   (C) the contaminated fish were found at the seaport and not the river
   (D) they were unaware that the typhoon was coming
   (E) they believed cholera could only be contracted through eating fruits

**Step 1** *Read the relevant lines*

Read from where you left off, paying attention to the cited lines.

> It is very hot. All summer has this great heat continued, and it makes one nervous. Over all the land it is like this, this heavy, sultry heat. It is no cooler when it rains, no dryer when the hot sun shines. A junk gets loose from its moorings, and drifts down stream, stern first, on the slow current. Who cares? No one. It will beach itself presently, on a mud flat, and can be recovered towards evening. The great heat lies over all the land, and cholera is in the slowly flowing water, and the fishermen and the children live and work and play by the river bank, and they have no fear of it, because they are ignorant.

**Step 2** *Passage 2400 Golden Strategy: WYPAD*

don't know danger

**Step 3** *Eliminate answer choices that disagree with WYPAD*

(A) ?

(B) ✗

(C) ✗

(D) ?

(E) ?

**Step 4** *Apply Passage 2400 Strategies to the remaining answer choices*

(A) *Passage 2400 Strategy 10: Choose general over specific*
Is this a general answer choice with evidence in the passage? Yes.

(D) *Passage 2400 Strategy 6: Avoid assumptions*
Does the passage mention "they were unaware that the typhoon was coming"? No.

(E) *Passage 2400 Strategy 7: Avoid extremes*
Does the answer choice avoid extremes like "only"? No.

**Step 5** *Confirm your potential answer choice with evidence in the passage*

(A) Do people live near the water because they do "not realize that the cholera was in the water"? Yes.

> cholera is in the slowly flowing water, and the fishermen and the children live and work and play by the river bank, and they have no fear of it, because they are ignorant.

Select (A) as your answer choice.

Step 3
Master
WYPAD and
other keys
to success on
SAT Reading

......................

192

**5.** At the end of the passage, the author suggests that people who are afraid of cholera

(A) have unrealistic expectations about the severity and duration of the illness
(B) may have a long and difficult wait before their fears can be alleviated
(C) should be more concerned about the oppressive heat than about the cholera
(D) are not nearly as lucky as the cholera victims, who only suffer for a few days
(E) will not get sick once the typhoon finally arrives and drives away the heat

### Step 1 — Read the relevant lines

Finish reading the passage.

> They say a typhoon is coming. Word has come from Formosa that a typhoon is rushing up from the southern seas. It will reach us tonight. That will be better. This unnatural heat will go then, blown from the land by the gigantic blast of the typhoon.
>
> Only it did not come—the typhoon. They said it would, but it failed. So the damp, stifling heat lingers, and the toll of cholera rolls slowly upward day by day. Here in the hospital they lie in rows, very quiet. Not an outcry, not a murmur.
>
> So there is cholera in the land, and fear of cholera. Those who were not afraid have cholera. With them it is a matter of a few days only, one way or the other. But those who have fear of cholera have something which lasts much longer, weeks and weeks. Till the heat breaks. Till the typhoon comes.

### Step 2 — Passage 2400 Strategy 3: Make paragraph summaries

When there is a lot to read, summarize only the main points.

*typhoon coming, but didn't, cholera still there*

### Step 3 — Revisit the main idea

Reacquaint yourself with the main idea before answering general questions. You may need to adjust the main idea after you've read the entire passage.

*Educated fear cholera . . . uneducated don't.*

### Step 4 — Passage 2400 Golden Strategy: WYPAD

*fear it a long time*

**Step 5** ✏ *Eliminate answer choices that disagree with WYPAD*

(A) ✗
(B) ?
(C) ✗
(D) ?
(E) ✗

**Step 6** ✏ *Apply Passage 2400 Strategies to the remaining answer choices*

(B) *Passage 2400 Strategy 10: Choose general over specific*
   Is this a general answer choice with evidence in the passage? Yes.
(D) *Passage 2400 Strategy 7: Avoid extremes*
   Does the answer choice avoid extremes like "only"? No.

**Step 7** ✏ *Confirm your potential answer choice with evidence in the passage*

(B) Does the author suggest that people who are afraid of cholera "may have a long and difficult wait before their fears can be alleviated"? Yes.

> But those who have fear of cholera have something which lasts much longer, weeks and weeks.

Select (B) as your answer choice.

**Practice problem set**   *Medium standard passages*

The answer key for this problem set is on page 284.

---

> Each passage below is followed by questions based on its content. Answer the questions on the basis of what is <u>stated</u> or <u>implied</u> in the passage and in any introductory material that <u>may be</u> provided.

---

**Questions 1–9 are based on the following passage.**

*This passage is taken from a 1794 essay by a German philosopher.*

First, then, aesthetics has for its object the vast realm of the beautiful, and it may be most adequately defined as the philosophy of art or of the fine arts. To some the
Line definition may seem arbitrary, as excluding the beautiful
5 in nature; but it will cease to appear so if it is remarked that the beauty which is the work of art is higher than natural beauty, because it is the offspring of the mind. Moreover, if, in conformity with a certain school of modern philosophy, the mind be viewed as the true
10 being, including all in itself, it must be admitted that beauty is only truly beautiful when it shares in the nature of mind, and is mind's offspring.

**Step 3**
Master
WYPAD and
other keys
to success on
SAT Reading

**194**

Viewed in this light, the beauty of nature is only a
reflection of the beauty of the mind, only an imperfect
15  beauty, which as to its essence is included in that of the
mind. Nor has it ever entered into the mind of any thinker
to develop the beautiful in natural objects, so as to convert
it into a science and a system. The field of natural beauty
is too uncertain and too fluctuating for this purpose.
20  Moreover, the relation of beauty in nature and beauty
in art forms a part of the science of aesthetics, and finds
again its proper place.
    But it may be urged that art is not worthy of a scientific
treatment. Art is no doubt an ornament of our life and a
25  charm to the fancy; but has it a more serious side? When
compared with the absorbing necessities of human existence,
it might seem a luxury, a superfluity, calculated to enfeeble
the heart by the assiduous worship of beauty, and thus to be
actually prejudicial to the true interest of practical life. This
30  view seems to be largely countenanced by a dominant party
in modern times, and practical men, as they are styled, are
only too ready to take this superficial view of the office of art.
    Nevertheless, art is worthy of science; aesthetics is a true
science, and the office of art is as high as that assigned to it
35  in the pages of Schiller. We admit that art viewed only as an
ornament and a charm is no longer free, but a slave. But this
is a perversion of its proper end. Science has to be considered
as free in its aim and in its means, and it is only free when
liberated from all other considerations; it rises up to truth,
40  which is its only real object, and can alone fully satisfy it.
Art in like manner is alone truly art when it is free and
independent.

1. All of the following could be considered to fit the definition
   of aesthetics in the first paragraph (lines 1–12) EXCEPT

   (A) a beautiful painting
   (B) a beautiful poem
   (C) a beautiful mountain
   (D) a beautiful sculpture
   (E) a beautiful song

2. The primary purpose of the first paragraph (lines 1–12) is to

   (A) describe multiple sides of a debate
   (B) explain the definition of a certain term
   (C) establish a particular mood
   (D) disprove a common misconception
   (E) provide concrete examples to substantiate a theory

3. Based on information in the passage, which of the following is most likely to be a belief held by those who are part of the "school of modern philosophy" (lines 8–9)?

   (A) People who are surrounded by natural beauty have a greater appreciation for all types of beauty.
   (B) Art is not science.
   (C) The mind is the essence of one's self.
   (D) Art that has been created by someone is far more beautiful than art that exists in nature.
   (E) Aesthetics has more to do with internal beauty than with external beauty.

4. In line 25, "fancy" most nearly means

   (A) complexity
   (B) elegance
   (C) decoration
   (D) imagination
   (E) luxury

5. According to the passage, all of the following are characteristics of natural beauty EXCEPT that it

   (A) is merely a reflection of the beauty that can be created by the human mind
   (B) is part of the science of aesthetics, along with artistic beauty
   (C) can be considered less beautiful than the art produced by the human mind
   (D) is frequently thought of as "mind's offspring"
   (E) is too changeable and uncertain to be used as a system or a science

6. Which of the following statements best summarizes the "superficial view" mentioned in line 32?

   (A) Art has a more serious side than many people realize.
   (B) Art is merely a luxury and is not a fundamental part of a practical way of life.
   (C) The necessities of human existence are often complemented by artistic works.
   (D) People who don't appreciate the beauty of art are often labeled as impractical.
   (E) All human beings can find enjoyment in a work of art.

7. In context of the passage as a whole, the purpose of the third paragraph (lines 23–32) is to

   (A) answer a question that had previously been raised
   (B) call for a greater understanding of a certain concept
   (C) describe a controversial new discovery
   (D) provide evidence to corroborate a particular claim
   (E) describe a point of view that is later refuted

Step 3
Master
WYPAD and
other keys
to success on
SAT Reading
..................
196

**8.** According to the passage, what is one characteristic that art and science have in common?

(A) They are both favored equally by modern philosophers.
(B) They must both be independent in order to truly satisfy their objectives.
(C) They are both considered an inherent part of natural beauty.
(D) Neither of them fit into the definition of aesthetics.
(E) Neither of them can be thought of as an ornament or a luxury.

**9.** Based on information provided in the final paragraph (lines 33–42), which of the following is the goal of science?

(A) Natural beauty
(B) Aesthetics
(C) Systematic order
(D) Truth
(E) Artistic beauty

**Questions 10–15 are based on the following passage.**

*This passage is taken from a 1905 compilation of articles about important events in world history.*

Now commenced a new era. Many English kings had occasionally committed unconstitutional acts; but none had ever systematically attempted to make himself a
*Line* despot, and to reduce the Parliament to a nullity. Such
5 was the end which Charles distinctly proposed to himself. From March, 1629, to April, 1640, the Houses were not convoked. Never in our history had there been an interval of eleven years between Parliament and Parliament. Only once had there been an interval of even half that length.
10 This fact alone is sufficient to refute those who represent Charles as having merely trodden in the footsteps of the Plantagenets and Tudors.

It is proved, by the testimony of the King's most strenuous supporters, that, during this part of his reign, the
15 provisions of the Petition of Right were violated by him, not occasionally, but constantly, and on system; that a large part of the revenue was raised without any legal authority; and that persons obnoxious to the government languished for years in prison, without being ever called upon to
20 plead before any tribunal.

For these things history must hold the King himself chiefly responsible. From the time of his third Parliament he was his own prime minister. Several persons, however, whose temper and talents were suited to his purposes,
25 were at the head of different departments of the administration.

Thomas Wentworth, successively created Lord Wentworth and Earl of Strafford, a man of great abilities,
eloquence, and courage, but of a cruel and imperious
30  nature, was the counsellor most trusted in political and
military affairs. He had been one of the most distinguished
members of the opposition, and felt toward those whom he
had deserted that peculiar malignity which has, in all ages,
been characteristic of apostates. He perfectly understood the
35  feelings, the resources, and the policy of the party to which
he had lately belonged, and had formed a vast and deeply
meditated scheme which very nearly confounded even the
able tactics of the statesmen by whom the House of Commons
had been directed. To this scheme, in his confidential
40  correspondence, he gave the expressive name of Thorough.

His object was to do in England all, and more than all, that
Richelieu was doing in France: to make Charles a monarch as
absolute as any on the Continent; to put the estates and the
personal liberty of the whole people at the disposal of the
45  crown; to deprive the courts of law of all independent
authority, even in ordinary questions of civil right between
man and man; and to punish with merciless rigor all who
murmured at the acts of the government, or who applied,
even in the most decent and regular manner, to any
50  tribunal for relief against those acts.

10. The author's tone in this passage could best be described as

    (A) ashamed
    (B) critical
    (C) indifferent
    (D) mournful
    (E) furious

11. All of the following was proved by the testimony of the
"King's most strenuous supporters" (lines 13–14) EXCEPT

    (A) People who objected to the government were
        imprisoned without receiving a fair hearing.
    (B) The King raised a large amount of funds illegally.
    (C) The King was in a close alliance with Thomas
        Wentworth.
    (D) The King broke the law frequently and systematically,
        not just every now and then.
    (E) The King was in violation of the Petition of the Right.

12. In line 24, "temper" most nearly means

    (A) character
    (B) rage
    (C) resentment
    (D) irritation
    (E) moderation

**13.** The author of this passage would mostly likely characterize Thomas Wentworth as

(A) lazy and corrupt
(B) vile and devious
(C) inefficient and useless
(D) violent and deranged
(E) eccentric and unintelligent

**14.** It can be inferred from the passage that the main reason Thomas Wentworth posed such a threat to the opposition was that he

(A) had once been a member of the opposition and could use his insider knowledge to his advantage
(B) was friends with several influential members of Parliament
(C) was able to fool others by hiding his intelligence and power behind a seemingly timid manner
(D) had absolute authority over everyone, even the King
(E) was universally well-liked and trusted by everyone

**15.** The primary purpose of this passage is to

(A) lament the loss of a government ruled by a strong Parliament
(B) illustrate how easily kings can be controlled by their advisors
(C) describe the oppressive and unjust reign of King Charles
(D) draw a comparison between Thomas Wentworth in England and Richelieu in France
(E) explain the process by which a tyrant gains power over the whole country

## Example passages 3 • *Long standard passage*

### Questions 1–12 are based on the following passage.

*This passage is taken from a novel set in 19th-century England.*

I have often noticed that almost everyone has his own individual small economies—careful habits of saving fractions of pennies in some one peculiar direction—
Line any disturbance of which annoys him more than spending
5 shillings or pounds on some real extravagance. An old gentleman of my acquaintance, who took the intelligence of the failure of a Joint-Stock Bank, in which some of his money was invested, with stoical mildness, worried his family all through a long summer's day because one of
10 them had torn (instead of cutting) out the written leaves of his now useless bank-book; of course, the correspond-ing pages at the other end came out as well, and this little

Step 3
Master
WYPAD and
other keys
to success on
SAT Reading

198

unnecessary waste of paper (his private economy) chafed
him more than all the loss of his money. I am not above
15 owning that I have this human weakness myself. String
is my foible. My pockets get full of little hanks of it,
picked up and twisted together, ready for uses that
never come. I am seriously annoyed if any one cuts
the string of a parcel instead of patiently and faithfully
20 undoing it fold by fold.

Now Miss Matty Jenkyns was chary of candles. We
had many devices to use as few as possible. In the winter
afternoons she would sit knitting for two or three hours—
she could do this in the dark, or by firelight—and when I
25 asked if I might not ring for candles to finish stitching my
wristbands, she told me to "keep blind man's holiday."

One night, I remember this candle economy particularly
annoyed me. I had been very much tired of my compulsory
"blind man's holiday," especially as Miss Matty had fallen
30 asleep, and I did not like to stir the fire and run the risk of
awakening her; so I could not even sit on the rug, and
scorch myself with sewing by firelight, according to my
usual custom. When Martha brought in the lighted candle
and tea, Miss Matty started into wakefulness, with a
35 strange, bewildered look around, as if we were not the
people she expected to see about her. There was a little
sad expression that shadowed her face as she recognized
me; but immediately afterwards she tried to give me her
usual smile.
40 All through tea-time her talk ran upon the days of her
childhood and youth. Perhaps this reminded her of the
desirableness of looking over all the old family letters,
and destroying such as ought not to be allowed to fall
into the hands of strangers; for she had often spoken
45 of the necessity of this task, but had always shrunk
from it, with a timid dread of something painful. Tonight,
however, she rose up after tea and went for them—in the
dark; for she piqued herself on the precise neatness of all
her chamber arrangements, and used to look uneasily at
50 me when I lighted a bed-candle to go to another room for
anything.

When she returned there was a faint, pleasant smell
of Tonquin beans in the room. I had always noticed this
scent about any of the things which had belonged to her
55 mother; and many of the letters were addressed to her—
yellow bundles of love-letters, sixty or seventy years old.

Miss Matty undid the packet with a sigh; but she stifled
it directly, as if it were hardly right to regret the flight of
time, or of life either. We agreed to look them over separately,
60 each taking a different letter out of the same bundle and
describing its contents to the other before destroying it. I
never knew what sad work the reading of old-letters was

Step 3
Master
WYPAD and
other keys
to success on
SAT Reading

200

before that evening, though I could hardly tell why. The
letters were as happy as letters could be—at least those
65 early letters were. There was in them a vivid and intense
sense of the present time, which seemed so strong and full,
as if it could never pass away, and as if the warm, living
hearts that so expressed themselves could never die, and
be as nothing to the sunny earth. I should have felt less
70 melancholy, I believe, if the letters had been more so. I saw
the tears stealing down the well-worn furrows of Miss Matty's
cheeks, and her spectacles often wanted wiping. I trusted at
last that she would light the other candle, for my own eyes
were rather dim, and I wanted more light to see the pale,
75 faded ink; but no, even through her tears, she saw and
remembered her little economical ways.

**1.** The narrator most likely mentions the "old gentleman"
in lines 5–14 in order to

(A) raise a question
(B) mock an emotion
(C) illustrate an attitude
(D) criticize an idea
(E) quote an authority

**2.** In line 6, "intelligence" most nearly means

(A) aptitude
(B) news
(C) alertness
(D) cleverness
(E) espionage

**3.** The primary purpose of the first paragraph (lines 1–20)
is to show that

(A) only very wealthy people can afford certain luxury
items
(B) frugal people are the ones who succeed in life
(C) nearly everyone shares a particular character trait
(D) bank failures were common events in the narrator's
time
(E) people who make extravagant purchases often waste
smaller items like paper or string

**4.** In line 15, "owning" most nearly means

(A) possessing
(B) admitting
(C) receiving
(D) maintaining
(E) controlling

**5.** The narrator's comments about not stirring the fire in lines 28–33 ("I had been . . . custom") suggest that the narrator possesses which of the following personality traits?

(A) courtesy
(B) hostility
(C) elegance
(D) stubbornness
(E) exuberance

**6.** Miss Matty's behavior in lines 33–36 ("When . . . about her") implies that she was

(A) baffled by the chaotic scene around her
(B) annoyed at being awoken so abruptly by Martha
(C) embarrassed because she had been asleep for so long
(D) angry at the narrator for wasting too many candles
(E) disoriented for a moment by her surroundings

**7.** Which of the following can be inferred from the comment about Miss Matty's attempt to give her "usual smile" (lines 36–39)?

(A) The narrator physically resembled a person that Miss Matty had disliked many years ago.
(B) Miss Matty was ordinarily quite cheerful after waking up from a nap.
(C) The narrator had annoyed Miss Matty by asking for a candle earlier in the evening, and Miss Matty was trying to be polite in spite of this irritation.
(D) Miss Matty had been momentarily disappointed because the narrator's appearance was a reminder that Miss Matty was living in the present and not the past.
(E) Miss Matty was usually happier to see the narrator than she was to see Martha, but for some reason Miss Matty preferred Martha's company that night.

**8.** According to the fourth paragraph (lines 40–51), Miss Matty wanted to destroy the old letters because

(A) her relatives had asked her to burn them after she read them
(B) they evoked too many sad memories
(C) she did not want anyone from outside the family to read their contents
(D) they took up too much space in her house
(E) the ink was so faded it was no longer legible

**9.** It can be inferred from lines 41–56 that Miss Matty had previously approached the task of destroying the old letters with

(A) eagerness
(B) apathy
(C) disdain
(D) resistance
(E) animosity

**10.** The use of the phrase "in the dark" (lines 47–48) suggests that Miss Matty did not need to take a candle to her room because she

(A) could see better in the dark than the narrator could
(B) kept her room so tidy that she could easily move around it in the dark
(C) lived in a room with abundant natural light
(D) was more familiar with the layout of the house than the narrator was
(E) often fell asleep in front of the fireplace instead of in her room

**11.** Lines 69–70 ("I should . . . more so") suggest that the narrator feels sadness because

(A) the letters were so cheerful and vibrant that it was difficult to realize their authors were no longer alive
(B) she had never gotten the opportunity to meet Miss Matty's mother
(C) the letters reminded her of a much happier time, when she and Miss Matty were both young and carefree
(D) she regretted the fact that she had treated Miss Matty with disrespect earlier in the evening
(E) the letters made her think of her own family members

**12.** In the final paragraph (lines 57–76), the narrator mentions Miss Matty's "little economical ways" primarily in order to

(A) dismiss an unimportant idea
(B) ridicule a personal belief
(C) lament an unfortunate event
(D) challenge a commonly held notion
(E) reinforce an earlier claim

## General Reading 2400 Strategy Part 1 ▪ *Write your main idea down*

### Step 1 ✐ *Read the beginning of the passage*

I have often noticed that almost everyone has his own individual small economies—careful habits of saving fractions of pennies in some one peculiar direction— any disturbance of which annoys him more than spending shillings or pounds on some real extravagance. An old gentleman of my acquaintance, who took the intelligence of the failure of a Joint-Stock Bank, in which some of his money was invested, with stoical mildness, worried his family all through a long summer's day because one of them had torn (instead of cutting) out the written leaves of his now useless bank-book; of course, the corresponding pages at the other end came out as well, and this little unnecessary waste of paper (his private economy) chafed him more than all the loss of his money.

Step 3

Master
WYPAD and
other keys
to success on
SAT Reading

202

### Step 2 ✎ WYMID

*Ppl have own idiosyncratic ways of saving $$$.*

### General Reading 2400 Strategy Part 2 • *Answer all line-specific questions*

**1.** The narrator most likely mentions the "old gentleman" in lines 5–14 in order to

(A) raise a question
(B) mock an emotion
(C) illustrate an attitude
(D) criticize an idea
(E) quote an authority

### Step 1 ✎ *Read the relevant lines*

Re-read the lines, but with the question in mind this time.

> An old gentleman of my acquaintance, who took the intelligence of the failure of a Joint-Stock Bank, in which some of his money was invested, with stoical mildness, worried his family all through a long summer's day because one of them had torn (instead of cutting) out the written leaves of his now useless bank-book; of course, the corresponding pages at the other end came out as well, and this little unnecessary waste of paper (his private economy) chafed him more than all the loss of his money.

### Step 2 ✎ *Passage 2400 Golden Strategy: WYPAD*

*example of odd economical ways*

### Step 3 ✎ *Eliminate answer choices that disagree with WYPAD*

(A) X
(B) X
(C) ?
(D) ?
(E) X

### Step 4 ✎ *Apply Passage 2400 Strategies to the remaining answer choices*

(C) *Passage 2400 Strategy 6: Avoid assumptions*
   There seem to be no assumptions.

(D) *Passage 2400 Strategy 9: Criticize every word*
   Does the author "criticize" the old gentleman? No.

**Step 5** *Confirm your potential answer choice with evidence in the passage*

(C) Does the author mention the old gentleman in order to "illustrate an attitude"? Yes.

> and this little unnecessary waste of paper (his private economy) chafed him more than all the loss of his money.

Select (C) as your answer choice.

**Step 3**
Master
WYPAD and
other keys
to success on
SAT Reading

. . . . . . . . . . . . . . . . . . . . .

**204**

---

**2.** In line 6, "intelligence" most nearly means

(A) aptitude
(B) news
(C) alertness
(D) cleverness
(E) espionage

**Step 1** *Read the relevant lines*

> An old gentleman of my acquaintance, who took the intelligence of the failure of a Joint-Stock Bank, in which some of his money was invested, with stoical mildness

**Step 2** *Passage 2400 Golden Strategy: WYPAD*

*news*

**Step 3** *Eliminate answer choices that disagree with WYPAD*

(A) aptitude    ≠ *news*
(B) news       = *news* ?
(C) alertness  ≠ *news*
(D) cleverness ≠ *news*
(E) espionage  ≠ *news*

Selected definitions

aptitude   = ability
espionage  = spying

**Step 4** *Apply Passage 2400 Strategies to the remaining answer choices*

This is unnecessary: WYPAD is sufficient.

**Step 5** ✎ *Confirm your potential answer choice with evidence in the passage*

(B) Does "intelligence" mean "news" in the passage? Yes.

> An old
> gentleman of my acquaintance, who took the **news**
> of the failure of a Joint-Stock Bank, in which some of his
> money was invested, with stoical mildness

Select (B) as your answer choice.

---

3. The primary purpose of the first paragraph (lines 1–20) is to show that

   (A) only very wealthy people can afford certain luxury items
   (B) frugal people are the ones who succeed in life
   (C) nearly everyone shares a particular character trait
   (D) bank failures were common events in the narrator's time
   (E) people who make extravagant purchases often waste smaller items like paper or string

**Step 1** ✎ *Read the relevant lines*

> I have often noticed that almost everyone has his own
> individual small economies—careful habits of saving
> fractions of pennies in some one peculiar direction—
> any disturbance of which annoys him more than spending
> shillings or pounds on some real extravagance. An old
> gentleman of my acquaintance, who took the intelligence
> of the failure of a Joint-Stock Bank, in which some of his
> money was invested, with stoical mildness, worried his
> family all through a long summer's day because one of
> them had torn (instead of cutting) out the written leaves
> of his now useless bank-book; of course, the correspond-
> ing pages at the other end came out as well, and this little
> unnecessary waste of paper (his private economy) chafed
> him more than all the loss of his money. I am not above
> owning that I have this human weakness myself. String
> is my foible. My pockets get full of little hanks of it,
> picked up and twisted together, ready for uses that
> never come. I am seriously annoyed if any one cuts
> the string of a parcel instead of patiently and faithfully
> undoing it fold by fold.

**Step 2** ✎ *Passage 2400 Golden Strategy: WYPAD*

show people's weird quirks

Step 3
Master
WYPAD and
other keys
to success on
SAT Reading
..........................
**206**

**Step 3** ☞ *Eliminate answer choices that disagree with WYPAD*

(A) ✗
(B) ✗
(C) ?
(D) ✗
(E) ✗

**Step 4** ☞ *Apply Passage 2400 Strategies to the remaining answer choices*

This is unnecessary: WYPAD is sufficient.

**Step 5** ☞ *Confirm your potential answer choice with evidence in the passage*

(C) Is the purpose of the first paragraph to show that "nearly everyone shares a particular character trait"? Yes.

> almost everyone has his own individual small economies

Select (C) as your answer choice.

---

**4.** In line 15, "owning" most nearly means

    (A) possessing
    (B) admitting
    (C) receiving
    (D) maintaining
    (E) controlling

**Step 1** ☞ *Read the relevant lines*

Re-read the lines, but with the question in mind this time.

> I am not above owning that I have this human weakness myself.

**Step 2** ☞ *Passage 2400 Golden Strategy: WYPAD*

*confessing*

**Step 3** ☞ *Eliminate answer choices that disagree with WYPAD*

(A) possessing    ≠ *confessing*
(B) admitting    = *confessing* ?
(C) receiving    ≠ *confessing*
(D) maintaining ≠ *confessing*
(E) controlling    ≠ *confessing*

**Step 4** ☞ *Apply Passage 2400 Strategies to the remaining answer choices*

This is unnecessary: WYPAD is sufficient.

**Step 5** ⌐ *Confirm your potential answer choice with evidence in the passage*

(B) Does "owning" mean "admitting" in the passage? Yes.

> I am not above
> **admitting** that I have this human weakness myself.

Select (B) as your answer choice.

----

**5.** The narrator's comments about not stirring the fire in lines 28–33 ("I had been . . . custom") suggest that the narrator possesses which of the following personality traits?

    (A) courtesy
    (B) hostility
    (C) elegance
    (D) stubbornness
    (E) exuberance

**Step 1** ⌐ *Read the relevant lines*

Read from where you left off, paying attention to the cited lines.

> Now Miss Matty Jenkyns was chary of candles. We had many devices to use as few as possible. In the winter afternoons she would sit knitting for two or three hours— she could do this in the dark, or by firelight—and when I asked if I might not ring for candles to finish stitching my wristbands, she told me to "keep blind man's holiday."
> One night, I remember this candle economy particularly annoyed me. I had been very much tired of my compulsory "blind man's holiday," especially as Miss Matty had fallen asleep, and I did not like to stir the fire and run the risk of awakening her; so I could not even sit on the rug, and scorch myself with sewing by firelight, according to my usual custom.

**Step 2** ⌐ *Passage 2400 Strategy 3: Make paragraph summaries*

When there is a lot to read, summarize only the main points.

*Miss Matty doesn't like using candles; author annoyed.*

**Step 3** ⌐ *Passage 2400 Golden Strategy: WYPAD*

*not combative*

**Step 4** ⌐ *Eliminate answer choices that disagree with WYPAD*

(A) courtesy      = *not combative* ?
(B) hostility      ≠ *not combative*
(C) elegance      ≠ *not combative*
(D) stubbornness ≠ *not combative*
(E) exuberance      ≠ *not combative*

Selected definitions

hostility    = resentment, aggression
elegance     = grace
exuberance = enthusiasm, liveliness

**Step 3**
Master
WYPAD and
other keys
to success on
SAT Reading
..................
**208**

**Step 5** ✎ *Apply Passage 2400 Strategies to the remaining answer choices*

This is unnecessary: WYPAD is sufficient.

**Step 6** ✎ *Confirm your potential answer choice with evidence in the passage*

(A) Do the narrator's comments represent "courtesy"? Yes.

> I did not like to stir the fire and run the risk of awakening her

Select (A) as your answer choice.

---

**6.** Miss Matty's behavior in lines 33–36 ("When . . . about her") implies that she was

    (A) baffled by the chaotic scene around her
    (B) annoyed at being awoken so abruptly by Martha
    (C) embarrassed because she had been asleep for so long
    (D) angry at the narrator for wasting too many candles
    (E) disoriented for a moment by her surroundings

**Step 1** ✎ *Read the relevant lines*

> When Martha brought in the lighted candle and tea, Miss Matty started into wakefulness, with a strange, bewildered look around, as if we were not the people she expected to see about her.

**Step 2** ✎ *Passage 2400 Golden Strategy: WYPAD*

surprised

**Step 3** ✎ *Eliminate answer choices that disagree with WYPAD*

(A) ?
(B) ?
(C) ✗
(D) ✗
(E) ?

**Step 4** ✎ *Apply Passage 2400 Strategies to the remaining answer choices*

(A) *Passage 2400 Strategy 10: Choose general over specific*
Is "a chaotic scene" a general qualification with evidence in the passage?
No.

(B) *Passage 2400 Strategy 6: Avoid assumptions*
Does the passage mention that Miss Matty was "annoyed"? No.

(E) *Passage 2400 Strategy 10: Choose general over specific*
Is this a general answer choice with evidence in the passage? Yes.

### Step 5 ⟋ Confirm your potential answer choice with evidence in the passage

(E) Does Miss Matty's behavior imply that she was "disoriented for a moment by her surroundings"? Yes.

> Miss Matty started into wakefulness, with a strange, bewildered look around

Select (E) as your answer choice.

----

7. Which of the following can be inferred from the comment about Miss Matty's attempt to give her "usual smile" (lines 36–39)?

(A) The narrator physically resembled a person that Miss Matty had disliked many years ago.

(B) Miss Matty was ordinarily quite cheerful after waking up from a nap.

(C) The narrator had annoyed Miss Matty by asking for a candle earlier in the evening, and Miss Matty was trying to be polite in spite of this irritation.

(D) Miss Matty had been momentarily disappointed because the narrator's appearance was a reminder that Miss Matty was living in the present and not the past.

(E) Miss Matty was usually happier to see the narrator than she was to see Martha, but for some reason Miss Matty preferred Martha's company that night.

### Step 1 ⟋ Read the relevant lines

> There was a little sad expression that shadowed her face as she recognized me; but immediately afterwards she tried to give me her usual smile.

### Step 2 ⟋ Passage 2400 Golden Strategy: WYPAD

WYPAD can't be applied, because the question doesn't give us enough clues about what to look for.

### Step 3 ⟋ Apply Passage 2400 Strategies directly to the answer choices

(A) *Passage 2400 Strategy 6: Avoid assumptions*
Does the passage mention the narrator's resemblance to "a person that Miss Matty had disliked many years ago"? No.

(B) *Passage 2400 Strategy 6: Avoid assumptions*
Does the passage mention that Miss Matty was normally "quite cheerful after waking up from a nap"? No.

(C) *Passage 2400 Strategy 6: Avoid assumptions*
Does the passage mention Miss Matty's "asking for a candle earlier in the evening"? No.

(D) *Passage 2400 Strategy 6: Avoid assumptions*
Does the passage mention Miss Matty's disappointment with "living in the present and not the past"? No.

(E) *Passage 2400 Strategy 6: Avoid assumptions*
Does the passage mention that Miss Matty preferred "Martha's company that night"? No.

Step 3
Master
WYPAD and
other keys
to success on
SAT Reading
..............................
210

Sometimes, you will eliminate all of the answer choices! This is actually a good sign, because it means that you are being critical of every word and phrase.

### Step 4 ⚊ Reevaluate the relevant lines

The answer to a line-specific question may be a line or two above or below the lines cited in the question.

> When Martha brought in the lighted candle and tea, Miss Matty started into wakefulness, with a strange, bewildered look around, as if we were not the people she expected to see about her. There was a little sad expression that shadowed her face as she recognized me; but immediately afterwards she tried to give me her usual smile.
> All through tea-time her talk ran upon the days of her childhood and youth. Perhaps this reminded her of the desirableness of looking over all the old family letters

### Step 5 ⚊ Reapply Passage 2400 Strategies directly to the answer choices

(A) *Passage 2400 Strategy 6: Avoid assumptions*
Does the passage mention the narrator's resemblance to "a person that Miss Matty had disliked many years ago"? No.

(B) *Passage 2400 Strategy 6: Avoid assumptions*
Does the passage mention that Miss Matty was normally "quite cheerful after waking up from a nap"? No.

(C) *Passage 2400 Strategy 6: Avoid assumptions*
Does the passage mention Miss Matty's "asking for a candle earlier in the evening"? No.

(D) *Passage 2400 Strategy 6: Avoid assumptions*
Does the passage mention Miss Matty's disappointment with "living in the present and not the past"? Yes.

(E) *Passage 2400 Strategy 6: Avoid assumptions*

Does the passage mention that Miss Matty preferred "Martha's company that night"? No.

## Step 6 ✒ *Confirm your potential answer choice with evidence in the passage*

(D) Can you infer that "Miss Matty had been momentarily disappointed because the narrator's appearance was a reminder that Miss Matty was living in the present and not the past" from her attempt to give her "usual smile"? Yes.

> as if we were not the people she expected to see about her. There was a little sad expression that shadowed her face as she recognized me; but immediately afterwards she tried to give me her usual smile.
> All through tea-time her talk ran upon the days of her childhood and youth. Perhaps this reminded her of the desirableness of looking over all the old family letters

Select (D) as your answer choice.

---

8. According to the fourth paragraph (lines 40–51), Miss Matty wanted to destroy the old letters because

   (A) her relatives had asked her to burn them after she read them
   (B) they evoked too many sad memories
   (C) she did not want anyone from outside the family to read their contents
   (D) they took up too much space in her house
   (E) the ink was so faded it was no longer legible

## Step 1 ✒ *Read the relevant lines*

> All through tea-time her talk ran upon the days of her childhood and youth. Perhaps this reminded her of the desirableness of looking over all the old family letters, and destroying such as ought not to be allowed to fall into the hands of strangers; for she had often spoken of the necessity of this task, but had always shrunk from it, with a timid dread of something painful. Tonight, however, she rose up after tea and went for them—in the dark; for she piqued herself on the precise neatness of all her chamber arrangements, and used to look uneasily at me when I lighted a bed-candle to go to another room for anything.

## Step 2 ✒ *Passage 2400 Golden Strategy: WYPAD*

*prevent strangers from seeing*

**Step 3**

Master
WYPAD and
other keys
to success on
SAT Reading
..........................

**212**

**Step 3** ⚞ *Eliminate answer choices that disagree with WYPAD*

(A) ✗
(B) ?
(C) ?
(D) ✗
(E) ✗

**Step 4** ⚞ *Apply Passage 2400 Strategies to the remaining answer choices*

(B) *Passage 2400 Strategy 6: Avoid assumptions*

Does the passage mention that the old letters "evoked too many sad memories"? No.

(C) *Passage 2400 Strategy 6: Avoid assumptions*

Does the passage mention that Miss Matty "did not want anyone from outside the family to read their contents"? Yes.

**Step 5** ⚞ *Confirm your potential answer choice with evidence in the passage*

(C) Did Miss Matty want to destroy the old letters because "she did not want anyone from outside the family to read their contents." Yes.

> destroying such as ought not to be allowed to fall
> into the hands of strangers

Select (C) as your answer choice.

---

> **9.** It can be inferred from lines 41–56 that Miss Matty had previously approached the task of destroying the old letters with
>
> (A) eagerness
> (B) apathy
> (C) disdain
> (D) resistance
> (E) animosity

**Step 1** ⚞ *Read the relevant lines*

> Perhaps this reminded her of the desirableness of looking over all the old family letters, and destroying such as ought not to be allowed to fall into the hands of strangers; for she had often spoken of the necessity of this task, but had always shrunk from it, with a timid dread of something painful. Tonight, however, she rose up after tea and went for them—in the dark; for she piqued herself on the precise neatness of all her chamber arrangements, and used to look uneasily at me when I lighted a bed-candle to go to another room for anything.

When she returned there was a faint, pleasant smell
of Tonquin beans in the room. I had always noticed this
scent about any of the things which had belonged to her
mother; and many of the letters were addressed to her—
yellow bundles of love-letters, sixty or seventy years old.

## Step 2 ⌁ Passage 2400 Golden Strategy: WYPAD

*fear*

## Step 3 ⌁ Eliminate answer choices that disagree with WYPAD

(A) eagerness ≠ *fear*
(B) apathy ≠ *fear*
(C) disdain ≠ *fear*
(D) resistance = *fear* ?
(E) animosity ≠ *fear*

Selected definitions

apathy = indifference
disdain = scorn, contempt; despise
animosity = hostility, loathing

## Step 4 ⌁ Apply Passage 2400 Strategies to the remaining answer choices

This is unnecessary: WYPAD is sufficient.

## Step 5 ⌁ Confirm your potential answer choice with evidence in the passage

(D) Did Miss Matty previously approach destroying the old letters with "resistance"? Yes.

> she had often spoken
> of the necessity of this task, but had always shrunk
> from it, with a timid dread of something painful.

Select (D) as your answer choice.

_____

**10.** The use of the phrase "in the dark" (lines 47–48) suggests
that Miss Matty did not need to take a candle to her room
because she

(A) could see better in the dark than the narrator could
(B) kept her room so tidy that she could easily move
   around it in the dark
(C) lived in a room with abundant natural light
(D) was more familiar with the layout of the house than
   the narrator was
(E) often fell asleep in front of the fireplace instead of
   in her room

Step 3

Master
WYPAD and
other keys
to success on
SAT Reading

214

**Step 1**  *Read the relevant lines*

> Tonight, however, she rose up after tea and went for them—in the dark; for she piqued herself on the precise neatness of all her chamber arrangements, and used to look uneasily at me when I lighted a bed-candle to go to another room for anything.

**Step 2**  *Passage 2400 Golden Strategy: WYPAD*

*knew her way around*

**Step 3**  *Eliminate answer choices that disagree with WYPAD*

(A) ✗
(B) ?
(C) ✗
(D) ?
(E) ✗

**Step 4**  *Apply Passage 2400 Strategies to the remaining answer choices*

(B) *Passage 2400 Strategy 6: Avoid assumptions*
Does the passage mention that the room was "tidy"? Yes.

(D) *Passage 2400 Strategy 6: Avoid assumptions*
Does the passage mention how "familiar with the layout of the house" the narrator was? No.

**Step 5**  *Confirm your potential answer choice with evidence in the passage*

(B) Did Miss Matty not need a candle to enter her room because she "kept her room so tidy that she could easily move around it in the dark"? Yes.

> she rose up after tea and went for them—in the dark; for she piqued herself on the precise neatness of all her chamber arrangements

Select (B) as your answer choice.

---

**11.** Lines 69–70 ("I should . . . more so") suggest that the narrator feels sadness because

(A) the letters were so cheerful and vibrant that it was difficult to realize their authors were no longer alive
(B) she had never gotten the opportunity to meet Miss Matty's mother
(C) the letters reminded her of a much happier time, when she and Miss Matty were both young and carefree
(D) she regretted the fact that she had treated Miss Matty with disrespect earlier in the evening
(E) the letters made her think of her own family members

**Step 1** ↗ *Read the relevant lines*

Read from where you left off, paying attention to the cited lines.

> Miss Matty undid the packet with a sigh; but she stifled
> it directly, as if it were hardly right to regret the flight of
> time, or of life either. We agreed to look them over separately,
> each taking a different letter out of the same bundle and
> describing its contents to the other before destroying it. I
> never knew what sad work the reading of old-letters was
> before that evening, though I could hardly tell why. The
> letters were as happy as letters could be—at least those
> early letters were. There was in them a vivid and intense
> sense of the present time, which seemed so strong and full,
> as if it could never pass away, and as if the warm, living
> hearts that so expressed themselves could never die, and
> be as nothing to the sunny earth. I should have felt less
> melancholy, I believe, if the letters had been more so.

**Step 2** ↗ *Passage 2400 Golden Strategy: WYPAD*

*letters so happy*

**Step 3** ↗ *Eliminate answer choices that disagree with WYPAD*

(A) ?
(B) ✗
(C) ?
(D) ✗
(E) ✗

**Step 4** ↗ *Apply Passage 2400 Strategies to the remaining answer choices*

(A) *Passage 2400 Strategy 6: Avoid assumptions*
Does the passage mention that the letters' "authors were no longer alive"?
Yes.

(C) *Passage 2400 Strategy 6: Avoid assumptions*
Does the passage mention "when she and Miss Matty were both young and
carefree"? No.

**Step 5** ↗ *Confirm your potential answer choice with evidence in the passage*

(A) Did the narrator feel sadness because "the letters were so cheerful and
vibrant that it was difficult to realize their authors were no longer alive"?
Yes.

> as if the warm, living
> hearts that so expressed themselves could never die, and
> be as nothing to the sunny earth. I should have felt less
> melancholy, I believe, if the letters had been more so.

Select (A) as your answer choice.

Step 3
Master
WYPAD and
other keys
to success on
SAT Reading

216

**12.** In the final paragraph (lines 57–76), the narrator mentions Miss Matty's "little economical ways" primarily in order to

(A) dismiss an unimportant idea
(B) ridicule a personal belief
(C) lament an unfortunate event
(D) challenge a commonly held notion
(E) reinforce an earlier claim

**Step 1** *Read the relevant lines*

Miss Matty undid the packet with a sigh; but she stifled it directly, as if it were hardly right to regret the flight of time, or of life either. We agreed to look them over separately, each taking a different letter out of the same bundle and describing its contents to the other before destroying it. I never knew what sad work the reading of old-letters was before that evening, though I could hardly tell why. The letters were as happy as letters could be—at least those early letters were. There was in them a vivid and intense sense of the present time, which seemed so strong and full, as if it could never pass away, and as if the warm, living hearts that so expressed themselves could never die, and be as nothing to the sunny earth. I should have felt less melancholy, I believe, if the letters had been more so. I saw the tears stealing down the well-worn furrows of Miss Matty's cheeks, and her spectacles often wanted wiping. I trusted at last that she would light the other candle, for my own eyes were rather dim, and I wanted more light to see the pale, faded ink; but no, even through her tears, she saw and remembered her little economical ways.

**Step 2** *Passage 2400 Golden Strategy: WYPAD*

*show the permanence of Miss Matty's quirks*

**Step 3** *Eliminate answer choices that disagree with WYPAD*

(A) X
(B) X
(C) X
(D) X
(E) ?

**Step 4** *Apply Passage 2400 Strategies to the remaining answer choices*

This is unnecessary: WYPAD is sufficient.

**Step 5** ⌐ *Confirm your potential answer choice with evidence in the passage*

(E) Do Miss Matty's "little economic ways" confirm an earlier claim in the passage? Yes.

> almost everyone has his own individual small economies

Select (E) as your answer choice.

## General Reading 2400 Strategy Part 3 ▪ *Answer all general questions*

There are no general questions.

### Practice problem set ▪ *Long standard passages*

The answer key for this problem set is on page 284.

> Each passage below is followed by questions based on its content. Answer the questions on the basis of what is <u>stated</u> or <u>implied</u> in the passage and in any introductory material that may be provided.

### Questions 1–13 are based on the following passage.

*This passage is from an 1898 essay by a Scottish literary scholar. It discusses the Icelandic Sagas, a series of stories describing events in Iceland in the 10th and 11th centuries.*

Iceland was more than an island of refuge for muddled and blundering souls that had found the career of the great world too much for them. The ideas of an old-fashioned society migrated
*Line* to Iceland, but they did not remain there unmodified. The modes
5 of thought in Iceland, as is proved by its historical literature, were distinguished by their freedom from extravagances. While the life represented in the Icelandic Sagas is more primitive, less civilized, than the life of the great Southern nations in the Middle Ages, the record of that life is by a still
10 greater interval in advance of all the common modes of narrative then known to the more fortunate or more luxurious parts of Europe. The conventional form of the Icelandic Saga has none of the common medieval restrictions of view. It is accepted at once by modern readers without deduction or apology on the
15 score of antique fashion, because it is in essentials the form with which modern readers are acquainted in modern story-telling; and more especially because the language is unaffected and idiomatic, not "quaint" in any way, and because the conversations are like the talk of living people.
20 The Sagas are stories of characters who speak for themselves, and who are interesting on their own merits. There are good and bad Sagas, and the good ones are not all equally good throughout. The mistakes and misuses of the inferior parts of the literature do not, however, detract from the sufficiency of the common form,
25 as represented at its best.

Step 3
Master
WYPAD and
other keys
to success on
SAT Reading
..........................
218

It is no small part of the force of the Sagas that they have so much of reality behind them. The element of history in them, and their close relation to the lives of those for whom they were made, have given them a substance and solidity beyond anything else in
30 the imaginative stories of the Middle Ages. It may be that this advantage is gained rather unfairly. The art of the Sagas, which is so modern in many things, and so different from the medieval conventions in its selection of matter and its development of the plot, is largely indebted to circumstances outside of art. In its
35 rudiments it was always held close to the real and material interests of the people; it was not like some other arts which in their beginning are fanciful, or dependent on myth or legend for their subject-matter, as in the medieval schools of painting or sculpture generally, or in the medieval drama. Its imaginative
40 methods were formed through essays in the representation of actual life; its first artists were impelled by historical motives, and by personal and local interests.

The Sagas differ in value, according to their use and arrange-ment of these matters, in relation to a central or imaginative
45 conception of the main story and the characters engaged in it. Some of the best Sagas are among those which make most of the history and, like *Njála* and *Laxdæla,* act out their tragedies in a commanding way that carries along with it the whole crowd of minor personages, yet so that their minor
50 and particular existences don't interfere with the story, but help it and give it substantiality.

The loose assemblage of stories current in Iceland before the Sagas were composed in writing must, of course, have been capable of all kinds of variation. The written Sagas
55 gave a check to oral variations and rearrangements; but many of them in alternative versions keep the traces of the original story-teller's freedom of selection, while all the Sagas together in a body acknowledge themselves practically as a selection from traditional report. This solidarity and
60 interconnection of the Sagas needs no explanation. It could not be otherwise in a country like Iceland; a community of neighbors (in spite of distances and difficulties of travelling) where there was nothing much to think about or to know except other people's affairs. The effect of this in the written
65 Sagas is to give them something like the system of the *Comédie Humaine.* There are new characters in each, but the old characters reappear. Sometimes there are discrepancies; the characters are not always treated from the same point of view. On the whole, however, there is agreement. The
70 character of Gudmund the Great, for example, is well drawn, with zest, and some irony, in his own Saga (*Ljósvetninga*); he is the prosperous man, the "rich glutton," fond of praise and of influence, but not as sound as he looks, and not invulnerable. His many appearances in other Sagas all go
75 to strengthen this impression of the full-blown great man and his ambiguous greatness.

**1.** The principal function of the opening paragraph is to

(A) introduce the topic of sagas in relation to actual historical events
(B) illustrate the trend toward reinterpreting Icelandic Sagas in a modern light
(C) provide an explanation for the barbaric language used in the Icelandic Sagas
(D) explore the connection between modern Icelandic literature and the medieval Icelandic Sagas
(E) point out the differences between the Icelandic Sagas and other medieval European sagas

**2.** It can be inferred from the first sentence (lines 1–3) that some people thought of medieval Iceland as

(A) a place where people went when they could not keep up with the pace of the rest of the world
(B) a refuge for people who were persecuted for their religious or political beliefs
(C) a land populated by predominantly lazy or unintelligent people
(D) a nation that only welcomed immigrants from certain European countries
(E) a place where people felt overwhelmed by the relentless demands of their neighbors

**3.** The author would most likely agree that medieval Iceland, as compared with the rest of medieval Europe, could best be described as

(A) more civilized
(B) less dangerous
(C) less accepting
(D) more relaxed
(E) less luxurious

**4.** According to the first paragraph, modern readers are likely to appreciate the Icelandic Sagas because

(A) they can relate very easily to the struggles of the characters
(B) life in modern Iceland is surprisingly similar to life in medieval Iceland
(C) the language used in the Icelandic Sagas is straightforward and realistic
(D) they are already familiar with the sagas of the rest of medieval Europe
(E) they consist of simple, interconnected stories

**5.** In line 14, "deduction" most nearly means

(A) concession
(B) inference
(C) conclusion
(D) discount
(E) logic

Step 3
Master
WYPAD and
other keys
to success on
SAT Reading
.....................
**220**

**6.** In line 18, the use of the word "quaint" in quotation marks most likely suggests that

(A) there is no direct Icelandic translation for that word
(B) medieval European sagas often included unusual or quirky characters
(C) modern critics have used that term to describe the language in other medieval European sagas
(D) Icelandic literature in general has a tendency to use old-fashioned terms
(E) the dialogue in many of the Icelandic Sagas was peculiar and elaborate

**7.** It can be inferred from the second paragraph (lines 20–25) that the author believes which of the following about the Icelandic Sagas?

(A) The problems in many of the earlier Icelandic Sagas were corrected in the later Icelandic Sagas.
(B) Though the Icelandic Sagas have their faults, as a whole they are generally deserving of praise.
(C) The Icelandic Sagas are too different from one another to flow together in a logical order.
(D) The inconsistencies in many of the "good" Icelandic Sagas cause the entire series to seem highly unrealistic.
(E) The only remarkable aspect of the Icelandic Sagas is the fact that they exhibit fascinating character development.

**8.** In line 26, "force" most nearly means

(A) intensity
(B) drive
(C) vigor
(D) effectiveness
(E) coercion

**9.** According to the passage, the Icelandic Sagas have "substance and solidity" (line 29) because they

(A) progress smoothly from one story to another without interruption
(B) make use of dialogue that is pleasant and old-fashioned
(C) stem from actual historical events and real people's actions rather than fictional myths
(D) contain highly developed plots that are actually quite modern
(E) rely primarily on the myths and legends of the local people

**10.** The third paragraph (lines 26–42) primarily serves to

(A) criticize the way in which modern scholars interpret the Icelandic Sagas
(B) list the artistic sources that the authors of the Icelandic Sagas drew on for inspiration
(C) question the importance of realism in great works of literature
(D) describe the differences between the art of the Sagas and other medieval art
(E) assess the positive impact of the Icelandic Sagas on the body of medieval literature as a whole

**11.** Based on the information in the passage, which of the following scenarios about creating artwork is most similar to the process by which the Icelandic Sagas were initially developed?

(A) A fashion artist designs a new clothing line after being inspired by a trip to the beach.
(B) A writer publishes an article about Russia after reading several great works in classic Russian literature.
(C) A sculptor creates a new sculpture using recycled scrap metal after attending a seminar on the environmental benefits of recycling.
(D) An architect designs a modern office building in a Greco-Roman style after reading a book about ancient Roman mythology.
(E) A novelist writes a book about a small town after meeting the people who actually live there and then documenting their real-life stories.

**12.** The author mentions specific Icelandic Sagas in line 47 primarily in order to

(A) provide examples of sagas in which the minor characters add to rather than detract from the work as a whole
(B) illustrate how important plot development is to the effectiveness of a saga
(C) highlight some unique aspects of medieval Icelandic language
(D) explain why so many sagas are tragedies rather than comedies
(E) show how real stories about local people can be transformed into great works of art

**13.** The author refers to Gudmund the Great (lines 69–76) most nearly in order to

(A) discuss the relationship between character development and plot development in the Sagas
(B) explain how a reappearing character is generally depicted the same way in different Sagas
(C) indicate that a minor character can be just as important as a major character
(D) lament the vulnerabilities of many of the characters who frequently appear in the Sagas
(E) convey the need for a more thorough scholarly study of some of the more obscure Sagas

**Questions 14–25 are based on the following passage.**

*This passage is taken from a 1908 novel by an American author.*

The time was the year 1872, and the place a bend in the river above a long pond terminating in a dam. On the bank, and in a small woods-opening, burned two fires,
Line their smoke ducking and twisting under the buffeting of
5 the wind. The first of these fires occupied a shallow trench dug for its accommodation, and was overarched by a rustic framework from which hung several pails, kettles, and pots. An injured-looking, chubby man in a battered brown derby hat moved here and there. He divided his time between the
10 utensils and an indifferent youth—his "cookee." The other, and larger, fire centered a rectangle composed of tall racks, built of saplings and intended for the drying of clothes. Two large tents gleamed white among the trees.
About the drying-fire were gathered thirty-odd men.
15 Some were half-reclining before the blaze; others sat in rows on logs drawn close for the purpose; still others squatted like Indians on their heels, their hands thrown forward to keep the balance. Nearly all were smoking pipes.
Every age was represented in this group, but young men
20 predominated. All wore woollen trousers stuffed into leather boots reaching just to the knee. These boots were armed on the soles with rows of formidable sharp spikes or caulks, a half and sometimes even three quarters of an inch in length. The tight driver's shoe and "stagged" trousers had not then
25 come into use. From the waist down these men wore all alike, as though in a uniform, the outward symbol of their calling. From the waist up was more latitude of personal taste. One young fellow sported a bright-coloured Mackinaw blanket jacket; another wore a red knit sash, with tasselled
30 ends; a third's fancy ran to a bright bandana about his neck. Head-gear, too, covered wide variations of broader or narrower brim, of higher or lower crown; and the faces beneath those hats differed as everywhere the human countenance differs. Only when the inspection, passing

**Step 3**
Master
WYPAD and
other keys
to success on
SAT Reading

222

the gradations of broad or narrow, thick or thin, bony or
rounded, rested finally on the eyes, would the observer
have caught again the caste-mark which stamped these
men as belonging to a distinct order, and separated them
essentially from other men in other occupations. Blue
and brown and black and gray these eyes were, but all
steady and clear with the steadiness and clarity that comes
to those whose daily work compels them under penalty to
pay close and undeviating attention to their surroundings.
This is true of sailors, hunters, plainsmen, cowboys, and
tugboat captains. It was especially true of the old-fashioned
river-driver, for a misstep, a miscalculation, a moment's
forgetfulness of the sullen forces shifting and changing
about him could mean for him maiming or destruction.
So, finally, to one of an imaginative bent, these eyes, like
the "cork boots," grew to seem part of the uniform, one of
the marks of their caste, the outward symbol of their calling.

Ordinarily from very early in the morning until very late
at night the riverman is busy every instant at his dangerous
and absorbing work. Those affairs which don't immediately
concern his task—as the swiftness of rapids, the state of flood,
the curves of streams, the height of water, the obstructions of
channels, the quantities of logs—pass by the outer fringe of
his consciousness, if indeed they reach him at all. Thus, often
he works all day up to his waist in a current bearing the rotten
ice of the first break-up, or endures the drenching of an early
spring rain, or battles the rigors of a belated snow with
apparent indifference. You or I would be exceedingly
uncomfortable; would require an effort of fortitude to make
the plunge. Yet these men, absorbed in the mighty problems
of their task, have little attention to spare to such things. The
cold, the wet, the discomfort, the hunger, the weariness, all
pass as shadows on the background. In like manner the softer
moods of the spring rarely penetrate through the concentration
of faculties on the work. The warm sun shines; the birds by
thousands flutter and twitter and sing their way north; the delicate
green of spring, showered from the hand of the passing Sower,
sprinkles the tops of the trees, and gradually sifts down through
the branches; the great, beautiful silver clouds sail down the
horizon like ships of a statelier age, as totally without actual
existence to these men. The logs, the river—those are enough
to strain all the faculties a man possesses, and more.

**14.** In line 2, "terminating in" most nearly means

    (A) concluding in
    (B) destroying in
    (C) bounded by
    (D) issued by
    (E) dismissed by

Step 3

Master
WYPAD and
other keys
to success on
SAT Reading

........................

224

**15.** The primary purpose of the first paragraph (lines 1–13) is to

(A) dismiss a commonly held idea
(B) document an actual event
(C) disprove an erroneous theory
(D) establish a setting
(E) describe several main characters

**16.** In line 16, "the purpose" most nearly refers to

(A) sitting in a way that facilitates easy conversation
(B) moving closer to the fire for warmth
(C) positioning themselves in a circle for protection against wildlife
(D) finding a use for the logs that the men had fished from the river
(E) placing themselves around the fire to cook their food

**17.** According to the passage, the group of rivermen consisted mostly of men who

(A) tended to be younger in age
(B) were unaccustomed to being outdoors for long periods of time
(C) could not afford expensive clothing
(D) had spent many years working along the river
(E) were of the same ethnic group

**18.** The "outward symbol of their calling" (line 26) refers to

(A) "hands thrown forward" (line 17)
(B) "woollen trousers" (line 20) and "boots" (line 21)
(C) "driver's shoe" and "stagged trousers" (line 24)
(D) "bright bandana" (line 30)
(E) "head-gear" (line 31)

**19.** In line 27, "latitude" most nearly means

(A) location
(B) freedom
(C) distance
(D) capacity
(E) span

**20.** Which of the following can be inferred from the discussion about the rivermen's clothing "from the waist up" (line 27)?

    (A) The rivermen were rebelling against the uniform they were required to wear as part of their dress code.

    (B) The rivermen believed it was a good idea to wear bright clothing because it made you easier to spot if you got lost in the wilderness.

    (C) Due to the cold temperatures both in and out of the water, the men had to wear several layers above the waist to prevent hypothermia.

    (D) It was difficult to find waterproof fabrics, so the men made their clothing out of whatever material they could find.

    (E) The rivermen were only waist-deep in water and could therefore have more flexibility in choosing what to wear above the waist.

**21.** The author refers to the "inspection" (line 34) most nearly to

    (A) indicate that the rivermen were often judged too harshly based on their appearance

    (B) suggest that not everyone has the physical build to become a riverman

    (C) insinuate that the rivermen were not very fashionable according to the styles of the time

    (D) hint that the physical differences among the rivermen were obvious to most observers

    (E) imply that the rivermen often had to present themselves for dress code inspections

**22.** According to the passage, the rivermen's eyes all shared which of the following characteristics?

    (A) selfishness
    (B) attentiveness
    (C) eagerness
    (D) kindness
    (E) indifference

**23.** Examples of "those affairs which don't immediately concern his task" (lines 54–55) include all of the following EXCEPT

    (A) "the obstructions of channels" (line 56–57)
    (B) "the cold" (lines 65–66)
    (C) "the warm sun" (line 69)
    (D) "the delicate green of spring" (lines 70–71)
    (E) "the great, beautiful silver clouds" (line 73)

**24.** In line 74, "statelier" most nearly means

(A) more political
(B) more imposing
(C) more dignified
(D) more high-ranking
(E) more virtuous

**25.** In the final paragraph (lines 52–76), the author characterizes the rivermen as

(A) generally close-minded
(B) unobservant of the changing seasons
(C) foolish in the way they risk their personal safety
(D) focused on their work and nothing else
(E) unable to relax and enjoy themselves

**Step 3**
Master
WYPAD and
other keys
to success on
SAT Reading
.........................
**226**

## Example passages 4 • *Set of short comparison passages*

**Questions 1-5 are based on the following passages.**

### Passage 1

The term "Brutalism" refers to a style of architecture that was popular between 1950 and 1980 and is characterized by the use of large, blocky structures typically made of concrete.
*Line* Brutalism was a common choice for many architects in design-
5 ing office buildings, university structures, libraries, and other large commercial buildings. Brutalism was popular because of its simple, blunt style and because it did not require costly building materials—poured concrete is usually inexpensive and easy to acquire. Although many Brutalist structures are
10 now being demolished because they have not aged well, many others are considered quite iconic and representative of an architectural era. As a result, many people have petitioned to label such buildings as "historic" for preservation purposes.

### Passage 2

The recent effort to save buildings designed in the Brutalist
15 style is simply absurd. These buildings were constructed after World War II for one purpose and one purpose only: to rebuild bombed-out cities as quickly and cheaply as possible, without regard to the aesthetic effect they had on their surroundings. The ugly, soaring cement structures clashed horribly with the build-
20 ings around them. Now, years later, they are still cosmetic blights on our city skylines. Thankfully, many of them are now being torn down. The unattractive cement exteriors have not aged well in many cold, moist climates such as England's—they have become cracked, stained, discolored, and overridden with moss
25 and lichen. To claim that these monstrosities have any sort of "historic" value is akin to claiming that supermarket tabloid magazines have high literary value.

1. Which statement best characterizes the relationship between Passage 1 and Passage 2?

   (A) Passage 1 introduces a controversy that Passage 2 dismisses as unimportant.
   (B) Passage 1 praises a method of building construction that Passage 2 finds mediocre.
   (C) Passage 1 describes an architectural style that Passage 2 criticizes.
   (D) Passage 1 discusses the history of certain types of architecture, whereas Passage 2 debates the future of preservation efforts.
   (E) Passage 1 objects to the demolition of historical buildings, whereas Passage 2 argues for the necessity of tearing down old structures.

2. Unlike Passage 1, Passage 2 focuses primarily on Brutalism's

   (A) historical importance
   (B) aesthetic attributes
   (C) economic impact
   (D) structural integrity
   (E) universal appeal

3. The author of Passage 2 would most likely argue that the "people" mentioned in line 12 are

   (A) foolishly clinging to the outmoded belief that cement buildings can age gracefully
   (B) unaware of the exorbitant cost that comes with demolishing old structures
   (C) reasonably knowledgeable about both architecture and literature
   (D) overly concerned with the need to build structures as cheaply as possible
   (E) mistaken in their beliefs about what constitutes beautiful or important architecture

4. The authors of both passages agree that Brutalist structures

   (A) were cheap and easy to build in the post-war era
   (B) should be demolished in spite of protests about their historical importance
   (C) are more practical as commercial buildings rather than residential buildings
   (D) ought to be repainted more often, especially in cold and moist climates
   (E) may have some historical value in spite of their unattractiveness

**5.** Compared to the tone of Passage 2, Passage 1 is more

(A) whimsical
(B) impartial
(C) critical
(D) sympathetic
(E) sarcastic

Step 3

Master
WYPAD and
other keys
to success on
SAT Reading

228

## General Reading 2400 Strategy Part 1 • *Write your main idea down (both passages)*

### Step 1 ⟋ *Read the beginning of Passage 1*

Because there are few line-specific questions on short comparison passages, it often makes sense to read the entire passage.

> The term "Brutalism" refers to a style of architecture that was popular between 1950 and 1980 and is characterized by the use of large, blocky structures typically made of concrete. Brutalism was a common choice for many architects in designing office buildings, university structures, libraries, and other large commercial buildings. Brutalism was popular because of its simple, blunt style and because it did not require costly building materials—poured concrete is usually inexpensive and easy to acquire. Although many Brutalist structures are now being demolished because they have not aged well, many others are considered quite iconic and representative of an architectural era. As a result, many people have petitioned to label such buildings as "historic" for preservation purposes.

### Step 2 ⟋ *WYMID (Passage 1)*

*Brutalism = blocky & historical*

### Step 3 ⟋ *Read the beginning of Passage 2*

> The recent effort to save buildings designed in the Brutalist style is simply absurd. These buildings were constructed after World War II for one purpose and one purpose only: to rebuild bombed-out cities as quickly and cheaply as possible, without regard to the aesthetic effect they had on their surroundings. The ugly, soaring cement structures clashed horribly with the buildings around them. Now, years later, they are still cosmetic blights on our city skylines. Thankfully, many of them are now being torn down. The unattractive cement exteriors have not aged well in many cold, moist climates such as England's—they have become cracked, stained, discolored, and overridden with moss and lichen. To claim that these monstrosities have any sort of "historic" value is akin to claiming that supermarket tabloid magazines have high literary value.

### Step 4 ⟋ *WYMID (Passage 2)*

*Brutalism = ugly*

## General Reading 2400 Strategy Part 2 • *Answer all line-specific questions*

There are no line-specific questions. Although question 3 cites a specific line, it isn't a line-specific question, because its answer requires knowledge of the general main idea of Passage 2.

## General Reading 2400 Strategy Part 3 • *Answer all general questions*

1. Which statement best characterizes the relationship between Passage 1 and Passage 2?

   (A) Passage 1 introduces a controversy that Passage 2 dismisses as unimportant.
   (B) Passage 1 praises a method of building construction that Passage 2 finds mediocre.
   (C) Passage 1 describes an architectural style that Passage 2 criticizes.
   (D) Passage 1 discusses the history of certain types of architecture, whereas Passage 2 debates the future of preservation efforts.
   (E) Passage 1 objects to the demolition of historical buildings, whereas Passage 2 argues for the necessity of tearing down old structures.

### Step 1 ⤳ Revisit the main ideas

Before answering general questions, reacquaint yourself with the passages' main ideas.

Passage 1: *Brutalism = blocky & historical*
Passage 2: *Brutalism = ugly*

### Step 2 ⤳ Passage 2400 Golden Strategy: WYPAD

*Passage 1 describes features & history vs. Passage 2 criticizes aesthetic features.*

### Step 3 ⤳ Eliminate answer choices that disagree with WYPAD

(A) ✗
(B) ✗
(C) ?
(D) ✗
(E) ✗

### Step 4 ⤳ Apply Passage 2400 Strategies to the remaining answer choices

This is unnecessary: WYPAD is sufficient.

**Step 3**

Master
WYPAD and
other keys
to success on
SAT Reading
............................

**230**

**Step 5** *Confirm your potential answer choice with evidence in the passage*

(C) Does the following statement characterize the relationship between the two passages: "Passage 1 describes an architectural style that Passage 2 criticizes"? Yes.

(Passage 1)

> "Brutalism" . . . is characterized by the use of large, blocky structures typically made of concrete.

(Passage 2)

> The ugly, soaring cement [Brutalist] structures clashed horribly with the buildings around them.

Select (C) as your answer choice.

---

2. Unlike Passage 1, Passage 2 focuses primarily on Brutalism's

    (A) historical importance
    (B) aesthetic attributes
    (C) economic impact
    (D) structural integrity
    (E) universal appeal

**Step 1** *Revisit the main ideas*

Before answering general questions, reacquaint yourself with the passages' main ideas.

Passage 1: *Brutalism = blocky & historical*
Passage 2: *Brutalism = ugly*

**Step 2** *Passage 2400 Golden Strategy: WYPAD*

*ugly style*

**Step 3** *Eliminate answer choices that disagree with WYPAD*

(A) historical importance   *≠ ugly style*
(B) aesthetic attributes    *= ugly style  ?*
(C) economic impact      *≠ ugly style*
(D) structural integrity    *≠ ugly style*
(E) universal appeal     *= ugly style  ?*

**Step 4** *Apply Passage 2400 Strategies to the remaining answer choices*

(B) *Passage 2400 Strategy 6: Avoid assumptions*
   Does the passage mention "aesthetic attributes"? Yes.

(E) *Passage 2400 Strategy 7: Avoid extremes*
   Does the answer choice avoid extremes like "universal"? No.

**Step 5** ⌐ *Confirm your potential answer choice with evidence in the passage*

(B) Unlike Passage 1, does Passage 2 focus on "aesthetic attributes"? Yes.

(Passage 2)

> without regard to the aesthetic effect . . . The ugly, soaring cement structures . . . they are still cosmetic blights . . . The unattractive cement exteriors

Select (B) as your answer choice.

---

3. The author of Passage 2 would most likely argue that the "people" mentioned in line 12 are

   (A) foolishly clinging to the outmoded belief that cement buildings can age gracefully
   (B) unaware of the exorbitant cost that comes with demolishing old structures
   (C) reasonably knowledgeable about both architecture and literature
   (D) overly concerned with the need to build structures as cheaply as possible
   (E) mistaken in their beliefs about what constitutes beautiful or important architecture

**Step 1** ⌐ *Revisit the main ideas*

Before answering general questions, reacquaint yourself with the passages' main ideas.

Passage 1: *Brutalism = blocky & historical*
Passage 2: *Brutalism = ugly*

**Step 2** ⌐ *Read the relevant lines*

(Passage 1)

> As a result, many people have petitioned to label such buildings as "historic" for preservation purposes.

**Step 3** ⌐ *Passage 2400 Golden Strategy: WYPAD*

*not looking at ugliness and not aging well*

**Step 4** ⌐ *Eliminate answer choices that disagree with WYPAD*

(A) ?
(B) ✕
(C) ✕
(D) ✕
(E) ?

Selected definition

exorbitant = excessive, huge

**Step 3**
Master
WYPAD and
other keys
to success on
SAT Reading
..................
**232**

### Step 5 ⌁ Apply Passage 2400 Strategies to the remaining answer choices

(A) *Passage 2400 Strategy 6: Avoid assumptions*
   Does the passage mention an "outmoded belief that cement buildings can age gracefully"? No.

(E) *Passage 2400 Strategy 6: Avoid assumptions*
   Does the passage mention "what constitutes beautiful or important architecture"? Yes.

### Step 6 ⌁ Confirm your potential answer choice with evidence in the passage

(E) Would the author of Passage 2 argue that the "people" mentioned in line 12 are "mistaken in their beliefs about what constitutes beautiful or important architecture"? Yes.

> To claim that these monstrosities have any sort of "historic" value is akin to claiming that supermarket tabloid magazines have high literary value.

Select (E) as your answer choice.

----

**4.** The authors of both passages agree that Brutalist structures

   (A) were cheap and easy to build in the post-war era
   (B) should be demolished in spite of protests about their historical importance
   (C) are more practical as commercial buildings rather than residential buildings
   (D) ought to be repainted more often, especially in cold and moist climates
   (E) may have some historical value in spite of their unattractiveness

### Step 1 ⌁ Revisit the main ideas

Before answering general questions, reacquaint yourself with the passages' main ideas.

Passage 1: Brutalism = blocky & historical
Passage 2: Brutalism = ugly

### Step 2 ⌁ Passage 2400 Golden Strategy: WYPAD

are cheap cement constructions

**Step 3** *Eliminate answer choices that disagree with WYPAD*

(A) ?
(B) ✗
(C) ✗
(D) ✗
(E) ✗

**Step 4** *Apply Passage 2400 Strategies to the remaining answer choices*

This is unnecessary: WYPAD is sufficient.

**Step 5** *Confirm your potential answer choice with evidence in the passage*

(A) Would both authors agree that Brutalist structures "were cheap and easy to build in the post-war era"? Yes.

(Passage 1)

> [Brutalism] did not require costly building materials—poured concrete is usually inexpensive and easy to acquire.

(Passage 2)

> These buildings were constructed after World War II . . . as quickly and cheaply as possible

Select (A) as your answer choice.

_____

**5.** Compared to the tone of Passage 2, Passage 1 is more

   (A) whimsical
   (B) impartial
   (C) critical
   (D) sympathetic
   (E) sarcastic

**Step 1** *Revisit the main ideas*

Before answering general questions, reacquaint yourself with the passages' main ideas.

Passage 1: Brutalism = blocky & historical
Passage 2: Brutalism = ugly

**Step 2** *Passage 2400 Golden Strategy: WYPAD*

historical perspective

**Step 3**
Master
WYPAD and
other keys
to success on
SAT Reading
..........................
**234**

### Step 3 ⌁ Eliminate answer choices that disagree with WYPAD

(A) whimsical    ≠ *historical perspective*
(B) impartial     = *historical perspective ?*
(C) critical        = *historical perspective ?*
(D) sympathetic ≠ *historical perspective*
(E) sarcastic     ≠ *historical perspective*

### Selected definitions

whimsical = fanciful, eccentric, quirky
impartial  = unbiased, fair, objective

### Step 4 ⌁ Apply Passage 2400 Strategies to the remaining answer choices

(B) *Passage 2400 Strategy 9: Criticize every word*
    Is the author fairly "impartial" regarding Brutalism? Yes.
(C) *Passage 2400 Strategy 9: Criticize every word*
    Does the author "criticize" Brutalism? No.

### Step 5 ⌁ Confirm your potential answer choice with evidence in the passage

(B) Is the tone of Passage 1 more "impartial" than that of Passage 2? Yes.

(Passage 1)

> As a result, many people have petitioned
> to label such buildings as "historic" for preservation purposes.

(Passage 2)

> The recent effort to save buildings designed in the Brutalist
> style is simply absurd.

Select (B) as your answer choice.

---

**Practice problem set**   *Set of short comparison passages*

The answer key for this problem set is on page 284.

> The passages below are followed by questions based on their content
> or on the relationship between the two passages. Answer the questions
> on the basis of what is <u>stated</u> or <u>implied</u> in the passages and in any
> introductory material that may be provided.

**Questions 1–5 are based on the following passage.**

**Passage 1**

    Perhaps the most universally known fact in regard to bacteria
is that they are the cause of disease. It is this fact that has made
them objects of such wide interest. This is the side of the subject

Line that first attracted attention, has been most studied, and in regard
5 to which there has been the greatest accumulation of evidence.
So persistently has the relation of bacteria to disease been discussed and emphasized that the majority of readers are hardly
able to disassociate the two. To most people the very word
"bacteria" is almost equivalent to disease, and the thought of
10 swallowing microbes in drinking water or milk is decidedly
repugnant and alarming. In the public mind it is only necessary
to demonstrate that an article holds bacteria to throw it under
condemnation.

**Passage 2**

We must, from the very nature of our environment, be con-
15 stantly inhaling these germs as we pass through the wards of
our hospitals; yes, they are floating in the air of our streets and
dwellings. It becomes necessary then for us to inquire: If bacteria
cause disease, in what manner do they produce it? The healthy
organism is always beset with a multitude of non-pathogenic
20 bacteria. They occupy the natural cavities, especially the
alimentary canal. They feed on the substances lying in their
neighborhood, whether brought into the body or secreted by the
tissues. In so doing they set up chemical changes in their substances. Where the organs are acting normally these bacteria
25 work no mischief. The products of decomposition thus set up are
harmless, or are conveyed out of the body before they begin
to be active.

1. Unlike Passage 1, Passage 2 focuses primarily on bacteria's

   (A) constant and often harmless presence
   (B) dangers and health risks
   (C) similarity with disease
   (D) effects on people who are ill
   (E) image in the public eye

2. The primary purpose of Passage 1 is to

   (A) illustrate the health hazards of common bacteria
   (B) convey the misconceptions people have regarding
       various diseases
   (C) call for a greater understanding of the term "bacteria"
   (D) persuade people to accept the fact that not all bacteria
       causes disease
   (E) describe public perceptions about bacteria

3. According to Passage 1, the term "bacteria"

   (A) has revolutionized the way doctors explain infections
       to the public
   (B) is considered by most people to be interchangeable
       with the term "disease"
   (C) has neither positive nor negative connotations
   (D) is used more often by the public than by healthcare
       professionals
   (E) refers exclusively to disease-causing germs

**Step 3**
Master
WYPAD and
other keys
to success on
SAT Reading
.........................

**236**

**4.** The author of Passage 2 would most likely respond to the claim in lines 8–11 ("To most . . . alarming") by

(A) arguing that viruses cause disease more often than bacteria do
(B) stating that the bacteria in our food and drink are generally not the type that causes infection
(C) disputing the notion that bacteria exist in our internal organs
(D) claiming that people don't realize how widespread and innocuous most bacteria are
(E) citing examples of bacteria that have caused deadly diseases

**5.** In line 19, "beset with" most nearly means

(A) embellished with
(B) attacked by
(C) placed beside
(D) concerned about
(E) covered in

## Example passages 5 • *Set of long comparison passages*

**Questions 1–9 are based on the following passages.**

*The following passages discuss the possible link between cell phone use and cancer.*

### Passage 1

In most modern societies, it's nearly impossible to go anywhere without seeing someone talking on or tapping away on a cell phone. Cell phones have quickly become an
*Line* ingrained technology in our society. It's estimated that a
5 whopping five *billion* people on our planet use cell phones. And though these small and ubiquitous devices may seem innocuous enough, the reality may surprise you: cell phones emit radiofrequency energy, which may be a cancer risk.
Waves of radiofrequency energy, known more commonly
10 as "radio waves," are emitted by a variety of objects: satellite stations, microwave ovens, and radio towers, to name just a few. Why, then, are people so concerned about radio waves from cell phones? The trouble is that people get much more up close and personal with these waves: the phones are pressed
15 against our ears, carried in pockets, or held in our hands for a long time—often hours—each day. Very rarely will people stand next to a microwave oven or radio tower for so long, or within such close proximity.

The biggest concern so far seems to be that the radio waves
20 from a cell phone held against a person's ear will penetrate
through to the brain and cause damage to DNA that may in
turn lead to a brain tumor. In the past five years, there have
been an unnerving number of lawsuits brought against cell phone
manufacturers that allege the use of cell phones has caused
25 their owners to develop brain tumors. There has also been an
increase in brain tumors in recent years, which may correspond
to the rapid increase of cell phone use around the world.

Many studies have attempted to find a definite link between
cell phone use and the incidence of brain tumors. Unfortunately,
30 many of these studies have been inconclusive, no doubt due to
the lack of long-term research. One six-year international study
did find that after ten years of heavy cell phone use on one side
of the head, a person's risk of developing a tumor on that side
of the head did increase. (A Swedish study later came to the
35 same conclusion.) Furthermore, the six-year study found that after
1,640 hours of cell phone use, a person's risk of glioma (a type
of brain cancer) also increased. The 1,640 hours corresponds
to 30 minutes of use every day for ten years—a plausible amount
of cell phone usage for many people. With these troubling results,
40 it's likely that longer-term studies will find more and more cause
for concern.

**Passage 2**

Recent studies that call into question the safety of cell phones
have caused some people to panic and wonder whether they
should throw their cell phones out—or, at the very least, use them
45 much more sparingly. But there's no need for any drastic action—
not yet, anyway. The overwhelming majority of studies have not
found a definitive link between cell phone use and certain
cancers (specifically, brain tumors). Nearly all of these studies
report inconclusive findings and caution that much more research
50 is needed before a clear link can be established.

Furthermore, one of the largest international studies that did
find a possible correlation may itself be flawed. In this six-year
study, people were asked to remember certain patterns of cell
phone use from the past ten years. This introduces the substantial
55 problem of recall bias. Recall bias occurs when studies rely on
subjects' memories, which may very well be faulty. People may
easily exaggerate or simply misremember how often they used
a cell phone ten years ago, much less how often they held it to
one ear or the other. The six-year study relied on this type of
60 self-reported data and as a result may be flawed by recall bias.

With the inherent flaws in the six-year study, it's quite clear
that there need to be more studies—well-designed studies—
to determine whether cell phones do in fact cause cancer.

Step 3
Master
WYPAD and
other keys
to success on
SAT Reading
.....................
238

1. The authors of both passages agree that

   (A) the existing studies don't conclusively prove that cell phone use causes cancer
   (B) the six-year study is flawed because its subjects are prone to recall bias
   (C) lawsuits against cell phone manufacturers have dramatically increased in recent years
   (D) the six-year study is the only study of cell phones and cancer to be corroborated by a later study
   (E) cell phones are unquestionably more dangerous than microwave ovens or radio towers

2. In lines 4–5, the author of Passage 1 mentions the number of global cell phone users in order to

   (A) lament the potential cancer risk for a certain percentage of the global population
   (B) point out that many people are foolishly lulled into thinking cell phones are safe
   (C) emphasize the overwhelmingly widespread use of cell phones in modern societies
   (D) suggest that there is a need for more effective cancer treatment in many countries
   (E) explain why many studies about cell phones and cancer are international in nature

3. The question in lines 12–13 ("Why . . . phones") primarily serves to

   (A) suggest that people are often afraid of technology that they don't understand
   (B) indicate that people underestimate the dangers of devices such as microwave ovens
   (C) argue that radio waves play a crucially important role in modern technology
   (D) assert that all forms of radiation can cause cancer if a person is in close proximity to the source
   (E) imply that many people assume cell phones are as harmless as other devices that emit radio waves

4. In line 23, "unnerving" most nearly means

   (A) unsettling
   (B) bullying
   (C) flustering
   (D) bewildering
   (E) enfeebling

**5.** The author of Passage 1 mentions the Swedish study (lines 34–35) in order to

(A) point out that the Swedish study does not have the recall bias issues that the six-year study does
(B) compare the benefits and drawbacks of a long-term study and a short-term study
(C) emphasize the superiority of an international study over a study from a single country
(D) further bolster the findings of the six-year study by pointing out that they were independently verified in another study
(E) suggest that the six-year study was not inherently flawed because other studies were able to perfectly replicate it

**6.** In line 45, the phrase "no need for any drastic action" suggests that people

(A) tend to behave recklessly when they hear that they may have a brain tumor
(B) do not fully understand how their actions affect people with cancer
(C) should continue using cell phones because they have not yet been shown to cause cancer
(D) may be tempted to make rash decisions as a direct result of the recall bias in the six-year study
(E) ought to consider using their cell phones less often rather than throwing them out completely

**7.** In line 46, "overwhelming" most nearly means

(A) breathtaking
(B) stunning
(C) devastating
(D) overpowering
(E) vast

**8.** The author of Passage 1 would most likely respond to the final claim in Passage 2 (lines 61–63) by

(A) conceding that the existing studies have all been undermined by recall bias
(B) maintaining that a well-designed study would most likely find a link between cell phone use and cancer
(C) arguing that it is very difficult, if not impossible, to create a study without any inherent flaws at all
(D) disputing the notion that a long-term study would be the best way to determine whether cell phones cause cancer
(E) agreeing that people often exaggerate or misremember past events

**Step 3**

Master
WYPAD and
other keys
to success on
SAT Reading

**240**

**9.** The author of Passage 2 would most likely respond to
the reference to the Swedish study (lines 34–35) by

(A) suggesting that the Swedish study may also have been
prone to inherent flaws such as recall bias

(B) expressing reservation that the Swedish study might
have been inconclusive because it was not as
long-term as the six-year study

(C) denouncing the Swedish study as false and outmoded
because it relied on old data

(D) lamenting the fact that the Swedish study was not a
part of the international six-year study

(E) agreeing that the Swedish study may have uncovered
substantial evidence in support of a link between
cancer and cell phone use

## General Reading 2400 Strategy Part 1 · *Write your main idea down*

### Step 1 ⟋ *Read the beginning of Passage 1*

In most modern societies, it's nearly impossible to go
anywhere without seeing someone talking on or tapping
away on a cell phone. Cell phones have quickly become an
ingrained technology in our society. It's estimated that a
whopping five *billion* people on our planet use cell phones.
And though these small and ubiquitous devices may seem
innocuous enough, the reality may surprise you: cell phones
emit radiofrequency energy, which may be a cancer risk.

### Step 2 ⟋ *WYMID (Passage 1)*

*cell phones common but maybe cancer risk*

### Step 3 ⟋ *Read the beginning of Passage 2*

Recent studies that call into question the safety of cell phones
have caused some people to panic and wonder whether they
should throw their cell phones out—or, at the very least, use them
much more sparingly. But there's no need for any drastic action—
not yet, anyway. The overwhelming majority of studies have not
found a definitive link between cell phone use and certain
cancers (specifically, brain tumors). Nearly all of these studies
report inconclusive findings and caution that much more research
is needed before a clear link can be established.

### Step 4 ⟋ *WYMID (Passage 2)*

*link between cell phones and cancer unclear*

**2.** In lines 4–5, the author of Passage 1 mentions the number of global cell phone users in order to

(A) lament the potential cancer risk for a certain percentage of the global population
(B) point out that many people are foolishly lulled into thinking cell phones are safe
(C) emphasize the overwhelmingly widespread use of cell phones in modern societies
(D) suggest that there is a need for more effective cancer treatment in many countries
(E) explain why many studies about cell phones and cancer are international in nature

**Step 1** ⌐ *Read the relevant lines*

Cell phones have quickly become an ingrained technology in our society. It's estimated that a whopping five *billion* people on our planet use cell phones.

**Step 2** ⌐ *Passage 2400 Golden Strategy: WYPAD*

demonstrate how common cell phone use is

**Step 3** ⌐ *Eliminate answer choices that disagree with WYPAD*

(A) ?
(B) ?
(C) ?
(D) X
(E) X

**Step 4** ⌐ *Apply Passage 2400 Strategies to the remaining answer choices*

(A) *Passage 2400 Strategy 6: Avoid assumptions*
Does the passage mention that the author "lament[s] the potential cancer risk"? No.

(B) *Passage 2400 Strategy 6: Avoid assumptions*
Does the passage mention people being "foolishly lulled into thinking cell phones are safe"? No.

(C) *Passage 2400 Strategy 10: Choose general over specific*
Is this a general answer choice with evidence in the passage? Yes.

**Step 5** ✎ *Confirm your potential answer choice with evidence in the passage*

(C) Does the author mention the number of global cell phone users in order to "emphasize the overwhelmingly widespread use of cell phones in modern societies"? Yes.

> Cell phones have quickly become an ingrained technology in our society. It's estimated that a whopping five *billion* people on our planet use cell phones.

Select (C) as your answer choice.

---

**3.** The question in lines 12–13 ("Why . . . phones") primarily serves to

(A) suggest that people are often afraid of technology that they don't understand

(B) indicate that people underestimate the dangers of devices such as microwave ovens

(C) argue that radio waves play a crucially important role in modern technology

(D) assert that all forms of radiation can cause cancer if a person is in close proximity to the source

(E) imply that many people assume cell phones are as harmless as other devices that emit radio waves

**Step 1** ✎ *Read the relevant lines*

Read from where you left off, paying attention to the cited lines.

> Waves of radiofrequency energy, known more commonly as "radio waves," are emitted by a variety of objects: satellite stations, microwave ovens, and radio towers, to name just a few. Why, then, are people so concerned about radio waves from cell phones? The trouble is that people get much more up close and personal with these waves: the phones are pressed against our ears, carried in pockets, or held in our hands for a long time—often hours—each day.

**Step 2** ✎ *Passage 2400 Golden Strategy: WYPAD*

point out an inconsistency

**Step 3** ✎ *Eliminate answer choices that disagree with WYPAD*

(A) X

(B) X

(C) ?

(D) ?

(E) ?

### Step 4 ✒ Apply Passage 2400 Strategies to the remaining answer choices

(C) *Passage 2400 Strategy 6: Avoid assumptions*
Does the passage mention that radio waves "play a crucially important role in modern technology"? No.

(D) *Passage 2400 Strategy 6: Avoid extremes*
Does the answer choice avoid extremes like "all"? No.

(E) *Passage 2400 Strategy 10: Choose general over specific*
Is this a general answer choice with evidence in the passage? Yes.

### Step 5 ✒ Confirm your potential answer choice with evidence in the passage

(E) Does the question primarily serve to "imply that many people assume cell phones are as harmless as other devices that emit radio waves"? Yes.

> Waves of radiofrequency energy, known more commonly as "radio waves," are emitted by a variety of objects: satellite stations, microwave ovens, and radio towers, to name just a few. Why, then, are people so concerned about radio waves from cell phones?

Select (E) as your answer choice.

---

**4.** In line 23, "unnerving" most nearly means

    (A) unsettling
    (B) bullying
    (C) flustering
    (D) bewildering
    (E) enfeebling

### Step 1 ✒ Read the relevant lines

Read from where you left off, paying attention to the cited lines.

> Very rarely will people stand next to a microwave oven or radio tower for so long, or within such close proximity.
> The biggest concern so far seems to be that the radio waves from a cell phone held against a person's ear will penetrate through to the brain and cause damage to DNA that may in turn lead to a brain tumor. In the past five years, there have been an unnerving number of lawsuits brought against cell phone manufacturers that allege the use of cell phones have caused their owners to develop brain tumors.

### Step 2 ✒ Passage 2400 Golden Strategy: WYPAD

*scary*

Step 3

Master
WYPAD and
other keys
to success on
SAT Reading
. . . . . . . . . . . . . . . . . . . . . .
244

## Step 3 ☞ *Eliminate answer choices that disagree with WYPAD*

(A) unsettling   = scary ?
(B) bullying     ≠ scary
(C) flustering   ≠ scary
(D) bewildering ≠ scary
(E) enfeebling  ≠ scary

## Selected definitions

unsettle  = worry, disturb
fluster    = confuse, agitate
bewilder = confuse
enfeeble = weaken

## Step 4 ☞ *Apply Passage 2400 Strategies to the remaining answer choices*

This is unnecessary: WYPAD is sufficient.

## Step 5 ☞ *Confirm your potential answer choice with evidence in the passage*

(A) Does "unnerving" most nearly mean "unsettling"? Yes.

> In the past five years, there have been an **unsettling** number of lawsuits brought against cell phone manufacturers that allege the use of cell phones have caused their owners to develop brain tumors.

Select (A) as your answer choice.

---

**5.** The author of Passage 1 mentions the Swedish study (lines 34–35) in order to

(A) point out that the Swedish study does not have the recall bias issues that the six-year study does
(B) compare the benefits and drawbacks of a long-term study and a short-term study
(C) emphasize the superiority of an international study over a study from a single country
(D) further bolster the findings of the six-year study by pointing out that they were independently verified in another study
(E) suggest that the six-year study was not inherently flawed because other studies were able to perfectly replicate it

**Step 1** ⌐ *Read the relevant lines*

Read from where you left off, paying attention to the cited lines.

> There has also been an
> increase in brain tumors in recent years, which may correspond
> to the rapid increase of cell phone use around the world.
>     Many studies have attempted to find a definite link between
> cell phone use and the incidence of brain tumors. Unfortunately,
> many of these studies have been inconclusive, no doubt due to
> the lack of long-term research. One six-year international study
> did find that after ten years of heavy cell phone use on one side
> of the head, a person's risk of developing a tumor on that side
> of the head did increase. (A Swedish study later came to the
> same conclusion.)

**Step 2** ⌐ *Passage 2400 Golden Strategy: WYPAD*

help support the conclusion of other study

**Step 3** ⌐ *Eliminate answer choices that disagree with WYPAD*

(A) ✗
(B) ✗
(C) ✗
(D) ?
(E) ?

**Step 4** ⌐ *Apply Passage 2400 Strategies to the remaining answer choices*

(D) *Passage 2400 Strategy 9: Criticize every word*
   Does every word appear to match the WYPAD? Yes.

(E) *Passage 2400 Strategy 7: Avoid extremes*
   Does the answer choice avoid extremes like "perfectly"? No.

**Step 5** ⌐ *Confirm your potential answer choice with evidence in the passage*

(D) Does the author of Passage 1 mention the Swedish study in order to "further bolster the findings of the six-year study by pointing out that they
   were independently verified in another study"? Yes.

> One six-year international study
> did find that after ten years of heavy cell phone use on one side
> of the head, a person's risk of developing a tumor on that side
> of the head did increase. (A Swedish study later came to the
> same conclusion.)

Select (D) as your answer choice.

**Step 3**
Master
WYPAD and
other keys
to success on
SAT Reading

· · · · · · · · · · · · · · · · · · · · ·

246

**6.** In line 45, the phrase "no need for any drastic action" suggests that people

(A) tend to behave recklessly when they hear that they may have a brain tumor
(B) do not fully understand how their actions affect people with cancer
(C) should continue using cell phones because they have not yet been shown to cause cancer
(D) may be tempted to make rash decisions as a direct result of the recall bias in the six-year study
(E) ought to consider using their cell phones less often rather than throwing them out completely

### Step 1 ☞ Read the relevant lines

Finish reading Passage 1 first.

> Furthermore, the six-year study found that after 1,640 hours of cell phone use, a person's risk of glioma (a type of brain cancer) also increased. The 1,640 hours corresponds to 30 minutes of use every day for ten years—a plausible amount of cell phone usage for many people. With these troubling results, it's likely that longer-term studies will find more and more cause for concern.

Then read the relevant lines of Passage 2.

> Recent studies that call into question the safety of cell phones have caused some people to panic and wonder whether they should throw their cell phones out—or, at the very least, use them much more sparingly. But there's no need for any drastic action— not yet, anyway. The overwhelming majority of studies have not found a definitive link between cell phone use and certain cancers (specifically, brain tumors).

### Step 2 ☞ Passage 2400 Golden Strategy: WYPAD

*no imminent danger*

### Step 3 ☞ Eliminate answer choices that disagree with WYPAD

(A) ✗
(B) ✗
(C) ?
(D) ✗
(E) ?

**Step 4** ‒ *Apply Passage 2400 Strategies to the remaining answer choices*

(C) *Passage 2400 Strategy 6: Avoid assumptions*
Does the passage mention that cell phones "have not yet been shown to cause cancer"? Yes.

(E) *Passage 2400 Strategy 6: Avoid assumptions*
Does the passage mention that people should "consider using their cell phones less"? No.

**Step 5** ‒ *Confirm your potential answer choice with evidence in the passage*

(C) Does the phrase "no need for any drastic action" suggest that people "should continue using cell phones because they have not yet been shown to cause cancer "? Yes.

> But there's no need for any drastic action— not yet, anyway. The overwhelming majority of studies have not found a definitive link between cell phone use and certain cancers (specifically, brain tumors).

Select (C) as your answer choice.

---

**7.** In line 46, "overwhelming" most nearly means

    (A) breathtaking
    (B) stunning
    (C) devastating
    (D) overpowering
    (E) vast

**Step 1** ‒ *Read the relevant lines*

> The overwhelming majority of studies have not found a definitive link between cell phone use and certain cancers (specifically, brain tumors).

**Step 2** ‒ *Passage 2400 Golden Strategy: WYPAD*

*most*

**Step 3** ‒ *Eliminate answer choices that disagree with WYPAD*

(A) breathtaking  ≠ *most*
(B) stunning      ≠ *most*
(C) devastating   ≠ *most*
(D) overpowering ≠ *most*
(E) vast          = *most* ?

Selected definition

vast = huge, great, enormous

**Step 4** ✎ *Apply Passage 2400 Strategies to the remaining answer choices*

This is unnecessary: WYPAD is sufficient.

**Step 5** ✎ *Confirm your potential answer choice with evidence in the passage*

(E) Does "overwhelming" most nearly mean "vast"? Yes.

**Step 3**
Master
WYPAD and
other keys
to success on
SAT Reading
..........................
**248**

> The **vast** majority of studies have not
> found a definitive link between cell phone use and certain
> cancers (specifically, brain tumors).

Select (E) as your answer choice.

## General Reading 2400 Strategy Part 3 • *Answer all general questions*

**1.** The authors of both passages agree that

    (A) the existing studies don't conclusively prove that cell
         phone use causes cancer
    (B) the six-year study is flawed because its subjects are
         prone to recall bias
    (C) lawsuits against cell phone manufacturers have
         dramatically increased in recent years
    (D) the six-year study is the only study of cell phones and
         cancer to be corroborated by a later study
    (E) cell phones are unquestionably more dangerous than
         microwave ovens or radio towers

**Step 1** ✎ *Read the relevant lines*

Finish reading Passage 2.

> Nearly all of these studies
> report inconclusive findings and caution that much more research
> is needed before a clear link can be established.
>     Furthermore, one of the largest international studies that did
> find a possible correlation may itself be flawed. In this six-year
> study, people were asked to remember certain patterns of cell
> phone use from the past ten years. This introduces the substantial
> problem of recall bias. Recall bias occurs when studies rely on
> subjects' memories, which may very well be faulty. People may
> easily exaggerate or simply misremember how often they used
> a cell phone ten years ago, much less how often they held it to
> one ear or the other. The six-year study relied on this type of
> self-reported data and as a result may be flawed by recall bias.
>     With the inherent flaws in the six-year study, it's quite clear
> that there need to be more studies—well-designed studies—
> to determine whether cell phones do in fact cause cancer.

**Step 2** ✦ *Passage 2400 Golden Strategy: WYPAD*

When there is a lot to read, summarize only the main points.

*studies inconclusive; 6-yr study = recall bias problem*

**Step 3** ✦ *Revisit the main ideas*

Before answering general questions, reacquaint yourself with the passages' main ideas.

Passage 1: *cell phones common but maybe cancer risk*
Passage 2: *link between cell phones and cancer unclear*

**Step 4** ✦ *Passage 2400 Golden Strategy: WYPAD*

*not 100% clear if cell phones = cancer*

**Step 5** ✦ *Eliminate answer choices that disagree with WYPAD*

(A) ?
(B) ✗
(C) ✗
(D) ?
(E) ?

**Step 6** ✦ *Apply Passage 2400 Strategies to the remaining answer choices*

(A) *Passage 2400 Strategy 6: Avoid assumptions*
   Do both passages mention that "existing studies don't conclusively prove that cell phone use causes cancer"? Yes.
(D) *Passage 2400 Strategy 7: Avoid extremes*
   Does the answer choice avoid extremes like "only"? No.
(E) *Passage 2400 Strategy 7: Avoid extremes*
   Does the answer choice avoid extremes like "unquestionably"? No.

**Step 7** ✦ *Confirm your potential answer choice with evidence in the passage*

(A) Would the authors of both passages agree that "existing studies don't conclusively prove that cell phone use causes cancer"? Yes.

   (Passage 1)

                                                 Unfortunately,
             many of these studies have been inconclusive

   (Passage 2)

                                   Nearly all of these studies
             report inconclusive findings and caution that much more research
             is needed before a clear link can be established.

Select (A) as your answer choice.

**Step 3**

Master
WYPAD and
other keys
to success on
SAT Reading

· · · · · · · · · · · · · · · · · · ·

**250**

**8.** The author of Passage 1 would most likely respond to the final claim in Passage 2 (lines 61–63) by

(A) conceding that the existing studies have all been undermined by recall bias
(B) maintaining that a well-designed study would most likely find a link between cell phone use and cancer
(C) arguing that it is very difficult, if not impossible, to create a study without any inherent flaws at all
(D) disputing the notion that a long-term study would be the best way to determine whether cell phones cause cancer
(E) agreeing that people often exaggerate or misremember past events

### Step 1 ⚞ Revisit the main ideas

Before answering general questions, reacquaint yourself with the passages' main ideas.

Passage 1:  *cell phones common but maybe cancer risk*
Passage 2:  *link between cell phones and cancer unclear*

### Step 2 ⚞ Read the relevant lines

With the inherent flaws in the six-year study, it's quite clear that there need to be more studies—well-designed studies— to determine whether cell phones do in fact cause cancer.

### Step 3 ⚞ Passage 2400 Golden Strategy: WYPAD

*Swedish study reaffirmed 6-yr study.*

### Step 4 ⚞ Eliminate answer choices that disagree with WYPAD

(A) X
(B) ?
(C) X
(D) ?
(E) X

Sometimes, WYPAD doesn't result in an answer similar to any of the choices.

### Step 5 ⚞ Apply Passage 2400 Strategies to the remaining answer choices

(B) *Passage 2400 Strategy 6: Avoid assumptions*
Does Passage 1 mention that "a well-designed study would most likely find a link between cell phone use and cancer"? Yes.

(D) *Passage 2400 Strategy 7: Avoid extremes*
Does the answer choice avoid extremes like "best"? No.

**Step 6** ⚬ *Confirm your potential answer choice with evidence in the passage*

(B) Does Passage 1 agree that "a well-designed study would most likely find a link between cell phone use and cancer"? Yes.

> many of these studies have been inconclusive, no doubt due to the lack of long-term research . . . it's likely that longer-term studies will find more and more cause for concern.

Select (B) as your answer choice.

9. The author of Passage 2 would most likely respond to the reference to the Swedish study (lines 34–35) by

   (A) suggesting that the Swedish study may also have been prone to inherent flaws such as recall bias
   (B) expressing reservation that the Swedish study might have been inconclusive because it was not as long-term as the six-year study
   (C) denouncing the Swedish study as false and outmoded because it relied on old data
   (D) lamenting the fact that the Swedish study was not a part of the international six-year study
   (E) agreeing that the Swedish study may have uncovered substantial evidence in support of a link between cancer and cell phone use

**Step 1** ⚬ *Revisit the main ideas*

Before answering general questions, reacquaint yourself with the passages' main ideas.

Passage 1: *cell phones common but maybe cancer risk*
Passage 2: *link between cell phones and cancer unclear*

**Step 2** ⚬ *Read the relevant lines*

> One six-year international study did find that after ten years of heavy cell phone use on one side of the head, a person's risk of developing a tumor on that side of the head did increase. (A Swedish study later came to the same conclusion.)

**Step 3** ⚬ *Passage 2400 Golden Strategy: WYPAD*

*Swedish study could also have issue.*

**Step 4** ⚬ *Eliminate answer choices that disagree with WYPAD*

(A) ?
(B) ?
(C) ✗
(D) ✗
(E) ✗

**Step 3**

Master
WYPAD and
other keys
to success on
SAT Reading

........................

252

**Step 5** ⟋ *Apply Passage 2400 Strategies to the remaining answer choices*

(A) *Passage 2400 Strategy 6: Avoid assumptions*

Does Passage 2 mention that studies can have "inherent flaws such as recall bias"? Yes.

(B) *Passage 2400 Strategy 6: Avoid assumptions*

Does Passage 2 mention that the Swedish study could have been "inconclusive because it was not as long-term as the six-year study"? No.

**Step 6** ⟋ *Confirm your potential answer choice with evidence in the passage*

(A) Does the author of Passage 2 suggest "that the Swedish study may also have been prone to inherent flaws such as recall bias"? Yes.

> Recall bias occurs when studies rely on subjects' memories, which may very well be faulty. . . .
> With the inherent flaws in the six-year study, it's quite clear that there need to be more studies—well-designed studies— to determine whether cell phones do in fact cause cancer.

Select (A) as your answer choice.

---

**Practice problem set**   *Set of long comparison passages*

The answer key for this problem set is on page 284.

> The passages below are followed by questions based on their content or on the relationship between the two passages. Answer the questions on the basis of what is <u>stated</u> or <u>implied</u> in the passages and in any introductory material that may be provided.

### Questions 1–13 are based on the following passages.

### Passage 1

There is certainly some connection between the brain and intelligent behavior. While the spinal cord and brain stem vary according to the size of the body, and the cere-
*Line* bellum with the motility of the species of animal, the size
5 of the cerebrum varies more or less closely with the intelligence of the species. It does vary also with bodily size, as illustrated by the whale and elephant, which have the largest cerebrum of all animals, including man. But the monkey, which shows more intelligence than most animals,
10 has also a very large cerebrum for his size of body; and the chimpanzee and gorilla, considerably surpassing the ordinary monkeys in intelligence, have also a much larger cerebrum. The cerebrum of man, in proportion to the size of his body, far surpasses that of the chimpanzee or gorilla.
15     The cerebrum varies considerably in size from one human individual to another. In some adults it is twice as large as in

others, and the question arises whether greater intelligence goes with a larger brain. Now, it appears that an extremely small cerebrum spells idiocy; not all idiots have small brains, but all men with extremely small brains are idiots. The brain weight of quite a number of highly gifted men has been measured in post-mortem examination, and many of these gifted men have had a very large cerebrum. On the whole, the gifted individual seems to have a large brain, but there are exceptions, and the relationship between brain size and intelligence cannot be very close. Other factors must enter, one factor being undoubtedly the fineness of the internal structure of the cortex. Brain function depends on dendrites and end-brushes, forming synapses in the cortex, and such minute structures make little impression on the total brain weight.

While intelligence is related to the cerebrum as a whole, rather than to any particular "intelligence center," there is some likelihood that the special aptitudes are related to special parts of the cortex. However, it must be admitted that few aptitudes have as yet been localized.

**Passage 2**

Until a year or two ago it was customary to state that in cranial capacity also—that is to say, in the volume of brain-matter that the skull might contain—the Neanderthal race was intermediate between the Ape-Man and modern man. We have seen that the cranial capacity of the highest ape is about 600 cubic centimeters, and that of the Ape-Man (variously given as 850 and 950) is about 900. It was then added that the capacity of the Neanderthal race was about 1200, and that of civilized man (on the average) 1600.

Largeness of brain in an individual is no indication of intelligence, and smallness of brain no proof of low mentality. Some of the greatest thinkers, such as Aristotle and Leibniz, had abnormally small heads. Further, the size of the brain is of no significance whatever except in strict relation to the size and weight of the body. Woman has five or six ounces less brain-matter than man, but in proportion to her average size and the weight of the vital tissue of her body (excluding fat) she has as respectable a brain as man. When, however, these allowances have been made, it has usually been considered that the average brain of a race is in proportion to its average intelligence. This is not strictly true. The rabbit has a larger proportion of brain to body than the elephant or horse, and the canary a larger proportion than the chimpanzee.

Clearly the question is very complex, and some of these recent authorities conclude that the cranial capacity, or volume of the brain, has no relation to intelligence. Nevertheless, we hesitate to accept the statement that primitive man had as large a brain, if not a larger brain, than a modern race. The basis is slender, and the proportion of brain to body-

tissue has not been taken into account. On the other hand, the remains of this early race are, Professor Sollas says, "obviously more brutal than existing men in all the other ascertainable characters by which they differ from them."

70

Step 3
Master
WYPAD and
other keys
to success on
SAT Reading
......................
254

1. The argument in Passage 1 is supported primarily by

   (A) a description of the author's personal experiences in studying the brain
   (B) specific examples of different brain sizes in animals and people
   (C) a theory about why the brain cortex may be linked to specialized talents
   (D) an emotional appeal to raise more funding for scientists to examine the human brain
   (E) concrete evidence that proves intelligence is solely determined by brain size

2. Which of the following best summarizes the main point of Passage 1?

   (A) There is at least some connection between brain size and intelligence, but there are many other factors involved.
   (B) People may have various special aptitudes due to the presence of unique structures in the cortex.
   (C) The brain of a modern human being cannot be compared to that of a Neanderthal man.
   (D) Highly intelligent and talented people tend to have much larger brains than other people.
   (E) The size of an animal's brain varies in relation to the size of that animal's body.

3. The author of Passage 1 mentions the whale and elephant (line 7) most nearly in order to

   (A) support the argument that all large animals are intelligent creatures
   (B) prove that the size of the cerebrum is more important than the size of the cortex in determining an animal's intelligence
   (C) provide an example of how the cerebrum varies with body size
   (D) offer a parallel between a large animal that lives in the sea and one that lives on land
   (E) show that the brain stem, cerebellum, and spinal cord don't have any effect on an animal's level of intelligence

4. In line 30, "minute" most nearly means

   (A) fragile
   (B) temporary
   (C) detailed
   (D) precise
   (E) tiny

**5.** According to Passage 1, one difference between the brain of a gorilla and the brain of a human being is that

    (A) the gorilla's brain stem and spinal cord are smaller than those of a human being
    (B) there is less variation in brain size among gorillas than there is among human beings
    (C) the human being's cerebrum is proportionately larger than the gorilla's cerebrum
    (D) the gorilla's cortex is not as specialized as the human being's cortex
    (E) a human being's brain is capable of growing larger over time while the gorilla's is not

**6.** The author of Passage 1 mentions the "minute structures" (line 30) most nearly in order to

    (A) explain that intelligence may be determined by more than just the weight of the brain
    (B) justify the argument that special talents can be linked to specialized structures in the cortex
    (C) describe the process by which dendrites and end-brushes create synapses in the cortex
    (D) provide an example of the highly delicate nature of the human brain
    (E) suggest that the cerebrum determines a person's intelligence while the cortex determines a person's unique skills

**7.** The statement in lines 35–36 of Passage 1 ("However . . . localized") is best described as an example of

    (A) an emotional plea
    (B) a moral proclamation
    (C) a definition of an important term
    (D) an ironic remark
    (E) a statement of concession

**8.** The primary purpose of Passage 2 is to

    (A) explain why men and women have different brain sizes
    (B) demonstrate the importance of the cerebrum in determining a person's intelligence
    (C) assert that brain size is not necessarily representative of an animal's intelligence
    (D) trace the evolution of the brain from primitive man to modern man
    (E) argue that cranial capacity is not related to the size of an animal's body

Step 3

Master
WYPAD and
other keys
to success on
SAT Reading
· · · · · · · · · · · · · · · · · · · ·

**256**

**9.** It can be inferred from the passage that the term "highest" (lines 41–42) most nearly refers to

(A) the elevation at which the ape lives
(B) the very large size of the ape
(C) the shrill sound that the ape makes
(D) the level of domestication shown by the ape
(E) the ape's level of intelligence

**10.** The author mentions Aristotle and Leibniz (lines 48–49) most nearly in order to

(A) describe how brain size has remained fairly stable throughout history
(B) point out that people with smaller brains have plenty of special talents
(C) suggest that some highly intelligent people have smaller cerebrums and larger cortexes
(D) provide evidence that intelligence is not necessarily linked to the size of the brain
(E) demonstrate that people of smaller stature do have proportionately smaller brains

**11.** In line 54, "respectable" most nearly means

(A) sizeable
(B) proper
(C) honest
(D) passable
(E) admired

**12.** The authors of both passages would most likely agree with which of the following statements?

(A) There is no difference in brain size between the male and female of any animal species.
(B) The relationship between brain size and intelligence is complex and there are still many questions that need to be answered.
(C) The cortex is at least as important as the cerebrum in determining an animal's intelligence.
(D) The Neanderthal was probably not as intelligent as modern man.
(E) Chimpanzees and gorillas are far more intelligent than they were previously thought to be.

13. Which is a likely response by the author of Passage 1 to the claim in Passage 2 that "some of the greatest thinkers . . . had abnormally small heads" (lines 48–49)?

(A) It is likely that all of the greatest thinkers were also small in stature and had proportionately small brains as a result.

(B) A small head does not necessarily indicate a small cerebrum, and only a port-mortem examination could have told us with certainty whether Aristotle or Leibniz had large cerebrums.

(C) Many of the greatest thinkers probably had very large cortexes and very small cerebrums.

(D) It is highly likely that reports about the size of Aristotle's and Leibniz's heads are not accurate anyway.

(E) There is no link between having intelligence and having a large brain.

# SAT vocabulary

Vocabulary memorization will probably be your least favorite part of SAT preparation. It is boring and robotic. It requires months of absolute dedication, painstaking effort, and meticulous attention to detail. But you must do it.

I won't leave you stranded with a list of vocabulary words. Instead, I will share the tools and methods I used to memorize SAT words efficiently.

## The benefits of memorizing vocabulary

You will be hugely rewarded by memorizing SAT vocabulary—far beyond the help it provides on SENTENCE COMPLETION questions. I didn't realize many of the advantages until after I had completed my vocabulary memorization. I was sufficiently motivated to memorize vocabulary words without regard for the other benefits. But in case you are not . . .

### Vocabulary benefit 1: Score higher on SAT sentence completion

Many words on the *Vocabulary 2400* list will appear in SENTENCE COMPLETION questions on your SAT test. Even though there are only 19 SENTENCE COMPLETION questions on the SAT, memorizing hundreds of vocabulary words for these questions is not a waste. If your new vocabulary helps you correctly answer just three questions that you wouldn't have otherwise (a modest estimate), your score could improve by as much as 60 points. Imagine if that vocabulary helps you answer 6, 8, or even 10 more SENTENCE COMPLETION questions correctly!

**Step 3**
Master
WYPAD and
other keys
to success on
SAT Reading
............................
**258**

## Vocabulary benefit 2: Score higher on SAT passage-based reading

Many words on the *Vocabulary 2400* list will appear in the PASSAGE-BASED READING sections of your SAT test. While these sections primarily measure comprehension, they also test vocabulary. After I had memorized hundreds of vocabulary words late in my SAT training, I realized that I could better comprehend reading passages I had trouble with before. *Vocabulary 2400* words show up both in passages and in associated questions. Rather than guess what words mean from context, you will know what they mean.

## Vocabulary benefit 3: Ace the SAT essay

*Essay 2400 Strategy 3* (Use big words) is one of the best ways to impress SAT essay graders. And the *Vocabulary 2400* list is the perfect resource for incorporating large words into your SAT essay. Re-read my 2400 SAT essay (pages 45–46) and notice all of the large vocabulary words I included. I didn't write that way naturally—I was able to include them because I had just memorized hundreds of SAT vocabulary words. If you memorize the *Vocabulary 2400* list, your SAT essay score will surely go up!

## Vocabulary benefit 4: Ace all other essays

You will use words from the *Vocabulary 2400* list in your college, scholarship, and English essays. Not only will you sound more sophisticated, but you will also be abundantly rewarded for doing so. My "intelligent" vocabulary helped me gain admission to prestigious colleges and win several scholarships, as well as get lots of A's on English papers. Big words don't guarantee well-written compositions, but they certainly help.

## Vocabulary benefit 5: Become articulate and eloquent

The vocabulary you learn from the *Vocabulary 2400* list will be yours forever. A sophisticated vocabulary will benefit you in all of your future endeavors. I spent many hours memorizing SAT vocabulary in high school, and one result is that I now write with greater sophistication, understand complex literature better, and communicate more effectively. Hard work pays off . . . for the rest of your life.

# Vocabulary 2400 Strategy

You will have to memorize SAT vocabulary words while taking difficult high school courses, participating in sports, playing in the band/orchestra, and engaging in countless other extracurricular activities. It's important to tackle memorization with a strategy that is both efficient and effective.

## Vocabulary 2400 Strategy

STEP 1 · Eliminate familiar words
STEP 2 · Repeat unfamiliar words seven times
STEP 3 · Perform 2400 Review of the day's words
STEP 4 · Perform 2400 Review of previous days' words
STEP 5 · Perform 2400 Review of previous weeks' words

## Vocabulary 2400 Step 1 *Eliminate familiar words*

Save time by scanning a vocabulary set for words you already know. To be sure that you know what a particular word means, write your definition down in the "Synonym" column of the *Vocabulary 2400* list, and confirm that your definition agrees with the one provided.

## Vocabulary 2400 Step 2 *Repeat unfamiliar words seven times*

My eighth-grade science teacher told us that research shows that after people see something seven times, they remember it. I'm not sure that this is true, but my memorization method is based on this premise. For each word you don't already know, repeat the definition or synonym seven times, either aloud or silently. Cover the definition/synonym with your hand, focus your eyes on the SAT vocabulary word, and focus your mind on the definition/synonym. After seven repetitions, quiz yourself on the definition of the word. If you can recall it, move on to the next word. If you can't, repeat until you can.

## Vocabulary 2400 Step 3 *Perform 2400 Review of the day's words*

Review vocabulary words you've just memorized. For example, after you repeat word 2 seven times, quiz yourself on the definition of word 1. After you memorize word 8, quiz yourself on the definitions of words 7 through 1, in that order.

## Vocabulary 2400 Step 4 *Perform 2400 Review of previous days' words*

Review vocabulary words you memorized on previous days. If you are on Day 3 of your vocabulary memorization schedule, quiz yourself on all vocabulary words from Day 2 and Day 1.

Here's the good news: You only need to review vocabulary words from the previous week. For example, if you are on Day 4 of Week 5 of your vocabulary memorization schedule, you only have to review Week 5's Day 3, Day 2, and Day 1.

## Vocabulary 2400 Step 5 *Perform 2400 Review of previous weeks' words*

Review vocabulary words you memorized in previous weeks. This step sounds like it contradicts Step 4, but you only need to pick one day each week to review

words from previous weeks. For example, if you are in Week 4 of your vocabulary memorization schedule, choose one day in Week 4 to quiz yourself on all vocabulary words from Weeks 3, 2, and 1.

## The art of memorizing vocabulary

Step 3
Master
WYPAD and
other keys
to success on
SAT Reading

**260**

The key to the *Vocabulary 2400 Strategy* is review. Most students avoid review when they memorize. As a result, they forget many of the words they had previously learned. *2400 Review* of previous words helps you retain words from earlier in the day. *2400 Review* of previous days' words helps you retain words from earlier in the week. And *2400 Review* of previous weeks' words helps you retain all previously learned words.

Have you heard the adage "Repetition is the mother of all learning"? This is more relevant to vocabulary memorization than to any other aspect of SAT preparation. If you can't recall some words during *2400 Review,* write them down in the "Sentence Completion/Vocabulary" section of your 2400 notebook; it will take additional work to memorize these problematic words.

### Reverse review

*2400 Review* requires that you work backwards chronologically: You review words from Day 3 before words from Day 2 before words from Day 1. Here's the reason: You are more likely to forget words you have memorized recently. By reviewing these words first, you are more likely to recall them. In addition, the words you review last are the ones you've reviewed most, which means that they are easier to recall.

### The time involved

Although the review cycle requires more time in vocabulary memorization, it may not take as much dedication as you think. *2400 Review* of previous vocabulary should take only a few seconds per word. Reviewing vocabulary words takes significantly less time and effort than memorizing them.

### The pain involved

You may sometimes feel that you are working backwards because of this constant review cycle, when all you want to do is go forward and learn the next set of vocabulary words. But review is essential in imprinting words permanently in your mind.

### Acing all memorization

You can use this method of seven repetitions and review in any subject that requires rote memorization—biology, for example.

## Vocabulary 2400 schedule

You must have a schedule for SAT vocabulary memorization. You can't just memorize vocabulary words whenever you feel like it—because you will never feel like it.

Vocabulary memorization is different from other SAT preparation, which typically requires that you master *2400 Strategies*, learn from *2400 Examples*, rehearse *2400 Practice Problem Sets*, and perform *2400 Review*. SAT vocabulary requires that you memorize hundreds of words robotically, which means it is absolutely essential to stick to a schedule for this phase of SAT preparation.

## Tips

### Break up

Breaking up your day's SAT vocabulary memorization into individual sessions is an effective way to avoid feeling overwhelmed. If your schedule requires you to memorize 10 vocabulary words per day, try memorizing five in the morning and five at night. Look for moments in your schedule when you can memorize a word or two. Do you have five minutes before class, during lunch, or before an after-school activity? Finding small periods of time throughout the day to memorize vocabulary not only reduces the amount of work you have to spend in one sitting, but also keeps your mind engaged with SAT vocabulary.

### Don't make up

Your SAT vocabulary memorization schedule needs to be flexible. High school is an erratic place: One week can be super busy, and the next can be vacation-like. If you don't memorize all of a day's vocabulary words, don't try to make it up. If you try to memorize more words the next day, the words will pile up and you will eventually get discouraged. Focus on small vocabulary goals each day rather than on compensating for missed words. Not only will you deepen your understanding of each word, but you will also remember more words in the long run. If you don't meet your word quota on one day, try to meet it the next day. Of course, you should limit how many days a week you allow yourself to fall below your vocabulary goal. Inability to meet your quota should be a special circumstance, not a normal occurrence.

## Sample schedules

The schedule you adopt depends on how much time you have before the actual SAT; you can use one of the sample vocabulary memorization schedules suggested below, or you can create your own schedule. Above all, develop a schedule that is practical; don't choose an unrealistic vocabulary goal that will cause you to fall behind. If you set a reasonable goal, you will build confidence by hitting that goal each week.

The two sample schedules below mesh with the 2400 six-phase schedule outlined on pages 17–19.

Step 3
Master
WYPAD and
other keys
to success on
SAT Reading

262

## Sample schedule 1

In this schedule, you memorize 20 words (a *Vocabulary 2400* set) every week for 25 weeks—500 words in all. Dedicate three or four days to memorizing 5 to 7 words each day. Every day, you should also review words from earlier in the week. In addition, set aside one or two days every week for *2400 Review* of all vocabulary words from previous weeks.

| | | |
|---|---|---|
| **Phase 1** | Week 1 | ☐ Memorize Set 1<br>☐ Review Set 1 |
| | Week 2 | ☐ Memorize Set 2<br>☐ Review Sets 1–2 |
| | Week 3 | ☐ Memorize Set 3<br>☐ Review Sets 1–3 |
| | Week 4 | ☐ Memorize Set 4<br>☐ Review Sets 1–4 |
| **Phase 2** | Week 5 | ☐ Memorize Set 5<br>☐ Review Sets 1–5 |
| | Week 6 | ☐ Memorize Set 6<br>☐ Review Sets 1–6 |
| | Week 7 | ☐ Memorize Set 7<br>☐ Review Sets 1–7 |
| | Week 8 | ☐ Memorize Set 8<br>☐ Review Sets 1–8 |
| **Phase 3** | Week 9 | ☐ Memorize Set 9<br>☐ Review Sets 1–9 |
| | Week 10 | ☐ Memorize Set 10<br>☐ Review Sets 1–10 |
| | Week 11 | ☐ Memorize Set 11<br>☐ Review Sets 1–11 |
| | Week 12 | ☐ Memorize Set 12<br>☐ Review Sets 1–12 |
| **Phase 4** | Week 13 | ☐ Memorize Set 13<br>☐ Review Sets 1–13 |
| | Week 14 | ☐ Memorize Set 14<br>☐ Review Sets 1–14 |
| | Week 15 | ☐ Memorize Set 15<br>☐ Review Sets 1–15 |
| | Week 16 | ☐ Memorize Set 16<br>☐ Review Sets 1–16 |

**Phase 5**   Week 17   ☐ Memorize Set 17
   ☐ Review Sets 1–17

   Week 18   ☐ Memorize Set 18
   ☐ Review Sets 1–18

   Week 19   ☐ Memorize Set 19
   ☐ Review Sets 1–19

   Week 20   ☐ Memorize Set 20
   ☐ Review Sets 1–20

   Week 21   ☐ Memorize Set 21
   ☐ Review Sets 1–21

**Phase 6**   Week 22   ☐ Memorize Set 22
   ☐ Review Sets 1–22

   Week 23   ☐ Memorize Set 23
   ☐ Review Sets 1–23

   Week 24   ☐ Memorize Set 24
   ☐ Review Sets 1–24

   Week 25   ☐ Memorize Set 25
   ☐ Review Sets 1–25

## Sample schedule 2

In this schedule, you memorize 40 words (two *Vocabulary 2400* sets) every week for 12 weeks (except for week 9, when you memorize 60 words)—500 words in all. Dedicate four or five days per week to memorizing 8 to 10 words each day. Every day, you should also review words from earlier in the week. In addition, set aside one or two days every week for *2400 Review* of all vocabulary words from previous weeks.

**Phase 1**   Week 1   ☐ Memorize Sets 1–2
   ☐ Review Sets 1–2

   Week 2   ☐ Memorize Sets 3–4
   ☐ Review Sets 1–4

**Phase 2**   Week 3   ☐ Memorize Sets 5–6
   ☐ Review Sets 1–6

   Week 4   ☐ Memorize Sets 7–8
   ☐ Review Sets 1–8

**Phase 3**   Week 5   ☐ Memorize Sets 9–10
   ☐ Review Sets 1–10

   Week 6   ☐ Memorize Sets 11–12
   ☐ Review Sets 1–12

| | | |
|---|---|---|
| **Phase 4** | Week 7 | ☐ Memorize Sets 13–14 |
| | | ☐ Review Sets 1–14 |
| | Week 8 | ☐ Memorize Sets 15–16 |
| | | ☐ Review Sets 1–16 |
| **Phase 5** | Week 9 | ☐ Memorize Sets 17–19 |
| | | ☐ Review Sets 1–19 |
| | Week 10 | ☐ Memorize Sets 20–21 |
| | | ☐ Review Sets 1–21 |
| **Phase 6** | Week 11 | ☐ Memorize Sets 22–23 |
| | | ☐ Review Sets 1–23 |
| | Week 12 | ☐ Memorize Sets 24–25 |
| | | ☐ Review Sets 1–25 |

**Step 3**
Master
WYPAD and
other keys
to success on
SAT Reading

**264**

## Vocabulary 2400 example

The best way to learn *2400 Strategies* is to study *2400 Examples*. And the *Vocabulary 2400 Strategy* is no exception. Here's a *Vocabulary 2400* set of 20 words:

1 synthesize    *v.* create, produce    SYNONYM

   SENTENCE

2 advocate    *v.* support; *n.* supporter    SYNONYM

   SENTENCE

3 dogmatic    *adj.* firm/rigid in beliefs    SYNONYM

   SENTENCE

4 deleterious    *adj.* harmful    SYNONYM

   SENTENCE

5 ominous    *adj.* threatening, foreboding    SYNONYM

   SENTENCE

6 foreboding    *adj.* threatening; *n.* apprehension    SYNONYM

   SENTENCE

7 apprehension    *n.* anxiety, fear    SYNONYM

   SENTENCE

8 magnanimous    *adj.* noble, generous, giving    SYNONYM

   SENTENCE

9 pedantic    *adj.* academic, worried about rules    SYNONYM

   SENTENCE

| 10 | rural | *adj.* nonurban, in the country | SYNONYM |
|---|---|---|---|
| | SENTENCE | | |
| 11 | pastoral | *adj.* rural, nonurban | SYNONYM |
| | SENTENCE | | |
| 12 | rustic | *adj.* rural, nonurban | SYNONYM |
| | SENTENCE | | |
| 13 | bucolic | *adj.* rural, nonurban | SYNONYM |
| | SENTENCE | | |
| 14 | contemporary | *adj.* modern, current | SYNONYM |
| | SENTENCE | | |
| 15 | capricious | *adj.* unpredictable, impulsive | SYNONYM |
| | SENTENCE | | |
| 16 | arduous | *adj.* laborious, strenuous, difficult | SYNONYM |
| | SENTENCE | | |
| 17 | painstaking | *adj.* careful, thorough, meticulous | SYNONYM |
| | SENTENCE | | |
| 18 | meticulous | *adj.* careful, detailed, scrupulous | SYNONYM |
| | SENTENCE | | |
| 19 | scrupulous | *adj.* careful, thorough, fastidious | SYNONYM |
| | SENTENCE | | |
| 20 | fastidious | *adj.* excessively careful, fussy | SYNONYM |
| | SENTENCE | | |

◄ In the "Sentence Completion/Vocabulary" section of your 2400 note-book, create vocabulary word sets using the words and definitions in the sets on pages 270–282. Each page should have four columns: Number, Word, Synonym, and Sentence.

◄ Write your own one- or two-word definition under the "Synonym" column. Memorizing the synonym that you personally devised is a very effective recall method.

◄ Write a sample sentence using the vocabulary word under the "Sentence" column. The funnier or more relevant the sentence is, the more likely you are to remember the word. Try to include people you know (like teachers) in your sentences.

## Vocabulary 2400 Strategy

Let's say that you are currently in Week 1 of sample schedule 2. You have set a schedule to memorize 10 words every day for four days, with a total of 40 words per week. You will work through this vocabulary set as if it were Day 2, so words 1–10 from Day 1 are grayed out.

### Step 1 ⟋ *Eliminate familiar words*

First, eliminate the vocabulary words that you already know from the 10 words you need to memorize for the day. To make sure you know the meaning of the words, write your own synonym and sentence for each.

| # | Word | Definition | | SYNONYM |
|---|------|-----------|---|---------|
| 1 | synthesize | *v.* create, produce | SYNONYM | create |
| | SENTENCE | I just <u>synthesized</u> my own synonym. | | |
| 2 | advocate | *v.* support; *n.* supporter | SYNONYM | support |
| | SENTENCE | I <u>advocate</u> vegetarianism. | | |
| 3 | dogmatic | *adj.* firm/rigid in beliefs | SYNONYM | inflexible |
| | SENTENCE | I am not <u>dogmatic</u> about others' being vegetarian. | | |
| 4 | deleterious | *adj.* harmful | SYNONYM | harmful |
| | SENTENCE | To delete my computer's hard drive would be <u>deleterious</u>. | | |
| 5 | ominous | *adj.* threatening, foreboding | SYNONYM | sinister |
| | SENTENCE | A black cat is usually an <u>ominous</u> sign. | | |
| 6 | foreboding | *adj.* threatening; *n.* apprehension | SYNONYM | threatening |
| | SENTENCE | The dark clouds in the sky seem <u>foreboding</u>. | | |
| 7 | apprehension | *n.* anxiety, fear | SYNONYM | dread |
| | SENTENCE | The SAT causes a lot of students <u>apprehension</u>. | | |
| 8 | magnanimous | *adj.* noble, generous, giving | SYNONYM | dignified |
| | SENTENCE | Mother Teresa was <u>magnanimous</u>. | | |
| 9 | pedantic | *adj.* academic, worried about rules | SYNONYM | academic |
| | SENTENCE | Ms. Robinson is very <u>pedantic</u> about her English class. | | |
| 10 | rural | *adj.* nonurban, in the country | SYNONYM | farmlike |
| | SENTENCE | I grew up in Las Vegas, which is definitely not <u>rural</u>. | | |
| 11 | pastoral | *adj.* rural, nonurban | SYNONYM | |
| | SENTENCE | | | |
| 12 | rustic | *adj.* rural, nonurban | SYNONYM | |
| | SENTENCE | | | |

| 13 | bucolic | *adj.* rural, nonurban | SYNONYM | |
| | SENTENCE | | | |

| 14 | contemporary | *adj.* modern, current | SYNONYM | *current* |
| | SENTENCE | *I like <u>contemporary</u> furniture rather than antiques.* | | |

| 15 | capricious | *adj.* unpredictable, impulsive | SYNONYM | *changes mind* |
| | SENTENCE | *Mr. Harrington is <u>capricious</u> and always changes his mind.* | | |

| 16 | arduous | *adj.* laborious, strenuous, difficult | SYNONYM | |
| | SENTENCE | | | |

| 17 | painstaking | *adj.* careful, thorough, meticulous | SYNONYM | |
| | SENTENCE | | | |

| 18 | meticulous | *adj.* careful, detailed, scrupulous | SYNONYM | *very careful* |
| | SENTENCE | *Renee is <u>meticulous</u> about the seating arrangement.* | | |

| 19 | scrupulous | *adj.* careful, thorough, fastidious | SYNONYM | |
| | SENTENCE | | | |

| 20 | fastidious | *adj.* excessively careful, fussy | SYNONYM | |
| | SENTENCE | | | |

## Step 2 ⁄ *Repeat unfamiliar words seven times*

You now have only seven words left to memorize. Begin with "pastoral"; write down a synonym ("rural," for example) and sentence based on the definition provided. Then, repeat "pastoral means rural" seven times silently or aloud as you cover the word and definition with your hand.

| 11 | pastoral | *adj.* rural, nonurban | SYNONYM | *rural* |
| | SENTENCE | *<u>The Grapes of Wrath</u> takes place in <u>pastoral</u> settings.* | | |

Next, write down a synonym and sentence for "rustic" ("countryside," for example). Repeat "rustic means countryside" seven times silently or aloud as you cover the word and definition with your hand.

| 12 | rustic | *adj.* rural, nonurban | SYNONYM | *countryside* |
| | SENTENCE | *"Rural" and "<u>rustic</u>" sound similar and mean similar things.* | | |

Repeat this step with "bucolic," word 13. Then, perform a *2400 Review* of words 14 and 15 before moving on to "arduous," word 16.

Repeat this step until you have finished your vocabulary words for the day. Be sure to review previous words as you go.

**Step 3**
Master
WYPAD and
other keys
to success on
SAT Reading
........................
**268**

| 11 | pastoral | *adj.* rural, nonurban | SYNONYM | *rural* |
| | SENTENCE | The Grapes of Wrath takes place in pastoral settings. | | |
| 12 | rustic | *adj.* rural, nonurban | SYNONYM | *countryside* |
| | SENTENCE | "Rural" and "rustic" sound similar and mean similar things. | | |
| 13 | bucolic | *adj.* rural, nonurban | SYNONYM | *rural* |
| | SENTENCE | Many children like to frolic in bucolic places. | | |
| 14 | contemporary | *adj.* modern, current | SYNONYM | *current* |
| | SENTENCE | I like contemporary furniture rather than antiques. | | |
| 15 | capricious | *adj.* unpredictable, impulsive | SYNONYM | *changes mind* |
| | SENTENCE | Mr. Harrington is capricious and always changes his mind. | | |
| 16 | arduous | *adj.* laborious, strenuous, difficult | SYNONYM | *grueling* |
| | SENTENCE | SAT prep is arduous. | | |
| 17 | painstaking | *adj.* careful, thorough, meticulous | SYNONYM | *demanding* |
| | SENTENCE | Any task that takes pains is painstaking. | | |
| 18 | meticulous | *adj.* careful, detailed, scrupulous | SYNONYM | *very careful* |
| | SENTENCE | Renee is meticulous about the seating arrangement. | | |
| 19 | scrupulous | *adj.* careful, thorough, fastidious | SYNONYM | *thorough* |
| | SENTENCE | You must be scrupulous when it comes to SAT vocab. | | |
| 20 | fastidious | *adj.* excessively careful, fussy | SYNONYM | *fussy* |
| | SENTENCE | My mom is fastidious about making sure my room is tidy. | | |

## Step 3 ⟋ *Perform 2400 Review of the day's words*

Quiz yourself on the synonyms of the day's words in reverse order (20 to 11). Cover the entry except for the word itself, state your synonym ("fastidious means fussy"), then uncover the synonym to check your response. Write down troublesome words in your 2400 notebook.

| 11 | pastoral | *adj.* rural, nonurban | SYNONYM | *rural* |
| | SENTENCE | The Grapes of Wrath takes place in pastoral settings. | | |
| 12 | rustic | *adj.* rural, nonurban | SYNONYM | *countryside* |
| | SENTENCE | "Rural" and "rustic" sound similar and mean similar things. | | |
| 13 | bucolic | *adj.* rural, nonurban | SYNONYM | *rural* |
| | SENTENCE | Many children like to frolic in bucolic places. | | |
| 14 | contemporary | *adj.* modern, current | SYNONYM | *current* |
| | SENTENCE | I like contemporary furniture rather than antiques. | | |

| 15 | capricious | *adj.* unpredictable, impulsive | SYNONYM | *changes mind* |
|---|---|---|---|---|
| | SENTENCE | *Mr. Harrington is <u>capricious</u> and always changes his mind.* | | |
| 16 | arduous | *adj.* laborious, strenuous, difficult | SYNONYM | *grueling* |
| | SENTENCE | *SAT prep is <u>arduous</u>.* | | |
| 17 | painstaking | *adj.* careful, thorough, meticulous | SYNONYM | *demanding* |
| | SENTENCE | *Any task that takes pains is <u>painstaking</u>.* | | |
| 18 | meticulous | *adj.* careful, detailed, scrupulous | SYNONYM | *very careful* |
| | SENTENCE | *Renee is <u>meticulous</u> about the seating arrangement.* | | |
| 19 | scrupulous | *adj.* careful, thorough, fastidious | SYNONYM | *thorough* |
| | SENTENCE | *You must be <u>scrupulous</u> when it comes to SAT vocab.* | | |
| 20 | fastidious | *adj.* excessively careful, fussy | SYNONYM | *fussy* |
| | SENTENCE | *My mom is <u>fastidious</u> about making sure my room is tidy.* | | |

## Step 4 ⌁ *Perform 2400 Review of previous days' words*

Because this is Day 2 of Week 1, quiz yourself on the synonyms from Day 1 (words 1–10). Write down troublesome words in your 2400 notebook.

| 1 | synthesize | *v.* create, produce | SYNONYM | *create* |
|---|---|---|---|---|
| | SENTENCE | *I just <u>synthesized</u> my own synonym.* | | |
| 2 | advocate | *v.* support; *n.* supporter | SYNONYM | *support* |
| | SENTENCE | *I <u>advocate</u> vegetarianism.* | | |
| 3 | dogmatic | *adj.* firm/rigid in beliefs | SYNONYM | *inflexible* |
| | SENTENCE | *I am not <u>dogmatic</u> about others' being vegetarian.* | | |
| 4 | deleterious | *adj.* harmful | SYNONYM | *harmful* |
| | SENTENCE | *To delete my computer's hard drive would be <u>deleterious</u>.* | | |
| 5 | ominous | *adj.* threatening, foreboding | SYNONYM | *sinister* |
| | SENTENCE | *A black cat is usually an <u>ominous</u> sign.* | | |
| 6 | foreboding | *adj.* threatening; *n.* apprehension | SYNONYM | *threatening* |
| | SENTENCE | *The dark clouds in the sky seem <u>foreboding</u>.* | | |
| 7 | apprehension | *n.* anxiety, fear | SYNONYM | *dread* |
| | SENTENCE | *The SAT causes a lot of students <u>apprehension</u>.* | | |
| 8 | magnanimous | *adj.* noble, generous, giving | SYNONYM | *dignified* |
| | SENTENCE | *Mother Teresa was <u>magnanimous</u>.* | | |

| 9 | pedantic | *adj.* academic, worried about rules | SYNONYM | *academic* |
|---|---|---|---|---|
| | SENTENCE | *Ms. Robinson is very <u>pedantic</u> about her English class.* | | |
| 10 | rural | *adj.* nonurban, in the country | SYNONYM | *farmlike* |
| | SENTENCE | *I grew up in Las Vegas, which is definitely not <u>rural</u>.* | | |

**Step 3**
Master
WYPAD and
other keys
to success on
SAT Reading
..........
**270**

### Step 5 ⟋ *Perform 2400 Review of previous weeks' words*

Because this is a day on which you're memorizing new vocabulary words, don't review words from previous weeks. (Since this is Week 1, there are no previous weeks anyway.) On your designated *2400 Review* days, however, review all the words/synonyms from previous weeks. Write down troublesome words in your 2400 notebook.

## Vocabulary 2400 list

You are now ready to tackle the *Vocabulary 2400* list. Don't let the size of the list intimidate you; break it down into manageable chunks. I memorized *all* of these words during my SAT preparation, and many of them appeared on the actual test. Because the SAT is a standardized test, it is extremely likely that many of these words will appear on your SAT too!

### Vocabulary 2400 — Set 1

| | | |
|---|---|---|
| 1 | synthesize | *v.* create, produce |
| 2 | advocate | *v.* support; *n.* supporter |
| 3 | dogmatic | *adj.* firm/rigid in beliefs |
| 4 | deleterious | *adj.* harmful |
| 5 | foreboding | *adj.* threatening; *n.* apprehension |
| 6 | ominous | *adj.* threatening, foreboding |
| 7 | apprehension | *n.* anxiety, fear |
| 8 | magnanimous | *adj.* noble, generous, giving |
| 9 | pedantic | *adj.* academic, worried about rules |
| 10 | rural | *adj.* nonurban, in the country |
| 11 | pastoral | *adj.* rural, nonurban |
| 12 | rustic | *adj.* rural, nonurban |
| 13 | bucolic | *adj.* rural, nonurban |
| 14 | contemporary | *adj.* modern, current |
| 15 | capricious | *adj.* unpredictable, impulsive |
| 16 | arduous | *adj.* laborious, strenuous, difficult |
| 17 | painstaking | *adj.* careful, thorough, meticulous |
| 18 | meticulous | *adj.* careful, detailed, scrupulous |
| 19 | scrupulous | *adj.* careful, thorough, fastidious |
| 20 | fastidious | *adj.* excessively careful, fussy |

| 1 | belittle | *v.* degrade, demean |
| 2 | abase | *v.* belittle, degrade, demean |
| 3 | disparage | *v.* belittle, ridicule, mock |
| 4 | condescend | *v.* look down on, patronize |
| 5 | reprimand | *v.* criticize, lecture, reprove |
| 6 | admonish | *v.* reprimand, warn |
| 7 | condemn | *v.* criticize, censure, rebuke |
| 8 | censure | *v.* criticize, reprimand, condemn |
| 9 | decry | *v.* criticize, belittle, disparage |
| 10 | denounce | *v.* criticize, censure, condemn |
| 11 | disdain | *n.* scorn, contempt; *v.* despise |
| 12 | impugn | *v.* dispute the validity of, challenge |
| 13 | patronize | *v.* belittle, be condescending to |
| 14 | pejorative | *adj.* derogatory, negative |
| 15 | reproach | *n.* criticism; *v.* criticize, reprove |
| 16 | rebuke | *v.* reprimand, censure, reproach |
| 17 | scoff | *v.* ridicule, mock |
| 18 | reprove | *v.* criticize, rebuke |
| 19 | abhor | *v.* hate, detest |
| 20 | cynical | *adj.* pessimistic, distrustful |

| 1 | amiable | *adj.* friendly, amicable, sociable |
| 2 | affable | *adj.* friendly, genial, sociable |
| 3 | gregarious | *adj.* friendly, outgoing, sociable |
| 4 | congenial | *adj.* friendly, sociable |
| 5 | convivial | *adj.* welcoming, hospitable, friendly |
| 6 | cordial | *adj.* warm, pleasant, friendly |
| 7 | rapport | *n.* good relationship, bond |
| 8 | altruistic | *adj.* selfless, philanthropic |
| 9 | benevolent | *adj.* nice, kind, generous |
| 10 | benign | *adj.* harmless, gentle, mild |
| 11 | solicitous | *adj.* caring, considerate |
| 12 | alacrity | *n.* eagerness, enthusiasm |
| 13 | ebullient | *adj.* enthusiastic, excited, cheerful |
| 14 | effusive | *adj.* demonstrative, gushy |
| 15 | elation | *n.* happiness, joy, delight |
| 16 | enthralling | *adj.* captivating, enchanting |
| 17 | exuberant | *adj.* enthusiastic, lively, energetic |
| 18 | fervent | *adj.* passionate, ardent, avid |
| 19 | aesthetic | *adj.* artistic, relating to beauty |
| 20 | eclectic | *adj.* all-embracing, diverse |

**Step 3**
Master
WYPAD and
other keys
to success on
SAT Reading

272

## Vocabulary 2400 · Set 4

| | | |
|---|---|---|
| 1 | baneful | *adj.* harmful, destructive, deadly |
| 2 | eradicate | *v.* eliminate, destroy |
| 3 | exacerbate | *v.* worsen, aggravate, intensify |
| 4 | innocuous | *adj.* harmless, inoffensive |
| 5 | insidious | *adj.* sinister, menacing, ominous |
| 6 | machination | *n.* scheme, plot |
| 7 | pernicious | *adj.* evil, destructive, harmful |
| 8 | rancor | *n.* resentment, bitterness, malice |
| 9 | vitiate | *v.* make defective/inefficient |
| 10 | vulgar | *adj.* rude, crude, offensive |
| 11 | callous | *adj.* insensitive, heartless |
| 12 | effrontery | *n.* insolence, impudence, nerve |
| 13 | indignant | *adj.* angry, resentful |
| 14 | malice | *n.* hatred, ill will |
| 15 | nefarious | *adj.* evil, immoral |
| 16 | precarious | *adj.* risky, unstable, uncertain |
| 17 | disrepute | *n.* disgrace, discredit, notoriety |
| 18 | degenerate | *adj.* immoral, corrupt; *v.* deteriorate |
| 19 | accost | *v.* approach aggressively, confront |
| 20 | imminent | *adj.* approaching, about to occur |

## Vocabulary 2400 · Set 5

| | | |
|---|---|---|
| 1 | abridge | *v.* shorten, condense |
| 2 | curtail | *v.* limit, cut short |
| 3 | diminutive | *adj.* tiny, small, little |
| 4 | ephemeral | *adj.* short-lived, transient, fleeting |
| 5 | intermittent | *adj.* sporadic, fragmentary |
| 6 | laconic | *adj.* terse, brief, succinct |
| 7 | modicum | *n.* small amount |
| 8 | negligible | *adj.* insignificant, small, trivial |
| 9 | nominal | *adj.* insignificant, trivial |
| 10 | precipitous | *adj.* steep, abrupt, sudden |
| 11 | succinct | *adj.* concise, brief, pithy |
| 12 | terse | *adj.* brief, abrupt |
| 13 | transitory | *adj.* short-lived, fleeting |
| 14 | circumscribe | *v.* limit, restrict, enclose, confine |
| 15 | conditional | *adj.* restricted, contingent |
| 16 | debilitate | *v.* weaken |
| 17 | feeble | *adj.* weak, frail |
| 18 | futile | *adj.* useless, pointless, unsuccessful |
| 19 | tenuous | *adj.* fragile, feeble, weak |
| 20 | undermine | *v.* challenge, sabotage, erode |

## Vocabulary 2400 — Set 6

| 1 | prodigious | *adj.* large, vast |
| 2 | proximity | *n.* closeness, nearness |
| 3 | purveyor | *n.* supplier, vendor |
| 4 | opulent | *adj.* lavish, rich |
| 5 | affluence | *n.* wealth, prosperity, opulence |
| 6 | avarice | *n.* greed, materialism |
| 7 | dearth | *n.* lack, scarcity, famine |
| 8 | exorbitant | *adj.* excessive, very expensive |
| 9 | felicitous | *adj.* fortunate, blessed |
| 10 | gaudy | *adj.* showy, flashy, garish |
| 11 | insatiable | *adj.* voracious, greedy |
| 12 | insolvent | *adj.* broke, bankrupt |
| 13 | inundate | *v.* flood, overwhelm |
| 14 | serendipity | *n.* luck, happy chance |
| 15 | voracious | *adj.* ravenous, insatiable |
| 16 | aggregate | *v.* combine/group together |
| 17 | amalgamation | *n.* merger, mixture |
| 18 | supplant | *v.* replace |
| 19 | gluttony | *n.* greed, eating to excess |
| 20 | hedonistic | *adj.* pleasure-seeking |

## Vocabulary 2400 — Set 7

| 1 | arrogant | *adj.* conceited, self-important |
| 2 | haughty | *adj.* arrogant, conceited, proud |
| 3 | hubris | *n.* arrogance, excessive pride |
| 4 | ostentatious | *adj.* showy |
| 5 | pretentious | *adj.* pompous |
| 6 | salient | *adj.* striking, noticeable, prominent |
| 7 | smug | *adj.* self-satisfied, arrogant |
| 8 | supercilious | *adj.* arrogant, pompous |
| 9 | portentous | *adj.* pompous, ominous |
| 10 | descend | *v.* go down |
| 11 | superfluous | *adj.* extra, surplus, unnecessary |
| 12 | extraneous | *adj.* unnecessary, irrelevant |
| 13 | preeminent | *adj.* greatest, foremost, outstanding |
| 14 | prolific | *adj.* productive, abundant |
| 15 | adept | *adj.* expert, skilled, proficient |
| 16 | adroit | *adj.* skilled, clever |
| 17 | consummate | *adj.* highly skilled, perfect, complete |
| 18 | deft | *adj.* skilled, proficient, adroit |
| 19 | inept | *adj.* incompetent, unskilled |
| 20 | precedent | *n.* established example, model |

Step 3
Master
WYPAD and
other keys
to success on
SAT Reading
..........................
274

## Vocabulary 2400   Set 8

| | | |
|---|---|---|
| 1 | prudent | *adj.* careful, cautious, sensible |
| 2 | circumspect | *adj.* careful, cautious, prudent |
| 3 | conscientious | *adj.* careful, cautious, scrupulous |
| 4 | cursory | *adj.* hasty, quick |
| 5 | diligent | *adj.* hard-working, meticulous |
| 6 | onerous | *adj.* burdensome, arduous, difficult |
| 7 | perfunctory | *adj.* cursory, brief, hasty |
| 8 | peruse | *v.* read carefully, scrutinize |
| 9 | assiduous | *adj.* meticulous, careful, diligent |
| 10 | punctilious | *adj.* meticulous, assiduous |
| 11 | remiss | *adj.* careless, negligent |
| 12 | vigilant | *adj.* watchful, alert, attentive |
| 13 | wary | *adj.* careful, cautious, suspicious |
| 14 | fidelity | *n.* faithfulness, loyalty |
| 15 | foreshadow | *v.* portend, warn of |
| 16 | avow | *v.* confess, affirm |
| 17 | corroborate | *v.* support, confirm, substantiate |
| 18 | fortify | *v.* strengthen, reinforce |
| 19 | foster | *v.* develop, nurture, support |
| 20 | insinuate | *v.* imply, suggest, hint |

## Vocabulary 2400   Set 9

| | | |
|---|---|---|
| 1 | bureaucracy | *n.* administrative system with many rules |
| 2 | demagogue | *n.* political agitator |
| 3 | diplomatic | *adj.* political, tactful |
| 4 | egalitarian | *adj.* democratic, promoting equality |
| 5 | elitist | *adj.* snobbish, arrogant |
| 6 | inferior | *adj.* lower in rank, substandard |
| 7 | mandate | *n.* order, command |
| 8 | manifesto | *n.* proclamation, political platform |
| 9 | mercenary | *n.* hired soldier |
| 10 | monarch | *n.* king or queen, absolute ruler |
| 11 | nepotism | *n.* favoritism toward relatives |
| 12 | officious | *adj.* bossy, self-important |
| 13 | pacifist | *n.* peace-lover, antiwar advocate |
| 14 | partisan | *adj.* biased, taking political sides |
| 15 | perquisite | *n.* perk, a right based on position |
| 16 | propaganda | *n.* bogus publicity, misinformation |
| 17 | relegate | *v.* downgrade, demote |
| 18 | sedition | *n.* rebellion, treason |
| 19 | autonomous | *adj.* independent, self-sufficient |
| 20 | sovereign | *adj.* independent, autonomous |

## Vocabulary 2400 — Set 10

| | | |
|---|---|---|
| 1 | artificial | *adj.* fake, unnatural |
| 2 | belie | *v.* contradict, show to be false |
| 3 | chicanery | *n.* trickery, deceit |
| 4 | delude | *v.* deceive, mislead, cheat |
| 5 | disillusioned | *adj.* disappointed, disenchanted |
| 6 | disingenuous | *adj.* insincere, deceitful, untruthful |
| 7 | duplicity | *n.* deceit, double-dealing |
| 8 | embellish | *v.* exaggerate, decorate, adorn |
| 9 | fabrication | *n.* lie, falsehood |
| 10 | guile | *n.* cunning, slyness, craftiness |
| 11 | mendacity | *n.* dishonesty, deceit, lie |
| 12 | perfidy | *n.* treachery, disloyalty, duplicity |
| 13 | spurious | *adj.* false, fake |
| 14 | candid | *adj.* frank, sincere, honest |
| 15 | tenet | *n.* belief, principle, precept |
| 16 | conviction | *n.* belief, principle, tenet |
| 17 | immutable | *adj.* unchangeable, incontrovertible |
| 18 | anomaly | *n.* deviation, abnormality |
| 19 | aberration | *n.* deviation, anomaly |
| 20 | orthodox | *adj.* conventional, traditional |

## Vocabulary 2400 — Set 11

| | | |
|---|---|---|
| 1 | aloof | *adj.* distant, unconcerned |
| 2 | indifferent | *adj.* uninterested, uncaring |
| 3 | apathetic | *adj.* indifferent, uncaring |
| 4 | detachment | *n.* aloofness, indifference |
| 5 | devoid | *adj.* lacking, free from |
| 6 | elusive | *adj.* hard to find/achieve, evasive |
| 7 | estranged | *adj.* alienated, distant, separated |
| 8 | phlegmatic | *adj.* calm, placid |
| 9 | recluse | *n.* hermit, loner |
| 10 | reticent | *adj.* reserved, withdrawn |
| 11 | taciturn | *adj.* reserved, silent, reticent |
| 12 | contempt | *n.* disdain, disrespect, disregard |
| 13 | deferential | *adj.* respectful, reverent, admiring |
| 14 | flippant | *adj.* facetious, irreverent |
| 15 | impudent | *adj.* insolent, disrespectful, rude |
| 16 | insolence | *n.* disrespect, impudence |
| 17 | venerate | *v.* respect, honor, revere |
| 18 | ameliorate | *v.* improve, make better, reform |
| 19 | ascend | *v.* go up, rise, climb |
| 20 | bolster | *v.* support, boost, strengthen |

Step 3
Master
WYPAD and
other keys
to success on
SAT Reading

276

## Vocabulary 2400  Set 12

| 1 | exonerate | *v.* absolve, acquit, set free |
| 2 | impartial | *adj.* unbiased, fair, objective |
| 3 | objective | *adj.* unbiased, impartial |
| 4 | nullify | *v.* cancel, annul, invalidate |
| 5 | culpable | *adj.* guilty, deserving of blame |
| 6 | reprehensible | *adj.* culpable, guilty |
| 7 | tenable | *adj.* defensible, plausible |
| 8 | vindicate | *v.* justify, free from guilt/blame |
| 9 | totalitarian | *adj.* autocratic, authoritarian |
| 10 | oppressive | *adj.* domineering, harsh |
| 11 | tyrannical | *adj.* oppressive, autocratic |
| 12 | pompous | *adj.* self-important, pretentious |
| 13 | bombastic | *adj.* pompous, pretentious |
| 14 | adage | *n.* proverb, aphorism, saying |
| 15 | discourse | *n.* formal discussion/conversation |
| 16 | disjointed | *adj.* rambling, incoherent |
| 17 | loquacious | *adj.* talkative, wordy |
| 18 | garrulous | *adj.* talkative, chatty |
| 19 | verbose | *adj.* wordy, loquacious, garrulous |
| 20 | brevity | *n.* conciseness, shortness |

## Vocabulary 2400  Set 13

| 1 | cogent | *adj.* convincing, compelling, logical |
| 2 | concord | *n.* agreement, accord, harmony |
| 3 | debunk | *v.* expose, show to be false |
| 4 | demur | *v.* object, voice reservations |
| 5 | deride | *v.* ridicule, mock, scoff at |
| 6 | deter | *v.* stop, prevent, discourage |
| 7 | detract | *v.* belittle, devalue, lessen |
| 8 | diatribe | *n.* tirade, verbal attack |
| 9 | digress | *v.* deviate, stray, get off the subject |
| 10 | dispel | *v.* dismiss, make disappear |
| 11 | divisive | *adj.* causing disagreement |
| 12 | dubious | *adj.* doubtful, unsure, uncertain |
| 13 | myopic | *adj.* narrow-minded, short-sighted |
| 14 | obstinate | *adj.* stubborn, inflexible |
| 15 | polarize | *v.* divide into contrasting groups |
| 16 | pragmatic | *adj.* practical, sensible |
| 17 | presumption | *n.* supposition, assumption |
| 18 | query | *n.* inquiry, question |
| 19 | quizzical | *adj.* questioning, curious |
| 20 | reconnaissance | *n.* investigation, exploration |

## Vocabulary 2400 Set 14

| | | |
|---|---|---|
| 1 | refute | *v.* prove wrong, disprove, counter |
| 2 | rhetoric | *n.* persuasive/effective language |
| 3 | tangential | *adj.* mostly irrelevant, peripheral |
| 4 | tirade | *n.* harangue, rant, diatribe |
| 5 | divulge | *v.* reveal, make known |
| 6 | ambiguous | *adj.* unclear, imprecise, arguable |
| 7 | ambivalent | *adj.* unsure, indecisive |
| 8 | delineate | *v.* describe, define, explain |
| 9 | diaphanous | *adj.* almost transparent, translucent |
| 10 | discern | *v.* distinguish, tell the difference |
| 11 | discriminate | *v.* differentiate, distinguish |
| 12 | edify | *v.* enlighten, inform, instruct |
| 13 | elucidate | *v.* clarify, make clear, explain |
| 14 | enlighten | *v.* inform, make clear, edify |
| 15 | epitome | *n.* essence, embodiment |
| 16 | equivocal | *adj.* ambiguous, vague |
| 17 | impervious | *adj.* impenetrable, impermeable |
| 18 | incisive | *adj.* clear, insightful |
| 19 | lucid | *adj.* clear, coherent |
| 20 | induction | *n.* drawing a conclusion based on evidence |

## Vocabulary 2400 Set 15

| | | |
|---|---|---|
| 1 | consecrate | *v.* bless, sanctify, make sacred |
| 2 | desecrate | *v.* defile, violate, debase |
| 3 | iconoclast | *n.* skeptic, heretic, dissenter |
| 4 | ignoble | *adj.* dishonorable, shameful |
| 5 | invocation | *n.* chant, spell, incantation |
| 6 | blasphemy | *n.* irreverence, profanity |
| 7 | prophecy | *n.* divine prediction, foretelling |
| 8 | portent | *n.* bad sign, omen |
| 9 | renaissance | *n.* rebirth, revival of the arts |
| 10 | reverence | *n.* respect, veneration |
| 11 | sanctimonious | *adj.* hypocritically devout/pious |
| 12 | surfeit | *n.* excess, overindulgence |
| 13 | assimilate | *v.* integrate, absorb, incorporate |
| 14 | didactic | *adj.* educational, relating to teaching |
| 15 | covert | *adj.* secretive, clandestine |
| 16 | furtive | *adj.* secretive, surreptitious |
| 17 | latent | *adj.* hidden, dormant |
| 18 | opaque | *adj.* obscure, difficult to see through |
| 19 | clandestine | *adj.* secretive, stealthy, covert |
| 20 | surreptitious | *adj.* furtive, sneaky, covert |

Step 3
Master
WYPAD and
other keys
to success on
SAT Reading
..................
278

## Vocabulary 2400    Set 16

| | | |
|---|---|---|
| 1 | insipid | *adj.* boring, bland, dull |
| 2 | jaded | *adj.* bored, tired |
| 3 | monotonous | *adj.* boring, dull |
| 4 | mundane | *adj.* ordinary, boring, dull |
| 5 | banal | *adj.* commonplace, trite |
| 6 | platitude | *n.* cliché, banality |
| 7 | prosaic | *adj.* ordinary, mundane, banal |
| 8 | soporific | *adj.* boring, dull, sleep-inducing |
| 9 | trite | *adj.* overused, hackneyed |
| 10 | aphorism | *n.* cliché, adage, proverb |
| 11 | vapid | *adj.* dull, bland, insipid |
| 12 | nebulous | *adj.* unclear, vague, hazy |
| 13 | obscure | *adj.* unclear, hidden, puzzling |
| 14 | disseminate | *v.* distribute, circulate, spread |
| 15 | hackneyed | *adj.* overused, trite |
| 16 | incorrigible | *adj.* habitual, impossible to change |
| 17 | indelible | *adj.* permanent, unfading |
| 18 | inveterate | *adj.* habitual |
| 19 | perennial | *adj.* perpetual, endless, recurring |
| 20 | pervasive | *adj.* extensive, present everywhere |

## Vocabulary 2400    Set 17

| | | |
|---|---|---|
| 1 | daunting | *v.* intimidating, frightening, scary |
| 2 | gallantry | *n.* bravery, courage, daring |
| 3 | resolute | *adj.* determined, firm, unyielding |
| 4 | steadfast | *adj.* resolute, unwavering, loyal |
| 5 | valor | *n.* bravery, courage |
| 6 | vanquish | *v.* conquer, defeat |
| 7 | byzantine | *adj.* complex, convoluted, intricate |
| 8 | implausible | *adj.* improbable, unlikely |
| 9 | ironic | *adj.* paradoxical, incongruous |
| 10 | juxtapose | *v.* put side by side, contrast |
| 11 | misnomer | *n.* incorrect name/term |
| 12 | ostensible | *adj.* apparent, supposed |
| 13 | palpable | *adj.* tangible, obvious, touchable |
| 14 | tactile | *adj.* concrete, tangible, palpable |
| 15 | covet | *v.* yearn for, crave, desire to have |
| 16 | ascertain | *v.* make certain of, establish |
| 17 | libel | *n.* slander, defamation; *v.* slander, defame |
| 18 | notorious | *adj.* infamous, scandalous |
| 19 | defame | *v.* libel, slander, insult |
| 20 | slander | *n.* defamation, libel |

## Vocabulary 2400 — Set 18

| | | |
|---|---|---|
| 1 | mitigate | *v.* moderate, alleviate, lessen, ease |
| 2 | moderate | *adj.* restrained, temperate; *v.* curb |
| 3 | mollify | *v.* appease, mitigate, pacify, soften |
| 4 | palliative | *adj.* soothing, calming, sedative |
| 5 | placid | *adj.* peaceful, calm, easygoing |
| 6 | subordinate | *adj.* inferior, secondary, lesser |
| 7 | temperate | *adj.* moderate, mild |
| 8 | tranquil | *adj.* peaceful, calm, serene |
| 9 | waning | *adj.* diminishing, fading |
| 10 | intrinsic | *adj.* inherent, innate, essential |
| 11 | progeny | *n.* offspring |
| 12 | proliferate | *v.* reproduce, grow, propagate |
| 13 | redolent | *adj.* fragrant, suggestive |
| 14 | indigenous | *adj.* native |
| 15 | supple | *adj.* flexible, bending, lithe |
| 16 | liberate | *v.* free, release |
| 17 | dormant | *adj.* inactive, asleep, resting, latent |
| 18 | incredulous | *adj.* disbelieving, skeptical, doubtful |
| 19 | indolent | *adj.* lazy, idle, lethargic |
| 20 | neglect | *v.* abandon, ignore, fail to do |

## Vocabulary 2400 — Set 19

| | | |
|---|---|---|
| 1 | bereavement | *n.* grief, sorrow, mourning |
| 2 | desolate | *adj.* isolated, alone, depressed |
| 3 | hermit | *n.* loner, recluse |
| 4 | lament | *v.* grieve, mourn |
| 5 | lugubrious | *adj.* gloomy, mournful, sad |
| 6 | melancholy | *adj.* sad, depressed, gloomy |
| 7 | morose | *adj.* gloomy, miserable, depressed |
| 8 | morbid | *adj.* unhealthy, gruesome, morose |
| 9 | solemn | *adj.* stately, grave, serious, stern |
| 10 | sullen | *adj.* gloomy, morose |
| 11 | repeal | *v.* cancel, rescind, annul |
| 12 | repudiate | *v.* reject, deny |
| 13 | rescind | *v.* cancel, withdraw |
| 14 | caustic | *adj.* abrasive, sarcastic, scathing |
| 15 | acrid | *adj.* bitter, pungent, caustic, harsh |
| 16 | acrimony | *n.* bitterness, animosity |
| 17 | corrosive | *adj.* abrasive, damaging |
| 18 | confound | *v.* confuse, baffle, surprise |
| 19 | convoluted | *adj.* complicated, hard to follow |
| 20 | inane | *adj.* silly, ridiculous, absurd |

Step 3
Master
WYPAD and
other keys
to success on
SAT Reading
..........................
**280**

**Vocabulary 2400**  **Set 20**

| | | |
|---|---|---|
| 1 | anachronistic | *adj.* inappropriate to a time period |
| 2 | antiquated | *adj.* outdated, obsolete |
| 3 | archaic | *adj.* ancient, old, outdated |
| 4 | cosmopolitan | *adj.* multicultural, international |
| 5 | encroach | *v.* trespass, infringe, intrude |
| 6 | itinerant | *adj.* traveling, wandering |
| 7 | respite | *n.* rest, break |
| 8 | arid | *adj.* dry, barren |
| 9 | flotsam | *n.* ship wreckage, debris |
| 10 | contiguous | *adj.* adjoining, adjacent |
| 11 | derivative | *adj.* unoriginal, imitative |
| 12 | acquiesce | *v.* agree, accept, comply |
| 13 | docile | *adj.* passive, submissive, compliant |
| 14 | abstract | *adj.* conceptual, not physical |
| 15 | compulsory | *adj.* mandatory, obligatory, required |
| 16 | innate | *adj.* present at birth, intrinsic |
| 17 | apprentice | *n.* trainee, novice, beginner |
| 18 | dilettante | *n.* amateur, novice |
| 19 | gaffe | *n.* mistake, error, blunder |
| 20 | naive | *adj.* inexperienced, unsophisticated |

**Vocabulary 2400**  **Set 21**

| | | |
|---|---|---|
| 1 | catalyst | *n.* stimulus, spur, impetus |
| 2 | languid | *adj.* relaxed, lethargic, lazy |
| 3 | nonchalant | *adj.* casual, relaxed |
| 4 | cantankerous | *adj.* irritable, bad-tempered |
| 5 | exasperation | *n.* irritation, annoyance |
| 6 | impetuous | *adj.* impulsive, hasty, reckless, rash |
| 7 | petulant | *adj.* irritable, bad-tempered |
| 8 | vex | *v.* irritate, annoy, irk |
| 9 | plight | *n.* predicament, difficult situation |
| 10 | quagmire | *n.* swamp, predicament, quandary |
| 11 | repugnant | *adj.* disgusting, repulsive, offensive |
| 12 | motley | *adj.* colorful, varied, diverse |
| 13 | variegated | *adj.* diverse, multicolored |
| 14 | ornate | *adj.* elaborately decorated, fancy |
| 15 | versatile | *adj.* adaptable, multipurpose |
| 16 | empathy | *n.* sensitivity to another's situation |
| 17 | empirical | *adj.* based on observation/evidence |
| 18 | ineffable | *adj.* indescribable, inexpressible |
| 19 | introspective | *adj.* inward-looking, thoughtful |
| 20 | nostalgia | *n.* emotional recollection of the past |

## Vocabulary 2400  Set 22

| | | |
|---|---|---|
| 1 | jocular | *adj.* joking, humorous |
| 2 | levity | *n.* lightheartedness, liveliness |
| 3 | commend | *v.* praise, compliment, applaud |
| 4 | exalt | *v.* praise, revere, pay homage to |
| 5 | extol | *v.* praise enthusiastically, exalt |
| 6 | laud | *v.* praise, commend, extol |
| 7 | paragon | *n.* best example, model, archetype |
| 8 | burgeon | *v.* grow quickly, flourish, thrive |
| 9 | jubilation | *n.* joy, elation |
| 10 | provocative | *adj.* annoying, controversial |
| 11 | rousing | *adj.* stimulating, inspiring |
| 12 | enigma | *n.* mystery, puzzle |
| 13 | cryptic | *adj.* mysterious, puzzling |
| 14 | esoteric | *adj.* mysterious, obscure, cryptic |
| 15 | arcane | *adj.* mysterious, cryptic |
| 16 | cajole | *v.* persuade, coax |
| 17 | coerce | *v.* force, pressure |
| 18 | complacent | *adj.* self-satisfied, smug, content |
| 19 | supplement | *v.* add to, increase, augment |
| 20 | miscreant | *n.* criminal, wrongdoer, delinquent |

## Vocabulary 2400  Set 23

| | | |
|---|---|---|
| 1 | belligerent | *adj.* aggressive, combative, militant |
| 2 | quarrel | *v.* argue, fight |
| 3 | pugnacious | *adj.* aggressive, quarrelsome, hostile |
| 4 | salvo | *n.* barrage, sudden burst |
| 5 | incongruous | *adj.* mismatched, incompatible |
| 6 | paucity | *n.* scarcity, lack |
| 7 | destitute | *adj.* poor, impoverished |
| 8 | penurious | *adj.* poor, impoverished, destitute |
| 9 | indigent | *adj.* poor, impoverished, destitute |
| 10 | arbitrary | *adj.* capricious, random, illogical |
| 11 | erratic | *adj.* unpredictable, often changing |
| 12 | fickle | *adj.* changeable, volatile, capricious |
| 13 | mercurial | *adj.* excitable, temperamental |
| 14 | sporadic | *adj.* random, infrequent |
| 15 | whimsical | *adj.* fanciful, eccentric, quirky |
| 16 | conform | *v.* follow, comply, meet, match |
| 17 | conventional | *adj.* normal, usual, traditional |
| 18 | stringent | *adj.* strict, rigorous, demanding |
| 19 | tenacious | *adj.* persistent, stubborn, inflexible |
| 20 | flounder | *v.* struggle, have difficulty |

Step 3
Master
WYPAD and
other keys
to success on
SAT Reading
..................
**282**

## Vocabulary 2400   Set 24

| | | |
|---|---|---|
| 1 | austerity | *n.* strictness, sternness, frugality |
| 2 | crude | *adj.* simple, basic, rudimentary |
| 3 | forbearance | *n.* tolerance, patience, restraint |
| 4 | humility | *n.* humbleness, modesty |
| 5 | husbandry | *n.* farm management, thrift |
| 6 | rudimentary | *adj.* basic, simple |
| 7 | astute | *adj.* smart, sharp, clever |
| 8 | erudite | *adj.* educated, learned, scholarly |
| 9 | shrewd | *adj.* astute, sharp, perceptive |
| 10 | perspicacious | *adj.* insightful, perceptive, shrewd |
| 11 | sagacious | *adj.* wise, perceptive, shrewd |
| 12 | trenchant | *adj.* incisive, sharp, insightful |
| 13 | anarchy | *n.* lawlessness, chaos, disorder |
| 14 | inhibit | *v.* hinder, slow down, prevent |
| 15 | prohibit | *v.* forbid, ban, prevent |
| 16 | preclude | *v.* prevent, stop, prohibit |
| 17 | stagnate | *v.* languish, be sluggish, decline |
| 18 | suppress | *v.* subdue, stop, hold back, conceal |
| 19 | potent | *adj.* powerful, strong, convincing |
| 20 | robust | *adj.* healthy, strong, vigorous |

## Vocabulary 2400   Set 25

| | | |
|---|---|---|
| 1 | conflagration | *n.* fire, blaze, inferno |
| 2 | conjecture | *n.* guess, speculation, theory |
| 3 | corollary | *n.* consequence, result |
| 4 | repercussion | *n.* consequence, ramification |
| 5 | correlation | *n.* connection, relationship |
| 6 | deliberate | *adj.* intentional, willful, on purpose |
| 7 | dichotomy | *n.* contrast/division between two things |
| 8 | harmony | *n.* agreement, balance, symmetry |
| 9 | cacophony | *n.* noise, racket, discord |
| 10 | inclination | *n.* tendency, leaning |
| 11 | penchant | *n.* liking, preference |
| 12 | predilection | *n.* liking, fondness, preference |
| 13 | propensity | *n.* tendency, inclination |
| 14 | antagonist | *n.* opponent, enemy, adversary |
| 15 | trivial | *adj.* unimportant, petty, small |
| 16 | frivolous | *adj.* superficial, facetious, trivial |
| 17 | relinquish | *v.* abandon, give up, stop |
| 18 | phobic | *adj.* fearful |
| 19 | eccentric | *adj.* unconventional, strange, odd |
| 20 | idiosyncratic | *adj.* peculiar, odd, eccentric |

## Answer key for practice problem set · *Order of difficulty*

1. B
2. B
3. A
4. None
5. C
6. None
7. B
8. C
9. None
10. B

## Answer key for practice problem sets · *Sentence completion*

### WYPAD

1. E
2. C
3. B
4. D
5. A
6. A
7. C
8. E

### Work one at a time

1. A
2. B
3. A
4. C
5. A
6. B
7. C

### Fill in the exact same word

1. C
2. C
3. C
4. C
5. B
6. E

### Fill in the exact opposite word

1. E
2. D
3. E
4. B

### Fill in +/−

1. C
2. A
3. E
4. E

### Identify the double-blank relationship

1. B
2. C
3. D
4. A

## Short standard passages

1. D
2. B
3. D
4. E
5. E
6. C
7. E
8. C
9. A
10. D

## Medium standard passages

1. C
2. B
3. C
4. D
5. D
6. B
7. E
8. B
9. D
10. B
11. C
12. A
13. B
14. A
15. C

## Long standard passages

1. E
2. A
3. E
4. C
5. A
6. C
7. B
8. D
9. C

10. D
11. E
12. A
13. B
14. C
15. D
16. B
17. A
18. B
19. B
20. E
21. D
22. B
23. A
24. C
25. D

## Set of short comparison passages

1. A
2. E
3. B
4. B
5. E

## Set of long comparison passages

1. B
2. A
3. C
4. E
5. C
6. A
7. E
8. C
9. E
10. D
11. A
12. B
13. B

# Use unconventional methods to score high on SAT Math

Which of the following statements describes you best?

- ◄ Your bedroom is filled with math awards and trophies; SAT Math won't be a problem.
- ◄ You breeze through the first half of an SAT Math section, then stumble over more complex problems later.
- ◄ You cringe every time you encounter an SAT Math question.

No matter which of these statements applies to you, you can ace SAT Math. Why? Because SAT Math is simpler and easier than high school math, including arithmetic, algebra, and geometry.

In high school, teachers expect you to know specific formulas and concepts they cover in class. However, since high school math courses vary from region to region and from teacher to teacher, SAT test writers can't expect students to know specific formulas. This means that you don't need to memorize any particular material from your high school math courses as you prepare for SAT Math. In fact, each math section begins with the information chart reproduced at the bottom of this page.

Of course, you still need to have a basic understanding of arithmetic, algebra, and geometry in order to ace SAT Math. The key word here is "basic." You don't need to know specific mathematical concepts, such as how to prove a theorem in geometry. As long as you have completed courses in arithmetic, algebra, and geometry, you should have enough basic knowledge for SAT Math.

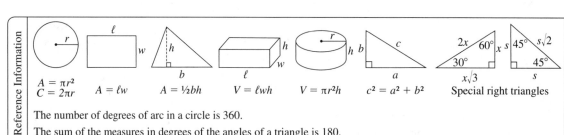

_(Reference Information)_

$A = \pi r^2$
$C = 2\pi r$  $A = \ell w$  $A = \frac{1}{2}bh$  $V = \ell wh$  $V = \pi r^2 h$  $c^2 = a^2 + b^2$  Special right triangles

The number of degrees of arc in a circle is 360.
The sum of the measures in degrees of the angles of a triangle is 180.

## SAT Math question types

There are two major types of SAT Math questions. The same set of *Math 2400 Strategies* applies to both types.

**Step 4**
Use
unconventional
methods
to score high
on SAT Math
.........................
**286**

1. **Multiple-choice questions** These questions offer five answer choices.
2. **Student-produced response questions** These questions offer no answer options; instead, you fill in your answer on a special section of the answer sheet.

Unlike a multiple-choice question, a student-produced response question may have several correct answers. For example, a question may ask for one *possible* value of *x*, which implies that there could be more than one correct answer to the question. You only need to fill in one of the correct answers to receive full credit.

If you answer a student-produced response question incorrectly, ¼ point isn't subtracted from your SAT raw score, in contrast to all other questions on the SAT. The SAT calculates your incorrect answer as +0, which is equivalent to leaving it blank. Because you won't be penalized, it's in your best interest to guess.

## Directions

Read the directions for SAT Math questions now so that you don't waste time reading them during the actual test.

The two boxes below appear at the beginning of each SAT Math section. The box at the bottom of page 287 appears before the SAT student-produced response section.

---

Notes

1. The use of a calculator is permitted.
2. All numbers used are real numbers.
3. Figures that accompany problems in this test are intended to provide information useful in solving the problems. They are drawn as accurately as possible EXCEPT when it is stated in a specific problem that the figure is not drawn to scale. All figures lie in a plane unless otherwise indicated.
4. Unless otherwise specified, the domain of any function *f* is assumed to be the set of all real numbers *x* for which $f(x)$ is a real number.

---

Reference Information

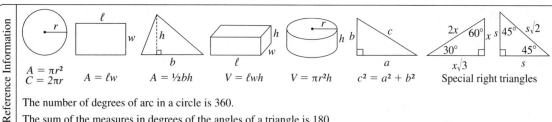

$A = \pi r^2$
$C = 2\pi r$
$A = \ell w$
$A = \frac{1}{2}bh$
$V = \ell wh$
$V = \pi r^2 h$
$c^2 = a^2 + b^2$
Special right triangles

The number of degrees of arc in a circle is 360.
The sum of the measures in degrees of the angles of a triangle is 180.

# Directions for SAT Math multiple-choice questions

> **Directions:** Solve each of the following problems, using any available space in your test booklet for scratchwork. When you have selected the answer you think is best, fill in the corresponding circle on the answer sheet.

# Directions for SAT Math student-produced response questions

> **Directions:** For student-produced response questions, use the grids at the bottom of the answer sheet page on which you have answered the multiple-choice math questions. Mark the grids as shown in the examples below.

---

**Directions: For student-produced response questions 9–18, use the grids at the bottom of the answer sheet page on which you have answered questions 1–8.**

Each of the remaining 10 questions requires you to solve the problem and enter your answer by marking the circles in the special grid, as shown in the examples below. You may use any available space for scratchwork.

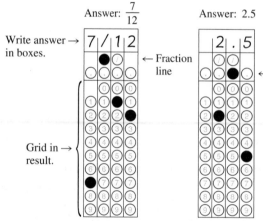

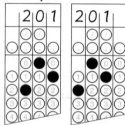

**Note:** You may start your answers in any column, space permitting. Columns not needed should be left blank.

- Mark no more than one circle in any column.

- Because the answer sheet will be machine-scored, **you will receive credit only if the circles are filled in correctly**.

- Although not required, it is suggested that you write your answer in the boxes at the top of the columns to help you fill in the circles accurately.

- Some problems may have more than one correct answer. In such cases, grid only one answer.

- No question has a negative answer.

- **Mixed numbers** such as $3\frac{1}{2}$ must be gridded as 3.5 or 7/2. (If $\boxed{3\,1\,/\,2}$ is gridded, it will be interpreted as $\frac{31}{2}$, not $3\frac{1}{2}$.)

- **Decimal answers:** If you obtain a decimal answer with more digits than the grid can accommodate, it may be either rounded or truncated, but it must fill the entire grid. For example, if you obtain an answer such as 0.6666..., you should record your result as .666 or .667. **A less accurate value such as .66 or .67 will be scored as incorrect.** Acceptable ways to grid $\frac{2}{3}$ are:

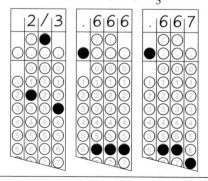

All student-produced response answers must fit in the four-column grid, as shown in the box at the bottom of page 287. The following types of answers are therefore impossible:

- ◄ A number with more than four digits
- ◄ A negative number
- ◄ An irrational number

If your answer is one of these types of numbers, you have made a mistake and should rework the problem.

## Format

There are 54 math questions in three sections on the SAT. If an SAT test has four math sections rather than three, one of the four sections is a "variable" section and doesn't count toward your score; it is used for diagnostic test purposes only.

The three math sections are organized as follows.

- ◄ A 25-minute section
  - 20 multiple-choice questions
- ◄ A 25-minute section
  - 8 multiple-choice questions
  - 10 student-produced response questions
- ◄ A 20-minute section
  - 16 multiple-choice questions

# Math 2400 Strategies

You don't need to be a whiz at arithmetic, geometry, and algebra to succeed in SAT Math. *Math 2400 Strategies* offer key approaches, many of which you probably didn't learn in high school. Unlike most high school math exams, SAT Math includes primarily multiple-choice questions, and it rewards students who can recognize patterns, uncover "hidden" concepts, and solve math questions using unconventional methods. *Math 2400 Strategies* focus on solving SAT Math questions in the most efficient way possible. Most high school students have been programmed to approach math questions in the conventional way, which is rarely the most efficient way for the SAT. Once you begin to instinctively solve questions using *Math 2400 Strategies*, you will succeed in SAT Math.

## Math 2400 Strategies

1 · Use order of difficulty to your advantage
2 · Write, don't visualize
3 · Avoid the calculator
4 · Circle the unknown
5 · Check your work as you go
6 · Do the first step
7 · Plug in numbers (PIN)
8 · Test answer choices (TAC)
9 · Simplify impractical problems
10 · Label givens
11 · Draw a picture
12 · Know your angles
13 · Know your triangles
14 · Know your circles
15 · Know your graphs

These 15 strategies apply to all SAT Math questions and concepts. You should use *Math 2400 Strategies 1* through *5* on every SAT Math question you tackle. *Math 2400 Strategies 6* through *15* are specific tactics that are applied to particular question types.

## Math 2400 Strategy 1 *Use order of difficulty to your advantage*

SAT Math questions are arranged in order of difficulty. The first questions in each section are easy; most test takers answer them correctly. Difficult questions that most students answer incorrectly appear at the end of the section. In the SAT Math section that includes 8 multiple-choice questions and 10 student-produced response questions, the two types of questions are grouped separately. The first few multiple-choice questions are easy, and the last few are hard. Then the order of difficulty is reset, so that the first few student-produced response questions are easy and the last few are hard.

Order of difficulty in SAT Math is useful on two types of problems:

1. Easy questions, which typically have obvious answers and are quickly and easily solved
2. Hard questions, which typically have answers that are not obvious and are difficult and time-consuming to solve

**Step 1** — *Read an easy question (early in the section)*

> If $1/7 + 1/8 + 1/9 < 1/x + 1/8 + 1/9$, then $x$ could be which of the following?
>
> (A) 6
> (B) 7
> (C) 8
> (D) 9
> (E) 10

**Step 2** — *Begin solving*

$1/7 + 1/8 + 1/9 = ?$

Common denominator $\rightarrow 7 \times 8 \times 9 = 504$

**Step 3** — *Use order of difficulty to your advantage*

Because this is an easy SAT Math question, the solution should be quick and easy. A fraction with a denominator of 504 indicates that this is probably not the simplest method to solve this question.

**Step 4** — *Try another solution*

The SAT rewards students who recognize the big picture. Both sides of the inequality have common terms that can be subtracted out.

$$1/7 + 1/8 + 1/9 < 1/x + 1/8 + 1/9$$
$$\underline{\phantom{1/7}- 1/8 - 1/9 \qquad - 1/8 - 1/9}$$
$$1/7 \qquad\qquad < 1/x$$

$x$ must be less than 7.

Select (A) as your answer choice.

**Step 1** — *Read a hard question (late in the section)*

> $$2, 4, 8, 16, \ldots$$
>
> In the geometric sequence above, 2 is the first term. What is the ratio of the eleventh term to the fifth term?
>
> (A) 6 to 1
> (B) 9 to 5
> (C) 16 to 1
> (D) 32 to 1
> (E) 64 to 1

**Step 2** ✏ *Use order of difficulty to your advantage*

Before you begin solving a hard SAT Math question, you should have a hunch about what the answer is. Because hard SAT Math questions typically have difficult answers, the answer to this question is probably (D) or (E).

**Step 3** ✏ *Solve the question*

2, 4, 8, 16, 32, 64, 128, 256, 512, 1024, 2048

Ratio → 2048 : 32 → 64 : 1

Select (E) as your answer choice.

## Math 2400 Strategy 2 ✏ *Write, don't visualize*

This strategy, which is a restatement of *General 2400 Strategy 2* (Write everything down), is more important in SAT Math than in any other section of the test. You must write down every number, variable, equation, and detail as you solve a math problem. Don't try to visualize how a problem should be worked; you will be overloaded with information as you try to remember the details of your solution. Think with your pencil!

### Math 2400 Example   *Write, don't visualize*

**Step 1** ✏ *Read the student-produced response question*

| If $2 < 3x + 2 < 4$, what is one possible value for $x$ ?

**Step 2** ✏ *Write, don't visualize*

Don't try to visualize what the answer should be. Immediately begin to write.

$$\begin{array}{ccccc} 2 & < 3x + 2 & < & 4 \\ -2 & \ \ \ \ -2 & & -2 \\ \hline \dfrac{0}{3} & < \dfrac{3x}{3} & < & \dfrac{2}{3} \end{array}$$

$0 < x < 2/3$

$x$ could equal 1/2.

Fill in 1/2 as your answer.

## Math 2400 Strategy 3 ⁄ *Avoid the calculator*

Some students take comfort in knowing that they can use a calculator in SAT Math. In reality, the calculator is more a handicap than an advantage. Every SAT Math question can be solved without a calculator.

If you try to "solve" a problem using a calculator, you often aren't able to completely "think through" the problem with your pencil. In this sense, avoiding a calculator complements *Math 2400 Strategy 2* (Write, don't visualize). You will see some students approach an SAT Math section with their calculators in their hands. Don't do this! Keep your pencil in contact with your test booklet and work the problems on paper.

Act as if you aren't allowed to use a calculator. This will force you to focus on working math problems on paper and to look for the SAT-friendly method of working each problem. While there is often a calculator-heavy approach to a problem, the SAT-friendly method is easier. SAT test writers reward the SAT-friendly approach, which allows you to do much less work than a student who uses the calculator-heavy method.

You can use your calculator to check your written calculations, but only *after* you have set up the entire problem on paper. Solve the problem on paper, then check your calculations on your calculator—paper first, calculator second.

### Math 2400 Example    *Avoid the calculator*

### Step 1 ⁄ *Read the question*

For all numbers $x$ and $y$, let $x \Delta y$ be defined as $x^2 - xy - y^2$. What is the value of $(3\Delta1)\Delta1$ ?

(A) 6
(B) 12
(C) 19
(D) 140
(E) 163

### Step 2 ⁄ *Avoid the calculator*

Don't try to solve the problem on your calculator. Instead, work each step out on paper.

$3\Delta1 \rightarrow x = 3$ and $y = 1$
$x^2 - xy - y^2$
$3^2 - 3(1) - 1^2$
$9 - 3 - 1$
$3\Delta1 = 5$

$(3\triangle1)\triangle1 \rightarrow 5\triangle1$

$5\triangle1 \rightarrow x = 5$ and $y = 1$
$x^2 - xy - y^2$
$5^2 - 5(1) - 1^2$
$25 - 5 - 1$
$5\triangle1 = 19$

Select (C) as your answer choice.

## Math 2400 Strategy 4 ⁻ *Circle the unknown*

Always circle what a question is asking for. Although this strategy is simple, it is a powerful tool that will prevent small mistakes on SAT Math. Have you ever gotten a math question wrong because you solved for $x$, when the question actually asked for the value of $x/2$? You sometimes get so engrossed in a math problem that you forget what the problem was asking for in the first place. Before you put your final answer in the test booklet, look back at what you circled and make sure that you solved for the correct unknown.

### Math 2400 Example   *Circle the unknown*

**Step 1** ⁻ *Read the question*

> For all numbers $x$ and $y$, let $x \odot y$ be defined as $x \odot y = x^2 + y^2$.
> If $a \odot 3 = 90$, what is the value of $\sqrt{a}$ ?
> (A) 3
> (B) 4
> (C) 9
> (D) 16
> (E) 81

**Step 2** ⁻ *Circle the unknown*

> For all numbers $x$ and $y$, let $x \odot y$ be defined as $x \odot y = x^2 + y^2$.
> If $a \odot 3 = 90$, what is the value of $\sqrt{a}$?

**Step 3** ⁻ *Solve the problem*

$a \odot 3 = 90$
$a^2 + 3^2 = 90$
$a^2 + 9 = 90$
$a^2 = 81$
$\sqrt{a^2} = \sqrt{81}$
$a = 9$

Look back at the circled unknown: value of $\sqrt{a}$.

$\sqrt{a} = \sqrt{9} = 3$

Select (A) as your answer choice.

Step 4
Use
unconventional
methods
to score high
on SAT Math

294

## Math 2400 Strategy 5 — Check your work as you go

Do you wait to check your work until you've finished an SAT Math section? You shouldn't. If you wait to check your work, you probably won't find many errors. You are more likely to reaffirm your initial work, because you have only a few minutes left—not enough time to reacquaint yourself with the problems. Instead, you should check your work while you are still engaged in a problem. Verify previous steps as you work. Make sure you didn't make a simple arithmetic error, didn't approach the problem incorrectly from the beginning, and didn't use the wrong formula. Checking your work as you go prevents frustration, saves time, and avoids errors.

### Math 2400 Example    Check your work as you go

### Step 1 — Read the question

> A movie theater charges $4 less for a child's ticket than for an adult's ticket. If a group of 5 children and 6 adults spent $79 on tickets, what is the price of one adult ticket?
>
> (A) $7
> (B) $9
> (C) $11
> (D) $12
> (E) $13

### Step 2 — Check your work as you go

$x$ = adult ticket price
$x - 4$ = child ticket price

> *Verify previous step: Is this the easiest way to approach problem? No. Instead, can test answer choices.* (See Math 2400 Strategy 8 below.)

If an adult's ticket costs $11 (answer choice (C)), the total cost for 5 children and 6 adults would be as follows.

$5(\$7) + 6(\$11) = \$35 + \$66 = \$101$

> *Verify previous step: Did I do the calculation correctly? Check. 5 x 7 = 35? 6 x 11 = 66? 35 + 66 = 101?*

Because the total price is too high, test answer choice (B).

If an adult's ticket costs $9, then the total cost of 5 children and 6 adults would be as follows.

$5(\$5) + 6(\$9) = \$25 + \$54 = \$79$

> *Verify previous step: Did I do the calculation correctly? Check. 5 x 5 = 25? 6 x 9 = 54? 25 + 54 = 79?*

Select (B) as your answer choice.

---

*Italic handwriting indicates problem-solving steps that are performed mentally.

## Math 2400 Strategy 6 — *Do the first step*

Do the first step of a problem, even if you don't know how to solve it entirely. In high school, you have been trained to tackle problems only when you know how to solve them; you are expected to have a solution plan in your head before you begin.

    Don't be afraid to begin a problem even if you have no idea what the next step is! I have seen many students simply stare blankly at a problem. They read the problem over and over, trying to come up with a plan for solving it. You don't have to think of a road map before you start—you can draw the road map as you do each step.

    Doing the first step of an SAT Math problem very often leads to the next step, which leads to the next step, and eventually you will have solved the problem. This strategy works especially well on long, complex problems with a lot of words, variables, and terms. Instead of looking at the problem as a whole, break it down into pieces and do the first step for each piece. For example, if the problem states that a variable is equivalent to some value, write it down. If you can multiply two terms, multiply. If you can divide two terms, divide. If you can factor something, factor. Even if you have no idea whether the step will help you . . . just do it!

### Math 2400 Example  *Do the first step*

#### Step 1 — *Read the question*

If $nx - 7 = (n - 1)x$, which of the following must be true?

(A) $x = 4$
(B) $x = 7$
(C) $n = 4$
(D) $n = 5$
(E) $n = 7x$

#### Step 2 — *Do the first step*

Multiply.

$$nx - 7 = (n - 1)x$$
$$nx - 7 = nx - x$$

#### Step 3 — *Do the next step*

Subtract.

$$
\begin{array}{rcr}
nx - 7 = & nx - x \\
-nx & -nx \\
\hline
-7 = & -x
\end{array}
$$

$$7 = x$$

Select (B) as your answer choice.

## Math 2400 Strategy 7 — Plug in numbers (PIN)

This powerful strategy makes the abstract tangible. Many problems contain abstract concepts, but by plugging in numbers, you will have concrete numbers to help you solve these problems with ease.

    You should use PIN when a problem contains algebraic variables in both the question and the answer choices. You make up your own numbers to substitute for the variables, then check to see which answer choice, given your substitutions, yields the correct answer.

    However, PIN works on more than just algebra questions. You can often use PIN on problems that involve geometry, number properties, and graphing. You will be introduced to the wide variety of PIN uses in the *Math 2400 Practice* problem sets later in this chapter.

**Step 4**
Use
unconventional
methods
to score high
on SAT Math
..........................

**296**

### Math 2400 Example — *Plug in numbers (PIN)*

#### Step 1 — *Read the question*

If 75% of $x$ is $y$ and $y$ is 200% of $z$, what is the ratio of $z$ to $x$ ?
(A) 1/8
(B) 1/4
(C) 3/8
(D) 1/2
(E) 3/4

#### Step 2 — *Plug in numbers*

75% of $x$ is $y$.

If x = 100, then y = 75 (can solve by doing (.75)100 = y)
75% of 100 is 75

#### Step 3 — *Plug in numbers again*

$y$ is 200% of $z$.

If y = 75, then z = 37.5 (can solve by doing 75 = (2.0)z)
75 is 200% of 37.5

Determine the ratio of $z$ to $x$.

z = 37.5
x = 100
z/x = 37.5/100
    = 3/8

Select (C) as your answer choice.

## Math 2400 Strategy 8 ⚊ *Test answer choices (TAC)*

TAC is very similar to PIN. TAC is typically used, however, when a problem contains algebraic variables in the question, but concrete numbers in the answer choices. Using TAC, you test the concrete numbers to see if they work in the algebraic expressions in the question. I usually started in the middle by testing answer choice (C), because answer choices are usually arranged from smallest (A) to largest (E). If answer choice (C) is too large when I test it, I test answer choice (B) or (A) next; if answer choice (C) is too small when I test it, I test answer choice (D) or (E) next.

Because multiple-choice exams are rare in high school algebra classes, this strategy may seem foreign to you. High school math teachers generally make you solve for variables on tests. But on the SAT, the answers are right there in front of you—you just need to test them!

### Math 2400 Example ⚊ *Test answer choices (TAC)*

#### Step 1 ⚊ *Read the question*

If $(n + m)/(n - m) = 3$, what is the value of $n/m$ ?
(A) $-8/3$
(B) $-2$
(C) $1/2$
(D) $2$
(E) $8/3$

#### Step 2 ⚊ *Test the middle answer choice*

(C) $1/2$

If $(n/m) = 1/2$ , then $n = 1$ and $m = 2$
$(n + m)/(n - m) = (1 + 2)/(1 - 2) = 3/{-1} = -3$

Answer choice (C) is too small.

#### Step 3 ⚊ *Test another answer choice*

(D) $2$

If $(n/m) = 2$, then $n = 2$ and $m = 1$
$(n + m)/(n - m) = (2 + 1)/(2 - 1) = 3/1 = 3$

Select (D) as your answer choice.

Step 4
Use
unconventional
methods
to score high
on SAT Math
..........................
298

## Math 2400 Strategy 9 ⚊ *Simplify impractical problems*

You will sometimes encounter an SAT Math problem that seems impractical to do in a reasonable amount of time. For example, the question may ask you to add a ridiculous number of integers, or find the 99th term in a sequence, or to perform another task that simply would take too long to write out on paper.

The typical high school solution to one of these problems is to find a formula and calculate from there. But if you would rather work with tangible numbers than with abstract variables, you have an alternative: Solve a simpler version of the impractical problem and try to find a pattern that you can apply to the larger problem. For example, if a problem asks you to find the 70th term in a sequence, find the 7th term instead. Then try to figure out the relationship between the 7th term and the rest of the sequence. Finally, extrapolate that relationship for the 70th term.

### Math 2400 Example    *Simplify impractical problems*

**Step 1** ⚊ *Read the student-produced response question*

> The sum of the positive odd integers less than 80 is subtracted from the sum of the positive even integers less than or equal to 80. What is the resulting difference?

**Step 2** ⚊ *Simplify impractical problems*

Try 8 instead of 80.

Sum the positive odd integers less than 8.

$1 + 3 + 5 + 7 = 16$

Sum the positive even integers less than or equal to 8.

$2 + 4 + 6 + 8 = 20$

Determine the difference.

$20 - 16 = 4$

**Step 3** ⚊ *Find a pattern*

How is 4 related to 8?

4 is 50% of 8.

The likely solution to this "impractical" problem is 40 (50% of 80).

Fill in 40 as your answer.

## Math 2400 Strategy 10 ⚊ *Label givens*

If there is a diagram associated with an SAT Math problem, label all givens. If there are two vertical angles, label those two angles as congruent. If there are two supplementary angles and you know the degree measure of one angle,

label the degree measure of the other. Label givens even if you don't know whether such labeling will help you solve the problem.

This strategy goes hand in hand with *Math 2400 Strategy 6* (Do the first step). The first step on most SAT Math problems that contain diagrams is to label the diagrams. It is especially important to label triangles and 90° angles.

### Math 2400 Example  *Label givens*

**Step 1** ☞ **Read the question**

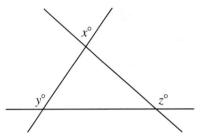

Note: Figure not drawn to scale.

In the figure above, if $x = 50$ and $z = 100$, what is the value of $y$ ?
(A) 50
(B) 70
(C) 90
(D) 110
(E) 130

**Step 2** ☞ **Label givens**

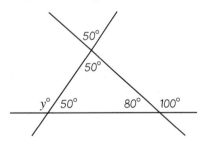

Vertical angles are congruent. (See *Math 2400 Strategy 12* below.)
Supplementary angles add up to 180°.
The angles of a triangle add up to 180°.

**Step 3** ☞ **Solve the problem**

Supplementary angles add up to 180°.

$$y + 50° = 180°$$
$$y = 130°$$

Select (E) as your answer choice.

**Step 4**
Use
unconventional
methods
to score high
on SAT Math
................................

**300**

## Math 2400 Strategy 11 ✒ *Draw a picture*

If an SAT Math problem describes a diagram but doesn't show the diagram, draw a picture yourself. If the problem describes a cube, draw a cube. If the problem describes a line on a graph, draw a graph.

Drawing a picture helps make abstract concepts tangible, which is key to acing SAT Math. This strategy goes hand in hand with *Math 2400 Strategy 2* (Write, don't visualize). Don't try to visualize a diagram in your head—draw a picture instead!

### Math 2400 Example   *Draw a picture*

### Step 1 ✒ *Read the question*

The base of an isosceles triangle is 2 feet more than each of the two other equal sides. If the base of the triangle is 12 feet, what is its area?
(A)  24 feet²
(B)  48 feet²
(C)  96 feet²
(D)  192 feet²
(E)  384 feet²

### Step 2 ✒ *Draw a picture*

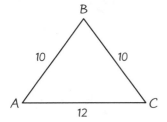

### Step 3 ✒ *Make right triangles*

Drawing your own lines on pictures you draw (as well as on diagrams provided on the SAT) is key to solving many SAT Math questions.

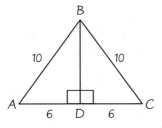

**Step 4** ✎ *Find the length of BD*

Use the Pythagorean Theorem.

$a^2 + b^2 = c^2$
$6^2 + BD^2 = 10^2$
$36 + BD^2 = 100$
$BD^2 = 64$
$BD = 8$

**Step 5** ✎ *Find the area of the isosceles triangle*

First, find the area of each right triangle.

$A = \frac{1}{2} bh$
$\quad = \frac{1}{2}(6)(8)$
$\quad = 24$

Now, find the area of the isosceles triangle.

$A = 2 \times 24$
$\quad = 48$

Select (B) as your answer choice.

———————————

The final four *Math 2400 Strategies* cover major mathematical concepts that you must be familiar with in order to succeed in SAT Math.

## Math 2400 Strategy 12 ✎ *Know your angles*

Angles are crucial in SAT Math. Here are the basics:

**Vertical angles** These are formed when two angles are directly opposite each other. Vertical angles are congruent.

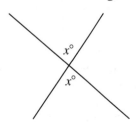

**Straight line** Angles that form a straight line must add up to 180°.

**Step 4**
Use
unconventional
methods
to score high
on SAT Math

**302**

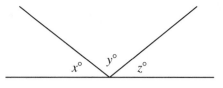

$$x° + y° + z° = 180°$$

**Parallel lines** Parallel lines lie in the same plane and never intersect. When a line passes through a set of parallel lines, special angles are formed.

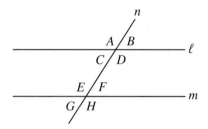

**Corresponding angles** Corresponding angles are congruent. Here are examples of such angles in the diagram above:

$A$ and $E$
$B$ and $F$
$C$ and $G$
$D$ and $H$

**Alternate interior angles** Alternate interior angles are congruent. Here are examples of such angles in the diagram above:

$C$ and $F$
$D$ and $E$

**Perpendicular lines** Perpendicular lines form a 90° angle.

**Polygons** The sum of the interior angle measure of any polygon with $n$ sides is $(n - 2) \times 180°$.

**Bisected angle** An angle that is bisected is split into two equivalent angles.

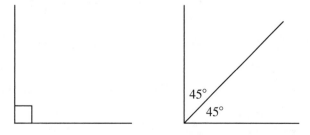

## Math 2400 Example   *Know your angles*

### Step 1 ⌁ *Read the question*

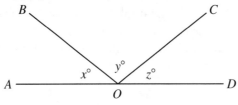

Note: Figure not drawn to scale.

In the figure above, point $O$ lies on line segment AD. Line segment OC bisects angle BOD. If $y = 55$, what is the value of $x$ ?

(A) 45
(B) 50
(C) 55
(D) 70
(E) 110

### Step 2 ⌁ *Know your angles*

An angle that is bisected is split into two equivalent angles.

$y° = z°$
$55° = 55°$

Angles that form a straight line must add up to 180°.

$x° + y° + z° = 180°$
$x° + 55° + 55° = 180°$
$x° = 70°$

Select (D) as your answer choice.

## Math 2400 Strategy 13 ⸺ *Know your triangles*

The triangle is the central geometric figure in SAT Math. You can often draw your own triangles (especially right triangles) for questions that don't appear to relate to triangles at all. For example, you never need the distance formula to calculate the distance between two points on an SAT problem. Instead, you calculate the distance between two points by drawing your own right triangles. Here are the triangle basics you need to know:

**Step 4**
Use
unconventional
methods
to score high
on SAT Math

· · · · · · · · · · · · · · · · · · · · ·

**304**

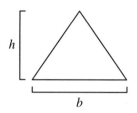

### Basics

◂ The area of a triangle is given by the formula $A = \frac{1}{2}bh$.

    $b$ = base of the triangle
    $h$ = height of the triangle

◂ The third side of a triangle must be greater than the difference of the other two sides *and* less than the sum of the other two sides.

    EXAMPLE    If two sides of a triangle are 6 and 8, the third side must be greater than 2 *and* less than 14.

### Angles

◂ All angles in a triangle add up to 180°.
◂ The angles opposite congruent sides of a triangle are also congruent, and vice versa.
◂ The angle opposite the longest side of a triangle is the largest.
◂ The angle opposite the shortest side of a triangle is the smallest.

### Right triangles

◂ A right triangle has one 90° angle.
◂ Pythagorean Theorem: $a^2 + b^2 = c^2$

◄ Pythagorean Triples

    ◄ Two common right triangles have specific side lengths: 3-4-5 and 5-12-13.

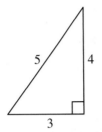 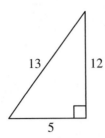

    ◄ Multiples of these Pythagorean Triples are common on the SAT; for example, a 6-8-10 triangle is a multiple of a 3-4-5 triangle.

## Special right triangles

### 45°/45°/90° triangle

    ◄ This is a right triangle with two congruent side lengths.

    ◄ The side lengths have the following relationship.

**EXAMPLE**

 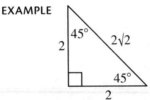

    ◄ One can often create two 45°/45°/90° triangles by drawing a diagonal across a square.

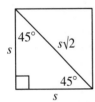

**Step 4**
Use
unconventional
methods
to score high
on SAT Math

306

### 30°/60°/90° triangle

◄ The side lengths have the following relationship.

EXAMPLE

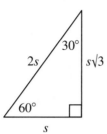
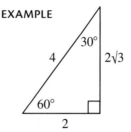

◄ One can often recognize a 30°/60°/90° triangle even if all the details are not given.

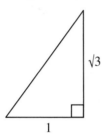

### Equilateral triangle

◄ All sides of an equilateral triangle are congruent.
◄ All angles of an equilateral triangle are equal to 60°.
◄ When an equilateral triangle is bisected, two 30°/60°/90° triangles are formed.

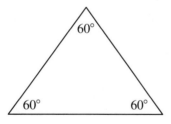
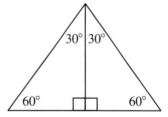

### Isosceles triangle

◄ Two sides of an isosceles triangle are congruent.
◄ Two angles of an isosceles triangle are congruent (the angles opposite the congruent sides).

## Math 2400 Example    *Know your triangles*

### Step 1 — *Read the question*

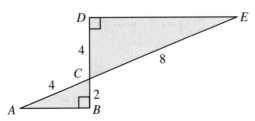

What is the area of the shaded region in the figure above (units²)?

(A) 3
(B) 4√3
(C) 8√3
(D) 10√3
(E) 18

### Step 2 — *Know your triangles*

Because the hypotenuse of each right triangle in the diagram is double the short side, you should immediately recognize these as 30°/60°/90° triangles.

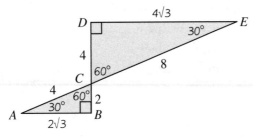

Since you know the base and height of each triangle, you can calculate the area.

*Triangle ABC*
  *A* = ½ bh
    = ½ (2√3)(2)
    2√3

*Triangle CDE*
  *A* = ½ bh
    = ½ (4√3)(4)
    = 8√3

*Total area*
  *A* = 2√3 + 8√3 = 10√3

Select (D) as your answer choice.

## Math 2400 Strategy 14 ⚞ *Know your circles*

It is very important to be familiar with circles in SAT Math. Although squares and rectangles appear more often than circles on the SAT, most students have more trouble with circles than with quadrilaterals.

**Step 4**
Use
unconventional
methods
to score high
on SAT Math
·······················
**308**

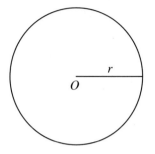

### Basics

◄ The radius of a circle is represented by $r$.

   $r$ = radius of the circle

◄ The area of a circle is given by the formula $A = \pi r^2$.

   $A$ = area of the circle

◄ The circumference of a circle is given by the formula $C = 2\pi r$.

   $C$ = length around the perimeter of the circle

◄ The diameter of a circle is given by the formula $d = 2r$.

   $d$ = length directly across the circle passing through its center

### Angles (sectors)

◄ A circle is made up of 360°.

◄ An arc is a connected portion of a circle's circumference.

◄ A sector is a pie-shaped portion of a circle.

   ◄ The ratio of a sector's central angle to 360° is equivalent to

      1. The ratio of the sector's area to the circle's area

      2. The ratio of the sector's arc length to the circle's circumference

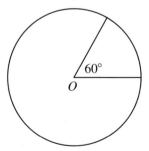

   ◄ The sector is 1/6 of the circle's area (60°/360°).

   ◄ The sector's arc is 1/6 of the circle's circumference (60°/360°).

## Circles and triangles

Special triangles are often formed by drawing line segments on sectors.

### Equilateral triangle

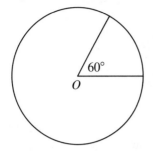
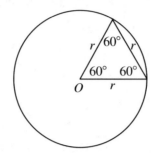

### 45°/45°/90° triangle

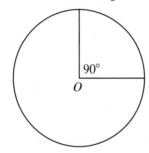
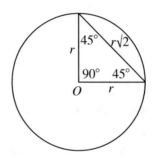

**Step 1**  *Read the question*

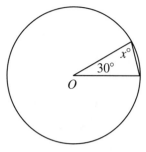

<u>Note</u>: Figure not drawn to scale.

In the figure above, point $O$ is the center of the circle. What is the value of $x$ ?

(A) 30
(B) 60
(C) 75
(D) 90
(E) 120

**Step 2**  *Know your triangles*

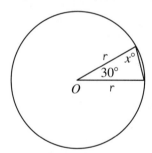

Radii ($r$) are always congruent in a circle.

In this case, $r$ happens to be two sides of the triangle, which makes the triangle isosceles.

**Step 3**  *Know your triangles*

All angles in a triangle add up to 180°.

The angles opposite congruent sides of a triangle are also congruent.

The unlabeled angle in the isosceles triangle must be equivalent to $x°$.

$x° + x° + 30° = 180°$
$2x° + 30° = 180°$
$2x° = 150°$
$x° = 75°$

Select (C) as your answer choice.

## Math 2400 Strategy 15 ∕ *Know your graphs*

Graphing is an important concept in SAT Math.

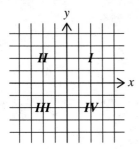

## Basics

◄ The horizontal axis on a graph represents the *x*-axis.

    *x*-intercept = the point at which a graph crosses the *x*-axis (*x* value when *y* = 0)

◄ The vertical axis on a graph represents the *y*-axis.

    *y*-intercept = the point at which a graph crosses the *y*-axis (*y* value when *x* = 0)

◄ The points designated on a graph are written in the form (*x*, *y*).

◄ The origin of a graph is designated as (0, 0).

◄ Quadrants (see the graph above) have the following designations:

    I     positive *x*, positive *y*   (*x*, *y*)
    II    negative *x*, positive *y*  (−*x*, *y*)
    III   negative *x*, negative *y*  (−*x*, −*y*)
    IV   positive *x*, negative *y*  (*x*, −*y*)

## Slope

◄ The slope (*m*) between any two points $(x_1, y_1)$ and $(x_2, y_2)$ is determined as follows.

$$m = \frac{(y_2 - y_1)}{(x_2 - x_1)}$$

◄ Parallel lines have equal slopes.

◄ Perpendicular lines have slopes that are opposite reciprocals of each other.

    EXAMPLE   Line *r* is perpendicular to line *s*. If line *r* has a slope of 1/2, line *s* has a slope of −2.

◄ A horizontal line indicates a slope of 0.

◄ A vertical line indicates an undefined slope.

### Point-slope form

The point-slope form of a line appears as $y = mx + b$.

  $m$ = slope of the line
  $b$ = $y$-intercept of the line

**Step 4**
Use
unconventional
methods
to score high
on SAT Math

**312**

If a line passes through the origin, $b = 0$.

### Rates

When time is on the $x$-axis of a graph, rate is typically represented by a slope.

  Positive slope   = Increasing rate
  Constant slope = Constant rate (horizontal line)
  Negative slope  = Decreasing rate

### Reflection

◄ Reflections of graphs about the $x$-axis flip upside down.

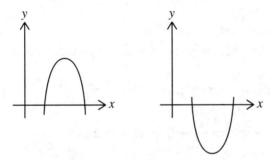

◄ Reflections of graphs about the $y$-axis flip horizontally across the $y$-axis.

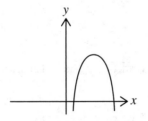 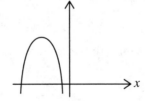

## Graph movements

$f(x)$ can represent any line or graph on a curve.

| | |
|---|---|
| $f(x) + m$ | The graph shifts up $m$ units. |
| $f(x) - m$ | The graph shifts down $m$ units. |
| $f(x + m)$ | The graph shifts left $m$ units. |
| $f(x - m)$ | The graph shifts right $m$ units. |

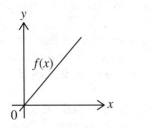
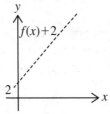

### Math 2400 Example   *Know your graphs*

**Step 1** *Read the student-produced response question*

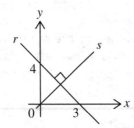

In the xy-coordinate plane above, line $m$ is perpendicular to line $n$. What is the slope of line $m$?

**Step 2** *Know your graphs*

Determine the two points of line $n$.

$(0, 4)$
$(3, 0)$

Calculate the slope of line $n$.

$$m = \frac{(4 - 0)}{(0 - 3)} = -4/3$$

The slope of line $m$ is the opposite reciprocal of the slope of line $n$.

Fill in 3/4 as your answer.

# Math 2400 Practice: 50 problems

Now that you've learned to tackle any SAT Math problem using the 15 *Math 2400 Strategies* above, let's tackle 50 problems . . . step by step, together.

**Step 4**
Use unconventional methods to score high on SAT Math
........................

**314**

Most SAT prep books follow the same approach as your high school math teachers: review math concepts in general, then leave you to apply these concepts to standardized exams on your own. This approach simply doesn't work. It is far better to focus on the standardized exam questions and learn how specific concepts are tested.

In addition, most SAT prep books cover math concepts as distinct topics. An SAT Math question, however, rarely involves a single mathematical concept; instead, a typical question requires you to integrate several math concepts in order to solve it.

I approach preparation for SAT Math differently; this walk-through provides typical SAT questions *first* and general math concepts *second*. By reviewing the math concepts that you need to know for each problem and by explaining each answer step by step, you will learn to apply the 15 *Math 2400 Strategies* so that you can think like a 2400 SAT student.

Many of the solutions to these 50 problems may not have occurred to you, because you are still thinking in terms of high school math. The solutions presented frequently take advantage of the multiple-choice nature of the SAT test—a format that isn't common in high school math classrooms. As you perform more and more *2400 Practice,* you will change your approach to SAT Math questions, which will result in your SAT Math score skyrocketing!

## Example SAT Math problems

In the 50 problems that follow, only the last ten *Math 2400 Strategies* are referenced. The first five *Math 2400 Strategies* are general approaches that you should apply to every question.

### Example SAT Math Problem 1

If $m$ and $n$ are positive even integers and $p$ is a positive odd integer, which of the following could be prime?

(A) $mp$
(B) $mn$
(C) $mn + p$
(D) $mp + n$
(E) $np + m$

**Primary Math 2400 Strategy** • *Plug in numbers*

**Primary math concept**

Number properties

◄ Integers are whole numbers that do not have fractions or decimals (for example, $-2, -1, 0, 1, 2$).

◄ An even integer is divisible by two.
◄ An odd integer is not divisible by two.
◄ A prime number is a positive integer that is only divisible by 1 and itself.

**Solution**

**1** • *Plug in numbers*

$m = 2$
$n = 4$
$p = 3$

**2** • *Substitute numbers into the answer choices*

(A) $mp$ $= 6$
(B) $mn$ $= 8$
(C) $mn + p$ $= 11$
(D) $mp + n$ $= 10$
(E) $np + m$ $= 14$

**3** • *Determine the prime number*

Only 11 is prime.

Select (C) as your answer choice.

NOTE You could have plugged in numbers that made answer choice (C) a composite (nonprime) number. For example, if you had plugged in $m = 6$, $n = 4$, and $p = 11$, (C) would have been 35, a composite number. If none of the answer choices yields a prime number, continue plugging in numbers until one answer choice does yield a prime number.

## Example SAT Math Problem 2

If $3a + 6b = 12$, then $a + 2b =$
(A) 3
(B) 4
(C) 5
(D) 6
(E) 7

**Primary Math 2400 Strategy** • *Do the first step*

**Solution**

**1** • *Do the first step: Divide the original equation by 3*

$$\frac{3a}{3} + \frac{6b}{3} = \frac{12}{3}$$

$a + 2b = 4$

Select (B) as your answer choice.

### Example SAT Math Problem 3

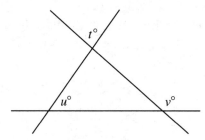

Note: Figure not drawn to scale.

In the figure above, if $t = 30$ and $v = 100$, what is the value of $u$ ?
(A) 50
(B) 60
(C) 70
(D) 80
(E) 90

**Step 4**
Use
unconventional
methods
to score high
on SAT Math
·······················
**316**

**Primary Math 2400 Strategies** • *Label givens* **+** *Know your triangles*

**Solution**

1 • *Label givens*

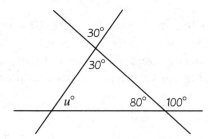

2 • *Know your triangles*

$30° + 80° + u° = 180°$
$u° = 70°$

Select (C) as your answer choice.

## Example SAT Math Problem 4

If Anne makes $d$ dollars for working $h$ hours, which of the following represents her hourly earnings, in dollars per hour?

(A) $\dfrac{d}{h}$

(B) $\dfrac{h}{d}$

(C) $\dfrac{1}{dh}$

(D) $dh$

(E) $d^2h$

**Primary Math 2400 Strategy** • *Plug in numbers*

**Solution**

**1** • *Plug in numbers*

$d = \$10$

$h = 5$ hours

**2** • *Determine hourly earnings*

$\$10 / 5$ hours $= \$2$ per hour

**3** • *Substitute numbers into the answer choices*

(A) $\dfrac{d}{h}$ $= 2$ ✓

(B) $\dfrac{h}{d}$ $= 1/2$

(C) $\dfrac{1}{dh}$ $= 1/50$

(D) $dh$ $= 50$

(E) $d^2h$ $= 500$

Select (A) as your answer choice.

## Example SAT Math Problem 5

In the coordinate plane, the points $A$ $(2, 3)$, $B$ $(4, 6)$, and $C$ are on a line. Which of the following could be the coordinates of $C$ ?
(A) $(0, 0)$
(B) $(3, 5)$
(C) $(6, 10)$
(D) $(9, -6)$
(E) $(12, -8)$

**Primary Math 2400 Strategy** ▫ *Know your graphs*

**Solution**

**1** ▫ *Determine the slope between A and B*

$m = (y_2 - y_1)/(x_2 - x_1)$
$\quad = (6 - 3)/(4 - 2) = 3/2$

**2** ▫ *Plug the slope into the point-slope form*

$y = mx + b$
$y = (3/2)x + b$

**3** ▫ *Plug in either point A or point B to determine b*

$A$ $(2, 3)$

$y = (3/2)x + b$
$3 = (3/2)2 + b$
$3 = 3 + b$
$0 = b$

The point-slope equation is $y = (3/2)x + 0$.

**4** ▫ *Plug each answer choice into the point-slope equation*

(A) $(0, 0)$ $\quad$ $0 = (3/2)(0) + 0$ $\quad$ $0 = 0$ $\quad$ ✓
(B) $(3, 5)$ $\quad$ $5 = (3/2)(3) + 0$ $\quad$ $5 \neq 9/2$
(C) $(6, 10)$ $\quad$ $10 = (3/2)(6) + 0$ $\quad$ $10 \neq 9$
(D) $(9, -6)$ $\quad$ $-6 = (3/2)(9) + 0$ $\quad$ $-6 \neq 27/2$
(E) $(12, -8)$ $\quad$ $-8 = (3/2)(12) + 0$ $\quad$ $-8 \neq 18$

Select (A) as your answer choice.

## Example SAT Math Problem 6

For all numbers $x$ and $y$, let $x \odot y$ be defined as $x \odot y = x^2 - y^2$.
If $a \odot 3 = 91$, what is the value of $\sqrt{a - 1}$ ?

(A) 3
(B) 4
(C) 7
(D) 9
(E) 10

**Primary Math 2400 Strategy** • *Do the first step*

**Solution**

**1** • *Do the first step: Interpret $a \odot 3$*

$$a \odot 3 = x^2 - y^2$$
$$= a^2 - 3^2$$
$$= a^2 - 9$$

**2** • *Do the next step: Solve for a*

$$a^2 - 9 = 91$$
$$a^2 = 100$$
$$a = 10$$

**3** • *Solve for the unknown*

$$\sqrt{a - 1} = \sqrt{(10 - 1)} = \sqrt{9} = 3$$

Select (A) as your answer choice.

## Example SAT Math Problem 7

On three equally weighted tests, Ceril scores $k$, $k + 2$, and $k - 2$. If Ceril's score on the fourth test is the same as his average (arithmetic mean) for the first three tests, what is his score on the fourth test in terms of $k$ ?

(A) $k/2$
(B) $k$
(C) $2k$
(D) $3k$
(E) $4k$

**Step 4**
Use
unconventional
methods
to score high
on SAT Math

**320**

**Primary Math 2400 Strategy** • *Plug in numbers*

**Primary math concept**

Number properties

◂ The average (arithmetic mean) is the quantity calculated when the sum of a set of values is divided by the number of values in the set.

**Solution**

**1** • *Plug in numbers*

$k = 10$

**2** • *Determine the average of the first three tests*

$k = 10$

$k + 2 = 12$

$k - 2 = 8$

$$\frac{10 + 12 + 8}{3} = 10$$

**3** • *Determine Ceril's score on the fourth test*

The fourth test score is the average of the first three test scores: 10.

**4** • *Substitute numbers into the answer choices*

(A) $k/2 = 5$
(B) $k\ \ \ = 10$ ✓
(C) $2k\ = 20$
(D) $3k\ = 30$
(E) $4k\ = 40$

Select (B) as your answer choice.

## Example SAT Math Problem 8

> If $4 < 3x + 2 < 8$, what is one possible value for $x$ ?

**Primary Math 2400 Strategy** • *Plug in numbers*

**Solution**

**1** • *Plug in numbers*

Choose any value between 4 and 8 and set $3x + 2$ equal to it.

$$3x + 2 = 6$$
$$3x \quad\;\; = 4$$

**2** • *Find the unknown*

$x = 4/3$

Fill in 4/3 (or any value that satisfies $2/3 < x < 2$) as your answer.

## Example SAT Math Problem 9

> For positive integers $a$ and $b$, $(a + b)^2 = 36$ and $(a - b)^2 = 4$.
> If $a \le b$, what is the value of $b$ ?

**Primary Math 2400 Strategy** • *Plug in numbers*

**Solution**

**1** • *Simplify the relationship between the variables*

$$(a + b)^2 = 36$$
$$\sqrt{(a + b)^2} = \sqrt{36}$$
$$a + b = 6$$

The answer must be positive, because the question states "positive integers."

$$(a - b)^2 = 4$$
$$\sqrt{(a - b)^2} = \sqrt{4}$$
$$a - b = 2 \text{ or } -2$$

**2** • *Plug in numbers (guess and check)*

$$a + b = 6$$
$$a - b = 2 \text{ or } -2$$

Guess: $a = 1$ and $b = 5$.

$$a + b = 6 \quad ✓$$
$$a - b = -4 \quad ✗$$

Guess: $a = 2$ and $b = 4$.

$$a + b = 6 \quad ✓$$
$$a - b = -2 \quad ✓$$

Fill in 4 as your answer.

## Example SAT Math Problem 10

**Step 4**
Use
unconventional
methods
to score high
on SAT Math

322

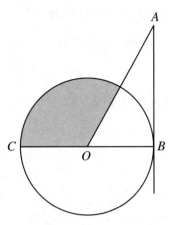

In the figure above, line segment $AB$ is tangent to circle $O$ at $B$. If $AO = BC = 12$, what fraction of the circle is shaded?

**Primary Math 2400 Strategies** • *Label givens + Know your triangles + Know your circles*

**Primary math concept**

Lines and angles

◄ Line $OB$ must form a $90°$ angle with line $AB$, which is tangent to it.

**Solution**

**1** • *Label givens*

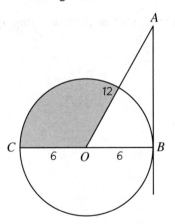

**2** • *Know your triangles*

Triangle *AOB* must be a 30°/60°/90° triangle, because the hypotenuse is double the short side.

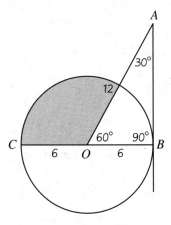

**3** • *Know your circles*

The area of the shaded region is one-half the circle minus the area of the 60° sector formed by angle *AOB*.

AREA OF THE CIRCLE

$A = \pi r^2$

$\quad = \pi 6^2$

$\quad = \pi 36$

AREA OF THE HALF-CIRCLE

$A = 18\pi$

AREA OF THE 60° SECTOR

$A = 6\pi$

Why 6π?

$$\frac{60°}{360°} = \frac{1}{6}$$

$1/6$ of $A\,(36\pi) = 6\pi$

AREA OF THE SHADED AREA

$18\pi - 6\pi = 12\pi$

**4** • *Solve for the unknown*

$$\frac{12\pi}{36\pi} = \frac{1}{3}$$

Fill in 1/3 as your answer.

Step 4
Use
unconventional
methods
to score high
on SAT Math
....................
324

## Example SAT Math Problem 11

If $a^3 \times a^3 = 25^3$, what is the value of $a$ ?

(A) 1
(B) 2
(C) 5
(D) 10
(E) 25

### Primary Math 2400 Strategy ▫ *Do the first step*

### Primary math concept

Exponents

◂ Add exponents when multiplying numbers with the same base.
◂ Multiply exponents when one number is to the power of another.

### Solution

**1** ▫ *Do the first step*

$a^3 \times a^3 = 25^3$

$a^6 = 25^3$

**2** ▫ *Do the next step*

$a^6 = (5^2)^3$

$\quad = 5^6$

Select (C) as your answer choice.

## Example SAT Math Problem 12

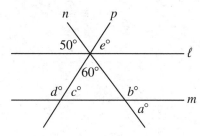

Note: Figure not drawn to scale.

In the figure above $\ell \parallel m$ and $\ell$, $n$, and $p$ intersect at a point. Which of the following is least?

(A) $a$
(B) $b$
(C) $c$
(D) $d$
(E) $e$

**Solution**

*1 • Know your angles*

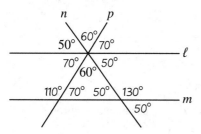

Select (A) as your answer choice.

## Example SAT Math Problem 13

If $f(x) = x^2 + 3$ and $f(a) = b$, which of the following is $f(b)$ ?
(A) $a^2 + 3$
(B) $a^2 + 6$
(C) $(a^2 + 3)^2$
(D) $(a^2 + 3)^2 + 3$
(E) $a^4 + 12$

**Primary Math 2400 Strategy** • *Do the first step*

**Solution**

*1 • Do the first step*

$f(a) = a^2 + 3 = b$

*2 • Do the next step*

$f(b) = b^2 + 3$, where $b = a^2 + 3$
$f(b) = (a^2 + 3)^2 + 3$

Select (D) as your answer choice.

## Example SAT Math Problem 14

**Step 4**
Use unconventional methods to score high on SAT Math

In the figure above $\ell \perp m$ and $\ell$ intersects $m$ at $(a, b)$ and passes through the origin. What is the slope of $m$ ?

(A) $\dfrac{b}{a}$

(B) $\dfrac{a}{b}$

(C) $1$

(D) $-\dfrac{a}{b}$

(E) $-\dfrac{b}{a}$

**Primary Math 2400 Strategies** • *Plug in numbers + Know your graphs*

**Solution**

**1** • *Plug in numbers*

NOTE Since $(a, b)$ is in quadrant I, you may choose any positive numbers for them.

$a = 2$
$b = 4$

**2** • *Determine the slope of $\ell$*

$y = mx + b$
$y = mx + 0$ (because $\ell$ passes through the origin)
$(4) = m(2)$
$m = 2$

**3** • *Determine the slope of $m$*

The opposite reciprocal of 2 is $-\frac{1}{2}$ (reverse the sign and invert).

**4** • *Substitute numbers into the answer choices*

(A) $\dfrac{b}{a}$ $\quad = 2$

(B) $\dfrac{a}{b}$ $\quad = 1/2$

(C) $1 \quad = 1$

(D) $-\dfrac{a}{b} \quad = -1/2$ ✓

(E) $-\dfrac{b}{a} \quad = -2$

Select (D) as your answer choice.

## Example SAT Math Problem 15

| $x$ | $f(x)$ | $g(x)$ |
|---|---|---|
| 1 | 7 | −2 |
| 2 | 2 | −4 |
| 3 | 4 | −8 |
| 4 | 9 | 0 |

In the table above, $f$ and $g$ are defined only for the points indicated. What is the value of $f(4) + g(2)$ ?
(A) −4
(B) −2
(C) 3
(D) 5
(E) 6

**Primary Math 2400 Strategy** ▪ *Do the first step*

**Solution**

**1** ▪ *Do the first step*

What is $f(4)$?

In the $x$ column, scroll down to 4.

In the $f(x)$ column, find the corresponding value (9).

**2** ▪ *Do the next step*

What is $g(2)$?

In the $x$ column, scroll down to 2.

In the $g(x)$ column, find the corresponding value (−4).

**3** ▪ *Determine the value of $f(4) + g(2)$*

$f(4) + g(2)$

$9 + -4$

$5$

Select (D) as your answer choice.

## Example SAT Math Problem 16

If 50% of $x$ is $y$ and $y$ is 150% of $z$, what is the ratio of $z$ to $x$ ?

(A) $\dfrac{1}{3}$

(B) $\dfrac{3}{4}$

(C) 1

(D) $\dfrac{4}{3}$

(E) 3

**Step 4**
Use
unconventional
methods
to score high
on SAT Math

**328**

**Primary Math 2400 Strategy** • *Plug in numbers*

**Solution**

**1** • *Plug in numbers*

50% of $x$ is $y$.

If $x = 60$, then $y = 30$.  $((.5)(60) = y)$

50% of 60 is 30.

**2** • *Plug in numbers again*

$y$ is 150% of $z$.

If $y = 30$, then $z = 20$.  $(30 = 1.5z)$

30 is 150% of 20.

**3** • *Determine the ratio of z to x*

$z = 20$
$x = 60$
$z/x = 20/60 = 1/3$

Select (A) as your answer choice.

## Example SAT Math Problem 17

A taxi charges $a$ dollars for a pickup fee and $b$ dollars per quarter-mile of the ride. How much will be charged for a taxi ride of $c$ miles?

(A) $bc$
(B) $4abc$
(C) $a + bc$
(D) $a + 4b$
(E) $a + 4bc$

**Primary Math 2400 Strategy** • *Plug in numbers*

**Solution**

**1** • *Plug in numbers*

$a = \$2 \qquad b = \$1 \qquad c = 3 \text{ miles}$

**2** ▫ *Determine the charge*

Pickup = $2

3 miles = 12 ¼ miles = 12 × $1 = $12

Total charge = $2 + $12 = $14

**3** ▫ *Substitute numbers into the answer choices*

(A) $bc$ = 3
(B) $4abc$ = 24
(C) $a + bc$ = 5
(D) $a + 4b$ = 6
(E) $a + 4bc$ = 14 ✓

Select (E) as your answer choice.

## Example SAT Math Problem 18

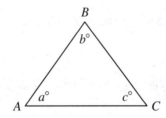

Note: Figure not drawn to scale.

If $\triangle ABC$ is isosceles and $a < b$, then which of the following could be true?

   I.  $b = c$
  II.  $a > c$
 III.  $a = c$

(A) I only
(B) II only
(C) III only
(D) I and III only
(E) I, II, and III

**Primary Math 2400 Strategy** ▫ *Know your triangles*

**Solution**

**1** ▫ *Know your triangles*

If $a < b$, then $c$ could equal either $a$ or $b$ in order to form an isosceles triangle. (Therefore, I and III could both be true.)

If $c$ does equal $b$, then $a < c$. (Therefore, II could not be true.)

Select (D) as your answer choice.

## Example SAT Math Problem 19

**Step 4**
Use
unconventional
methods
to score high
on SAT Math

................................

**330**

Note: Figure not drawn to scale.

What is the sum of the perimeters of triangles *ABC* and *CDE* in the figure above?

(A) 20
(B) 42
(C) 44
(D) 50
(E) 52

**Primary Math 2400 Strategy** ◦ *Know your triangles*

**Solution**

**1** ◦ *Know your triangles*

Notice the Pythagorean Triples in the figure.

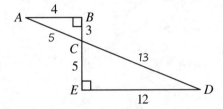

Alternatively, you could calculate the hypotenuse of each right triangle using the Pythagorean Theorem.

**2** ◦ *Calculate the total perimeter*

3 + 4 + 5 + 5 + 12 + 13 = 42

Select (B) as your answer choice.

## Example SAT Math Problem 20

If $\dfrac{j-k}{v+w} = \dfrac{7}{8}$, then $\dfrac{8j-8k}{21v+21w} =$

(A) $\dfrac{56}{3}$

(B) $\dfrac{15}{8}$

(C) $\dfrac{7}{8}$

(D) $\dfrac{8}{21}$

(E) $\dfrac{1}{3}$

**Primary Math 2400 Strategy** • *Plug in numbers*

**Solution**

**1** • *Plug in numbers*

NOTE  Use numbers that make the first equation true.

$j = 9$
$k = 2$
$v = 3$
$w = 5$

**2** • *Substitute numbers into the equations*

$\dfrac{j-k}{v+w} = \dfrac{7}{8} \qquad \dfrac{9-2}{3+5} = \dfrac{7}{8}$

$\dfrac{8j-8k}{21v+21w} \qquad \dfrac{8(9)-8(2)}{21(3)+21(5)} = \dfrac{72-16}{63+105} = \dfrac{56}{168} = \dfrac{1}{3}$

Select (E) as your answer choice.

Step 4
Use
unconventional
methods
to score high
on SAT Math

332

## Example SAT Math Problem 21

A certain menu has 5 appetizers, 7 entrées, and 3 desserts. How many different arrangements of one appetizer, one entrée, and one dessert are possible?

(A) 5
(B) 15
(C) 21
(D) 35
(E) 105

**Primary Math 2400 Strategy** ∘ *Do the first step*

**Solution**

**1** ∘ *Do the first step*

Determine how many possibilities are available.

$$\frac{\quad}{A} \ \frac{\quad}{E} \ \frac{\quad}{D} \qquad \frac{5}{A} \ \frac{7}{E} \ \frac{3}{D}$$

**2** ∘ *Multiply the possibilities*

$5 \times 7 \times 3 = 105$

NOTE Don't worry about combination/permutation formulas on the SAT; just think logically about the possibilities for each position.

Select (E) as your answer choice.

## Example SAT Math Problem 22

If $x^5k = a$ and $x^2k^2 = b$, what is the value of $x^3$ ?

(A) $\dfrac{a}{b}$

(B) $\dfrac{ak}{b}$

(C) $\dfrac{a^2k^2}{b}$

(D) $a - b$

(E) $a^2 - b^2$

**Primary Math 2400 Strategy** ∘ *Plug in numbers*

**Solution**

**1** ∘ *Plug in numbers*

$x = 2$
$k = 3$
$a = x^5k = (2^5)(3) = 96$
$b = x^2k^2 = (2^2)(3^2) = 36$

**2** • *Determine the value of the unknown*

$x^3 = 2^3 = 8$

**3** • *Substitute numbers into the answer choices*

(A) $\dfrac{a}{b}$ $= 2.67$

(B) $\dfrac{ak}{b}$ $= 8$ ✓

(C) $\dfrac{a^2k^2}{b}$ $= 2304$

(D) $a - b$ $= 60$

(E) $a^2 - b^2$ $= 7920$

Select (B) as your answer choice.

## Example SAT Math Problem 23

3, 6, 12, 24, …

In the geometric sequence above, 3 is the first term. What is the ratio of the ninth term to the fifth term?

(A) 6 to 1
(B) 9 to 5
(C) 16 to 1
(D) 64 to 1
(E) 256 to 1

**Primary Math 2400 Strategy** • *Do the first step*

**Solution**

**1** • *Do the first step*

Find the pattern.

Each term doubles the previous term.

**2** • *Do the next step*

Write out the sequence through the ninth term.

3, 6, 12, 24, 48, 96, 192, 384, 768

**3** • *Do the next step*

Determine the ratio of the ninth term to the fifth term.

$\dfrac{768}{48} = 16$

Select (C) as your answer choice.

# Example SAT Math Problem 24

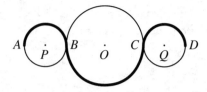

Note: Figure not drawn to scale.

In the figure above, circle $O$ has a radius of 3 and circles $P$ and $Q$ have diameters of 3. If the circles are tangent at points $B$ and $C$ as shown and the centers of the circles are collinear, what is the total length of the darkened curve?

(A) $6\pi$
(B) $8\pi$
(C) $9\pi$
(D) $10\pi$
(E) $12\pi$

**Primary Math 2400 Strategies** • *Label givens + Know your circles*

**Solution**

**1** • *Label givens*

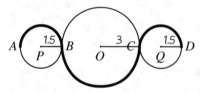

**2** • *Determine the circumference of each circle*

Circle $O$    $2\pi r = 2\pi(3)$  $= 6\pi$
Circle $P$    $2\pi r = 2\pi(1.5) = 3\pi$
Circle $Q$    $2\pi r = 2\pi(1.5) = 3\pi$

**3** • *Determine the length of the darkened curve*

$\frac{1}{2}C$ of $O$ + $\frac{1}{2}C$ of $P$ + $\frac{1}{2}C$ of $Q$
$3\pi + 1.5\pi + 1.5\pi$
$6\pi$

Select (A) as your answer choice.

## Example SAT Math Problem 25

If $-1 < x < 1$, which of the following could be true?

I.   $x^2 < x$
II.  $x^2 > x$
III. $x^2 < x^3$

(A) I only
(B) II only
(C) III only
(D) I and II only
(E) I, II, and III

**Primary Math 2400 Strategy** ▪ *Plug in numbers*

**Solution**

**1** ▪ *Plug in numbers*

x = 1/2 or x = −1/2

You must choose both positive and negative numbers in order to account for any differences the sign could make.

**2** ▪ *Substitute numbers into the answer choices*

x = ½                                                 x = −½

I.   $x^2 < x$     1/4 < 1/2  ✓          I.   $x^2 < x$     1/4 < −1/2
II.  $x^2 > x$     1/4 > 1/2             II.  $x^2 > x$     1/4 > −1/2  ✓
III. $x^2 < x^3$   1/4 < 1/8            III. $x^2 < x^3$   1/4 < −1/8

Select (D) as your answer choice.

## Example SAT Math Problem 26

All of Max's sisters can sing.

If the statement above is true, which of the following must also be true?

(A) If Sheila can sing, she is Max's sister.
(B) If Donna cannot sing, she is Max's sister.
(C) If Petra cannot sing, she is not Max's sister.
(D) None of Max's brothers can sing.
(E) All of Max's sisters can dance.

**Primary Math 2400 Strategy** ▪ *Do the first step*

**Solution**

**1** ▪ *Do the first step*

Determine the contrapositive (opposite) of the statement (which must also be true).

If a girl cannot sing, she is not one of Max's sisters.

Select (C) as your answer choice.

**Step 4**
Use
unconventional
methods
to score high
on SAT Math

**336**

## Example SAT Math Problem 27

If $x$ varies directly with $y$, which of the following could be the graph that shows the relationship between $x$ and $y$ ?

(A)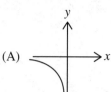

(B)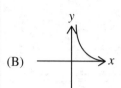

(C)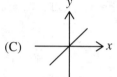

(D)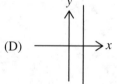

(E)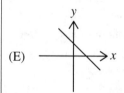

**Primary Math 2400 Strategy** ▪ *Know your graphs*

**Primary math concept**

Number properties

- ◄ If two numbers are directly proportional . . .
  - ◄ If one number increases, the other increases in the same proportion.
  - ◄ If one number decreases, the other decreases in the same proportion.
- ◄ If two numbers are inversely proportional . . .
  - ◄ If one number increases, the other decreases in the same proportion.
  - ◄ If one number decreases, the other increases in the same proportion.

**Solution**

**1** ● *Know your graphs*

Because *x* and *y* are directly proportional, when *x* increases (shifts right on the graph), *y* should also increase (shift up on the graph) in the same proportion. Interpret the graphs in the answer choices as follows.

(A) When *x* increases, *y* decreases.
(B) When *x* increases, *y* decreases.
(C) When *x* increases, *y* increases.
(D) *x* does not increase.
(E) When *x* increases, *y* decreases.

Select (C) as your answer choice.

## Example SAT Math Problem 28

$$4, 7, 10, 13, \ldots$$

In the sequence above, 4 is the first term and each term after the first is 3 more than the previous term. If *n* is the *n*th term, which of the following could be used to find the term equal to 100 ?

(A) $3(100) + 1 = n$
(B) $4(100) = n$
(C) $4n - 1 = 100$
(D) $3n - 2 = 100$
(E) $3n + 1 = 100$

**Primary Math 2400 Strategy** ● *Simplify impractical problems*

**Solution**

**1** ● *Simplify impractical problems*

Choose one of the terms given; for example, when $n = 3$, the term is 10.

Replace 100 with 10 in the answer choices, and find the one that works when $n = 3$.

(A) $3(100) + 1 = n$ $\quad$ $3(10) + 1 = n$
(B) $4(100) = n$ $\quad$ $4(10) = n$
(C) $4n - 1 = 100$ $\quad$ $4n - 1 = 10$
(D) $3n - 2 = 100$ $\quad$ $3n - 2 = 10$
(E) $3n + 1 = 100$ $\quad$ $3n + 1 = 10$ ✓

Because this formula works for one of the terms given, it must be the generic formula for the entire sequence.

Select (E) as your answer choice.

## Example SAT Math Problem 29

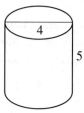

**Step 4**
Use
unconventional
methods
to score high
on SAT Math

**338**

Note: Figure not drawn to scale.

Which of the following right prisms has a volume closest to the volume of the cylinder above?

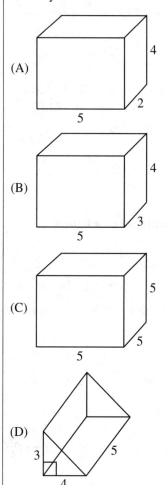

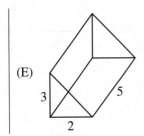

(E)

3

5

2

**Primary Math 2400 Strategy** ▪ *Do the first step*

**Primary math concept**

3-D geometry

- ◄ The volume of a cylinder is the area of the circle base multiplied by the height.
- ◄ The volume of a rectangular box is the area of the rectangular base multiplied by the height.
- ◄ The volume of a triangular prism is the area of the triangular base multiplied by the height.

**Solution**

**1** ▪ *Do the first step*

AREA OF THE CIRCLE BASE OF THE CYLINDER

$A = \pi r^2$

$\quad = \pi 2^2$

$\quad = \pi 4$

$\quad = \text{about } 12.5$

VOLUME OF THE CYLINDER

$V = A \times h$

$\quad \approx 12.5 \times 5$

$\quad \approx 62.5$

**2** ▪ *Calculate the volume of the answer choices*

(A) 40

(B) 60 ✓

(C) 125

(D) 30

(E) 15

Select (B) as your answer choice.

## Example SAT Math Problem 30

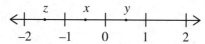

If $x$, $y$, and $z$ are the values indicated on the number line above, which of the following inequalities is true?

(A) $x^2 < y^3 < z^3$
(B) $x^2 < z^3 < y^3$
(C) $y^3 < x^2 < z^3$
(D) $z^3 < x^2 < y^3$
(E) $z^3 < y^3 < x^2$

**Step 4**
Use
unconventional
methods
to score high
on SAT Math

**340**

**Primary Math 2400 Strategy** • *Plug in numbers*

**Solution**

**1** • *Plug in numbers*

$x = -0.5$
$y = 0.5$
$z = -1.5$

**2** • *Substitute numbers into the answer choices*

(A) $x^2 < y^3 < z^3$   $.25 < .125 < -3.375$
(B) $x^2 < z^3 < y^3$   $.25 < -3.375 < .125$
(C) $y^3 < x^2 < z^3$   $.125 < .25 < -3.375$
(D) $z^3 < x^2 < y^3$   $-3.375 < .25 < .125$
(E) $z^3 < y^3 < x^2$   $-3.375 < .125 < .25$ ✓

Select (E) as your answer choice.

## Example SAT Math Problem 31

The win-loss-tie record for the soccer team is $4:3:2$, respectively. If the team played 36 matches in a season, how many more matches did they win than lose?

(A) 2
(B) 4
(C) 8
(D) 12
(E) 16

**Primary Math 2400 Strategy** • *Do the first step*

**Solution**

**1** • *Do the first step*

Add the ratio.

$4 + 3 + 2 = 9$

**2** • *Do the next step*

Divide the number of matches by the total.

$$\frac{36}{9} = 4$$

**3** • *Do the next step*

Multiply each individual number by 4.

$4:3:2 \rightarrow 16:12:8$

**4** • *Subtract the number of losses from the number of wins*

$16 - 12 = 4$

Select (B) as your answer choice.

### Example SAT Math Problem 32

**Step 4**
Use
unconventional
methods
to score high
on SAT Math

342

In the figure above, square $ABCD$ has an area of 24 and $E$, $F$, $G$, and $H$ are midpoints of the sides of the square. What is the area of the shaded region (units$^2$)?

(A) 6
(B) 9
(C) 15
(D) 24
(E) 30

**Primary Math 2400 Strategies** • *Label givens* + *Know your triangles*

**Solution**

**1** • *Label givens*

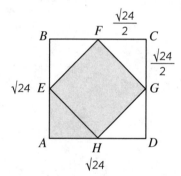

**2** • *Calculate the area of the nonshaded region*

$A = \frac{1}{2}bh$
$\quad = \frac{1}{2}(\sqrt{24}/2)(\sqrt{24}/2)$
$\quad = 3$

3 triangles of area 3 → 9

**3** • *Calculate the area of the shaded region*

$A = 24 - 9 = 15$

Select (C) as your answer choice.

## Example SAT Math Problem 33

If a number $n$ divided by 7 has a remainder of 4 and when divided by 9 has a remainder of 5, which of the following could be $n + 6$ ?

(A) 67
(B) 69
(C) 86
(D) 95
(E) 101

**Primary Math 2400 Strategy** ▪ *Test answer choices*

## Solution

**1** ▪ *Determine n from each answer choice*

(A) 67  $= n + 6 \rightarrow 61$
(B) 69  $= n + 6 \rightarrow 63$
(C) 86  $= n + 6 \rightarrow 80$
(D) 95  $= n + 6 \rightarrow 89$
(E) 101 $= n + 6 \rightarrow 95$

**2** ▪ *Test the new answer choices*

Divide each $n$ by 7.

(A) $61 / 7 \rightarrow$ *remainder of 5*
(B) $63 / 7 \rightarrow$ *remainder of 0*
(C) $80 / 7 \rightarrow$ *remainder of 3*
(D) $89 / 7 \rightarrow$ *remainder of 5*
(E) $95 / 7 \rightarrow$ *remainder of 4* ✓

Select (E) as your answer choice.

## Example SAT Math Problem 34

The line defined by equation $3x + 2y = 25$ intersects line $m$ at $(5, a)$.
If $m$ has a slope of 2, what is the $y$ intercept of $m$ ?

(A) $-5$
(B) $-3$
(C) 0
(D) 10
(E) 12.5

Step 4
Use
unconventional
methods
to score high
on SAT Math

344

**Primary Math 2400 Strategy** • *Know your graphs*

**Solution**

**1** • *Determine a*

$3x + 2y = 25$

Plug in point $(5, a)$.

$3(5) + 2a = 25$
$15 + 2a = 25$
$2a = 10$
$a = 5$

**2** • *Determine the point-slope form*

Given point $(5, 5)$ and slope $= 2$:

$y = mx + b$
$5 = 2(5) + b$
$-5 = b$

Select (A) as your answer choice.

## Example SAT Math Problem 35

| $x$ | $g(x)$ |
|-----|--------|
| 0   | 10     |
| 1   | 8      |
| 2   | 6      |
| 3   | 4      |

The table above shows the values of the function $g$ with four values of $x$.
If $g$ is linear, which of the following defines $g(x)$ ?

(A) $g(x) = x + 10$
(B) $g(x) = 2x + 10$
(C) $g(x) = 3x - 5$
(D) $g(x) = 10 - x$
(E) $g(x) = 10 - 2x$

**Solution**

**1** ▪ *Test the middle answer choice*

(C) $g(x) = 3x - 5$

When $x = 0$, does $g(x) = 10$?

$g(x) = 3(0) - 5 = -5$ ✘

**2** ▪ *Test the next answer choice*

(D) $g(x) = 10 - x$

When $x = 0$, does $g(x) = 10$?

$g(x) = 10 - (0) = 10$ ✔

When $x = 1$, does $g(x) = 8$?

$g(x) = 10 - (1) = 9$ ✘

**3** ▪ *Test the next answer choice*

(E) $g(x) = 10 - 2x$

When $x = 0$, does $g(x) = 10$?

$g(x) = 10 - 2(0) = 10$ ✔

When $x = 1$, does $g(x) = 8$?

$g(x) = 10 - 2(1) = 8$ ✔

When $x = 2$, does $g(x) = 6$?

$g(x) = 10 - 2(2) = 6$ ✔

When $x = 3$, does $g(x) = 4$?

$g(x) = 10 - 2(3) = 4$ ✔

Select (E) as your answer choice.

## Example SAT Math Problem 36

**Step 4**
Use
unconventional
methods
to score high
on SAT Math
.....................
**346**

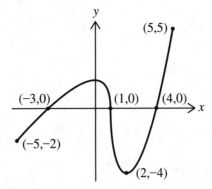

In the figure above, $f(x)$ is only defined for the values of $x$ such that $-5 \leq x \leq 5$. How many $x$ intercepts does $f(x) + 3$ have?

(A) One
(B) Two
(C) Three
(D) Four
(E) More than four

**Primary Math 2400 Strategy** ◦ *Know your graphs*

**Solution**

**1** ◦ *Know your graphs*

The graph currently has 3 $x$-intercepts: $(-3, 0)$, $(1, 0)$, and $(4, 0)$.

**2** ◦ *Shift the graph*

Shift the graph up 3 units.

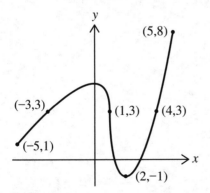

At how many points does the shifted graph cross the $x$-axis? Two.

Select (B) as your answer choice.

## Example SAT Math Problem 37

Jessica roller skates from home to school at 2 mph and returns home along the same route at 4 mph. If she spends 90 minutes commuting to and from school, how far is it from her home to school?

(A) 2 miles
(B) 2.25 miles
(C) 3.75 miles
(D) 4 miles
(E) 4.5 miles

**Primary Math 2400 Strategy** • *Test answer choices*

**Solution**

**1** • *Test the middle answer choice*

(C) 3.75 miles

If the route is 3.75 miles long, it would take Jessica 1.875 hours (3.75 miles / 2 miles per hour) to commute from home to school.

Answer choice (C) must be incorrect, because Jessica's entire round trip takes only 1.5 hours (= 90 minutes).

**2** • *Test another answer choice*

(A) 2 miles

If the route is 2 miles long, it would take Jessica 1 hour (= 2 miles / 2 miles per hour) to commute from home to school.

If the route is 2 miles long, it would take Jessica .5 hours (= 2 miles / 4 miles per hour) to commute from school to home.

The round trip takes 1.5 hours.

Select (A) as your answer choice.

### Example SAT Math Problem 38

If $a^b = 8$ for some integers $a$ and $b$, which of the following could be true?

   I.  $a < b$
  II.  $b < a$
 III.  $a = -2$

(A) I only
(B) II only
(C) I and II only
(D) II and III only
(E) I, II, and III

**Primary Math 2400 Strategy** • *Plug in numbers*

**Solution**

**1** • *Plug in numbers*

What are some common ways to produce 8 when one integer is raised to the power of another integer?

$2^3 = 8$
$8^1 = 8$

**2** • *Check the conditions*

   I.  Could $a < b$?     Yes. ($2^3 = 8$)
  II.  Could $b < a$?     Yes. ($8^1 = 8$)
 III.  Could $a = -2$?  No.

Select (C) as your answer choice.

### Example SAT Math Problem 39

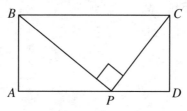

Note: Figure not drawn to scale.

If $CD = 4$ and $AP = 5$ in rectangle $ABCD$, what is the square of the length of $BP$?

**Primary Math 2400 Strategies** ▫ *Label givens ＋ Know your triangles*

**Primary math concept**

Rectangles

◂ All four angles in a rectangle are 90°.

**Solution**

**1** ▫ *Label givens*

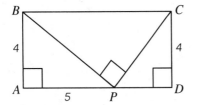

**2** ▫ *Know your triangles*

Use the Pythagorean Theorem.

$4^2 + 5^2 = BP^2$
$41 = BP^2$

Fill in 41 as your answer.

## Example SAT Math Problem 40

The sum of 5 consecutive odd integers is 65. What is the least of these 5 integers?

**Primary Math 2400 Strategy** ▫ *Do the first step*

**Solution**

**1** ▫ *Do the first step*

Because the numbers are consecutive, they must be close to the same value.

$65 / 5 \text{ values} = 13$

**2** ▫ *Do the next step*

The current sequence is 13, 13, 13, 13, 13 (sum = 65).

In order to make the above sequence consecutive odd integers without changing the sum, subtract 4 from the first term, subtract 2 from the second term, keep the middle term constant, add 2 to the fourth term, and add 4 to the fifth term.

The new sequence is 9, 11, 13, 15, 17 (sum = 65).

Fill in 9 as your answer.

Step 4
Use
unconventional
methods
to score high
on SAT Math

350

## Example SAT Math Problem 41

What is the units digit of $7^{2515}$ ?

**Primary Math 2400 Strategy** · *Simplify impractical problems*

**Solution**

**1** · *Simplify impractical problems*

Begin by putting 7 to the power of different integers.

$7^1 = 7$
$7^2 = 49$
$7^3 = 343$
$7^4 = 2401$
$7^5 = 16,807$
$7^6 = 117,649$
$7^7 = 823,543$

**2** · *Find a pattern*

The units digit seems to repeat the pattern 7 9 3 1.

**3** · *Divide*

Divide 2515 by 4.

$2515 / 4 = 628$ remainder 3 (or 628.75)

**4** · *Interpret the quotient*

The pattern 7 9 3 1 would repeat 628 times.

The units digit would correspond to the third term in the pattern.

Fill in 3 as your answer.

## Example SAT Math Problem 42

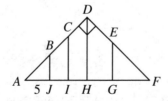

Note: Figure not drawn to scale.

In the figure above, $\triangle ADF$ is a right isosceles triangle and

$\overline{BJ} \parallel \overline{CI} \parallel \overline{DH} \parallel \overline{EG}$. $\overline{DH}$ bisects angle $ADF$. If $DE = EF = \dfrac{9\sqrt{2}}{2}$,

what is the length of $\overline{JF}$?

**Solution**

**1** • *Know your triangles*

A right isosceles triangle is also known as a 45°/45°/90° triangle.

When DH bisects angle ADF, it forms another 45°/45°/90° triangle: $\triangle DHF$.

**2** • *Calculate the length of $\overline{DF}$*

$\overline{DF} = \overline{DE} + \overline{EF}$

$\overline{DF} = \dfrac{9\sqrt{2}}{2} + \dfrac{9\sqrt{2}}{2}$

$\overline{DF} = 9\sqrt{2}$

**3** • *Know your triangles*

Because $\overline{DF}$ is the hypotenuse of $\triangle DHF$,

$\overline{DH} = \overline{HF} = \dfrac{9\sqrt{2}}{\sqrt{2}} = 9$

Because $\overline{DH}$ bisects an isosceles triangle, $\triangle DHF = \triangle DHA$.

$\overline{DH} = \overline{AH} = \dfrac{9\sqrt{2}}{\sqrt{2}} = 9$

**4** • *Calculate the length of $\overline{JF}$*

$\overline{JF} = \overline{JH} + \overline{HF}$

$\quad\quad = (\overline{AH} - \overline{AJ}) + 9$

$\quad\quad = (9 - 5) + 9$

$\quad\quad = (4) + 9$

$\quad\quad = 13$

Fill in 13 as your answer.

## Example SAT Math Problem 43

Step 4
Use
unconventional
methods
to score high
on SAT Math

352

For all integers $a$ and $b$, $a \odot b = 2^a 5^b$. If $p \odot q = \dfrac{1}{100}$, what is the value of $p - q$ ?

(A) $-10$
(B) $-4$
(C) $0$
(D) $10$
(E) It cannot be determined from the information provided.

**Primary Math 2400 Strategy** ⋅ *Plug in numbers*

**Solution**

**1** ⋅ *Plug in numbers*

Begin by listing the powers of 2 and 5.

$2^0 = 1$      $5^0 = 1$
$2^1 = 2$      $5^1 = 5$
$2^2 = 4$      $5^2 = 25$
$2^3 = 8$      $5^3 = 125$
$2^4 = 16$      $5^4 = 625$

**2** ⋅ *Examine the list*

Is there a way to produce 100 from the multiples of the powers of 2 and 5 listed above? Yes.

$2^2 \times 5^2 = 100$

**3** ⋅ *Calculate the reciprocal*

In order to get $\dfrac{1}{100}$, you must calculate $2^{-2} \times 5^{-2} = \dfrac{1}{100}$.

$a = -2$
$b = -2$

**4** ⋅ *Subtract*

$a - b = (-2) - (-2) = 0$

Select (C) as your answer choice.

## Example SAT Math Problem 44

Sue scored 85, 90, and $x$ on 3 equally weighted tests. If her average (arithmetic mean) test score is 91, what is the value of $x$ ?

(A) 91
(B) 92
(C) 93
(D) 98
(E) 99

**Primary Math 2400 Strategy** • *Test answer choices*

**Solution**

**1** • *Test the middle answer choice*

(C) 93

If $x = 93$, then Sue's average would be as follows.

$$\frac{85 + 90 + 93}{3} = 89.33$$

**2** • *Test the next answer choice*

(D) 98

If $x = 98$, then Sue's average would be as follows.

$$\frac{85 + 90 + 98}{3} = 91 \checkmark$$

Select (D) as your answer choice.

## Example SAT Math Problem 45

**Step 4**
Use
unconventional
methods
to score high
on SAT Math

354

Jana, Kat, and Laura spent 36 hours on a group project. Kat spent twice as long as Jana. Laura spent three times as long as Kat. How much time did Jana spend on the project?

(A)  4 hours
(B)  6 hours
(C)  8 hours
(D)  12 hours
(E)  24 hours

**Primary Math 2400 Strategy** • *Test answer choices*

**Solution**

**1** • *Test the middle answer choice*

(C)  8 hours

| Jana | 8 |
|------|-----|
| Kat | 16 |
| Laura | 48 |
| | 72 |

**2** • *Test another answer choice*

(A) 4 hours

| Jana | 4 |
|------|-----|
| Kat | 8 |
| Laura | 24 |
| | 36 |

Select (A) as your answer choice.

## Example SAT Math Problem 46

$m$, $x$, and $n$ are positive integers. If 20% of $m$ is $x$, and .02 percent of $n$ is $x$, which of the following must be true?

(A) $m > n$
(B) $m < x$
(C) $n > m$
(D) $x > n$
(E) $m = n$

**Primary Math 2400 Strategy** ▪ *Plug in numbers*

**Solution**

**1** ▪ *Plug in numbers*

$m = 10$

**2** ▪ *Calculate x*

20% of 10 = $x$ = 2

**3** ▪ *Calculate n*

.02% of $n$ = $x$
.0002$n$ = 2
$n$ = 10,000

**4** ▪ *Examine the values*

$m = 10$
$x = 2$
$n = 10,000$

Select (C) as your answer choice.

# Example SAT Math Problem 47

**Step 4**
Use
unconventional
methods
to score high
on SAT Math

356

Note: Figure not drawn to scale.

In the figure above, what is the value of $y$ ?

(A) 30
(B) 60
(C) 90
(D) 120
(E) 160

**Primary Math 2400 Strategy** ○ *Know your triangles*

**Solution**

**1** ○ *Know your triangles*

$2x° + 3x° + x° = 180°$
$6x° = 180°$
$x° = 30°$

**2** ○ *Know your angles*

$2x° = 2(30)° = 60°$

$2x° + y° = 180°$
$60° + y° = 180°$
$y° = 120°$

Select (D) as your answer choice.

## Example SAT Math Problem 48

Let the function $f$ be defined by $f(x) = x^2$ for all $x$. Which of the following is equal to $f(a - 2)$?

(A) $a^2 + 4$
(B) $a^2 - 4$
(C) $a^2 + 4a + 4$
(D) $a^2 - 4a - 4$
(E) $a^2 - 4a + 4$

**Primary Math 2400 Strategy** • *Plug in numbers*

## Solution

**1** • *Plug in numbers*

$a = 4$

**2** • *Solve $f(a - 2)$*

$$f(a - 2) = f(4 - 2)$$
$$= f(2)$$
$$= 2^2$$
$$= 4$$

**3** • *Substitute numbers into the answer choices*

$a = 4$

(A) $a^2 + 4$      $= 20$
(B) $a^2 - 4$      $= 12$
(C) $a^2 + 4a + 4$   $= 36$
(D) $a^2 - 4a - 4$   $= -4$
(E) $a^2 - 4a + 4$   $= 4$   ✓

Select (E) as your answer choice.

# Example SAT Math Problem 49

Step 4
Use
unconventional
methods
to score high
on SAT Math
..........................
358

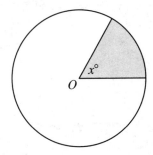

Note: Figure not drawn to scale.

In the figure above, the circle with center $O$ has a circumference of $12\pi$ and the area of the shaded region is $3\pi$. What is the value of $x$?

(A) 30
(B) 60
(C) 70
(D) 80
(E) 90

## Primary Math 2400 Strategy • *Know your circles*

## Solution

**1** • *Know your circles*

Find the radius ($r$).

$2\pi r = 12\pi$
$\pi r = 6\pi$
$r = 6$

**2** • *Calculate the area of the circle*

$A = \pi r^2$
$\phantom{A} = \pi 6^2$
$\phantom{A} = \pi 36$

**3** • *Determine the ratio*

Shaded region area    $3\pi$
Total circle area      $36\pi$

Ratio   $\dfrac{3\pi}{36\pi} = \dfrac{1}{12}$

**4** • *Convert the ratio to degrees*

$\dfrac{1}{12}$ of $360° = 30°$

Select (A) as your answer choice.

## Example SAT Math Problem 50

$$4x - 7y = 13$$

Which of the following equations, when graphed with the equation above, does not share any points in common?

(A) $4x + 7y = 13$
(B) $7x - 4y = 27$
(C) $8x - 14y = 27$
(D) $8x + 14y = 27$
(E) $8x + 14y = 26$

**Primary Math 2400 Strategy** • *Know your graphs*

**Primary math concept**

Graphs

◄ Parallel lines share no points in common.
◄ Parallel lines have the same slope.

## Solution

**1** • *Calculate the slope of the equation*

Convert the equation to point-slope form.

$4x - 7y = 13$

$-7y = -4x + 13$
$y = (4/7)x + -(13/7)$

$m \text{ (slope)} = 4/7$

**2** • *Calculate the slopes of the answer choices*

(A) $4x + 7y = 13$    $m = -4/7$
(B) $7x - 4y = 27$    $m = 7/4$
(C) $8x - 14y = 27$    $m = 4/7$    ✓
(D) $8x + 14y = 27$    $m = -4/7$
(E) $8x + 14y = 26$    $m = -4/7$

Select (C) as your answer choice.

# Practice with a simulated SAT test

To simulate SAT testing conditions, take this practice test in one sitting. Time each section as directed. Take a five-minute break after Sections 2, 4, and 6. The test should take about 3 hours and 45 minutes to complete. Mark your answers on the answer sheets on pages 363–366.

### Notes

1. The SAT variable section in this practice test is designated Section 10 and is omitted. (For details about the variable section, see page 3.)
2. Each multiple-choice section on the answer sheets has space for 40 answers. No section of the SAT has more than 35 questions.
3. Although the SAT is formatted in two columns per page, this practice test has only one column per page, providing more space for you to Write Everything Down (*General 2400 Strategy 2,* page 22).

After you have completed the test, proceed to Chapter 6, where the correct answers are given, along with my personal strategies for solving each question.

1  Ⓐ Ⓑ Ⓒ Ⓓ Ⓔ     11  Ⓐ Ⓑ Ⓒ Ⓓ Ⓔ     21  Ⓐ Ⓑ Ⓒ Ⓓ Ⓔ     31  Ⓐ Ⓑ Ⓒ Ⓓ Ⓔ
2  Ⓐ Ⓑ Ⓒ Ⓓ Ⓔ     12  Ⓐ Ⓑ Ⓒ Ⓓ Ⓔ     22  Ⓐ Ⓑ Ⓒ Ⓓ Ⓔ     32  Ⓐ Ⓑ Ⓒ Ⓓ Ⓔ
3  Ⓐ Ⓑ Ⓒ Ⓓ Ⓔ     13  Ⓐ Ⓑ Ⓒ Ⓓ Ⓔ     23  Ⓐ Ⓑ Ⓒ Ⓓ Ⓔ     33  Ⓐ Ⓑ Ⓒ Ⓓ Ⓔ
4  Ⓐ Ⓑ Ⓒ Ⓓ Ⓔ     14  Ⓐ Ⓑ Ⓒ Ⓓ Ⓔ     24  Ⓐ Ⓑ Ⓒ Ⓓ Ⓔ     34  Ⓐ Ⓑ Ⓒ Ⓓ Ⓔ
5  Ⓐ Ⓑ Ⓒ Ⓓ Ⓔ     15  Ⓐ Ⓑ Ⓒ Ⓓ Ⓔ     25  Ⓐ Ⓑ Ⓒ Ⓓ Ⓔ     35  Ⓐ Ⓑ Ⓒ Ⓓ Ⓔ
6  Ⓐ Ⓑ Ⓒ Ⓓ Ⓔ     16  Ⓐ Ⓑ Ⓒ Ⓓ Ⓔ     26  Ⓐ Ⓑ Ⓒ Ⓓ Ⓔ     36  Ⓐ Ⓑ Ⓒ Ⓓ Ⓔ
7  Ⓐ Ⓑ Ⓒ Ⓓ Ⓔ     17  Ⓐ Ⓑ Ⓒ Ⓓ Ⓔ     27  Ⓐ Ⓑ Ⓒ Ⓓ Ⓔ     37  Ⓐ Ⓑ Ⓒ Ⓓ Ⓔ
8  Ⓐ Ⓑ Ⓒ Ⓓ Ⓔ     18  Ⓐ Ⓑ Ⓒ Ⓓ Ⓔ     28  Ⓐ Ⓑ Ⓒ Ⓓ Ⓔ     38  Ⓐ Ⓑ Ⓒ Ⓓ Ⓔ
9  Ⓐ Ⓑ Ⓒ Ⓓ Ⓔ     19  Ⓐ Ⓑ Ⓒ Ⓓ Ⓔ     29  Ⓐ Ⓑ Ⓒ Ⓓ Ⓔ     39  Ⓐ Ⓑ Ⓒ Ⓓ Ⓔ
10 Ⓐ Ⓑ Ⓒ Ⓓ Ⓔ     20  Ⓐ Ⓑ Ⓒ Ⓓ Ⓔ     30  Ⓐ Ⓑ Ⓒ Ⓓ Ⓔ     40  Ⓐ Ⓑ Ⓒ Ⓓ Ⓔ

## Student-produced responses

9   10   11   12   13

14   15   16   17   18

## Section 6 Reading

1 Ⓐ Ⓑ Ⓒ Ⓓ Ⓔ    11 Ⓐ Ⓑ Ⓒ Ⓓ Ⓔ    21 Ⓐ Ⓑ Ⓒ Ⓓ Ⓔ    31 Ⓐ Ⓑ Ⓒ Ⓓ Ⓔ
2 Ⓐ Ⓑ Ⓒ Ⓓ Ⓔ    12 Ⓐ Ⓑ Ⓒ Ⓓ Ⓔ    22 Ⓐ Ⓑ Ⓒ Ⓓ Ⓔ    32 Ⓐ Ⓑ Ⓒ Ⓓ Ⓔ
3 Ⓐ Ⓑ Ⓒ Ⓓ Ⓔ    13 Ⓐ Ⓑ Ⓒ Ⓓ Ⓔ    23 Ⓐ Ⓑ Ⓒ Ⓓ Ⓔ    33 Ⓐ Ⓑ Ⓒ Ⓓ Ⓔ
4 Ⓐ Ⓑ Ⓒ Ⓓ Ⓔ    14 Ⓐ Ⓑ Ⓒ Ⓓ Ⓔ    24 Ⓐ Ⓑ Ⓒ Ⓓ Ⓔ    34 Ⓐ Ⓑ Ⓒ Ⓓ Ⓔ
5 Ⓐ Ⓑ Ⓒ Ⓓ Ⓔ    15 Ⓐ Ⓑ Ⓒ Ⓓ Ⓔ    25 Ⓐ Ⓑ Ⓒ Ⓓ Ⓔ    35 Ⓐ Ⓑ Ⓒ Ⓓ Ⓔ
6 Ⓐ Ⓑ Ⓒ Ⓓ Ⓔ    16 Ⓐ Ⓑ Ⓒ Ⓓ Ⓔ    26 Ⓐ Ⓑ Ⓒ Ⓓ Ⓔ    36 Ⓐ Ⓑ Ⓒ Ⓓ Ⓔ
7 Ⓐ Ⓑ Ⓒ Ⓓ Ⓔ    17 Ⓐ Ⓑ Ⓒ Ⓓ Ⓔ    27 Ⓐ Ⓑ Ⓒ Ⓓ Ⓔ    37 Ⓐ Ⓑ Ⓒ Ⓓ Ⓔ
8 Ⓐ Ⓑ Ⓒ Ⓓ Ⓔ    18 Ⓐ Ⓑ Ⓒ Ⓓ Ⓔ    28 Ⓐ Ⓑ Ⓒ Ⓓ Ⓔ    38 Ⓐ Ⓑ Ⓒ Ⓓ Ⓔ
9 Ⓐ Ⓑ Ⓒ Ⓓ Ⓔ    19 Ⓐ Ⓑ Ⓒ Ⓓ Ⓔ    29 Ⓐ Ⓑ Ⓒ Ⓓ Ⓔ    39 Ⓐ Ⓑ Ⓒ Ⓓ Ⓔ
10 Ⓐ Ⓑ Ⓒ Ⓓ Ⓔ   20 Ⓐ Ⓑ Ⓒ Ⓓ Ⓔ    30 Ⓐ Ⓑ Ⓒ Ⓓ Ⓔ    40 Ⓐ Ⓑ Ⓒ Ⓓ Ⓔ

## Section 7 Math

1 Ⓐ Ⓑ Ⓒ Ⓓ Ⓔ    11 Ⓐ Ⓑ Ⓒ Ⓓ Ⓔ    21 Ⓐ Ⓑ Ⓒ Ⓓ Ⓔ    31 Ⓐ Ⓑ Ⓒ Ⓓ Ⓔ
2 Ⓐ Ⓑ Ⓒ Ⓓ Ⓔ    12 Ⓐ Ⓑ Ⓒ Ⓓ Ⓔ    22 Ⓐ Ⓑ Ⓒ Ⓓ Ⓔ    32 Ⓐ Ⓑ Ⓒ Ⓓ Ⓔ
3 Ⓐ Ⓑ Ⓒ Ⓓ Ⓔ    13 Ⓐ Ⓑ Ⓒ Ⓓ Ⓔ    23 Ⓐ Ⓑ Ⓒ Ⓓ Ⓔ    33 Ⓐ Ⓑ Ⓒ Ⓓ Ⓔ
4 Ⓐ Ⓑ Ⓒ Ⓓ Ⓔ    14 Ⓐ Ⓑ Ⓒ Ⓓ Ⓔ    24 Ⓐ Ⓑ Ⓒ Ⓓ Ⓔ    34 Ⓐ Ⓑ Ⓒ Ⓓ Ⓔ
5 Ⓐ Ⓑ Ⓒ Ⓓ Ⓔ    15 Ⓐ Ⓑ Ⓒ Ⓓ Ⓔ    25 Ⓐ Ⓑ Ⓒ Ⓓ Ⓔ    35 Ⓐ Ⓑ Ⓒ Ⓓ Ⓔ
6 Ⓐ Ⓑ Ⓒ Ⓓ Ⓔ    16 Ⓐ Ⓑ Ⓒ Ⓓ Ⓔ    26 Ⓐ Ⓑ Ⓒ Ⓓ Ⓔ    36 Ⓐ Ⓑ Ⓒ Ⓓ Ⓔ
7 Ⓐ Ⓑ Ⓒ Ⓓ Ⓔ    17 Ⓐ Ⓑ Ⓒ Ⓓ Ⓔ    27 Ⓐ Ⓑ Ⓒ Ⓓ Ⓔ    37 Ⓐ Ⓑ Ⓒ Ⓓ Ⓔ
8 Ⓐ Ⓑ Ⓒ Ⓓ Ⓔ    18 Ⓐ Ⓑ Ⓒ Ⓓ Ⓔ    28 Ⓐ Ⓑ Ⓒ Ⓓ Ⓔ    38 Ⓐ Ⓑ Ⓒ Ⓓ Ⓔ
9 Ⓐ Ⓑ Ⓒ Ⓓ Ⓔ    19 Ⓐ Ⓑ Ⓒ Ⓓ Ⓔ    29 Ⓐ Ⓑ Ⓒ Ⓓ Ⓔ    39 Ⓐ Ⓑ Ⓒ Ⓓ Ⓔ
10 Ⓐ Ⓑ Ⓒ Ⓓ Ⓔ   20 Ⓐ Ⓑ Ⓒ Ⓓ Ⓔ    30 Ⓐ Ⓑ Ⓒ Ⓓ Ⓔ    40 Ⓐ Ⓑ Ⓒ Ⓓ Ⓔ

## Section 8 Reading

1 Ⓐ Ⓑ Ⓒ Ⓓ Ⓔ    11 Ⓐ Ⓑ Ⓒ Ⓓ Ⓔ    21 Ⓐ Ⓑ Ⓒ Ⓓ Ⓔ    31 Ⓐ Ⓑ Ⓒ Ⓓ Ⓔ
2 Ⓐ Ⓑ Ⓒ Ⓓ Ⓔ    12 Ⓐ Ⓑ Ⓒ Ⓓ Ⓔ    22 Ⓐ Ⓑ Ⓒ Ⓓ Ⓔ    32 Ⓐ Ⓑ Ⓒ Ⓓ Ⓔ
3 Ⓐ Ⓑ Ⓒ Ⓓ Ⓔ    13 Ⓐ Ⓑ Ⓒ Ⓓ Ⓔ    23 Ⓐ Ⓑ Ⓒ Ⓓ Ⓔ    33 Ⓐ Ⓑ Ⓒ Ⓓ Ⓔ
4 Ⓐ Ⓑ Ⓒ Ⓓ Ⓔ    14 Ⓐ Ⓑ Ⓒ Ⓓ Ⓔ    24 Ⓐ Ⓑ Ⓒ Ⓓ Ⓔ    34 Ⓐ Ⓑ Ⓒ Ⓓ Ⓔ
5 Ⓐ Ⓑ Ⓒ Ⓓ Ⓔ    15 Ⓐ Ⓑ Ⓒ Ⓓ Ⓔ    25 Ⓐ Ⓑ Ⓒ Ⓓ Ⓔ    35 Ⓐ Ⓑ Ⓒ Ⓓ Ⓔ
6 Ⓐ Ⓑ Ⓒ Ⓓ Ⓔ    16 Ⓐ Ⓑ Ⓒ Ⓓ Ⓔ    26 Ⓐ Ⓑ Ⓒ Ⓓ Ⓔ    36 Ⓐ Ⓑ Ⓒ Ⓓ Ⓔ
7 Ⓐ Ⓑ Ⓒ Ⓓ Ⓔ    17 Ⓐ Ⓑ Ⓒ Ⓓ Ⓔ    27 Ⓐ Ⓑ Ⓒ Ⓓ Ⓔ    37 Ⓐ Ⓑ Ⓒ Ⓓ Ⓔ
8 Ⓐ Ⓑ Ⓒ Ⓓ Ⓔ    18 Ⓐ Ⓑ Ⓒ Ⓓ Ⓔ    28 Ⓐ Ⓑ Ⓒ Ⓓ Ⓔ    38 Ⓐ Ⓑ Ⓒ Ⓓ Ⓔ
9 Ⓐ Ⓑ Ⓒ Ⓓ Ⓔ    19 Ⓐ Ⓑ Ⓒ Ⓓ Ⓔ    29 Ⓐ Ⓑ Ⓒ Ⓓ Ⓔ    39 Ⓐ Ⓑ Ⓒ Ⓓ Ⓔ
10 Ⓐ Ⓑ Ⓒ Ⓓ Ⓔ   20 Ⓐ Ⓑ Ⓒ Ⓓ Ⓔ    30 Ⓐ Ⓑ Ⓒ Ⓓ Ⓔ    40 Ⓐ Ⓑ Ⓒ Ⓓ Ⓔ

1 Ⓐ Ⓑ Ⓒ Ⓓ Ⓔ   11 Ⓐ Ⓑ Ⓒ Ⓓ Ⓔ   21 Ⓐ Ⓑ Ⓒ Ⓓ Ⓔ   31 Ⓐ Ⓑ Ⓒ Ⓓ Ⓔ
2 Ⓐ Ⓑ Ⓒ Ⓓ Ⓔ   12 Ⓐ Ⓑ Ⓒ Ⓓ Ⓔ   22 Ⓐ Ⓑ Ⓒ Ⓓ Ⓔ   32 Ⓐ Ⓑ Ⓒ Ⓓ Ⓔ
3 Ⓐ Ⓑ Ⓒ Ⓓ Ⓔ   13 Ⓐ Ⓑ Ⓒ Ⓓ Ⓔ   23 Ⓐ Ⓑ Ⓒ Ⓓ Ⓔ   33 Ⓐ Ⓑ Ⓒ Ⓓ Ⓔ
4 Ⓐ Ⓑ Ⓒ Ⓓ Ⓔ   14 Ⓐ Ⓑ Ⓒ Ⓓ Ⓔ   24 Ⓐ Ⓑ Ⓒ Ⓓ Ⓔ   34 Ⓐ Ⓑ Ⓒ Ⓓ Ⓔ
5 Ⓐ Ⓑ Ⓒ Ⓓ Ⓔ   15 Ⓐ Ⓑ Ⓒ Ⓓ Ⓔ   25 Ⓐ Ⓑ Ⓒ Ⓓ Ⓔ   35 Ⓐ Ⓑ Ⓒ Ⓓ Ⓔ
6 Ⓐ Ⓑ Ⓒ Ⓓ Ⓔ   16 Ⓐ Ⓑ Ⓒ Ⓓ Ⓔ   26 Ⓐ Ⓑ Ⓒ Ⓓ Ⓔ   36 Ⓐ Ⓑ Ⓒ Ⓓ Ⓔ
7 Ⓐ Ⓑ Ⓒ Ⓓ Ⓔ   17 Ⓐ Ⓑ Ⓒ Ⓓ Ⓔ   27 Ⓐ Ⓑ Ⓒ Ⓓ Ⓔ   37 Ⓐ Ⓑ Ⓒ Ⓓ Ⓔ
8 Ⓐ Ⓑ Ⓒ Ⓓ Ⓔ   18 Ⓐ Ⓑ Ⓒ Ⓓ Ⓔ   28 Ⓐ Ⓑ Ⓒ Ⓓ Ⓔ   38 Ⓐ Ⓑ Ⓒ Ⓓ Ⓔ
9 Ⓐ Ⓑ Ⓒ Ⓓ Ⓔ   19 Ⓐ Ⓑ Ⓒ Ⓓ Ⓔ   29 Ⓐ Ⓑ Ⓒ Ⓓ Ⓔ   39 Ⓐ Ⓑ Ⓒ Ⓓ Ⓔ
10 Ⓐ Ⓑ Ⓒ Ⓓ Ⓔ   20 Ⓐ Ⓑ Ⓒ Ⓓ Ⓔ   30 Ⓐ Ⓑ Ⓒ Ⓓ Ⓔ   40 Ⓐ Ⓑ Ⓒ Ⓓ Ⓔ

**Section 10** **Variable section** (omitted)

# SECTION 1
# ESSAY
### Time — 25 minutes

You have 25 minutes to write an essay on the topic assigned below.

On the actual SAT, you will write your essay on two lined sheets provided in your answer booklet. For this practice test, write your essay on two lined sheets of paper (25 lines per sheet).

Write your essay in pencil, as required on the actual test.

Do not write on another topic. An off-topic essay will receive a score of zero.

Read the excerpt below. Think about the issue presented in the excerpt and respond to the assignment that follows.

> We cannot expect that all nations will adopt like systems, for conformity is the jailer of freedom and the enemy of growth.
>
> —John F. Kennedy

**Assignment:** Should people conform to societal values? Plan and write an essay in which you develop your point of view on this issue. Support your position with reasoning and examples taken from your reading, studies, experiences, or observations.

# SECTION 2
# MATH

Time — 25 minutes
20 Questions

**Directions:** Solve each of the following problems, using any available space in your test booklet for scratchwork. When you have selected the answer you think is best, fill in the corresponding circle on the answer sheet.

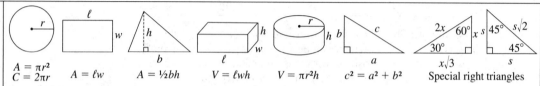
**1.** If Jill buys $k$ DVDs for $d$ dollars, what is the average (arithmetic mean) price of each DVD?

(A) $kd$

(B) $\dfrac{k}{d}$

(C) $\dfrac{d}{k}$

(D) $d + k$

(E) $d - k$

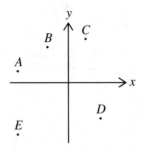

2. For which point in the *xy*-coordinate plane above is the product of the *x* and *y* coordinates the greatest?

(A) *A*
(B) *B*
(C) *C*
(D) *D*
(E) *E*

3. At Rose's Rose Market all the remaining 3100 roses are either red, yellow, or white. If 31% are red and 31% are white, what percent are yellow?

(A) 30%
(B) 31%
(C) 35%
(D) 38%
(E) 40%

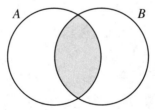

4. In the figure above, if set *A* represents the multiples of 5 and set *B* represents the factors of 100, which of the following numbers could be in the shaded region?

(A) 1
(B) 15
(C) 30
(D) 50
(E) 75

**5.** If $a + 10 + \dfrac{1}{10} < a + b + \dfrac{1}{10}$, which of the following
must be true?

(A) $b$ is a fraction
(B) $b$ is an integer
(C) $b = 10$
(D) $b < 10$
(E) $b > 10$

**6.** If $(m + 3)n = 13n$, which of the following must be true?

(A) $m = 3$
(B) $m = 10$
(C) $m = 13$
(D) $n - 3$
(E) $n = 10$

**Questions 7–9 refer to the following definition.**

Let $\varpi$ be defined by $p \varpi q = p(q + 1)$ for all numbers $p$ and $q$.

**7.** $3 \varpi 4 =$

(A) 7
(B) 12
(C) 14
(D) 15
(E) 16

**8.** If $2 \varpi a = 12$, then $a =$

(A) 5
(B) 6
(C) 7
(D) 8
(E) 9

**9.** If $m \neq 0$, for what value of $k$ will $m \varpi k = 0$ ?

(A) $-2$
(B) $-1$
(C) 0
(D) 1
(E) 2

**10.** If 2 is a root of the equation $x^2 + 3x = 10$, which of the following is another root?

(A) $-5$
(B) $-3$
(C) $-2$
(D) $3$
(E) $5$

**11.** If the diameter of a circle is $5c$, what is its area?

(A) $10\pi$
(B) $25\pi c$
(C) $25\pi c^2$
(D) $\dfrac{5\pi c}{2}$
(E) $\dfrac{25\pi c^2}{4}$

| $x$ | $f(x)$ |
|-----|--------|
| 3 | 19 |
| 6 | $a$ |
| 9 | $b$ |
| 12 | 46 |

**12.** In the table above, $f$ is a linear function. What is the value of $b - a$ ?

(A) $8$
(B) $9$
(C) $10$
(D) $11$
(E) $12$

RECORD HIGH AND LOW
TEMPERATURES FOR FIVE U.S. CITIES

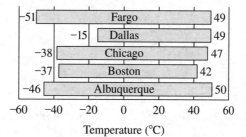

Temperature (°C)

**13.** The high and low record temperatures are displayed in
the chart above. If the cities were listed in order from
greatest temperature difference to least temperature
difference, which city would be third in the list?

(A) Albuquerque
(B) Boston
(C) Chicago
(D) Dallas
(E) Fargo

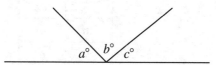

Note: Figure not drawn to scale.

**14.** In the figure above, $b < 90$ and $a = c + 1$. If $c$ is an integer,
what is the least possible value of $a$ ?

(A) 30
(B) 45
(C) 46
(D) 60
(E) 61

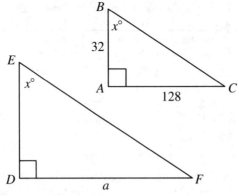

Note: Figure not drawn to scale.

**15.** In the figure above, what is the length of $\overline{DE}$ in terms of $a$ ?

(A) $a + 96$

(B) $2\sqrt{a}$

(C) $\dfrac{a}{4}$

(D) $4a$

(E) $\left(\dfrac{a}{2}\right)^2$

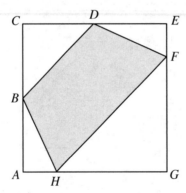

**16.** In the figure above, the probability that a point from square $ACEG$ is in the shaded region is $\dfrac{5}{8}$. What is the area of $\triangle HFG$ ?

(A) 5
(B) 10
(C) 25
(D) 50
(E) It cannot be determined from the information provided.

**17.** If the distance from Andrew's house to Betty's house is 5 miles and from Betty's to Candace's is 6 miles, which of the following could be the distance from Andrew's house to Candace's house?

(A) 10
(B) 12
(C) 13
(D) 15
(E) 16

**18.** At Hussain's Diner, if a burger is cooked for 5 minutes it burns, but if it cooks for 3 minutes it is undercooked. If $m$ is the number of minutes a burger at Hussain's Diner cooks that is nether burned nor undercooked, which of the following represents all the values of $m$ ?

(A) $|m| = 4$
(B) $|m - 3| < 5$
(C) $|m - 4| < 1$
(D) $|m - 4| < 5$
(E) $|m - 1| < 4$

**19.** If $\dfrac{1}{10ab}$ is the square of an integer and $\dfrac{1}{a}$ and $\dfrac{1}{b}$ are integers, which of the following could be the value of $ab$ ?

(A) 10

(B) 1

(C) $\dfrac{1}{9}$

(D) $\dfrac{1}{90}$

(E) $\dfrac{1}{100}$

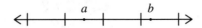

**20.** The tick marks on the number line above are equally spaced. If the average (arithmetic mean) of $a$ and $b$ is greater than the sum of $a$ and $b$, which of the following must be true?

    I. $a < 0$
   II. $|a| > b$
   III. $b < 0$

(A) I only
(B) II only
(C) I and II only
(D) I and III only
(E) II and III only

# STOP

**If you finish before time runs out,
you may check your work on this section only.
Do not turn to any other section of the test.**

Step 5
Practice with
a simulated
SAT test
............................
376

# SECTION 3
# WRITING

## Time — 25 minutes
## 35 Questions

**Directions:** Each question in this section has five answer choices labeled (A), (B), (C), (D), and (E). For each question, select the best answer from among the choices given and fill in the corresponding circle on the answer sheet.

The following sentences test correctness and effectiveness of expression. Part of each sentence or the entire sentence is underlined. Beneath each sentence are five ways of phrasing the underlined part. Choice (A) repeats the original phrasing. The other four choices are different. If you think the original phrasing is best, select choice (A). If not, select one of the other choices.

As you make your selection, follow the requirements of standard written English, paying attention to grammar, word choice, sentence construction, and punctuation. The correct choice should result in the most effective sentence—clear and precise, without awkwardness or ambiguity.

**Example**

The speaker praised the charitable organization but stressed that more funding is needed if the group is to continue its excellent work in the community.

(A) more funding is needed if the group is to continue its excellent work in the community
(B) more funding is needed for the group's continuing its excellent work in the community
(C) there is a need for more funding so the group continues its excellent work in the community
(D) a need for more funding for the group to continue its excellent work in the community
(E) they need more funding to continue its excellent work in the community

Correct answer: **(A)**

1. In the rainforests of Brazil, the Yanomami tribe often eat taro roots because of supposedly providing protection against malaria.

   (A) because of supposedly providing protection
   (B) for it is supposed that providing protection
   (C) for supposing that they would provide protection
   (D) because they supposedly provide protection
   (E) for being supposed that they provide protection

**2.** The ancient astronomer Ptolemy was a Roman citizen who lived in Egypt but actually writing most of his scientific works in Greek.

(A) The ancient astronomer Ptolemy was a Roman citizen who lived in Egypt but actually writing

(B) Despite being a Roman citizen, the ancient astronomer Ptolemy lived in Egypt, he actually wrote

(C) Although the ancient astronomer Ptolemy was a Roman citizen who lived in Egypt, he actually wrote

(D) Because he was a Roman citizen who lived in Egypt, the ancient astronomer Ptolemy actually writing

(E) Being that he was a Roman citizen who lived in Egypt, the ancient astronomer Ptolemy actually writing

**3.** Solar flares often release large amounts of x-rays and UV radiation, this may cause disruptions to radio communications on earth.

(A) radiation, this may cause

(B) radiation; causing

(C) radiation and causes

(D) radiation; for this reason they are causing

(E) radiation, which may cause

**4.** Excessive fishing in the waters off the Kamchatka peninsula, an area in eastern Russia, depleting fish populations and in turn harming the native brown bear, whose diet consists mainly of salmon.

(A) Russia, depleting fish populations and in turn harming

(B) Russia are depleting fish populations but they also harm

(C) Russia, depletes fish populations and in turn harms

(D) Russia, the depletion of fish populations and in turn harming

(E) Russia, which depletes fish populations and in turn harms

**5.** Crocodiles have the strongest bite in the entire animal kingdom; in fact, a crocodile bite is nearly twelve times more powerful than a great white shark.

(A) than a great white shark

(B) than those of a great white shark

(C) than those of a great white shark's

(D) than that of a great white shark

(E) than that of a great white shark's

6. Florists must use caution when handling a daffodil <u>because
its sap contains calcium oxalate</u>, a mild toxin that can cause
rashes and other skin problems.

  (A) because its sap contains calcium oxalate
  (B) due to the calcium oxalate contained in its sap
  (C) because of their sap which contains calcium oxalate
  (D) due to their sap containing calcium oxalate
  (E) because of the calcium oxalate contained in its sap

7. Rings around the moon can appear when tiny particles
of ice in the sky <u>causes light from a full moon</u> to refract
at a particular angle.

  (A) causes light from a full moon
  (B) causing a full moon's light
  (C) that causes light from a full moon
  (D) cause light from a full moon
  (E) which causes a full moon's light

8. In the equestrian sport of dressage, horses are judged on
their athletic ability, rhythm of gait, and <u>how willing they
are to obey</u> subtle commands.

  (A) how willing they are to obey
  (B) willingness to obey
  (C) whether or not they are willing to obey
  (D) how they willingly obey
  (E) willingness of their obeying

9. A virus does not just infect humans or other <u>animals, they
can also attack</u> plants, fungi, and even bacteria.

  (A) animals, they can also attack
  (B) animals, they are also attacking
  (C) animals; since it also can attack
  (D) animals, they also have attacked
  (E) animals; it can also attack

10. Rescuers spent thirteen days looking for Amelia Earhart
after her plane mysteriously vanished near Howland Island
in 1937, but <u>in searching the surrounding area, no trace of
her was found</u>.

  (A) in searching the surrounding area, no trace of her was
       found
  (B) with a search of the surrounding area, no trace of her
       was found
  (C) after searching the surrounding area, finding no trace
       of her
  (D) a search of the surrounding area resulted in no trace
       of her being found
  (E) when they searched the surrounding area, they found
       no trace of her

11. Artist Frederic Remington's illustrations of the American West were noteworthy not only because of their originality, but also because of them accurately depicting the motion of horses at full gallop.

(A) of them accurately depicting
(B) of their accuracy in depicting
(C) they were accurate when depicting
(D) of them depicting with accuracy
(E) they were accurate with the depicting of

**Directions:** The following sentences test your ability to recognize errors in grammar and usage. Each sentence contains either a single error or no error at all. The error, if there is one, is underlined and lettered. If the sentence contains an error, select the one underlined part that must be changed to make the sentence correct. If the sentence is correct as written, select choice E. As you choose your answers, follow the requirements of standard written English. No sentence contains more than one error.

**Example**

Geologists study data on recent earthquakes around the world
       A                                     B

as a means to predict when the next big quake might hit. No error
         C                              D      E

Correct answer: **C**

12. Although beluga whales like to congregate together
     A                       B

in pods, many belugas are transient and often prefer
                  C

to move restless from pod to pod. No error
        D              E

13. One of the greatest breakthroughs in the field of genetics
     A                            B

occurred when they discovered that the double helix is
          C

the basic structure of all DNA. No error
         D      E

14. The controversial new professor urged his students
       A

spending a night on the streets to experience firsthand
     B                     C

how it feels to be homeless. No error
          D    E

**Step 5**
Practice with
a simulated
SAT test
..........................
**380**

15. $\underset{\text{A}}{\underline{\text{More than}}}$ a century after the Mayan city of Chichen

Itza $\underset{\text{B}}{\underline{\text{is excavated}}}$ by researchers, we still $\underset{\text{C}}{\underline{\text{have not}}}$ yet

deciphered all of the hieroglyphics $\underset{\text{D}}{\underline{\text{that appear}}}$ on

its walls. $\underset{\text{E}}{\underline{\text{No error}}}$

16. The new mayor of the poverty-stricken city $\underset{\text{A}}{\underline{\text{quickly}}}$

implemented a plan to $\underset{\text{B}}{\underline{\text{reduce}}}$ violent crime, $\underset{\text{C}}{\underline{\text{and}}}$ just

a few years later, the homicide rate had $\underset{\text{D}}{\underline{\text{actually}}}$ tripled.

$\underset{\text{E}}{\underline{\text{No error}}}$

17. The Borzoi or Russian wolfhound is a breed of dog

that $\underset{\text{A}}{\underline{\text{is known for}}}$ its $\underset{\text{B}}{\underline{\text{surprising}}}$ graceful movements,

$\underset{\text{C}}{\underline{\text{especially}}}$ considering its $\underset{\text{D}}{\underline{\text{large size}}}$. $\underset{\text{E}}{\underline{\text{No error}}}$

18. $\underset{\text{A}}{\underline{\text{In Roman mythology}}}$, Romulus and Remus were twin

brothers who $\underset{\text{B}}{\underline{\text{were abandoned}}}$ in the wild as infants,

but they survived and $\underset{\text{C}}{\underline{\text{eventually}}}$ grew up to become

$\underset{\text{D}}{\underline{\text{the founder}}}$ of the city of Rome. $\underset{\text{E}}{\underline{\text{No error}}}$

19. Rebun Island in Japan $\underset{\text{A}}{\underline{\text{is known for}}}$ its spectacular

coastal scenery and its abundance of $\underset{\text{B}}{\underline{\text{rare}}}$ alpine flowers,

$\underset{\text{C}}{\underline{\text{which}}}$ grow there at sea level due to the $\underset{\text{D}}{\underline{\text{bitterly cold}}}$

climate. $\underset{\text{E}}{\underline{\text{No error}}}$

20. The Arenal volcano, $\underset{\text{A}}{\underline{\text{along with}}}$ four other volcanoes

in Costa Rica, $\underset{\text{B}}{\underline{\text{are}}}$ considered active and dangerous

$\underset{\text{C}}{\underline{\text{even though}}}$ recent reports show $\underset{\text{D}}{\underline{\text{no sign}}}$ of an

impending eruption. $\underset{\text{E}}{\underline{\text{No error}}}$

21. Due to the high cost of meat and fish during the Middle
    <u>A</u>                                        <u>B</u>
    Ages, the diet of medieval peasants consisted mainly
                    <u>C</u>                  <u>D</u>
    of cereals, fruits, cheeses, and vegetables. No error
                                                 <u>E</u>

22. Since 1890, the United States has hosted four Summer
    <u>A</u>                        <u>B</u>
    Olympic Games and four Winter Olympic Games,
                    <u>C</u>
    more than any nation. No error
            <u>D</u>        <u>E</u>

23. Of the two methods for predicting earthquakes, neither
                        <u>A</u>
    the search for geological "warning signs" nor the
        <u>B</u>
    statistical study of earthquake events are able to
                                        <u>C</u>
    accurately predict every earthquake. No error
        <u>D</u>                          <u>E</u>

24. When John first began training guide dogs for the
                <u>A</u>
    visually impaired, he had no idea that him and his dogs
                                        <u>B</u>
    would become so important to the whole community.
        <u>C</u>        <u>D</u>
    No error
    <u>E</u>

25. After the teacher realized that no students were doing
    <u>A</u>                                    <u>B</u>
    their nightly homework, she threatened giving a pop
                                        <u>C</u>
    quiz every week. No error
        <u>D</u>        <u>E</u>

26. The deforestation that has occurred in Madagascar is
                        <u>A</u>
    similar to Brazil, although the destruction of the Brazilian
        <u>B</u>
    rainforest has been more widely publicized. No error
            <u>C</u>          <u>D</u>              <u>E</u>

**Step 5**
Practice with
a simulated
SAT test
. . . . . . . . . . . . . . . . . . . .
**382**

27. Although the new documentary <u>met</u> with mixed results
                                   A

    <u>at the box office</u>, most film critics praised it <u>to be</u> an
         B                                              C

    excellent example <u>of investigative journalism</u>. <u>No error</u>
                              D                              E

28. At the Blue Hole sinkhole <u>in the Red Sea</u>, the
                                    A

    overwhelming number <u>of diving fatalities</u> <u>have prompted</u>
                                B                        C

    people <u>to name</u> the underwater sinkhole "the Diver's
               D

    Graveyard." <u>No error</u>
                    E

29. In economics, hyperinflation <u>occurs</u> when a nation's
                                     A

    currency <u>rapidly</u> loses <u>its</u> value, leading to an economic
                 B              C

    crisis and the likely <u>abandonment of</u> that currency.
                                   D

    <u>No error</u>
        E

---

**Directions:** The following passage is an early draft of an essay.
Some parts of the passage need to be rewritten to correct errors
in grammar and word choice or to improve the organization and
structure of the essay.

Read the passage and select the best answers for the questions that
follow it. Some questions are about particular sentences or parts
of sentences. Other questions ask you to consider organization and
development of the essay as a whole. In choosing answers, follow
the requirements of standard written English.

---

### Questions 30–35 are based on the following passage.

(1) There were many dinosaurs roaming the earth in the late
Jurassic period, but there is one that is especially famous
to people today. (2) The stegosaurus, with its spiked tail and
armored plates. (3) Paleontologists have argued about the
purpose of the armored plates that appear on the stegosaurus'
back. (4) It is generally agreed by them now that the plates
were used for defensive purposes, possibly to make the animal
look bigger and more threatening. (5) The four spikes on the
stegosaurus' tail were also used to protect the animal against
attack. (6) Some paleontologists initially thought that the
spikes were for display only because the tail would have had

very limited movement. **(7)** Therefore, paleontologists now believe the spikes were in fact used as a weapon because the stegosaurus probably swiveled its body in combat instead of lashing its tail.

**(8)** The stegosaurus was a large dinosaur with a heavy build, weighing up to five thousand kilograms. **(9)** They tended to have a body length of 20–30 feet. **(10)** An herbivorous animal, the stegosaurus mostly ate ferns, mosses, and low-hanging fruit. **(11)** Some paleontologists believe the stegosaurus could stand on its hind legs to reach fruit hanging from tall trees. **(12)** This is similar to the way bears today stand on their hind legs to reach high-growing berries.

**(13)** Though paleontologists know little about the stegosaurus' social habits, it's likely that the stegosaurus lived in large herds. **(14)** One piece of evidence in favor of the herd theory is the discovery of several baby stegosaurus tracks alongside the tracks of several adults. **(15)** Furthermore, the stegosaurus was a slow-moving creature, so living in a large herd would have provided extra protection against attacks.

**30.** Of the following, which is the best way to revise and combine the underlined portions of sentences 1 and 2 (reproduced below)?

*There were many dinosaurs roaming the earth in the late Jurassic period, but there is one that is especially famous to people today. The stegosaurus, with its spiked tail and armored plates.*

(A) famous to people today; because that is the stegosaurus
(B) of fame to people today, which is the stegosaurus
(C) famous to people today: the stegosaurus
(D) of fame to people today, it is the stegosaurus
(E) famous to people today being that it is the stegosaurus

**31.** Of the following, which is the best way to phrase the underlined portion of sentence 4 (reproduced below)?

*It is generally agreed by them now that the plates were used for defensive purposes, possibly to make the animal look bigger and more threatening.*

(A) (As it is now)
(B) Generally, they are now in agreement of the plates being
(C) Now, as generally agreed by them, the plates were
(D) In general agreement now, they believe that the plates being
(E) They now generally agree that the plates were

**Step 5**

Practice with
a simulated
SAT test

........................

**384**

**32.** In sentence 7, the word "Therefore" is best replaced by which of the following?

(A) However
(B) Moreover
(C) Likewise
(D) Consequently
(E) Incidentally

**33.** Which of the following sentences should be omitted to improve the unity of the second paragraph?

(A) Sentence 8
(B) Sentence 9
(C) Sentence 10
(D) Sentence 11
(E) Sentence 12

**34.** In context, which of the following is the best way to phrase the underlined portion of sentence 15 (reproduced below)?

*Furthermore, the stegosaurus was a slow-moving creature, so living in a large herd would have provided extra protection against attacks.*

(A) (As it is now)
(B) Furthering the fact that the stegosaurus was
(C) With further evidence that the stegosaurus being
(D) However, the stegosaurus was
(E) Considering this, the stegosaurus being

**35.** A strategy that the writer uses within the third paragraph is to

(A) Use exaggeration to make a point
(B) Attack certain false assumptions
(C) Provide evidence in support of an idea
(D) Show disdain for incorrect notions
(E) Stray from the main topic

# STOP

**If you finish before time runs out,
you may check your work on this section only.
Do not turn to any other section of the test.**

# SECTION 4
# READING

### Time — 25 minutes
### 24 Questions

**Directions:** Each sentence in this section has one or two blanks, each blank indicating that something has been omitted. Following each sentence are five words or sets of words labeled A through E. Choose the word or set of words that, when inserted in the sentence, best fits the meaning of the sentence as a whole. Mark your answer by filling in the corresponding circle on the answer sheet.

1. John is a ------- editor: he will catch every punctuation and spelling error, no matter how small, whenever he proofreads his essays.

   (A) flexible
   (B) misleading
   (C) captivating
   (D) meticulous
   (E) reserved

2. Although the talented young runner was not quite ready for the state competition, his coaches both agreed that he was a ------- champion who could win numerous trophies with more time and training.

   (A) questionable
   (B) nominal
   (C) passable
   (D) exorbitant
   (E) potential

3. Most people primarily think of yoga as a ------- discipline intended to improve strength and flexibility, but proponents of yoga claim that it is also ------- for the mind and soul.

   (A) strenuous . . severe
   (B) mild . . grueling
   (C) physical . . beneficial
   (D) fortuitous . . effective
   (E) vigorous . . effortless

4. Clinical trials that study the ------- of experimental cancer drugs are often ------- by the fact that many of the subjects still suffer serious long-term side effects from their first treatments, which were usually radiation or chemotherapy.

   (A) damages . . corrupted
   (B) advantages . . hindered
   (C) effectiveness . . anticipated
   (D) safety . . bolstered
   (E) marketability . . confirmed

5. The politician was the very essence of ------- behavior: he lied, cheated, and schemed incessantly.

(A) duplicitous
(B) repentant
(C) equitable
(D) refined
(E) garrulous

6. The head of the highly profitable corporation was known for his -------, and justifiably so: he donated more than two-thirds of his income to various charities each year and worked tirelessly for numerous humanitarian causes.

(A) altruism
(B) complicity
(C) prevarication
(D) acumen
(E) decorum

7. The importance of objectivity to a scientific study is -------: if any person or group with a vested interest in the outcome of a study has any influence whatsoever over the design of that study, the results will be considered biased and therefore must be -------.

(A) auspicious . . negated
(B) pragmatic . . augmented
(C) axiomatic . . repeated
(D) minimal . . curtailed
(E) monumental . . purged

8. Once the stubborn old mare decided she was not going to leave the warmth and comfort of her stall, not even a handful of sugar cubes could coax her to give up her ------- ways.

(A) precocious
(B) obsequious
(C) recalcitrant
(D) incontrovertible
(E) effulgent

**Directions:** Each passage below is followed by questions based on its content. Answer the questions on the basis of what is stated or implied in the passage and in any introductory material that may be provided.

**Questions 9–10 are based on the following passage.**

Certain learned college professors were once heard discussing methods of literary criticism and interpretation. They spoke of external and technical forms, and how

*Line* magnificently these were illustrated in the world's
5 acknowledged masterpieces of literature. Every work read or studied, they decided, should be carefully weighed, measured, and analyzed, and should be judged solely by the maxims and laws deduced from classical standards. The critical faculty must never be permitted to slumber or
10 to sleep. Above all, the literary student should beware of trusting to impressions.

9. It can be inferred from the passage that the college professors would most likely agree with which of the following statements?

   (A) Traditional literary analysis is essential to properly interpret a work.
   (B) Literary content is more important than technical skill.
   (C) Students may interpret classical literature based on assumptions.
   (D) There is no need to criticize every part of a literary work.
   (E) The greatest literature can be easily interpreted.

10. In line 11, "impressions" most nearly means

   (A) deductions
   (B) intuitions
   (C) certainties
   (D) notions
   (E) conclusions

**Questions 11–12 are based on the following passage.**

The years from about eight to twelve constitute a unique period of human life. The acute stage of teething is passing, the brain has acquired nearly its adult size and weight,

*Line* health is almost at its best, activity is greater and more
5 varied than it ever was before or ever will be again, and there is peculiar endurance, vitality, and resistance to fatigue. The child develops a life of its own outside the home circle, and its natural interests are never so independent of adult influence. Perception is very acute, and there is great immunity
10 to exposure, danger, accident, as well as to temptation. Reason, true morality, religion, sympathy, love, and esthetic enjoyment are but very slightly developed.

**11.** The primary purpose of the passage is to

    (A) convey the irrational emotions of being a child
    (B) describe growth during a certain period of childhood
    (C) argue that all children lack ethics
    (D) discuss the development of a child's brain
    (E) illustrate that adults have no control of their child's development

**12.** According to the passage, the author believes that a child possesses all of the following EXCEPT

    (A) distinct stamina
    (B) innate vigor
    (C) true empathy
    (D) astute awareness
    (E) apparent vivacity

**Questions 13–24 are based on the following passage.**

*This passage is from a collection of short stories by an Irish author and journalist.*

The name stood out in chaste white letters from the black background of the signboard. Indeed the name might be said to spring from the landscape, for this shop jumped from its
*Line* rural setting with an air of aggression. It was a commercial
5 oasis on a desert of grass. It proclaimed the clash of two civilizations. There were the hills, pitched round it like the galleries of some vast amphitheatre, rising tier upon tier to the blue of the sky. There was the yellow road, fantastic in its frolic down to the valley. And at one of its wayward
10 curves was the shop, the shop of Festus Clasby, a foreign growth upon the landscape, its one long window crowded with somber merchandise, its air that of established, cobweb respectability.

Inside the shop was Festus Clasby himself, like some
15 great masterpiece in its ancient frame. He was the product of the two civilizations, a charioteer who drove the two fiery steeds of Agricolo and Trade with a hand of authority. He was a man of lands and of shops. His voice was low, of an agreeable, even quality, floating over the boxes and barrels of his
20 shop like a chant. His words never jarred, his views were vaguely comforting, based on accepted conventions, expressed in round, soft, lulling platitudes. His manner was serious, his movements deliberate, the great bulk of the shoulders looming up in unconscious but dramatic poses in the curiously uneven
25 lighting of the shop. His hands gave the impression of slowness and a moderate skill; they could make up a parcel on the counter without leaving ugly laps; they could perform a minor surgical operation on a beast in the fields without degenerating to

butchery; and they would always be doing something, even
30  if it were only rolling up a ball of twine.

Festus Clasby would have looked the part in any notorious
position in life; his shoulders would have carried with dignity
the golden chain of office of the mayoralty of a considerable
city; as the Head of a pious Guild in a church he might almost
35  be confused with the figures of the stained glass windows;
marching at the head of a brass band he would symbolize
the conquering hero. As it was, Festus Clasby filled the
most fatal of all occupations to dignity without losing his
tremendous illusion of respectability. The hands which cut
40  the bacon and the tobacco, scooped bran and flour into scales,
took herrings out of their barrels, were hands whose movements
the eyes of no saucy customer dared follow with a gleam of
suspicion. Not once in a lifetime was that image tarnished; the
nearest he ever went to it was when he bought up—very cheaply,
45  as was his custom—a broken man's insurance policy a day after
the law made such a practice illegal. There was no haggling at
Festus Clasby's counter. There was only conversation, agreeable
conversation about things which Festus Clasby did not sell, such
as the weather and the results of races. These conversations were
50  not hurried or yet protracted. They came to a happy ending at
much the same moment as Festus Clasby made the knot on the
twine of your parcel. But to stand in the devotional lights in
front of his counter, wedged in between his boxes and barrels,
and to smell the good scents which exhaled from his shelves,
55  and to get served by Festus Clasby in person, was to feel that
you had been indeed served.

The small farmers and herds and the hardy little dark
mountainy men had this reverential feeling about the good
man and his shop. Festus Clasby waited on them with patience
60  and benignity. When he brought forth his great account book
and entered up their purchases they had strongly, deep down
in their souls, the conviction that they were then and for all time
debtors to Festus Clasby. Which, indeed and in truth, they were.
From year's end to year's end their accounts remained in that
65  book; in the course of their lives various figures rose and faded
after their names, recording the ups and downs of their financial
histories. It was only when Festus Clasby had supplied the
materials for their wakes that the great pencil, with one mighty
stroke of terrible finality, ran like a sword through their names,
70  wiping their very memories from the hillsides.

**13.** The "clash of two civilizations" (lines 5–6) most nearly
refers to the contrast between

(A) locals and foreigners
(B) hills and valleys
(C) land and commerce
(D) the refined and the uncivilized
(E) the fortunate and the unfortunate

**14.** In line 9, "wayward" most nearly means

(A) disobedient
(B) lost
(C) aimless
(D) disorderly
(E) random

**Step 5**
Practice with
a simulated
SAT test
..........................
**390**

**15.** In context of the passage as a whole, the word "foreign" (line 10) most likely indicates that

(A) the shop's presence was a strange intrusion on the natural scenery surrounding it
(B) the local townspeople refused to do business at Festus Clasby's shop
(C) Festus Clasby was actually an immigrant from another country
(D) the shop contained a great deal of goods imported from overseas
(E) foreigners were generally unwelcome in Festus Clasby's shop

**16.** The author most likely refers to Festus Clasby as a "charioteer" (line 16) in order to

(A) explain the degree of influence he had over his employees
(B) illustrate the talent he had for working with animals
(C) suggest that he was willing to ship his products over long distances
(D) convey his ease in handling matters related to both agriculture and commerce
(E) imply that he was by nature a highly competitive person

**17.** According to the passage, Festus Clasby's voice can best be described as

(A) vague
(B) soothing
(C) careless
(D) harsh
(E) enthusiastic

**18.** It can be inferred from lines 25–29 ("His hands . . . butchery") that Festus Clasby

(A) often was asked to perform surgery on sick livestock
(B) found working in a shop preferable to working on a farm
(C) was skilled at using his hands for a variety of purposes
(D) did not enjoy butchering the animals for the meat he sold in his store
(E) moved effortlessly from his shops to the fields when he was needed

**19.** Based on the description of Festus Clasby's hands (lines 25–30), it can be inferred that Festus

(A) was hardly ever idle
(B) had received formal training as a veterinarian
(C) was more carefree when he was not at work
(D) tended to rely on instinct rather than experience
(E) moved more slowly than he spoke

**20.** The author mentions the "mayoralty" (line 33), the "Head" of the church Guild (line 34), and the "conquering hero" (line 37) primarily in order to

(A) illustrate the diverse range of customers at Festus Clasby's shop
(B) emphasize how easy it was to imagine Festus Clasby in a dignified occupation
(C) suggest that Festus Clasby had missed his true calling in life
(D) indicate the superiority of Festus Clasby over the local townspeople
(E) imply that Festus Clasby had prior experience in political, religious, and military matters

**21.** The phrase "the most fatal of all occupations to dignity" (lines 37–38) primarily suggests that

(A) there were inherent dangers in the jobs that Festus Clasby did each day
(B) working as a shopkeeper was not nearly as fulfilling as tending to sick animals
(C) Festus Clasby was expected to remain a shopkeeper until the day he died
(D) the customers at Festus Clasby's store were surprised that he had not been more successful
(E) most people did not think of shopkeepers as being especially dignified or refined

Step 5
Practice with
a simulated
SAT test
......................

392

**22.** In line 42, "saucy" most nearly means

(A) rich
(B) impertinent
(C) mild
(D) agreeable
(E) corrupt

**23.** The reference to the "broken man's insurance policy" (line 45) suggests that Festus Clasby had which of the following attitudes toward people in need?

(A) compassionate
(B) stubborn
(C) disdainful
(D) confident
(E) abusive

**24.** The primary purpose of this passage is to

(A) illustrate how one man can shape the evolution
of an entire town
(B) suggest that people can be blinded by the faults
of a person they adore
(C) explain the differences between the lives of farmers
and the lives of shopkeepers
(D) convey the importance of a single shop in the lives
of so many different people
(E) provide a description of a unique man who was highly
regarded by his peers

# STOP

**If you finish before time runs out,
you may check your work on this section only.
Do not turn to any other section of the test.**

# SECTION 5
# MATH

**Time — 25 minutes**
**18 Questions**

---

**Directions:** Solve each of the following problems, using any available space in your test booklet for scratchwork. When you have selected the answer you think is best, fill in the corresponding circle on the answer sheet.

---

---

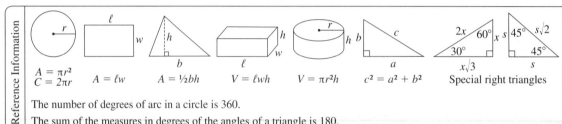
---

**1.** If $5a + b = 10$ and $a = -2$, what is the value of $b$ ?

(A) $-20$
(B) $-10$
(C) $0$
(D) $10$
(E) $20$

---

**2.** Six adults and three children pay $72 for admission tickets to a movie. If an adult ticket is $3 more than a child's ticket, what is the price of admission for one adult?

(A) $3
(B) $6
(C) $9
(D) $12
(E) $15

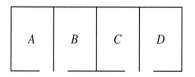

3. The figure above shows four cubicles in an office. Only one person uses each cubicle. Wendy's cubicle is next to Xavier's and Yolanda's cubicle is next to Wendy's and Zack's. Which could be the arrangement of the people in cubicles (A, B, C, D)?

(A) (Zack, Yolanda, Wendy, Xavier)
(B) (Zack, Wendy, Yolanda, Xavier)
(C) (Xavier, Yolanda, Wendy, Zack)
(D) (Xavier, Zack, Wendy, Yolanda)
(E) (Wendy, Xavier, Yolanda, Zack)

4. If circle $A$ has a radius of $a$ and circle $B$ has a radius of $b$, what is the ratio of the area of circle $A$ to the area of circle $B$?

(A) $1:2\pi$
(B) $a:b$
(C) $2a\pi:2b\pi$
(D) $a^2\pi:b^2$
(E) $a^2:b^2$

Janet either walks or rides the bus to school.
Janet never takes the bus when it is sunny.

5. Both statements above are true. If it rained on Tuesday and was sunny on Wednesday, which of the following statements must be true?

(A) Janet took the bus to school on Tuesday.
(B) Janet walked to school on Tuesday.
(C) Janet took the bus to school on Wednesday.
(D) Janet walked to school on Wednesday.
(E) Janet walked to school on Saturday.

$$\frac{1}{4}, 1, 4, \ldots$$

6. In the geometric sequence above, the first term is $\frac{1}{4}$ and the second term is 1. If $n$ is the 98th term and $p$ is the 100th term, what is the value of $\frac{p}{n}$?

(A) $\dfrac{1}{16}$

(B) $\dfrac{1}{4}$

(C) 4

(D) 16

(E) 32

7. If the diagonals of quadrilateral $Q$ are perpendicular, which of the following must be true?

(A) $Q$ is a rhombus
(B) $Q$ is a square
(C) $Q$ has 4 equal angles
(D) $Q$ is a trapezoid
(E) $Q$ is a rectangle

8. If $a^{10} = b^3$ and $b^4 = 5$, what is the value of $b^2$ in terms of $a$ ?

(A) $\dfrac{5}{a^{10}}$

(B) $\dfrac{25}{a^{10}}$

(C) $\dfrac{25}{a^{20}}$

(D) $\dfrac{a^{20}}{25}$

(E) $\dfrac{a^{10}}{5}$

**Directions: For student-produced response questions 9–18, use the grids at the bottom of the answer sheet page on which you have answered questions 1–8.**

Each of the remaining 10 questions requires you to solve the problem and enter your answer by marking the circles in the special grid, as shown in the examples below. You may use any available space for scratchwork.

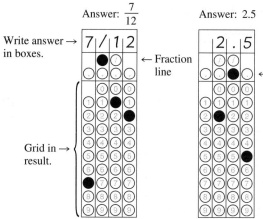

Answer: $\frac{7}{12}$

Write answer → in boxes.

← Fraction line

Grid in → result.

Answer: 2.5

← Decimal point

Answer: 201
Either position is correct.

**Note:** You may start your answers in any column, space permitting. Columns not needed should be left blank.

- Mark no more than one circle in any column.

- Because the answer sheet will be machine-scored, **you will receive credit only if the circles are filled in correctly**.

- Although not required, it is suggested that you write your answer in the boxes at the top of the columns to help you fill in the circles accurately.

- Some problems may have more than one correct answer. In such cases, grid only one answer.

- No question has a negative answer.

- **Mixed numbers** such as $3\frac{1}{2}$ must be gridded as 3.5 or 7/2. (If $\boxed{3\,1\,/\,2}$ is gridded, it will be interpreted as $\frac{31}{2}$, not $3\frac{1}{2}$.)

- **Decimal answers:** If you obtain a decimal answer with more digits than the grid can accommodate, it may be either rounded or truncated, but it must fill the entire grid. For example, if you obtain an answer such as 0.6666..., you should record your result as .666 or .667. **A less accurate value such as .66 or .67 will be scored as incorrect.** Acceptable ways to grid $\frac{2}{3}$ are:

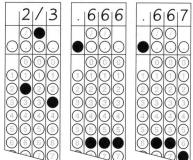

9. A gelato shop has 3 types of cones, 10 types of gelato, and 5 distinct toppings. What is the greatest number of different ways to create an order of 1 cone, 1 type of gelato, and 1 topping?

_____

10. If $10 < 3x + 2 < 20$ and $x$ is an integer, what is one possible value for $x$ ?

**11.** If two squares with areas of 49 are combined to form a rectangle with no overlap, what is the perimeter of the new rectangle that is formed?

**12.** If $2^a \times 3^b \times 5^c = 12 \times 15 \times 18$, what is the value of $a + b + c$?

**13.** If 10 divided by $x$ is 30, what is the value of $x$?

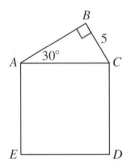

**14.** In the figure above, what is the area of square $ACDE$?

**15.** If $s$ is the sum of the positive even integers between 100 and 201 and $t$ is the sum of the positive odd integers between 100 and 200, what is the value of $s - t$?

**16.** For functions $f$ and $g$, $f(a) = b$ whenever $g(b) = a$. If $g(3) = k$, what is the value of $f(k)$?

**17.** During the last water polo season, Jami played 50% of the matches for 20 minutes, 30% of the matches for 25 minutes, and 20% of the matches for 10 minutes. What is the average (arithmetic mean) number of minutes Jamie played last season?

**18.** If the ratio of the volume of two cubes is 8 to 125, what is the ratio of the surface areas of the same cubes?

# STOP

**If you finish before time runs out,**
**you may check your work on this section only.**
**Do not turn to any other section of the test.**

**Step 5**
Practice with
a simulated
SAT test

..........................

**398**

**Directions:** Each sentence in this section has one or two blanks, each blank indicating that something has been omitted. Following each sentence are five words or sets of words labeled A through E. Choose the word or set of words that, when inserted in the sentence, best fits the meaning of the sentence as a whole. Mark your answer by filling in the corresponding circle on the answer sheet.

1. The dismal critical response to the film ------- the reputation of its young director, who had previously been regarded as an ------- artistic genius.

   (A) upheld . . endearing
   (B) tarnished . . emerging
   (C) affirmed . . indisputable
   (D) damaged . . unpredictable
   (E) cemented . . obvious

2. Most of the ambassadors agreed that the ------- of the large nation into many small, independent countries would be the best way to negotiate an ending to the long-lasting civil war.

   (A) enhancement
   (B) forbearance
   (C) incapacitation
   (D) disjointing
   (E) protraction

3. Over time, the shrewd young businessman built enough wealth and garnered enough power to be considered a ------- in his industry.

   (A) dichotomy
   (B) magnate
   (C) propagandist
   (D) rogue
   (E) miscreant

4. The talented athlete, who was typically known for her modest and ------- manner, surprised everyone with her arrogant and ------- behavior at the celebration after the game.

   (A) reserved . . reticent
   (B) ungainly . . snide
   (C) taciturn . . brash
   (D) unassuming . . beneficent
   (E) indolent . . conceited

**5.** The wealthy widow was well known for her -------: after she inherited her husband's fortune, she made regular and very generous donations to numerous charities.

(A) munificence
(B) jocularity
(C) intransigence
(D) mendacity
(E) erudition

**Directions:** The passages below are followed by questions based on their content. Answer the questions on the basis of what is <u>stated</u> or <u>implied</u> in the passages and in any introductory material that may be provided.

**Questions 6–9 are based on the following passages.**

**Passage 1**

Most people have heard of uranium, the element used as fuel in most nuclear reactors. But few people know what happens to the uranium that's left over.
*Line* Uranium works by splitting atoms, causing a fission
5 chain reaction that produces nuclear energy. But when the energy's been generated, some uranium remains. This depleted uranium ("DU") is twice as dense as lead, so it's useful in a variety of applications. The military uses DU to coat many of its weapons because it allows them to
10 to penetrate enemy armor. Hospitals use DU as shields in their radiation therapy machines. Airplanes use DU as counterweights. But despite its usefulness, DU is a controversial subject—it's toxic to our kidneys, lungs, brains, and many other organs, and with long-term exposure,
15 it could cause cancer and even organ failure.

**Passage 2**

War is terrible, no matter what. But there's a silent atrocity in modern warfare, one that few people know about and even fewer are willing to talk about. It's depleted uranium, or DU. Rockets, shells, and bombs
20 coated with this detestable material are raining down on unsuspecting people in war zones all over the world. Militaries cover their weapons with DU because it can penetrate almost any armor, and may even ignite on contact. It's deadly, horrible stuff, made much worse by
25 the fact that chronic exposure to DU leads to birth defects, cancer, organ failure, and genetic mutations that can last for generations. Thousands of children in the Middle East have already been affected by the horrors of DU exposure.

**Step 5**
Practice with
a simulated
SAT test
. . . . . . . . . . . . . . . . . . . . .

**400**

6. Compared to the tone of Passage 2, Passage 1 is more

(A) bitter
(B) uncertain
(C) tolerant
(D) neutral
(E) mocking

7. Both passages support which of the following conclusions about DU?

(A) Militaries should stop coating weapons with DU.
(B) Chronic exposure to DU has detrimental health effects.
(C) DU is far more dangerous than regular uranium.
(D) Children are the ones who are most at risk for health problems from DU exposure.
(E) Despite its potential health and safety risks, DU is a useful and versatile material.

8. Which of the following best characterizes the relationship between Passage 1 and Passage 2?

(A) Passage 1 describes a potential problem that Passage 2 dismisses.
(B) Passage 1 offers a theory that is criticized in Passage 2.
(C) Passage 2 provides evidence that refutes a claim made in Passage 1.
(D) Passage 1 defends a position that is hinted at in Passage 2.
(E) Passage 2 presents an argument that elaborates on a point made in Passage 1.

9. The author of Passage 2 would most likely respond to the claim in Passage 1 that DU is "useful" (line 8) by

(A) arguing that its adverse health effects far outweigh its potential usefulness
(B) calling for a more thorough scientific study of the effects of DU exposure on human organs
(C) conceding that DU is useful, but cautioning that it should only be used short-term
(D) admitting that the wide range of applications for using DU is a point in its favor
(E) claiming that long-term exposure to DU is not as worrisome as short-term exposure

**Questions 10–15 are based on the following passage.**

*The following passage is from a 1909 book about immigration and race in America.*

"All men are created equal." So wrote Thomas Jefferson, and so agreed with him the delegates from the American colonies. But we must not press them too closely nor insist
on the literal interpretation of their words. They were not
5   publishing a scientific treatise on human nature nor describing the physical, intellectual, and moral qualities of different races and different individuals, but they were bent upon a practical object in politics. They desired to sustain before the world the cause of independence by
10  such appeals as they thought would have effect; and certainly the appeal to the sense of equal rights before the law is the most powerful that can be addressed to the masses of any people. This is the very essence of American democracy, that one man should have just
15  as large an opportunity as any other to make the most of himself, to come forward and achieve high standing in any calling to which he is inclined. To do this, the bars of privilege have one by one been thrown down, the suffrage has been extended to every man, and public
20  office has been opened to any one who can persuade his fellow-voters or their representatives to select him.
But there is another side to the successful operations of democracy. It is not enough that equal opportunity to participate in voting on and enforcing the laws should be
25  vouchsafed to all—it is equally important that all should be capable of such participation. The individuals, or the classes, or the races, who through any mental or moral defect are unable to assert themselves beside other individuals, classes, or races, and to enforce their right to an
30  equal voice in determining the laws and conditions which govern all, are just as much deprived of the privilege as though they were excluded by the constitution. In the case of individuals, when they sink below the level of joint participation, we recognize them as belonging to a
35  defective or criminal or pauper class, and we provide for them, not on the basis of their rights, but on the basis of charity or punishment. Such classes are exceptions in point of numbers, and we do not feel that their non-participation is a flaw in the operations of democratic
40  government. But when a social class is unable to command that share in conducting government to which the laws entitle it, we recognize at once that democracy as a practical institution has in so far broken down, and that, under the forms of democracy, there has developed a class oligarchy.
45  The conditions necessary for democratic government are not merely the constitutions and laws which guarantee equality, liberty, and the pursuit of happiness, for these

**Step 5**
Practice with
a simulated
SAT test
...................

**402**

after all are but paper documents. They are not merely
freedom from foreign power, for the Australian colonies
50 enjoy the most democratic of all governments, largely
because they are owned by another country which has
protected them from foreign and civil wars. Neither are
wealth and prosperity necessary for democracy, for these
may tend to luxury, inequality, and envy. World power,
55 however glorious and enticing, is not helpful to democracy,
for it inclines to militarism and centralization, as did Rome
in the hands of an emperor, or Venice in the hands of an
oligarchy. The true foundations of democracy are in the
character of the people themselves, that is, of the individuals
60 who constitute the democracy.

**10.** In line 8, "bent" most nearly means

(A) prejudiced
(B) crooked
(C) determined
(D) molded
(E) stooped

**11.** In the first paragraph (lines 1–21), the author implies that
the framers of the Declaration of Independence wrote about
equal rights primarily because

(A) it was a compelling topic that would help them gain
supporters in their bid for independence
(B) they felt strongly that their own rights had been
violated for hundreds of years
(C) the issue of equality had never before been used as
a means to win political freedom
(D) it was a uniquely American issue that had been
ignored for too long
(E) they believed equality was the perfect solution for all
political problems

**12.** The author mentions the "bars of privilege" (line 18) most
probably in order to

(A) convey the overwhelming sense of imprisonment felt
by many Americans under British rule
(B) describe the inequality that existed between wealthy
city-dwellers and poor farmers in early America
(C) illustrate the political differences between democracy
and oligarchy
(D) imply that people are considered equal in an ideal
democracy, regardless of their wealth or social status
(E) suggest that gaining equality is a long, slow,
cumbersome process

**13.** The main point of the second paragraph (lines 22–44) is best expressed by which of the following statements?

(A) People who are not morally or mentally fit to vote should receive special treatment.
(B) It is highly unlikely that an entire social class should be unable to vote or otherwise join in a democratic government.
(C) It is unconstitutional to prohibit individuals from voting just because they have mental or moral deficiencies.
(D) Allowing everyone to vote, even if they do not want to, is one of the fundamental principles of democracy.
(E) A democracy will fail if an entire race or social class is not able to participate in the voting process.

**14.** The author mentions "the Australian colonies" (line 49) most nearly in order to

(A) suggest that the Americans could learn a lot about politics from the Australians
(B) provide an example of a democratic country that is still under foreign rule
(C) imply that democracy can take on many different forms around the world
(D) illustrate how easy it is for a democratic country to resist both foreign and civil wars
(E) hint that government in Australia may actually be an oligarchy and not a democracy

**15.** The primary purpose of the passage is best reflected in which of the following statements?

(A) Joint participation of the people is crucial for any form of government to survive.
(B) It is more important to allow everyone the right to vote than it is for everyone to be capable of voting.
(C) People are more enthusiastic about participating in a democratic government than in an oligarchy.
(D) For a democracy to be successful, the character of the people who make up that democracy is more important than the guarantee of wealth, freedom, or power.
(E) People should not interpret the words of Thomas Jefferson or other founding fathers too literally because their words can too easily be taken out of context.

## Questions 16–24 are based on the following passage.

*The following passage is from an 1888 novel by an English playwright and author.*

Little Sara Crewe never went in or out of the house
without reading that door-plate and reflecting upon it.
By the time she was twelve, she had decided that all
*Line* her trouble arose because, in the first place, she was not
5 "Select," and in the second she was not a "Young Lady."
When she was eight years old, she had been brought to
Miss Minchin as a pupil, and left with her. Her papa had
brought her all the way from India. Her mamma had died
when she was a baby, and her papa had kept her with him
10 as long as he could. And then, finding the hot climate was
making her very delicate, he had brought her to England
and left her with Miss Minchin, to be part of the Select
Seminary for Young Ladies. Sara, who had always been a
sharp little child, who remembered things, recollected hear-
15 ing him say that he had not a relative in the world whom he
knew of, and so he was obliged to place her at a boarding-
school, and he had heard Miss Minchin's establishment
spoken of very highly. The same day, he took Sara out and
bought her a great many beautiful clothes—clothes so grand
20 and rich that only a very young and inexperienced man would
have bought them for a mite of a child who was to be brought
up in a boarding-school. But the fact was that he was a rash,
innocent young man, and very sad at the thought of parting
with his little girl, who was all he had left to remind him of
25 her beautiful mother, whom he had dearly loved. And he
wished her to have everything the most fortunate little girl
could have; and so, when the polite saleswomen in the shops
said, "Here is our very latest thing in hats, the plumes are
exactly the same as those we sold to Lady Diana Sinclair
30 yesterday," he immediately bought what was offered to him,
and paid whatever was asked. The consequence was that Sara
had a most extraordinary wardrobe. Her dresses were silk and
velvet and India cashmere, her hats and bonnets were covered
with bows and plumes, her small undergarments were adorned
35 with real lace, and she returned in the cab to Miss Minchin's
with a doll almost as large as herself, dressed quite as grandly
as herself, too.

Then her papa gave Miss Minchin some money and went
away, and for several days Sara would neither touch the doll,
40 nor her breakfast, nor her dinner, nor her tea, and would do
nothing but crouch in a small corner by the window and cry.
She cried so much, indeed, that she made herself ill. She was a
queer little child, with old-fashioned ways and strong feelings,
and she had adored her papa, and could not be made to think
45 that India and an interesting bungalow were not better for her
than London and Miss Minchin's Select Seminary. The instant
she had entered the house, she had begun promptly to hate Miss

Minchin, and to think little of Miss Amelia Minchin, who was
smooth and dumpy, and lisped, and was evidently afraid of
50  her older sister. Miss Minchin was tall, and had large, cold,
fishy eyes, and large, cold hands, which seemed fishy, too,
because they were damp and made chills run down Sara's back
when they touched her, as Miss Minchin pushed her hair off her
forehead and said: "A most beautiful and promising little girl,
55  Captain Crewe. She will be a favorite pupil; quite a favorite
pupil, I see."

**16.** According to the passage, Sara attributed all of her problems
to the fact that

(A) her father had abandoned her at a place she did not like
(B) she did not live up to the expectations of her teachers
(C) her clothes were too fancy and expensive for her
   surroundings
(D) she felt she did not fit the description listed on the
   door-plate
(E) she had not made any new friends at the boarding-
   school

**17.** In line 11, "delicate" most nearly means

(A) fragile
(B) weak
(C) dainty
(D) refined
(E) subtle

**18.** According to Sara's memory, her father left her with Miss
Minchin because

(A) he had no family to leave her with and he needed to go
   back to India
(B) he had heard more praise for Miss Minchin's school
   than for any other school
(C) Miss Minchin had made many false promises to Sara's
   father
(D) Sara's mother had wanted her to go to Miss Minchin's
   school
(E) Miss Minchin's school was the only boarding-school
   in the area

**19.** In line 14, "sharp" most nearly means

(A) lively
(B) abrupt
(C) punctual
(D) intelligent
(E) stylish

**Step 5**
Practice with
a simulated
SAT test
..........................
**406**

20. The author refers to Sara as a "mite of a child" (line 21) most probably in order to

   (A) lament the fact that no one seemed to care about Sara except her absent father
   (B) suggest that Sara was like a parasite who was preying on the Minchin sisters' hospitality
   (C) indicate that Sara was so small and quiet that she was hardly noticeable at the boarding-school
   (D) imply that most parents would not have spent so much money on fancy clothes for a small young girl who would be growing up in a boarding-school
   (E) convey the belief that a lot of girls tend to get lost in the shuffle at a large, busy boarding-school like the one owned by the Minchin sisters

21. According to the passage, Sara's father spent money on expensive clothes for his daughter for all of the following reasons EXCEPT

   (A) He was morose at the thought of being separated from his daughter.
   (B) Sara was the last living reminder of his deceased wife.
   (C) He was young and naive.
   (D) Sara would refuse to wear anything but the finest dresses.
   (E) He wanted Sara to have everything that a little girl from a wealthy family could have.

22. Which of the following words best describes Sara's father as he is depicted in this passage?

   (A) gloomy
   (B) gullible
   (C) carefree
   (D) self-centered
   (E) old-fashioned

23. Sara's reaction to Miss Amelia Minchin can best be described as one of

   (A) fear
   (B) anger
   (C) dislike
   (D) disgust
   (E) tolerance

**24.** Based on the passage, on the day that Sara's father left, Sara thought that she

(A) could make new friends more easily than she actually had been able to so far
(B) would have been much happier to stay with her father in India
(C) was being neglected by the Minchin sisters
(D) would detest living in the boarding-house because the bungalow was much more interesting
(E) might be more ill from crying than she ever had been from the climate in India

# STOP

**If you finish before time runs out,
you may check your work on this section only.
Do not turn to any other section of the test.**

# SECTION 7
# MATH

**Time — 20 minutes**
**16 Questions**

---

**Directions:** Solve each of the following problems, using any available space in your test booklet for scratchwork. When you have selected the answer you think is best, fill in the corresponding circle on the answer sheet.

---

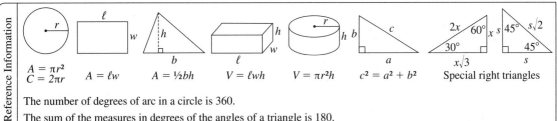
1. If 3200 people all donate $20.00 to the same charity, how much does the charity receive from these donations?

   (A) $64.00
   (B) $640.00
   (C) $6,400.00
   (D) $64,000.00
   (E) $640,000.00

---

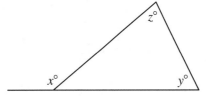

2. In the figure above, $y = 80$ and $z = 40$. What is the value of $x$ ?

   (A) 40
   (B) 80
   (C) 100
   (D) 120
   (E) 140

ESSAY LENGTH

| Pages | Words |
|-------|-------|
| 2 | 640 |
| 3 | 960 |
| 4 | 1280 |
| 8 | 2560 |
| 10 | 3200 |

**3.** The table above shows the essay length by number of words and pages for Karen's typical essay. If the relationship is constant, how many words would a 6-page essay contain?

(A) 1600
(B) 1850
(C) 1880
(D) 1920
(E) 2240

**4.** Pat's snake increased in length by 3 inches each month. If it was born 4 inches long, which of the following functions gives the length of the snake $n$ months after birth?

(A) $L(n) = 3n + 4$
(B) $L(n) = 4n + 3$
(C) $L(n) = 7n$
(D) $L(n) = 12n$
(E) $L(n) = 4n^3$

**5.** If $a$ is five times $b$ and $b$ is seven times $c$, what is $a$ in terms of $c$ ?

(A) $\dfrac{5}{7}c$

(B) $c$

(C) $\dfrac{7}{5}c$

(D) $12c$

(E) $35c$

**Step 5**

Practice with
a simulated
SAT test

..........................

**410**

6. If the average (arithmetic mean) of 5, 7, 12, and $c$ is 6, what is the average of $c$, 6, and 6 ?

(A) 3
(B) 4
(C) 6
(D) 9
(E) 12

7. If $\dfrac{2a}{b} = \dfrac{2}{3}$, what is the value of $\dfrac{3a}{4b}$ ?

(A) $\dfrac{2}{3}$

(B) $\dfrac{1}{2}$

(C) $\dfrac{1}{4}$

(D) $\dfrac{4}{3}$

(E) $\dfrac{3}{2}$

**Questions 8 and 9 refer to the following information.**

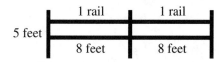

The figure above represents a fence that has two horizontal rails between vertical posts.

8. How many rails will be needed to build 80 feet of fence?

(A) 10
(B) 20
(C) 30
(D) 40
(E) 50

9. If Janice measures a total of 4184 linear feet of wood used in the rails and posts of a fence, how long is the fence?

(A) 262 feet
(B) 523 feet
(C) 1,592 feet
(D) 1,593 feet
(E) 25,472 feet

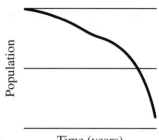

Time (years)

**10.** The graph above shows the population of a species of bird over a 100-year time span. Which of the following could be the data used to create the graph?

(A) | Time | Population |
|---|---|
| 0 | 80 |
| 50 | 100 |
| 100 | 200 |

(B) | Time | Population |
|---|---|
| 0 | 100 |
| 50 | 200 |
| 100 | 100 |

(C) | Time | Population |
|---|---|
| 0 | 100 |
| 50 | 80 |
| 100 | 10 |

(D) | Time | Population |
|---|---|
| 0 | 100 |
| 50 | 100 |
| 100 | 100 |

(E) | Time | Population |
|---|---|
| 0 | 100 |
| 50 | 50 |
| 100 | 100 |

---

$$\frac{1}{2}x - 5 = 7$$

**11.** While solving the equation above, Kevin subtracts 5 from 7, then multiplies the result by 2. What is the difference between Kevin's result and the value of $x$ ?

(A) 28
(B) 24
(C) 20
(D) 5
(E) 0

**12.** Which of the following is equivalent to $2^k + 2^k + 2^k + 2^k$, for all positive integers $k$ ?

(A) $2^k$
(B) $2^k + 2$
(C) $2^{k+2}$
(D) $4^k$
(E) $8^k$

**Step 5**
Practice with
a simulated
SAT test
. . . . . . . . . . . . . . . . .
**412**

**13.** Vern and Wesley use a coupon for 50% off the purchase of a second entrée at a local restaurant. They order the same entrée, and each of them gets a drink that costs $1.50 each. If the bill is $18 before tax, what is the original price of the entrée?

(A) $5
(B) $6
(C) $10
(D) $12
(E) $15

**14.** If $\dfrac{a^2}{b^4} = 1$ and $b^2 + a = 25$, what is the value of $2a$ ?

(A) 0
(B) 5
(C) 10
(D) 25
(E) It cannot be determined with the information provided.

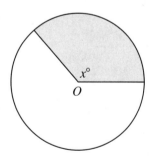

**15.** In the figure above, if the area of the circle is $36\pi$ and the distance around the shaded region is $12 + 4\pi$, what is the value of $x$ ?

(A) 30
(B) 60
(C) 90
(D) 120
(E) 160

**16.** In the coordinate plane, functions $h$ and $g$ intersect at two points, $g(x)$ is a line with a slope of 2, and $h(x) = x^2 + k$. If $h(t) = g(t) = 8$ and $h(-1) = g(-1) = t$, what is the value of $k$ ?

(A) 5
(B) 4
(C) 3
(D) 2
(E) 1

## STOP

**If you finish before time runs out,
you may check your work on this section only.
Do not turn to any other section of the test.**

# SECTION 8
# READING

Time — 20 minutes
19 Questions

**Directions:** Each sentence in this section has one or two blanks, each blank indicating that something has been omitted. Following each sentence are five words or sets of words labeled A through E. Choose the word or set of words that, when inserted in the sentence, best fits the meaning of the sentence as a whole. Mark your answer by filling in the corresponding circle on the answer sheet.

1. The revolutionary new ointment for treating burns is ------- encouraging skin to heal and should, therefore, be ------- more hospitals around the country.

   (A) untested for . . provided to
   (B) pivotal in . . recalled by
   (C) effective in . . distributed to
   (D) essential for . . restricted at
   (E) unconvincing at . . produced for

2. Hoping to ------- the ------- art gallery, artists and patrons joined together to raise funds in an effort to keep its doors open.

   (A) redeem . . nefarious
   (B) rescue . . struggling
   (C) release . . antiquated
   (D) restore . . desolate
   (E) rescind . . unpopular

3. Proponents of bilingual education believe that instructing children in both their native language and English ------- their academic performance, arguing that such ------- in learning leads to improved test scores and a more successful educational career overall.

   (A) bolsters . . multiplicity
   (B) demeans . . homogeneity
   (C) impedes . . eloquence
   (D) maintains . . forbearance
   (E) ameliorates . . mimicry

4. The trail up the mountain was undoubtedly -------: an impossibly steep wall of rock prevented us from even seeing where the path would lead.

   (A) immutable
   (B) circumspect
   (C) precipitous
   (D) ostentatious
   (E) conjunctive

**5.** The teacher, who normally spoke in a gentle and encouraging manner, surprised her students by adopting a ------- tone during a particularly difficult lesson.

(A) moderate
(B) pejorative
(C) melancholy
(D) reassuring
(E) capricious

**6.** The endless series of unbearably boring speeches at the conference left us all in a state of -------: we had no energy or desire to do anything but go home.

(A) effulgence
(B) vigilance
(C) ennui
(D) stupefaction
(E) irascibility

---

**Directions:** The passages below are followed by questions based on their content. Answer the questions on the basis of what is <u>stated</u> or <u>implied</u> in the passages and in any introductory material that may be provided.

---

**Questions 7–19 are based on the following passages.**

*Both passages discuss the issue of disciplining children. Passage 1 was written in 1910 by a well-regarded playwright and literary critic. Passage 2 was written in 1900 by a writer known for her works on parenting, education, and family life.*

**Passage 1**

Experienced parents, when children's rights are preached to them, very naturally ask whether children are to be allowed to do what they like. The best reply is
*Line* to ask whether adults are to be allowed to do what they
5   like. The two cases are the same. The adult who is nasty is not allowed to do what he likes: neither can the child who likes to be nasty. There is no difference in principle between the rights of a child and those of an adult: the difference in their cases is one of circumstance. An adult
10   is not supposed to be punished except by process of law; nor, when he is so punished, is the person whom he has injured allowed to act as judge, jury, and executioner. It is true that employers do act in this way every day to their workpeople; but this is not a justified and intended
15   part of the situation: it is an abuse of capitalism which nobody defends in principle. As between child and parent

**Step 5**
Practice with
a simulated
SAT test
....................

**416**

or nurse it is not argued about because it is inevitable. You
cannot hold an impartial judicial inquiry every time a child
misbehaves itself. To allow the child to misbehave without
20  instantly making it unpleasantly conscious of the fact
would be to spoil it. The adult has therefore to take action
of some sort with nothing but his conscience to shield the
child from injustice or unkindness. The action may be a
torrent of scolding culminating in a furious smack causing
25  terror and pain, or it may be a remonstrance causing remorse,
or it may be a sarcasm causing shame and humiliation, or it
may be a sermon causing the child to believe that it is a little
reprobate on the road to hell. The child has no defense in
any case except the kindness and conscience of the adult;
30  and the adult had better not forget this; for it involves a
heavy responsibility.

**Passage 2**

One often finds, in the modern system of training, the crude
desire for mastery still alive and breaking out when the child
is obstinate. "You won't!" say father and mother; "I will teach
35  you whether you have a will. I will soon drive self-will out
of you." But nothing can be driven out of the child; on the
other hand, much can be scourged into it which should be
kept far away. Only during the first few years of life is a kind
of drill necessary, as a pre-condition to a higher training. The
40  child is then in such a high degree controlled by sensation,
that a slight physical pain or pleasure is often the only
language he fully understands. Consequently for some
children discipline is an indispensable means of enforcing
the practice of certain habits. For other children, the stricter
45  methods are entirely unnecessary even at this early age, and
as soon as the child can remember a blow, he is too old to
receive one. The child must certainly learn obedience, and,
besides, this obedience must be absolute. If such obedience
has become habitual from the tenderest age, a look, a word,
50  an intonation is enough to keep the child straight. The dis-
satisfaction of those who are bringing him up can only be
made effective when it falls as a shadow in the usual sunny
atmosphere of home. And if people refrain from laying the
foundations of obedience while the child is small, and his
55  naughtiness is entertaining, Spencer's method undoubtedly
will be found unsuitable after the child is older and his
caprice disagreeable. With a very small child, one should
not argue, but act consistently and immediately. The effort
of training should be directed at an early period to arrange
60  the experiences in a consistent whole of impressions
according to Rousseau and Spencer's recommendation.
So certain habits will become impressed in the flesh and
blood of the child.

**7.** Unlike the author of Passage 1, the author of Passage 2 develops an argument primarily by

(A) revealing personal anecdotes
(B) referring to historical events
(C) reporting on a scientific observation
(D) challenging a common practice
(E) listing statistical evidence

**8.** The comment about asking whether adults should be allowed to do what they like (lines 3–5) suggests that the author of Passage 1 believes which of the following statements?

(A) Adults typically do not have to face the same level of peer pressure that children do.
(B) There are consequences for the actions of adults, just as there are consequences for the actions of children.
(C) Children are not judged every time they misbehave, so they have different rights than adults do.
(D) Disciplining a child is far more difficult than coping with a misbehaving adult.
(E) Employers are justified in their actions when they judge and punish their employees.

**9.** The difference of "circumstance" referred to in line 9 can best be described by which of the following statements?

(A) Adults who behave wrongly receive a fair trial and are judged by an impartial party, while children who misbehave are both judged and punished by the party they have injured.
(B) Because children are not legally responsible for their actions, they tend to get away with misbehaving far more often than adults.
(C) Parents or other caretakers are allowed to legally defend the actions of their children in a court of law.
(D) The injured party in a dispute between adults is not allowed to determine the punishment for the person who behaved wrongly.
(E) Children do not have any legal right to argue their side of the story and should therefore accept whatever punishment they receive for their actions.

**10.** In line 15, the "abuse of capitalism" most nearly refers to the

(A) neglect suffered by many children whose parents are working
(B) powerlessness that employees have in bringing legal action against their employers
(C) tendency of employers to unfairly judge and punish their employees
(D) popular belief that parents should ignore their children when they misbehave
(E) detrimental effect that a weak economy has on the upbringing of children

**11.** According to the author of Passage 1, children become spoiled when

(A) their parents rely on nurses or other caretakers to discipline them
(B) they receive mixed reactions after misbehaving on a regular basis
(C) their parents allow them to speak out on their own self-defense
(D) they have too much self-will
(E) their parents or caretakers do not immediately punish them for their poor behavior

**12.** In lines 23–28, the author of Passage 1 describes the different ways in which

(A) children may react to being disciplined
(B) society accepts different types of punishments
(C) people may observe the behavior of their peers
(D) parents may punish their children
(E) employers may deal with the poor behavior of employees

**13.** According to the author of Passage 1, using sarcasm to discipline a child often makes the child feel

(A) embarrassed
(B) terrified
(C) remorseful
(D) vindictive
(E) distressed

**14.** The main point of Passage 1 can best be described by which of the following statements?

(A) One of the worst problems in a capitalist society is the unfair treatment of employees at the hands of their employers.

(B) The burden of punishing a person for his or her bad behavior lies with the person most injured by that behavior.

(C) Adults have the responsibility of disciplining their children, but they must do so in a fair, just, and kind manner.

(D) Children do not have all the same rights as adults in terms of the consequences they must face for their actions.

(E) When parents drive out all traces of self-will in a child, that child is likely to become far more obedient.

**15.** According to the author of Passage 2, when a child is behaving stubbornly, parents tend to react by

(A) having a sudden impulse to hurt their child's feelings

(B) feeling the need to display an unquestionable authority

(C) issuing a series of unwarranted punishments

(D) setting down highly unrealistic expectations for their child's behavior

(E) looking only to other parents for advice and guidance

**16.** In line 32, "crude" most nearly means

(A) primitive
(B) raw
(C) coarse
(D) unskilled
(E) vulgar

**17.** It can be inferred from Passage 2 that children who have been disciplined from an early age are more likely to

(A) recognize almost instantly when a certain behavior displeases their parents

(B) blame their actions on themselves rather than on other people

(C) grow up to be obedient and dedicated employees

(D) discipline their own children without using physical force

(E) feel the need to be rebellious when they are older

**18.** In line 62, "impressed" most nearly means

(A) inspired
(B) delighted
(C) imprinted
(D) induced
(E) amazed

**19.** The author of Passage 2 would most likely respond to the claim in lines 19–21 ("To allow . . . spoil it") by

(A) arguing that it is more important to treat your child with kindness than to worry about spoiling it
(B) lamenting the fact that so many parents spoil their children without even realizing it
(C) conceding that some children are spoiled, but arguing that they will still grow up to be productive members of society
(D) agreeing that a parent should immediately punish a child for misbehavior, but further adding that the parent must make discipline a long-term habit and not a one-time event
(E) insisting that it is not about how quickly a parent should punish a child for misbehavior, but how fair the punishment is

# STOP

**If you finish before time runs out,
you may check your work on this section only.
Do not turn to any other section of the test.**

# SECTION 9
# WRITING

**Time — 10 minutes**
**14 Questions**

**Directions:** Each question in this section has five answer choices labeled (A), (B), (C), (D), and (E). For each question, select the best answer from among the choices given and fill in the corresponding circle on the answer sheet.

The following sentences test correctness and effectiveness of expression. Part of each sentence or the entire sentence is underlined. Beneath each sentence are five ways of phrasing the underlined part. Choice (A) repeats the original phrasing. The other four choices are different. If you think the original phrasing is best, select choice (A). If not, select one of the other choices.

As you make your selection, follow the requirements of standard written English, paying attention to grammar, word choice, sentence construction, and punctuation. The correct choice should result in the most effective sentence—clear and precise, without awkwardness or ambiguity.

**Example**

The speaker praised the charitable organization but stressed that more funding is needed if the group is to continue its excellent work in the community.

(A) more funding is needed if the group is to continue its excellent work in the community
(B) more funding is needed for the group's continuing its excellent work in the community
(C) there is a need for more funding so the group continues its excellent work in the community
(D) a need for more funding for the group to continue its excellent work in the community
(E) they need more funding to continue its excellent work in the community

Correct answer: **(A)**

1. People never expected the flood to do so much damage simply because of assuming that the levees would prevent the water from inundating the city.

   (A) of assuming that the levees would prevent
   (B) of having the assumption that the levees preventing
   (C) they assumed that the levees would prevent
   (D) they assumed that the levees' prevention of
   (E) of an assumption that the levees preventing

**Step 5**
Practice with
a simulated
SAT test
..........................

**422**

2. When the cost of gasoline begins <u>to rise, this is when many people begin thinking</u> about taking public transportation.

   (A) to rise, this is when many people begin thinking
   (B) to rise is when many people are beginning to think
   (C) to rise is why many people begin thinking
   (D) to rise, many people begin thinking
   (E) to rise, it is when many people are beginning to think

3. The wealthy young woman, after observing the suffering of the indigent people in her city, <u>there was suddenly a desire in herself to donate</u> most of her money to charity.

   (A) there was suddenly a desire in herself to donate
   (B) she suddenly was feeling a desire of donating
   (C) suddenly the feeling of a desire to donate
   (D) suddenly felt a desire to donate
   (E) she suddenly had the feeling of desiring to donate

4. Many people responded to the job advertisement, but the hiring managers found that most of the applicants were either odd characters or <u>people which did not have the</u> proper experience.

   (A) people which did not have
   (B) they found people without
   (C) people also they found without
   (D) some people which were without
   (E) people who did not have

5. After the tornado destroyed all of the homes in the neighborhood, police officers stood guard at various locations to deter people <u>about their entering</u> the dangerous wreckage to look for their belongings.

   (A) about their entering
   (B) from their entering
   (C) from entering
   (D) by not entering
   (E) not to enter

6. Although the new course sounded fascinating, the students quickly realized the workload was <u>far greater than they had expected.</u>

   (A) far greater than they had expected
   (B) far greater than that of their expectations
   (C) greater by far than their expectations
   (D) far greater than what they expected
   (E) greater by far than that of their expectations

7. The highest court in the United States is the Supreme Court; <u>it consists of a chief justice and eight associate justices, these people are appointed for life terms.</u>

    (A) it consists of a chief justice and eight associate justices, these people are appointed for life terms

    (B) the people who are appointed for life terms are the chief justice and eight associate justices

    (C) it consists of a chief justice and eight associate justices, who are appointed for life terms

    (D) consisting of a chief justice and eight associate justices, appointed for life terms

    (E) it consists of a chief justice and eight associate justices, they are appointed for life terms

8. <u>Funded by a federal art grant, parents from all over the country are clamoring to send their children to the new theatre school.</u>

    (A) Funded by a federal art grant, parents from all over the country are clamoring to send their children to the new theatre school.

    (B) Parents from all over the country are clamoring to send their children to the new theatre school, which is funded by a federal art grant.

    (C) Having been funded by a federal art grant, parents from all over the country clamor to send their children to the new theatre school.

    (D) Parents from all over the country are clamoring to send their children to the new theatre school being that it is funded by a federal art grant.

    (E) From all over the country, parents are clamoring to send their children to the new theatre school, having been funded by a federal art grant.

9. Botany is the study of plants and fungi, <u>especially their structure, development, classification, and ecological significance.</u>

    (A) especially their structure, development, classification, and ecological significance

    (B) and especially they are concerned with their structure, development, classification, and how they are significant ecologically

    (C) especially studying their structure, development, classification, and ecological significance

    (D) especially their structure, development, how they are classified, and their ecological significance

    (E) and especially their structure, development, classification, and with their ecological significance

10. The discussion about rezoning the coastal areas to allow developers to build beachfront skyscrapers <u>have angered many environmentalists and local residents</u>.

    (A) have angered many environmentalists and local residents
    (B) have caused anger for many environmentalists and local residents
    (C) has caused anger for many environmentalists and local residents as well
    (D) have caused anger for many environmentalists and also for local residents
    (E) has angered many environmentalists and local residents

11. The earthquake shook the house, rattled dishes in the china closet, knocked pictures down from the walls, and <u>even throwing appliances</u> off of the counter.

    (A) even throwing appliances
    (B) it threw appliances
    (C) causing the throwing of appliances
    (D) the result was throwing appliances
    (E) threw appliances

12. Survival shows that teach you how to stay alive in the wilderness should offer tips for both desert and mountain regions <u>because the one environment differs drastically from the other in terms of the climate and natural resources it has</u>.

    (A) because the one environment differs drastically from the other in terms of the climate and natural resources it has
    (B) because the two environments have drastically different climates and natural resources
    (C) because of the climates and natural resources they have, which are drastically different
    (D) inasmuch as there are different climates and natural resources in the two environments
    (E) because the one environment differs drastically from the other in terms of the climate and natural resources they have

13. The debate about the design of the new concert hall centered around two conflicting ideas: <u>making it an open-air amphitheater or, on the other hand, to keep it a traditional indoor space</u> with a regular stage.

(A) making it an open-air amphitheater or, on the other hand, to keep it a traditional indoor space

(B) to make it an open-air amphitheater or keeping it a traditional indoor space

(C) making it an open-air amphitheater or keeping it a traditional indoor space

(D) on the one hand, to make it an open-air amphitheatre, and on the other hand, keeping it a traditional indoor space

(E) making it on one hand an open-air amphitheater and on the other to keep it a traditional indoor space

14. After the devastating earthquakes and tsunamis that occurred around the world this year, <u>the number of volunteer nurses who are willing to travel overseas have been much higher</u> than in previous years.

(A) the number of volunteer nurses who are willing to travel overseas have been much higher

(B) the number of volunteer nurses which are willing to travel overseas being much higher

(C) volunteer nurses that are willing to travel overseas being much higher

(D) the number of volunteer nurses who are willing to travel overseas has been much higher

(E) volunteer nurses which are willing to travel overseas have been much higher

# STOP

**If you finish before time runs out,
you may check your work on this section only.
Do not turn to any other section of the test.**

## ⬅ Scoring instructions

Check your answers in Chapter 6. To calculate your approximate SAT score, use the **Conversion table for SAT raw and scaled scores** (pages 4–5).

# Use 2400 Strategies to analyze your answers

Analyzing your answers on the practice SAT test in Chapter 5 is crucial to learning how to think like a 2400 SAT student. This chapter includes a demonstration of how to solve every question on the practice test. By studying this analysis, you will learn how systematic the SAT really is.

The *2400 Strategies* in the explanations are not the only strategies that you can use. I've listed only the primary *2400 Strategies*. In fact, there are several "behind the scenes" *2400 Strategies* that are not listed, but that you should use to solve every question. For example, *Writing 2400 Strategy 1* (Ignore prepositional phrases), *Passage 2400 Strategy 2* (Read actively), and *Math 2400 Strategy 3* (Avoid the calculator) are examples of *2400 Strategies* that you should be using "behind the scenes," even though they are not mentioned in the answer explanations.

I encourage you to look over every SAT answer explanation, even for the questions you answered correctly. This will give you a very good idea of the thought processes that I used to score 2400 on my SAT. Pay particular attention to the SAT Reading and SAT Writing answer explanations, where I focus on eliminating incorrect answers rather than seeking correct answers.

I suggest that you revisit this chapter after you've read the entire book. Answer explanations and *2400 Strategies* that once seemed unfamiliar or even strange to you will now make complete sense.

**Step 6**
Use 2400
Strategies
to analyze
your answers

428

## Section 1   Essay

**Essay score of 6**
• Is 1.5–2 pages long
• Presents a logical and compelling argument
• Offers substantial, strong, academic evidence to support claims
• Has superbly organized ideas
• Displays a mastery of prose
• Contains few grammatical errors

**Essay score of 5**
• Is 1.5–2 pages long
• Presents a logical and persuasive argument
• Offers strong, academic evidence to support claims
• Has well-organized ideas
• Displays a proficient use of prose
• Contains few grammatical errors

**Essay score of 4**
• Is 1–2 pages long
• Presents a logical argument
• Offers academic evidence to support claims
• Has well-organized ideas
• Displays a capable use of prose
• Contains some grammatical errors

**Essay score of 3**
• Is 1–2 pages long
• Presents an argument
• Offers general or personal evidence to support claims
• Has satisfactorily organized ideas
• Displays a capable use of prose
• Contains some grammatical errors

**Essay score of 2**
• Is 0–1 pages long
• Lacks a sufficient argument
• Offers general or personal evidence to support claims
• Has poorly organized ideas
• Displays a mediocre use of prose
• Contains many grammatical errors

**Essay score of 1**
• Is 0–1 pages long
• Lacks an argument
• Hardly supports claims
• Has no organization of ideas

• Displays a poor use of prose
• Contains many grammatical errors

To obtain your SAT essay raw score of 2 to 12, double your self-assigned essay score. If you can't decide between two scores, double the average of the scores.

## Section 2   Math

**1.** (C)
Math 2400 Strategy 7 · *Plug in numbers*
① $k = 5$
  $d = 10$
② Average price = $10/5$ DVDs = $2
③ (A) $kd \quad \rightarrow 50$
  (B) $\dfrac{k}{d} \quad \rightarrow 1/2$
  (C) $\dfrac{d}{k} \quad \rightarrow 2 \quad$ ✓
  (D) $d + k \rightarrow 15$
  (E) $d - k \rightarrow 5$

**2.** (E)
Math 2400 Strategy 7 · *Plug in numbers*
① Point A   $(-4 , 1)$
  Point B   $(-1 , 2)$
  Point C   $(1 , 3)$
  Point D   $(3 , -3)$
  Point E   $(-4 , -4)$
② (A) $A \rightarrow -4 \times 1 = -4$
  (B) $B \rightarrow -1 \times 2 = -2$
  (C) $C \rightarrow 1 \times 3 = 3$
  (D) $D \rightarrow 3 \times -3 = -9$
  (E) $E \rightarrow -4 \times -4 = 16 \quad$ ✓

**3.** (D)
Math 2400 Strategy 6 · *Do the first step*
① $100\% - 31\% - 31\% = 38\%$

**4.** (D)
Math 2400 Strategy 8 · *Test answer choices*
① Test answer choice (C) $\rightarrow 30$
  Multiple of 5?   ✓
  Factor of 100?   ✗
② Test answer choice (D) $\rightarrow 50$
  Multiple of 5?   ✓
  Factor of 100?   ✓

**5.** (E)

Math 2400 Strategy 6 · *Do the first step*

① $a + 10 + \dfrac{1}{10} < a + b + \dfrac{1}{10}$

② $10 < b$

**6.** (B)

Math 2400 Strategy 6 · *Do the first step*

① $(m + 3)n = 13n$

$mn + 3n = 13n$

② $mn + 3n = 13n$

$\dfrac{-3n \qquad -3n}{mn \quad = \quad 10n}$

③ $\dfrac{mn}{n} = \dfrac{10n}{n}$

$m = 10$

**7.** (D)

Math 2400 Strategy 6 · *Do the first step*

① $3\varpi4 = 3(4 + 1)$

② $3\varpi4 = 3(5)$

$= 15$

**8.** (A)

Math 2400 Strategy 6 · *Do the first step*

① $12 = 2(a + 1)$

② $12 = 2a + 2$

$\dfrac{-2 \qquad -2}{10 = 2a}$

③ $10 = 2a$

$5 = a$

**9.** (B)

Math 2400 Strategy 8 · *Test answer choices*

① Test answer choice (C) → $k = 0$

$m(0 + 1) = 0$

$m = 0$ ✗ (problem states $m \neq 0$)

② Test answer choice (D) → $k = 1$

$m(1 + 1) = 0$

$2m = 0$ ✗

③ Test answer choice (B) → $k = -1$

$m(-1 + 1) = 0$

$0m = 0$ ✓

**10.** (A)

Math 2400 Strategy 6 · *Do the first step*

① $x^2 + 3x = 10$

$x^2 + 3x - 10 = 0$

② $x^2 + 3x - 10 = 0$

$(x - 2)(x + 5) = 0$

③ $x = 2$ or $-5$

**11.** (E)

Math 2400 Strategies 7 and 14 · *Plug in numbers and Know your circles*

① $c = 2$

② Diameter of circle = $5c = 5(2) = 10$

Radius of circle = $(1/2)(10) = 5$

③ (A) $10\pi$ → $10\pi$

(B) $25\pi(2)$ → $50\pi$

(C) $25\pi(2)^2$ → $100\pi$

(D) $\dfrac{5\pi(2)}{2}$ → $5\pi$

(E) $\dfrac{25\pi(2)^2}{4}$ → $25\pi$ ✓

**12.** (B)

Math 2400 Strategy 6 · *Do the first step*

① Number of terms: 4

Value of $f(x)$ for 1st term: 19

Value of $f(x)$ for 4th term: 46

② Difference between $f(x)$ for 1st and 4th

terms: $(46 - 19) = 27$

Difference between terms: 3

③ Each value increases by 27/3 = 9

④ Value of $a$: $(19 + 9) = 28$

Value of $b$: $(28 + 9) = 37$

⑤ Value of $b - a$: $(37 - 28) = 9$

**13.** (C)

Math 2400 Strategy 6 · *Do the first step*

① Fargo temperature difference:

$49 - (-51) = 100$

Dallas temperature difference:

$49 - (-15) = 64$

Chicago temperature difference:

$47 - (-38) = 85$

Boston temperature difference:

$42 - (-37) = 79$

Albuquerque temperature difference:

$50 - (-46) = 96$

② $100 > 96 > \mathbf{85} > 79 > 64$

**14.** (C)

Math 2400 Strategies 7 and 8 · *Plug in numbers and Test answer choices*

① $b = 89$

② Test answer choice (C) → $a = 46$

$a° + b° + c° = 180°$

$46° + 89° + c° = 180°$

$c° = 45°$

③ $a = c + 1$

$46 = 45 + 1$  ✓

**Step 6**
Use 2400
Strategies
to analyze
your answers

430

**15.** (C)

Math 2400 Strategy 13 · *Know your triangles*

① $\dfrac{\overline{AC}}{\overline{DF}} = \dfrac{\overline{AB}}{\overline{DE}}$

② $\dfrac{128}{a} = \dfrac{32}{\overline{DE}}$

$32a = 128(\overline{DE})$

$a = 4(\overline{DE})$

③ $\overline{DE} = \dfrac{a}{4}$

**16.** (E)

① Insufficient information

**17.** (A)

Math 2400 Strategy 11 · *Draw a picture*

① Straight line

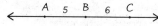

② The distance between Andrew and Candace's house must be 11 miles $(5 + 6)$ or less. (A straight line is the farthest distance three points can be apart.)

**18.** (C)

Math 2400 Strategy 7 · *Plug in numbers*

① Choose a number that makes the burger undercooked or overcooked: $m = 5$

② If the inequality is true, the answer choice is incorrect.

(A) $|m| = 4$  → False

(B) $|m - 3| < 5$ → True  ✗

(C) $|m - 4| < 1$ → False

(D) $|m - 4| < 5$ → True  ✗

(E) $|m - 1| < 4$ → True  ✗

③ Does $m$ always have to equal 4 (answer choice A)? No.

**19.** (D)

Math 2400 Strategy 8 · *Test answer choices*

① Test answer choice (C) → $ab = \dfrac{1}{9}$

$\dfrac{1}{10ab} = \dfrac{1}{10(1/9)}$

$= \dfrac{1}{(10/9)}$

$= \dfrac{9}{10}$  ✗

9/10 is not the square of an integer.

② Test answer choice (D) → $ab = \dfrac{1}{90}$

$\dfrac{1}{10ab} = \dfrac{1}{10(1/90)}$

$= \dfrac{1}{(10/90)}$

$= \dfrac{90}{10}$  ✓

90/10 (9) is the square of an integer (3).

**20.** (C)

Math 2400 Strategy 7 · *Plug in numbers*

① Try placing 0 at different points and plug in values for $a$ and $b$.

$a = -0.5$ and $b = 1.2$

$\dfrac{(-0.5 + 1.2)}{2} > (-0.5 + 1.2)$

$0.35 > 0.70$  ✗

$a = 0.5$ and $b = 2.2$

$\dfrac{(0.5 + 2.2)}{2} > (0.5 + 2.2)$

$1.35 > 1.7$  ✗

$a = -1.5$ and $b = 0.2$

$\dfrac{(-1.5 + 0.2)}{2} > (-1.5 + 0.2)$

$-0.65 > -2.3$  ✓

I. $a < 0$  ✓

II. $|a| > b$  ✓

III. $b < 0$

## Improving sentences

**1.** (D)
(A) Writing 2400 Strategy 11 · *Spot faulty transitions*: "providing" creates a fragment
(B) Writing 2400 Strategy 3 · *Catch unidentified pronouns*: "it"
(C) Writing 2400 Strategy 4 · *Check for verb tense agreement*: "supposing" does not agree with "eat"
(D) ✓
(E) Writing 2400 Strategy 15 · *Avoid awkward phrases*: "being"

**2.** (C)
(A) Writing 2400 Strategy 4 · *Check for verb tense agreement*: "writing" does not agree with "was"
(B) Writing 2400 Strategy 15 · *Avoid awkward phrases*: "being"
(C) ✓
(D) Writing 2400 Strategy 11 · *Spot faulty transitions*: "writing" creates a fragment
(E) Writing 2400 Strategy 15 · *Avoid awkward phrases*: "being"

**3.** (E)
(A) Writing 2400 Strategy 3 · *Catch unidentified pronouns*: "this"
(B) Writing 2400 Strategy 11 · *Spot faulty transitions*: both clauses separated by a semicolon must be complete sentences; "causing . . . earth" is not
(C) Writing 2400 Strategy 6 · *Check for subject-verb agreement*: "causes" (singular) is incorrectly paired with "solar flares" (plural)
(D) Writing 2400 Strategy 15 · *Avoid awkward phrases*: "for this reason"
(E) ✓

**4.** (C)
(A) Writing 2400 Strategy 11 · *Spot faulty transitions*: "depleting" creates a fragment
(B) Writing 2400 Strategy 6 · *Check for subject-verb agreement*: "are" (plural) is incorrectly paired with "excessive fishing" (singular)
(C) ✓
(D) Writing 2400 Strategy 10 · *Conjunct correctly*: no transition present between "peninsula" and "the depletion"
(E) Writing 2400 Strategy 11 · *Spot faulty transitions*: "which" creates a fragment

**5.** (D)
(A) Writing 2400 Strategy 12 · *Compare apples to apples*: cannot compare "a crocodile bite" to "a great white shark"
(B) Writing 2400 Strategy 12 · *Compare apples to apples*: cannot compare "a crocodile bite" (singular) to "those of a great white shark" (plural)
(C) Writing 2400 Strategy 12 · *Compare apples to apples*: cannot compare "a crocodile bite" (singular) to "those of a great white shark's" (plural)
(D) ✓
(E) Writing 2400 Strategy 12 · *Compare apples to apples*: cannot compare "a crocodile bite" to "that of a great white shark's" (great white shark's what?)

**6.** (A)
(A) ✓
(B) Writing 2400 Strategy 7 · *Identify misplaced modifiers*: "sap" is not a "mild toxin that can cause rashes and other skin problems"
(C) Writing 2400 Strategy 2: *Check for incorrect pronouns*: "their" cannot refer to "a daffodil"
(D) Writing 2400 Strategy 2 · *Check for incorrect pronouns*: "their" cannot refer to "a daffodil"
(E) Writing 2400 Strategy 7 · *Identify misplaced modifiers*: "sap" is not a "mild toxin that can cause rashes and other skin problems"

**Step 6**
Use 2400
Strategies
to analyze
your answers
................

432

**7.** (D)
(A) Writing 2400 Strategy 6 · *Check for subject-verb agreement*: "causes" (singular) is incorrectly paired with "particles" (plural)
(B) Writing 2400 Strategy 11 · *Spot faulty transitions*: "causing" creates a fragment
(C) Writing 2400 Strategy 6 · *Check for subject-verb agreement*: "causes" (singular) is incorrectly paired with "particles" (plural)
(D) ✓
(E) Writing 2400 Strategy 6 · *Check for subject-verb agreement*: "causes" (singular) is incorrectly paired with "particles" (plural)

**8.** (B)
(A) Writing 2400 Strategy 5 · *Get parallel*: "how willing they are to obey" is not parallel with the other items in the list
(B) ✓
(C) Writing 2400 Strategy 5 · *Get parallel*: "whether or not they are willing to obey" is not parallel with the other items in the list
(D) Writing 2400 Strategy 5 · *Get parallel*: "how they willingly obey" is not parallel with the other items in the list
(E) Writing 2400 Strategy 5 · *Get parallel*: "willingness of their obeying" is not parallel with the other items in the list

**9.** (E)
(A) Writing 2400 Strategy 2 · *Check for incorrect pronouns*: "they" cannot refer to "a virus"
(B) Writing 2400 Strategy 2 · *Check for incorrect pronouns*: "they" cannot refer to "a virus"
(C) Writing 2400 Strategy 11 · *Spot faulty transitions*: both clauses separated by a semicolon must be complete sentences; "since . . . bacteria" is not
(D) Writing 2400 Strategy 2 · *Check for incorrect pronouns*: "they" cannot refer to "a virus"
(E) ✓

**10.** (E)
(A) Writing 2400 Strategy 14 · *Avoid the passive voice*: "no trace of her was found" is passive because there is no subject doing the finding
(B) Writing 2400 Strategy 14 · *Avoid the passive voice*: "no trace of her was found" is passive because there is no subject doing the finding
(C) Writing 2400 Strategy 4 · *Check for verb tense agreement*: "searching" and "finding" do not agree with "spent" and "vanished"
(D) Writing 2400 Strategy 15 · *Avoid awkward phrases*: "being"
(E) ✓

**11.** (B)
(A) Writing 2400 Strategy 5 · *Get parallel*: "of them accurately depicting" is not parallel with "of their originality"
(B) ✓
(C) Writing 2400 Strategy 5 · *Get parallel*: "they were accurate when depicting" is not parallel with "of their originality"
(D) Writing 2400 Strategy 5 · *Get parallel*: "of them depicting with accuracy" is not parallel with "of their originality"
(E) Writing 2400 Strategy 5 · *Get parallel*: "they were accurate with the depicting of" is not parallel with "of their originality"

## Identifying sentence errors

**12.** (D)
Writing 2400 Strategy 13 · *Don't swap adjectives and adverbs*: the adverb "restlessly" should describe the verb "move"

**13.** (C)
Writing 2400 Strategy 3 · *Catch unidentified pronouns*: there is nothing in the sentence "they" could refer to

**14.** (B)
Writing 2400 Strategy 4 · *Check for verb tense agreement*: the infinitive "to spend" is the accurate "verb tense" in this particular sentence

**15.** (B)
Writing 2400 Strategy 4 · *Check for verb tense agreement*: "after" indicates that the past tense "was" should be used

**16.** (C)
Writing 2400 Strategy 10 · *Conjunct correctly*: the conjunction "but" would make logical sense in this sentence

**17.** (B)
Writing 2400 Strategy 13 · *Don't swap adjectives and adverbs*: the adverb "surprisingly" should describe "graceful"

**18.** (D)
Writing 2400 Strategy 2 · *Check for incorrect pronouns*: "founders" should be used instead to refer to both "Romulus and Remus." Although "founder" is not a pronoun, you can think of it as one in this sentence, because it is substituting for the nouns "Romulus and Remus."

**19.** (E)
No error

**20.** (B)
Writing 2400 Strategy 6 · *Check for subject-verb agreement*: "are" (plural) is incorrectly paired with "volcano" (singular)

**21.** (E)
No error

**22.** (D)
Writing 2400 Strategy 12 · *Compare apples to apples*: cannot compare the number of Olympic Games the United States has hosted to "any nation"

**23.** (C)
Writing 2400 Strategy 6 · *Check for subject-verb agreement*: "are" (plural) is incorrectly paired with "neither the search . . . nor the statistical study" (both singular)

**24.** (B)
Writing 2400 Strategy 2 · *Check for incorrect pronouns*: because the pronoun in the sentence is doing the action of the verb ("become"), the subject pronoun "he" should be used rather than the object pronoun "him"

**25.** (C)
Writing 2400 Strategy 4 · *Check for verb tense agreement*: the infinitive "to give" is the correct "verb tense" in this sentence

**26.** (B)
Writing 2400 Strategy 12 · *Compare apples to apples*: cannot compare "deforestation" to "Brazil"

**27.** (C)
Writing 2400 Strategy 9 · *Know your idioms*: "praised it as" is the idiomatically correct form

**28.** (C)
Writing 2400 Strategy 6 · *Check for subject-verb agreement*: "have" (plural) is incorrectly paired with "number" (singular)

**29.** (E)
No error

## Improving paragraphs

PASSAGE WYMID: "Stegosaurus stands out"

**30.** (C)
(A) Paragraph 2400 Strategy 3 · *Use correct grammar*: both clauses separated by a semicolon must be complete sentences; "because . . . plates" is not (see Writing 2400 Strategy 11)
(B) Paragraph 2400 Strategy 3 · *Use correct grammar*: unnecessary ", which" conjunction (see Writing 2400 Strategy 10)
(C) ✓
(D) Paragraph 2400 Strategy 3 · *Use correct grammar*: unidentified "it" pronoun (see Writing 2400 Strategy 3)
(E) Paragraph 2400 Strategy 3 · *Use correct grammar*: awkward phrase "being" (see Writing 2400 Strategy 15)

**Step 6**
Use 2400
Strategies
to analyze
your answers

434

**31.** (E)
(A) Paragraph 2400 Strategy 3 · *Use correct grammar*: "agreed by them" is passive voice (see Writing 2400 Strategy 14)
(B) Paragraph 2400 Strategy 3 · *Use correct grammar*: awkward phrase "being" (see Writing 2400 Strategy 15)
(C) Paragraph 2400 Strategy 3 · *Use correct grammar*: "agreed by them" is passive voice (see Writing 2400 Strategy 14)
(D) Paragraph 2400 Strategy 3 · *Use correct grammar*: awkward phrase "being" (see Writing 2400 Strategy 15)
(E) ✓

**32.** (A)
WYPAD SOLUTION: "but"
(A) ✓
(B) Paragraph 2400 Strategy 5 · *Revise the underlined portion*: does not agree with "but"
(C) Paragraph 2400 Strategy 5 · *Revise the underlined portion*: does not agree with "but"
(D) Paragraph 2400 Strategy 5 · *Revise the underlined portion*: does not agree with "but"
(E) Paragraph 2400 Strategy 5 · *Revise the underlined portion*: does not agree with "but"

**33.** (E)
WYPAD SOLUTION: "paragraph concerns stegosaurus"
(A) Paragraph 2400 Strategy 4 · *Check sentence and paragraph function*: describes stegosaurus
(B) Paragraph 2400 Strategy 4 · *Check sentence and paragraph function*: describes stegosaurus
(C) Paragraph 2400 Strategy 4 · *Check sentence and paragraph function*: describes stegosaurus
(D) Paragraph 2400 Strategy 4 · *Check sentence and paragraph function*: describes stegosaurus
(E) ✓

**34.** (A)
WYPAD SOLUTION: "transition should reinforce"
(A) ✓
(B) Paragraph 2400 Strategy 3 · *Use correct grammar*: "furthering the fact" is unnecessarily wordy (see Writing 2400 Strategy 8)
(C) Paragraph 2400 Strategy 3 · *Use correct grammar*: awkward phrase "being" (see Writing 2400 Strategy 15)
(D) Paragraph 2400 Strategy 4 · *Check sentence and paragraph function*: does not reinforce
(E) Paragraph 2400 Strategy 3 · *Use correct grammar*: awkward phrase "being" (see Writing 2400 Strategy 15)

**35.** (C)
WYPAD SOLUTION: "uses scientific evidence"
(A) Paragraph 2400 Strategy 4 · *Check sentence and paragraph function*: no "exaggeration"
(B) Paragraph 2400 Strategy 4 · *Check sentence and paragraph function*: no "attack"
(C) ✓
(D) Paragraph 2400 Strategy 4 · *Check sentence and paragraph function*: no "disdain"
(E) Paragraph 2400 Strategy 4 · *Check sentence and paragraph function*: no "stray from the main topic"

**Section 4**  *Reading*

## Sentence completions

**1.** (D)
WYPAD SOLUTION: "thorough"
(A) flexible   ≠ "thorough"
(B) misleading   ≠ "thorough"
(C) captivating   ≠ "thorough"
(D) meticulous   = "thorough"   ✓
(E) reserved   ≠ "thorough"
SELECTED DEFINITIONS
captivating = charming
meticulous = careful

**2.** (E)

WYPAD SOLUTION: "likely"
(A) questionable ≠ "likely"
(B) nominal ≠ "likely"
(C) passable ≠ "likely"
(D) exorbitant ≠ "likely"
(E) potential = "likely" ✓

SELECTED DEFINITIONS
nominal = small
exorbitant = excessive

**3.** (C)

FIRST WYPAD SOLUTION: "physical"
(A) strenuous ≠ "physical"
(B) mild ≠ "physical"
(C) physical = "physical" ?
(D) fortuitous ≠ "physical"
(E) vigorous = "physical" ?

SELECTED DEFINITION
fortuitous = lucky

SECOND WYPAD SOLUTION: "good"
(C) beneficial = "good" ✓
(E) effortless ≠ "good"

**4.** (B)

FIRST WYPAD SOLUTION: "effects"
(A) damages ≠ "effects"
(B) advantages = "effects" ?
(C) effectiveness = "effects" ?
(D) safety = "effects" ?
(E) marketability ≠ "effects"

SECOND WYPAD SOLUTION: "influenced negatively"
(B) hindered = "influenced negatively" ✓
(C) anticipated ≠ "influenced negatively"
(D) bolstered ≠ "influenced negatively"

SELECTED DEFINITIONS
hinder = hamper
bolster = boost

**5.** (A)

WYPAD SOLUTION: "bad"
(A) duplicitous = "bad" ✓
(B) repentant ≠ "bad"
(C) equitable ≠ "bad"
(D) refined ≠ "bad"
(E) garrulous ≠ "bad"

SELECTED DEFINITIONS
duplicitous = deceitful
repentant = regretful
equitable = fair
garrulous = talkative

**6.** (A)

WYPAD SOLUTION: "philanthropy"
(A) altruism = "philanthropy" ✓
(B) complicity ≠ "philanthropy"
(C) prevarication ≠ "philanthropy"
(D) acumen ≠ "philanthropy"
(E) decorum ≠ "philanthropy"

SELECTED DEFINITIONS
altruism = selflessness
complicity = collusion
prevarication = lie
acumen = sharpness
decorum = proper behavior

**7.** (E)

FIRST WYPAD SOLUTION: "crucial"
(A) auspicious ≠ "crucial"
(B) pragmatic ≠ "crucial"
(C) axiomatic = "crucial" ?
(D) minimal ≠ "crucial"
(E) monumental = "crucial" ?

SELECTED DEFINITIONS
auspicious = promising
pragmatic = practical
axiomatic = obvious

SECOND WYPAD SOLUTION: "thrown out"
(C) repeated ≠ "thrown out"
(E) purged = "thrown out" ✓

SELECTED DEFINITION
purge = remove

**Step 6**

Use 2400
Strategies
to analyze
your answers

· · · · · · · · · · · · · · ·

**436**

**8.** (C)

WYPAD SOLUTION: "stubborn"
(A) precocious    ≠ "stubborn"
(B) obsequious    ≠ "stubborn"
(C) recalcitrant    = "stubborn"   ✓
(D) incontrovertible   ≠ "stubborn"
(E) effulgent    ≠ "stubborn"

SELECTED DEFINITIONS
precocious    = intelligent
obsequious    = flattering
recalcitrant    = disobedient
incontrovertible = indisputable
effulgent    = glowing

## Passage-based reading

PASSAGE WYMID: "professors take lit analysis seriously"

**9.** (A)

WYPAD SOLUTION: "something that takes lit analysis seriously"
(A) ✓
(B) Passage 2400 Strategy 6 · *Avoid assumptions*: does the passage mention "literary content"?
(C) Passage 2400 Strategy 6 · *Avoid assumptions*: does the passage mention "assumptions"?
(D) Passage 2400 Strategy 9 · *Criticize every word*: criticize "no need"
(E) Passage 2400 Strategy 6 · *Avoid assumptions*: does the passage mention that "literature can be easily interpreted"?

**10.** (B)

WYPAD SOLUTION: "gut feelings"
(A) deductions    ≠ "gut feelings"
(B) intuitions    = "gut feelings"   ✓
(C) certainties    ≠ "gut feelings"
(D) notions    ≠ "gut feelings"
(E) conclusions    ≠ "gut feelings"

PASSAGE WYMID: "8–12 years old is a unique time in life"

**11.** (B)

WYPAD SOLUTION: "8–12 years old is a unique time in life"
(A) Passage 2400 Strategy 6 · *Avoid assumptions*: does the passage mention "irrational emotions"?
(B) ✓
(C) Passage 2400 Strategy 7 · *Avoid extremes*: avoid "all"
(D) Passage 2400 Strategy 9: *Criticize every word*: criticize "development"
(E) Passage 2400 Strategy 6: *Avoid assumptions*: does the passage mention that "adults have 'no control'"?

**12.** (C)

Try to find evidence in the passage for characteristics that are present.
(A) distinct stamina = "peculiar endurance"   ✗
(B) innate vigor = "vitality, and resistance to fatigue"   ✗
(C) true empathy = "sympathy . . . slightly developed"   ✓
(D) astute awareness = "perception is very acute"   ✗
(E) apparent vivacity = "vitality, and resistance to fatigue"   ✗

PASSAGE WYMID: "urban shop in rural setting"

**13.** (C)

WYPAD SOLUTION: "urban vs. rural"
(A) locals and foreigners ≠ "urban vs. rural"
(B) hills and valleys ≠ "urban vs. rural"
(C) land and commerce = "urban vs. rural"   ✓
(D) the refined and the uncivilized ≠ "urban vs. rural"
(E) the fortunate and the unfortunate ≠ "urban vs. rural"

**14.** (E)

WYPAD SOLUTION: "arbitrary"
(A) disobedient ≠ "arbitrary"
(B) lost ≠ "arbitrary"
(C) aimless ≠ "arbitrary"
(D) disorderly ≠ "arbitrary"
(E) random = "arbitrary" ✓

**15.** (A)

WYPAD SOLUTION: "shop doesn't fit in with surroundings"
(A) ✓
(B) Passage 2400 Strategy 10 · *Choose general over specific*: answer choice is too specific
(C) Passage 2400 Strategy 6 · *Avoid assumptions*: does the passage mention that Clasby was "an immigrant from another country"?
(D) Passage 2400 Strategy 6 · *Avoid assumptions*: does the passage mention "a great deal of goods imported from overseas"?
(E) Passage 2400 Strategy 6 · *Avoid assumptions*: does the passage mention that "foreigners were generally unwelcome"?

**16.** (D)

WYPAD SOLUTION: "could handle both farming and trade"
(A) Passage 2400 Strategy 7 · *Avoid extremes*: authors are rarely able to "explain" concepts in passages
(B) Passage 2400 Strategy 6 · *Avoid assumptions*: does the passage mention "animals"?
(C) Passage 2400 Strategy 10 · *Choose general over specific*: answer choice is too specific
(D) ✓
(E) Passage 2400 Strategy 6 · *Avoid assumptions*: does the passage mention that "he was by nature a highly competitive person"?

**17.** (B)

WYPAD SOLUTION: "chantlike"
(A) vague ≠ "chantlike"
(B) soothing = "chantlike" ✓
(C) careless ≠ "chantlike"
(D) harsh ≠ "chantlike"
(E) enthusiastic ≠ "chantlike"

**18.** (C)

WYPAD SOLUTION: "was skilled and busy"
(A) Passage 2400 Strategy 10 · *Choose general over specific*: answer choice is too specific
(B) Passage 2400 Strategy 6 · *Avoid assumptions*: does the passage mention that he "found working in a shop preferable"?
(C) ✓
(D) Passage 2400 Strategy 10 · *Choose general over specific*: answer choice is too specific
(E) Passage 2400 Strategy 6 · *Avoid assumptions*: does the passage mention that he "moved effortlessly from his shops to the fields"?

**19.** (A)

WYPAD SOLUTION: "was skilled and busy"
(A) ✓
(B) Passage 2400 Strategy 10 · *Choose general over specific*: answer choice is too specific
(C) Passage 2400 Strategy 6 · *Avoid assumptions*: does the passage mention that he "was more carefree when he was not at work"?
(D) Passage 2400 Strategy 6 · *Avoid assumptions*: does the passage mention that he "tended to rely on instinct"?
(E) Passage 2400 Strategy 6 · *Avoid assumptions*: does the passage mention that he "moved more slowly than he spoke"?

**20.** (B)

WYPAD SOLUTION: "Festus Clasby's demeanor exuded significance"
(A) Passage 2400 Strategy 9 · *Criticize every word*: criticize "diverse range of customers"
(B) ✓
(C) Passage 2400 Strategy 6 · *Avoid assumptions*: does the passage mention "his true calling in life"?
(D) Passage 2400 Strategy 6 · *Avoid assumptions*: does the passage mention "superiority . . . over the local townspeople"?
(E) Passage 2400 Strategy 10 · *Choose general over specific*: answer choice is too specific

**21.** (E)

WYPAD SOLUTION: "being a merchant was not respectable"

(A) Passage 2400 Strategy 6 · *Avoid assumptions*: does the passage mention "inherent dangers . . . Festus Clasby did each day"?

(B) Passage 2400 Strategy 10 · *Choose general over specific*: answer choice is too specific

(C) Passage 2400 Strategy 10 · *Choose general over specific*: answer choice is too specific

(D) Passage 2400 Strategy 6 · *Avoid assumptions*: does the passage mention that people "were surprised that he had not been more successful"?

(E) ✓

**22.** (B)

WYPAD SOLUTION: "impolite"

(A) rich           ≠ "impolite"

(B) impertinent = "impolite"   ✓

(C) mild          ≠ "impolite"

(D) agreeable     ≠ "impolite"

(E) corrupt      ≠ "impolite"

**23.** (A)

WYPAD SOLUTION: "sympathetic"

(A) compassionate = "sympathetic"   ✓

(B) stubborn       ≠ "sympathetic"

(C) disdainful      ≠ "sympathetic"

(D) confident       ≠ "sympathetic"

(E) abusive        ≠ "sympathetic"

**24.** (E)

WYPAD SOLUTION: "describe the character Fetus Clasby"

(A) Passage 2400 Strategy 7 · *Avoid extremes*: avoid "entire"

(B) Passage 2400 Strategy 6 · *Avoid assumptions*: does the passage mention that "people can be blinded by the faults . . ."?

(C) Passage 2400 Strategy 7 · *Avoid extremes*: authors are rarely able to "explain" concepts in passages

(D) Passage 2400 Strategy 6 · *Avoid assumptions*: does the passage mention "so many different people"?

(E) ✓

---

## Section 5   Math

**1.** (E)

Math 2400 Strategy 6 · *Do the first step*

① $5a + b = 10$

   $5(-2) + b = 10$

   $-10 + b = 10$

② $b = 20$

**2.** (C)

Math 2400 Strategy 8 · *Test answer choices*

① Test answer choice (C) →

   Adult ticket = $9

   Child's ticket = $9 − $3 = $6

   6 adults ($9) + 3 children ($6) = 6($9) + 3($6) = $54 + $18 = $72   ✓

**3.** (A)

Math 2400 Strategy 11 · *Draw a picture*

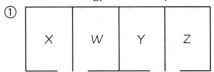

① 

| X | W | Y | Z |

or

② 

| Z | Y | W | X |

**4.** (E)

Math 2400 Strategies 7 and 14 · *Plug in numbers and Know your circles*

① $a = 2$

   $b = 3$

② Area of circle $A = \pi r^2 = \pi(2)^2 = 4\pi$

   Area of circle $B = \pi r^2 = \pi(3)^2 = 9\pi$

③ Ratio of the areas: $\dfrac{4\pi}{9\pi} = \dfrac{4}{9}$

④ (A) $1:2\pi$     → $1:2\pi$

   (B) $a:b$       → $2:3$

   (C) $2a\pi:2b\pi$ → $4\pi:6\pi$

   (D) $a^2\pi:b^2\pi$ → $4\pi:9\pi$

   (E) $a^2:b^2$    → $4:9$    ✓

**5.** (D)

Math 2400 Strategy 6 · *Do the first step*

① Janet must walk to school when it is sunny. It was sunny on Wednesday.

**6.** (D)

Math 2400 Strategy 9 · *Simplify impractical problems*

① First term    1/4
   Second term   1
   Third term    4

② Ratio of third term to first term:

$$\frac{4}{1/4} = 16$$

③ 98th term, 99th term, 100th term

④ Ratio of 100th term to 98th term $= 16$

**7.** (A)

Math 2400 Strategy 12 · *Know your angles*

① The diagonals of a rhombus are perpendicular. A square is a special type of rhombus, but quadrilateral $Q$ could be a rhombus without being a square.

**8.** (C)

Math 2400 Strategy 6 · *Do the first step*

① $b^4 = 5$         $\rightarrow (b^3)(b^1) = 5$

② $(b^3)(b^1) = 5$  $\rightarrow (a^{10})(b^1) = 5$

③ $(a^{10})(b^1) = 5 \rightarrow b = \dfrac{5}{a^{10}}$

④ $b^2 = \dfrac{5^2}{(a^{10})^2}$  $\rightarrow b^2 = \dfrac{25}{a^{20}}$

## Student-produced response section

**9.** 150

Math 2400 Strategy 6 · *Do the first step*

① $3 \times 10 \times 5 = 150$

**10.** 3, 4, or 5

Math 2400 Strategy 7 · *Plug in numbers*

① $x = 2$

② $10 < 3(2) + 2 < 20$
   $10 < 6 + 2 < 20$
   $10 < 8 < 20$        ✗

③ $x = 3$

④ $10 < 3(3) + 2 < 20$
   $10 < 9 + 2 < 20$
   $10 < 11 < 20$       ✓

**11.** 42

Math 2400 Strategy 11 · *Draw a picture*

①

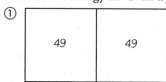

② $\sqrt{49} = 7$

③

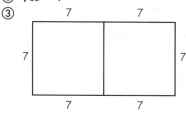

④ $7 + 7 + 7 + 7 + 7 + 7 = 42$

**12.** 8

Math 2400 Strategy 6 · *Do the first step*

① $12 \times 15 \times 18$
   $\rightarrow (2 \times 2 \times 3) \times (3 \times 5) \times (3 \times 3 \times 2)$

② $(2 \times 2 \times 3) \times (3 \times 5) \times (3 \times 3 \times 2)$
   $\rightarrow (2 \times 2 \times 2) \times (3 \times 3 \times 3 \times 3) \times (5)$

③ $(2 \times 2 \times 2) \times (3 \times 3 \times 3 \times 3) \times (5)$
   $\rightarrow 2^3 \times 3^4 \times 5^1$

④ $2^3 \times 3^4 \times 5^1 = 2^a \times 3^b \times 5^c$

⑤ $a + b + c = 3 + 4 + 1$

**13.** 1/3

Math 2400 Strategy 6 · *Do the first step*

① $\dfrac{10}{x} = 30 \rightarrow x = \dfrac{10}{30}$

② $x = 1/3$

**14.** 100

Math 2400 Strategy 13 · *Know your triangles*

① The short side is ½ the hypotenuse in a 30°/60°/90° triangle.

② $2 \times \overline{BC} = \overline{AC}$
   $2 \times 5 = \overline{AC}$

③ $\overline{AC} = 10$

④ Area of $ACDE = (\overline{AC})^2$
   $= (10)^2$
   $= 100$

**15.** 50

Math 2400 Strategy 9 · *Simplify impractical problems*

① Sum of positive even integers between 10 and 21
$\rightarrow 10 + 12 + 14 + 16 + 18 + 20 = 90$

② Sum of positive odd integers between 10 and 20
$\rightarrow 11 + 13 + 15 + 17 + 19 = 75$

③ Difference between 90 and 75 $\rightarrow 15$

④ How is 15 related to 10?
$\rightarrow +(1/2)(10) = +5$

⑤ Extrapolate how $s - t$ is related to 100
$\rightarrow +(1/2)(100) = +50$

**Step 6**
Use 2400 Strategies to analyze your answers

**440**

**16.** 3

Math 2400 Strategy 7 · *Plug in numbers*

① $b = 3$

② $g(b) = a$
$g(3) = a$

③ $g(3) = k$
$a = k$

④ $f(a) = b$
$f(k) = 3$

**17.** 39/2 or 19.5

Math 2400 Strategy 7 · *Plug in numbers*

① Plug in the number of games played $\rightarrow 10$

② 50% of games for 20 minutes
$\rightarrow 5$ games $\times 20$ minutes
30% of games for 25 minutes
$\rightarrow 3$ games $\times 25$ minutes
20% of games for 10 minutes
$\rightarrow 2$ games $\times 10$ minutes

③ 5 games $\times 20$ minutes $= 100$ minutes
3 games $\times 25$ minutes $= 75$ minutes
2 games $\times 10$ minutes $= 20$ minutes

④ 100 minutes $+ 75$ minutes $+ 20$ minutes
$= 195$ minutes

⑤ 195 minutes / 10 games
$= 19.5$ minutes / game

**18.** 4/25 or 0.16

Math 2400 Strategy 6 · *Do the first step*

① Cube *a* volume $= 8$
Sides of cube $a = \sqrt[3]{8} = 2$
Cube *b* volume $= 125$
Sides of cube $b = \sqrt[3]{125} = 5$

② Cube *a* surface area $= (2 \times 2) \times (6 \text{ sides})$
$= 24$
Cube *b* surface area $= (5 \times 5) \times (6 \text{ sides})$
$= 150$

③ Ratio of the surface area of cube *a* to cube *b* $\rightarrow 24 / 150 = 4/25$

## Section 6  *Reading*

### Sentence completions

**1.** (B)

FIRST WYPAD SOLUTION: "hurt"
(A) upheld      $\neq$ "hurt"
(B) tarnished   $=$ "hurt"   ?
(C) affirmed    $\neq$ "hurt"
(D) damaged     $=$ "hurt"   ?
(E) cemented    $\neq$ "hurt"

SELECTED DEFINITIONS
tarnish $=$ spoil
affirm  $=$ support

SECOND WYPAD SOLUTION: "amazing"
(B) emerging        $=$ "amazing"   ✓
(D) unpredictable  $\neq$ "amazing"

**2.** (D)

WYPAD SOLUTION: "break up"
(A) enhancement   $\neq$ "break up"
(B) forbearance   $\neq$ "break up"
(C) incapacitation $\neq$ "break up"
(D) disjointing   $=$ "break up"   ✓
(E) protraction   $\neq$ "break up"

SELECTED DEFINITIONS
forbearance  $=$ tolerance
incapacitate $=$ harm
disjointing  $=$ separation
protract     $=$ extend

**3.** (B)

WYPAD SOLUTION: "powerful person"
(A) dichotomy    ≠ "powerful person"
(B) magnate     = "powerful person"  ✓
(C) propagandist ≠ "powerful person"
(D) rogue       ≠ "powerful person"
(E) miscreant   ≠ "powerful person"
SELECTED DEFINITIONS
dichotomy   = division
magnate     = mogul
propaganda  = bogus publicity
rogue       = scoundrel
miscreant   = criminal

**4.** (C)

FIRST WYPAD SOLUTION: "calm"
(A) reserved   = "calm"  ?
(B) ungainly   ≠ "calm"
(C) taciturn   = "calm"  ?
(D) unassuming = "calm"  ?
(E) indolent   ≠ "calm"
SELECTED DEFINITIONS
ungainly    = awkward
taciturn    = reserved
unassuming  = humble
indolent    = lazy

SECOND WYPAD SOLUTION: "boisterous"
(A) reticent    ≠ "boisterous"
(C) brash       = "boisterous"  ✓
(D) beneficent  ≠ "boisterous"
SELECTED DEFINITIONS
reticent    = reserved
brash       = aggressive
beneficent  = compassionate

**5.** (A)

WYPAD SOLUTION: "generous giving"
(A) munificence  = "generous giving"  ✓
(B) jocularity   ≠ "generous giving"
(C) intransigence ≠ "generous giving"
(D) mendacity    ≠ "generous giving"
(E) erudition    ≠ "generous giving"
SELECTED DEFINITIONS
munificence   = generosity
jocular       = humorous
intransigence = stubbornness
mendacity     = deceit
erudition     = sophistication

## Passage-based reading

PASSAGE 1 WYMID: "discuss uses of DU"
PASSAGE 2 WYMID: "DU in warfare = really bad"

**6.** (D)

WYPAD SOLUTION: "informative"
(A) bitter     ≠ "informative"
(B) uncertain  ≠ "informative"
(C) tolerant   ≠ "informative"
(D) neutral    = "informative"  ✓
(E) mocking    ≠ "informative"

**7.** (B)

WYPAD SOLUTION: "toxic over long-term"
(A) Passage 2400 Strategy 6 · *Avoid assumptions*: do the passages mention that "militaries should stop coating weapons with DU"?
(B) ✓
(C) Passage 2400 Strategy 6 · *Avoid assumptions*: does Passage 2 mention "regular uranium"?
(D) Passage 2400 Strategy 10 · *Choose general over specific*: answer choice is too specific
(E) Passage 2400 Strategy 6 · *Avoid assumptions*: does Passage 2 mention that "DU is a useful and versatile material"?

Step 6

Use 2400
Strategies
to analyze
your answers

· · · · · · · · · · · · · · · · · · · · · · · ·

442

**8.** (E)

PASSAGE 1 WYPAD SOLUTION: "informative"

PASSAGE 2 WYPAD SOLUTION: "antagonistic"

(A) Passage 2400 Strategy 6 · *Avoid assumptions*: does Passage 2 dismiss "a potential problem"?

(B) Passage 2400 Strategy 9 · *Criticize every word*: criticize "theory"

(C) Passage 2400 Strategy 6 · *Avoid assumptions*: does Passage 2 refute "a claim made in Passage 1"?

(D) Passage 2400 Strategy 9 · *Criticize every word*: criticize "defends"

(E) ✓

**9.** (A)

WYPAD SOLUTION: "harmful effects override any usefulness"

(A) ✓

(B) Passage 2400 Strategy 10 · *Choose general over specific*: answer choice is too specific

(C) Passage 2400 Strategy 7 · *Avoid extremes*: avoid "only"

(D) Passage 2400 Strategy 6 · *Avoid assumptions*: does Passage 2 mention "the wide range of applications for using DU"?

(E) Passage 2400 Strategy 6 · *Avoid assumptions*: does Passage 2 mention "short-term exposure" to DU?

PASSAGE 3 WYMID: "examination of American democracy"

**10.** (C)

WYPAD SOLUTION: "focused"

(A) prejudiced    ≠ "focused"

(B) crooked       ≠ "focused"

(C) determined  = "focused"    ✓

(D) molded        ≠ "focused"

(E) stooped       ≠ "focused"

**11.** (A)

WYPAD SOLUTION: "to appeal to the masses"

(A) ✓

(B) Passage 2400 Strategy 6 · *Avoid assumptions*: does the passage mention that "they felt strongly that their own rights had been violated"?

(C) Passage 2400 Strategy 7 · *Avoid extremes*: avoid "never"

(D) Passage 2400 Strategy 7 · *Avoid extremes*: avoid "uniquely"

(E) Passage 2400 Strategy 7 · *Avoid extremes*: avoid "all"

**12.** (D)

WYPAD SOLUTION: "no qualifications needed for certain rights anymore"

(A) Passage 2400 Strategy 6 · *Avoid assumptions*: does the passage mention that "many Americans" felt imprisoned "under British rule"?

(B) Passage 2400 Strategy 10 · *Choose general over specific*: answer choice is too specific

(C) Passage 2400 Strategy 9 · *Criticize every word*: criticize "oligarchy"

(D) ✓

(E) Passage 2400 Strategy 6 · *Avoid assumptions*: does the passage mention a "long, slow, cumbersome process"?

**13.** (E)

WYPAD SOLUTION: "some groups are incapable of participating in democratic process"

(A) Passage 2400 Strategy 9 · *Criticize every word*: criticize "morally or mentally fit"

(B) Passage 2400 Strategy 6 · *Avoid assumptions*: does the passage mention that "it is highly unlikely that an entire social class should be unable to vote"?

(C) Passage 2400 Strategy 8 · *Avoid plagiarism*: "mental or moral deficiencies" plagiarizes "mental or moral defect"

(D) Passage 2400 Strategy 7 · *Avoid extremes*: avoid "everyone"

(E) ✓

**14.** (B)

WYPAD SOLUTION: "example of country owned by another, but still democratic"
(A) Passage 2400 Strategy 6 · *Avoid assumptions*: does the passage mention that "Americans could learn a lot about politics from the Australians"?
(B) ✓
(C) Passage 2400 Strategy 6 · *Avoid assumptions*: does the passage mention "different forms" of democracy?
(D) Passage 2400 Strategy 6 · *Avoid assumptions*: does the passage mention "how easy it is" to avoid wars?
(E) Passage 2400 Strategy 6 · *Avoid assumptions*: does the passage mention that "Australia may actually be an oligarchy"?

**15.** (D)

WYPAD SOLUTION: "democracy good, but not for everyone"
(A) Passage 2400 Strategy 7 · *Avoid extremes*: avoid "any"
(B) Passage 2400 Strategy 7 · *Avoid extremes*: avoid "everyone"
(C) Passage 2400 Strategy 6 · *Avoid assumptions*: does the passage mention that "people are more enthusiastic about participating in a democratic government"?
(D) ✓
(E) Passage 2400 Strategy 10 · *Choose general over specific*: answer choice is too specific

PASSAGE 4 WYMID: "dad put daughter in boarding school"

**16.** (D)

WYPAD SOLUTION: "she didn't think she fit in"
(A) Passage 2400 Strategy 6 · *Avoid assumptions*: does the passage mention that "her father had abandoned her"?
(B) Passage 2400 Strategy 6 · *Avoid assumptions*: does the passage mention that "she did not live up to the expectations of her teachers"?
(C) Passage 2400 Strategy 6 · *Avoid assumptions*: does the passage mention that "her clothes were too fancy and expensive"?
(D) ✓
(E) Passage 2400 Strategy 7 · *Avoid extremes*: avoid "any"

**17.** (B)

WYPAD SOLUTION: "feeble"
(A) fragile     ≠ "feeble"
(B) weak        = "feeble"     ✓
(C) dainty      ≠ "feeble"
(D) refined     ≠ "feeble"
(E) subtle      ≠ "feeble"

**18.** (A)

WYPAD SOLUTION: "had no relatives"
(A) ✓
(B) Passage 2400 Strategy 7 · *Avoid extremes*: avoid "any"
(C) Passage 2400 Strategy 6 · *Avoid assumptions*: does the passage mention "false promises to Sara's father"?
(D) Passage 2400 Strategy 6 · *Avoid assumptions*: does the passage mention that "Sara's mother had wanted her to go to Miss Minchin's school"?
(E) Passage 2400 Strategy 7 · *Avoid extremes*: avoid "only"

**19.** (D)

WYPAD SOLUTION: "smart"
(A) lively       ≠ "smart"
(B) abrupt       ≠ "smart"
(C) punctual     ≠ "smart"
(D) intelligent  = "smart"     ✓
(E) stylish      ≠ "smart"

**Step 6**
Use 2400
Strategies
to analyze
your answers
· · · · · · · · · · · · · · · · · · · · ·
**444**

**20.** (D)

WYPAD SOLUTION: "clothes too fancy for small child"
(A) Passage 2400 Strategy 7 · *Avoid extremes*: avoid "no one"
(B) Passage 2400 Strategy 6 · *Avoid assumptions*: does the passage mention that "Sara was like a parasite"?
(C) Passage 2400 Strategy 6 · *Avoid assumptions*: does the passage mention that Sara "was hardly noticeable" because she "was so small and quiet"?
(D) ✓
(E) Passage 2400 Strategy 6 · *Avoid assumptions*: does the passage mention that "a lot of girls tend to get lost in the shuffle at a large, busy boarding-school"?

**21.** (D)

WYPAD SOLUTION: "bought because loved Sara so much"
(A) True—"very sad at the thought of parting with his little girl"
(B) True—"all he had left to remind him of her beautiful mother"
(C) True—"he was a rash, innocent young man"
(D) ✓
(E) True—"he wished her to have everything the most fortunate little girl could have"

**22.** (B)

WYPAD SOLUTION: "naive"
(A) gloomy       ≠ "naive"
(B) gullible     = "naive"   ✓
(C) carefree     ≠ "naive"
(D) self-centered ≠ "naive"
(E) old-fashioned ≠ "naive"

**23.** (C)

WYPAD SOLUTION: "misery"
(A) fear     ≠ "misery"
(B) anger    ≠ "misery"
(C) dislike  = "misery"   ✓
(D) disgust  ≠ "misery"
(E) tolerance ≠ "misery"

**24.** (B)

WYPAD SOLUTION: "wanted to go back to papa"
(A) Passage 2400 Strategy 6 · *Avoid assumptions*: does the passage mention that Sara "could make new friends more easily than she actually had been able to so far"?
(B) ✓
(C) Passage 2400 Strategy 6 · *Avoid assumptions*: does the passage mention that Sara "was being neglected by the Minchin sisters"?
(D) Passage 2400 Strategy 8 · *Avoid plagiarism*: "bungalow was much more interesting" plagiarizes "interesting bungalow" in the passage
(E) Passage 2400 Strategy 10 · *Choose general over specific*: answer choice is too specific

## Section 7  *Math*

**1.** (D)
Math 2400 Strategy 6 · *Do the first step*
① 3200 × $20.00 = $64,000.00

**2.** (D)
Math 2400 Strategies 10 and 13 · *Label givens and Know your triangles*
①
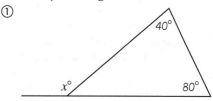
② 40° + 80° + third angle = 180°
   Third angle = 60°
③ Third angle + $x$° = 180°
   60° + $x$° = 180°
   $x$° = 120°

**3.** (D)
Math 2400 Strategy 6 · *Do the first step*
① 6 pages is halfway between 4 and 8 pages.
② What is halfway between 1280 and 2560 words?
   2560 − 1280 = 1280 words
③ Half of 1280 = 640 words
   1280 + 640 = 1920 words

**4.** (A)
Math 2400 Strategy 7 · *Plug in numbers*
① $n = 2$ months
② At birth    $\rightarrow 4$ inches
   1 month    $\rightarrow 7$ inches
   2 months $\rightarrow 10$ inches
③ (A) $3n + 4 \rightarrow 10$ inches   ✓
   (B) $4n + 3 \rightarrow 11$ inches
   (C) $7n$      $\rightarrow 14$ inches
   (D) $12n$    $\rightarrow 24$ inches
   (E) $4n^3$    $\rightarrow 32$ inches

**5.** (E)
Math 2400 Strategy 7 · *Plug in numbers*
① $c = 2$
② $c \times 7 = b$
   $2 \times 7 = b$
   $14 = b$
③ $b \times 5 = a$
   $14 \times 5 = a$
   $70 = a$
④ $\dfrac{a}{c} = \dfrac{70}{2}$
   $\dfrac{a}{c} = 35$
   $a = 35c$

**6.** (B)
Math 2400 Strategy 9 · *Test answer choices*
① Test answer choice (C) $\rightarrow \dfrac{6 + 6 + c}{3} = 6$
   $c = 6$
   $\dfrac{5 + 7 + 12 + 6}{4} = 7.5$   ✗
② Test answer choice (B) $\rightarrow \dfrac{6 + 6 + c}{3} = 4$
   $c = 0$
   $\dfrac{5 + 7 + 12 + 0}{4} = 6$   ✓

**7.** (C)
Math 2400 Strategy 9 · *Test answer choices*
① Test answer choice (C) $\rightarrow \dfrac{1}{4}$
   $\dfrac{3a}{4b} = \dfrac{1}{4}$
   $a$ could equal 1/3
   $b$ could equal 1
   $\dfrac{2(1/3)}{1} = \dfrac{2}{3}$   ✓

**8.** (B)
Math 2400 Strategy 6 · *Do the first step*
① Each fence section is 8 feet long.
   80 feet / 8 feet = 10 sections
② Each fence section has 2 rails.
   10 sections $\times$ 2 rails = 20 rails

**9.** (C)
Math 2400 Strategy 9 · *Test answer choices*
① Numbers (from the drawing):
   5 feet for each post
   16 feet for 2 rails in each section
   ($8 \times 2 = 16$)
   Extra 5 feet for post at end of the fence
② Test answer choice (C) $\rightarrow$ 1,592 feet
   1592 rail feet $\times$ 2 = 3184 rail feet
   3184 rail feet $\times \dfrac{5}{16} = 995$ post feet
   3184 rail feet + 995 post feet
      + 5 extra post feet = 4184 feet   ✓

**10.** (C)
Math 2400 Strategy 15 · *Know your graphs*
① As time increases, the population
   decreases.

**11.** (C)
Math 2400 Strategy 6 · *Do the first step*
① Kevin's method
   $1/2(x) - 5 = 7$
   $1/2(x) = 2$
   $x = 4$
② The correct method
   $1/2(x) - 5 = 7$
   $1/2(x) = 12$
   $x = 24$
③ The difference between the methods
   $24 - 4 = 20$

**12.** (C)
Math 2400 Strategy 7 · *Plug in numbers*
① $k = 3$
② $2^3 + 2^3 + 2^3 + 2^3 = ?$
   $8 + 8 + 8 + 8 = 32$
③ (A) $2^k$      $\rightarrow 8$
   (B) $2^k + 2 \rightarrow 10$
   (C) $2^{k+2}$   $\rightarrow 32$   ✓
   (D) $4^k$      $\rightarrow 64$
   (E) $8^k$      $\rightarrow 512$

**13.** (C)

Math 2400 Strategy 6 · *Do the first step*

① $18 − $1.50 − $1.50 = $15

② They paid only 1.5 times the normal price of one entrée.

$15 / 1.5 = $10

**Step 6**
Use 2400
Strategies
to analyze
your answers
······················
**446**

**14.** (D)

Math 2400 Strategy 9 · *Test answer choices*

① Test answer choice (C) → $2a = 10$

$2a = 10$

$a = 5$

$\dfrac{a^2}{b^4} = 1$

$\dfrac{25}{b^4} = 1$

$b^4 = 25$

$b = \sqrt{5}$

$b^2 + a = ?$

$5 + 5 = 10$  ✗

② Test answer choice (D) → $2a = 25$

$2a = 25$

$a = 12.5$

$\dfrac{a^2}{b^4} = 1$

$\dfrac{(12.5)^2}{b^4} = 1$

$b^4 = (12.5)^2$

$b = \sqrt{12.5}$

$b^2 + a = ?$

$12.5 + 12.5 = 25$  ✓

**15.** (D)

Math 2400 Strategy 14 · *Know your circles*

① $A = 36\pi$

$\pi r^2 = 36\pi$

$r^2 = 36$

$r = 6$

② $C = 2\pi r$

$= 12\pi$

③ Arc length of the shaded region:

$12 + 4\pi$

$\underline{-12\phantom{xxx}}$  (because there are two radii)

$4\pi$

④ Ratio of the arc length to $C$:

$4\pi / 12\pi = 1/3$

⑤ $x = 1/3(360°)$

$= 120°$

**16.** (B)

Math 2400 Strategy 15 · *Know your graphs*

① $g(-1) = t$

$g(x) = mx + b$

$t = (2)(-1) + b$

$t = -2 + b$

$t + 2 = b$

② $g(t) = 8$

$g(x) = mx + b$

$8 = (2)(t) + (t + 2)$

$8 = 2t + t + 2$

$8 = 3t + 2$

$6 = 3t$

$2 = t$

③ $h(t) = 8$

$h(x) = x^2 + k$

$8 = t^2 + k$

$8 = 2^2 + k$

$8 = 4 + k$

$4 = k$

**Section 8**  *Reading*

## Sentence completions

**1.** (C)

FIRST WYPAD SOLUTION: "working"

(A) untested for      ≠ "working"

(B) pivotal in        = "working"  ?

(C) effective in      = "working"  ?

(D) essential for     = "working"  ?

(E) unconvincing at  ≠ "working"

SECOND WYPAD SOLUTION: "available"

(B) recalled by       ≠ "available"

(C) distributed to  = "available"  ✓

(D) restricted at     ≠ "available"

**2.** (B)

FIRST WYPAD SOLUTION: "save"
(A) redeem = "save"    ?
(B) rescue = "save"    ?
(C) release ≠ "save"
(D) restore = "save"    ?
(E) rescind ≠ "save"
SELECTED DEFINITION
rescind = withdraw

SECOND WYPAD SOLUTION: "financially needy"
(A) nefarious ≠ "financially needy"
(B) struggling = "financially needy"    ✓
(D) desolate ≠ "financially needy"
SELECTED DEFINITIONS
nefarious = evil
desolate = lonely

**3.** (A)

FIRST WYPAD SOLUTION: "improves"
(A) bolsters = "improves"    ?
(B) demeans ≠ "improves"
(C) impedes ≠ "improves"
(D) maintains ≠ "improves"
(E) ameliorates = "improves"    ?
SELECTED DEFINITIONS
bolster = strengthen
demean = degrade
impede = hinder
ameliorate = improve

SECOND WYPAD SOLUTION: "diverseness"
(A) multiplicity = "diverseness"    ✓
(E) mimicry ≠ "diverseness"
SELECTED DEFINITIONS
multiplicity = variety
mimicry = imitation

**4.** (C)

WYPAD SOLUTION: "really steep"
(A) immutable ≠ "really steep"
(B) circumspect ≠ "really steep"
(C) precipitous = "really steep"    ✓
(D) ostentatious ≠ "really steep"
(E) conjunctive ≠ "really steep"
SELECTED DEFINITIONS
immutable = unchangeable
circumspect = careful
precipitous = steep
ostentatious = pretentious
conjunctive = connecting

**5.** (B)

WYPAD SOLUTION: "not gentle"
(A) moderate ≠ "not gentle"
(B) pejorative = "not gentle"    ✓
(C) melancholy ≠ "not gentle"
(D) reassuring ≠ "not gentle"
(E) capricious ≠ "not gentle"
SELECTED DEFINITIONS
pejorative = derogatory
melancholy = sad
capricious = whimsical

**6.** (C)

WYPAD SOLUTION: "boredom"
(A) effulgence ≠ "boredom"
(B) vigilance ≠ "boredom"
(C) ennui = "boredom"    ✓
(D) stupefaction ≠ "boredom"
(E) irascibility ≠ "boredom"
SELECTED DEFINITIONS
effulgence = brilliance
vigilance = attention
ennui = boredom
stupefaction = bewilderment
irascibility = irritability

PASSAGE 1 WYMID: "child similar to adult; shouldn't do what he/she likes"
PASSAGE 2 WYMID: "children learn obedience differently"

**7.** (D)

WYPAD SOLUTION: "doubt early discipline training"
(A) Passage 2400 Strategy 9 · *Criticize every word*: criticize "personal anecdotes"
(B) Passage 2400 Strategy 9 · *Criticize every word*: criticize "historical events"
(C) Passage 2400 Strategy 9 · *Criticize every word*: criticize "scientific observation"
(D) ✓
(E) Passage 2400 Strategy 9 · *Criticize every word*: criticize "statistical evidence"

**Step 6**
Use 2400
Strategies
to analyze
your answers

448

**8.** (B)

WYPAD SOLUTION: "children and adults are similar"

(A) Passage 2400 Strategy 10 · *Choose general over specific*: answer choice is too specific

(B) ✓

(C) Passage 2400 Strategy 7 · *Avoid extremes*: avoid "every time"

(D) Passage 2400 Strategy 6 · *Avoid assumptions*: does Passage 1 mention "coping with a misbehaving adult"?

(E) Passage 2400 Strategy 6 · *Avoid assumptions*: does Passage 1 mention that "employers are justified in their actions"?

**9.** (A)

WYPAD SOLUTION: "difference in societal situation"

(A) ✓

(B) Passage 2400 Strategy 6 · *Avoid assumptions*: does Passage 1 mention that children "tend to get away with misbehaving"?

(C) Passage 2400 Strategy 6 · *Avoid assumptions*: does Passage 1 mention "other caretakers"?

(D) Passage 2400 Strategy 10 · *Choose general over specific*: answer choice is too specific

(E) Passage 2400 Strategy 7 · *Avoid extremes*: avoid "any"

**10.** (C)

WYPAD SOLUTION: "employees being wrongly punished"

(A) Passage 2400 Strategy 6 · *Avoid assumptions*: does Passage 1 mention "neglect"?

(B) Passage 2400 Strategy 6 · *Avoid assumptions*: does Passage 1 mention "legal action against their employers"?

(C) ✓

(D) Passage 2400 Strategy 9 · *Criticize every word*: criticize "popular belief"

(E) Passage 2400 Strategy 6 · *Avoid assumptions*: does Passage 1 mention "a weak economy"?

**11.** (E)

WYPAD SOLUTION: "if don't make child immediately aware of misbehavior"

(A) Passage 2400 Strategy 6 · *Avoid assumptions*: does Passage 1 mention parents' reliance "on nurses or other caretakers"?

(B) Passage 2400 Strategy 6 · *Avoid assumptions*: does Passage 1 mention "mixed reactions"?

(C) Passage 2400 Strategy 9 · *Criticize every word*: criticize "self-defense"

(D) Passage 2400 Strategy 9 · *Criticize every word*: criticize "self-will"

(E) ✓

**12.** (D)

WYPAD SOLUTION: "ways to discipline a child"

(A) Passage 2400 Strategy 6 · *Avoid assumptions*: does Passage 1 mention how "children may react to being disciplined"?

(B) Passage 2400 Strategy 6 · *Avoid assumptions*: does Passage 1 mention how "society accepts different types of punishments"?

(C) Passage 2400 Strategy 6 · *Avoid assumptions*: does Passage 1 mention "peers"?

(D) ✓

(E) Passage 2400 Strategy 6 · *Avoid assumptions*: does Passage 1 mention the "poor behavior of employees"?

**13.** (A)

WYPAD SOLUTION: "embarrassed"

(A) embarrassed = "embarrassed"  ✓

(B) terrified      ≠ "embarrassed"

(C) remorseful    ≠ "embarrassed"

(D) vindictive    ≠ "embarrassed"

(E) distressed    ≠ "embarrassed"

**14.** (C)

WYPAD SOLUTION: "parents should discipline child immediately"

(A) Passage 2400 Strategy 6 · *Avoid assumptions*: does Passage 1 focus on "the unfair treatment of employees"?

(B) Passage 2400 Strategy 6 · *Avoid assumptions*: does Passage 1 mention that "the burden of punishing . . . lies with the person most injured"?

(C) ✓

(D) Passage 2400 Strategy 7 · *Avoid extremes*: avoid "all"

(E) Passage 2400 Strategy 7 · *Avoid extremes*: avoid "all"

**15.** (B)

WYPAD SOLUTION: "to eliminate what the child's will is"

(A) Passage 2400 Strategy 6 · *Avoid assumptions*: does Passage 2 mention "a child's feelings"?

(B) ✓

(C) Passage 2400 Strategy 9 · *Criticize every word*: criticize "series"

(D) Passage 2400 Strategy 10 · *Choose general over specific*: answer choice is too specific

(E) Passage 2400 Strategy 7 · *Avoid extremes*: avoid "only"

**16.** (A)

WYPAD SOLUTION: "primal"

(A) primitive = "primal"  ✓

(B) raw ≠ "primal"

(C) coarse ≠ "primal"

(D) unskilled ≠ "primal"

(E) vulgar ≠ "primal"

**17.** (A)

WYPAD SOLUTION: "to know wrong actions"

(A) ✓

(B) Passage 2400 Strategy 9 · *Criticize every word*: criticize "other people"

(C) Passage 2400 Strategy 6 · *Avoid assumptions*: does Passage 2 mention "employees"?

(D) Passage 2400 Strategy 6 · *Avoid assumptions*: does Passage 2 mention "without using physical force"?

(E) Passage 2400 Strategy 6 · *Avoid assumptions*: does Passage 2 mention "rebellious" children?

**18.** (C)

WYPAD SOLUTION: "permanent"

(A) inspired ≠ "permanent"

(B) delighted ≠ "permanent"

(C) imprinted = "permanent"  ✓

(D) induced ≠ "permanent"

(E) amazed ≠ "permanent"

**19.** (D)

WYPAD SOLUTION: "discipline should be continuing"

(A) Passage 2400 Strategy 6 · *Avoid assumptions*: does Passage 2 mention "spoiling" children?

(B) Passage 2400 Strategy 6 · *Avoid assumptions*: does Passage 2 mention that parents "spoil their children"?

(C) Passage 2400 Strategy 6 · *Avoid assumptions*: does Passage 2 mention "spoiling children"?

(D) ✓

(E) Passage 2400 Strategy 10 · *Choose general over specific*: answer choice is too specific

## Improving sentences

**1.** (C)
(A) Writing 2400 Strategy 4 · *Check for verb tense agreement*: "assuming" does not agree with "expected"
(B) Writing 2400 Strategy 4 · *Check for verb tense agreement*: "having" does not agree with "expected"
(C) ✓
(D) Writing 2400 Strategy 11 · *Spot faulty transitions*: "prevention of" creates a fragment
(E) Writing 2400 Strategy 4 · *Check for verb tense agreement*: "preventing" does not agree with "expected"

**2.** (D)
(A) Writing 2400 Strategy 3 · *Catch unidentified pronouns*: "this"
(B) Writing 2400 Strategy 15 · *Avoid awkward phrases*: "is when"
(C) Writing 2400 Strategy 15 · *Avoid awkward phrases*: "is why"
(D) ✓
(E) Writing 2400 Strategy 3 · *Catch unidentified pronouns*: "it"

**3.** (D)
(A) Writing 2400 Strategy 10 · *Conjunct correctly*: no transition present between "woman" and "there"
(B) Writing 2400 Strategy 8 · *Recognize redundancy*: "she" appears after "young woman"
(C) Writing 2400 Strategy 11 · *Spot faulty transitions*: "the feeling" creates a fragment
(D) ✓
(E) Writing 2400 Strategy 8 · *Recognize redundancy*: "she" appears after "young woman"

**4.** (E)
(A) Writing 2400 Strategy 2 · *Check for incorrect pronouns*: "which" cannot refer to "people"
(B) Writing 2400 Strategy 3 · *Catch unidentified pronouns*: "they" could refer to the "managers" or the "applicants"
(C) Writing 2400 Strategy 3 · *Catch unidentified pronouns*: "they" could refer to the "managers" or the "applicants"
(D) Writing 2400 Strategy 2 · *Check for incorrect pronouns*: "which" cannot refer to "people"
(E) ✓

**5.** (C)
(A) Writing 2400 Strategy 9 · *Know your idioms*: "deter about" is idiomatically incorrect
(B) Writing 2400 Strategy 8 · *Recognize redundancy*: "their" unnecessarily appears after "people"
(C) ✓
(D) Writing 2400 Strategy 9 · *Know your idioms*: "deter by" is idiomatically incorrect
(E) Writing 2400 Strategy 9 · *Know your idioms*: "deter not" is idiomatically incorrect

**6.** (A)
(A) ✓
(B) Writing 2400 Strategy 3 · *Catch unidentified pronouns*: "that"
(C) Writing 2400 Strategy 12 · *Compare apples to apples*: cannot compare "workload" to "expectations"
(D) Writing 2400 Strategy 4 · *Check for verb tense agreement*: because two or more events are occurring in the past in relation to one another, the past perfect tense is required, not the simple past tense
(E) Writing 2400 Strategy 3 · *Catch unidentified pronouns*: "that"

Step 6
Use 2400
Strategies
to analyze
your answers

450

**7.** (C)

(A) Writing 2400 Strategy 8 · *Recognize redundancy*: "these people" unnecessarily appears after "chief justice and eight associate justices"

(B) Writing 2400 Strategy 8 · *Recognize redundancy*: "are" appears twice

(C) ✓

(D) Writing 2400 Strategy 11 · *Spot faulty transitions*: both clauses separated by a semicolon must be complete sentences; "consisting . . . terms" is not

(E) Writing 2400 Strategy 8 · *Recognize redundancy*: "they" unnecessarily appears after "chief justice and eight associate justices"

**8.** (B)

(A) Writing 2400 Strategy 7 · *Identify misplaced modifiers*: "parents" are not "funded by a federal art grant"

(B) ✓

(C) Writing 2400 Strategy 7 · *Identify misplaced modifiers*: "parents" have not been "funded by a federal art grant"

(D) Writing 2400 Strategy 15 · *Avoid awkward phrases*: "being"

(E) Writing 2400 Strategy 4 · *Check for verb tense agreement*: "having been" does not agree with "are"

**9.** (A)

(A) ✓

(B) Writing 2400 Strategy 3 · *Catch unidentified pronouns*: "they"

(C) Writing 2400 Strategy 8 · *Recognize redundancy*: "studying" unnecessarily appears after "study"

(D) Writing 2400 Strategy 5 · *Get parallel*: "how they are classified" is not parallel with the other items in the list

(E) Writing 2400 Strategy 8 · *Recognize redundancy*: "their" appears twice

**10.** (E)

(A) Writing 2400 Strategy 6 · *Check for subject-verb agreement*: "have" (plural) is incorrectly paired with "discussion" (singular)

(B) Writing 2400 Strategy 6 · *Check for subject-verb agreement*: "have" (plural) is incorrectly paired with "discussion" (singular)

(C) Writing 2400 Strategy 8 · *Recognize redundancy*: unnecessarily wordy

(D) Writing 2400 Strategy 6 · *Check for subject-verb agreement*: "have" (plural) is incorrectly paired with "discussion" (singular)

(E) ✓

**11.** (E)

(A) Writing 2400 Strategy 5 · *Get parallel*: "even throwing appliances" is not parallel with the other items in the list

(B) Writing 2400 Strategy 8 · *Recognize redundancy*: "it" appears after "earthquake"

(C) Writing 2400 Strategy 5 · *Get parallel*: "causing the throwing of appliances" is not parallel with the other items in the list

(D) Writing 2400 Strategy 5 · *Get parallel*: "the result was throwing appliances" is not parallel with the other items in the list

(E) ✓

**12.** (B)

(A) Writing 2400 Strategy 3 · *Catch unidentified pronouns*: "it"

(B) ✓

(C) Writing 2400 Strategy 3 · *Catch unidentified pronouns*: "they"

(D) Writing 2400 Strategy 10 · *Conjunct correctly*: "inasmuch as" does not make sense in this sentence

(E) Writing 2400 Strategy 3 · *Catch unidentified pronouns*: "they"

**13.** (C)

(A) Writing 2400 Strategy 5 · *Get parallel*:
  "making it" is not parallel with "to keep it"

(B) Writing 2400 Strategy 5 · *Get parallel*: "to
  make it" is not parallel with "keeping it"

(C) ✓

(D) Writing 2400 Strategy 5 · *Get parallel*: "to
  make it" is not parallel with "keeping it"

(E) Writing 2400 Strategy 5 · *Get parallel*:
  "making it" is not parallel with "to keep it"

**14.** (D)

(A) Writing 2400 Strategy 6 · *Check for
  subject-verb agreement*: "have" (plural)
  is incorrectly paired with "number"
  (singular)

(B) Writing 2400 Strategy 15 · *Avoid awkward
  phrases*: "being"

(C) Writing 2400 Strategy 15 · *Avoid awkward
  phrases*: "being"

(D) ✓

(E) Writing 2400 Strategy 2 · *Check for
  incorrect pronouns*: "which" cannot refer
  to "nurses"

# Do's and don'ts for test day

The night before and the morning of your SAT test can be nerve-racking. Emotions run high, and your state of mind on test day can significantly impact your SAT score. Remember one thing on the day you take the SAT: Be calm.

## Checklists

The following checklists will help you keep your composure.

### Do's

- Do relax the week leading up to the SAT. Do only a light amount of *2400 Practice,* and don't worry about reviewing every concept.
- Do get a good night's sleep.
- Do eat a wholesome dinner the night before, and a wholesome breakfast the morning of, the test. Eat natural foods (fruit, for example) and whole grains (oats, for example) to assure sustained energy during the test.
- Do stay as focused as possible during the test.
- Do remain calm, even if there are concepts you don't recognize on the test. The questions you aren't familiar with will be in the minority.

### Don'ts

- Don't worry about SAT details that you haven't studied. Most of these details won't appear on the test.
- Don't worry that you might forget a particular *SAT 2400 Strategy*. You will be able to recall the strategy when you encounter a question that requires it.
- Don't take stimulants such as energy drinks; these will cause your heart to race during the test.
- Don't make the SAT a bigger deal than it is. Reassure yourself that you have prepared well for the test and that you can take it again, if necessary. Downplaying the test's importance will work to your advantage.

## My 2400 test day

**Step 7**
Do's and
don'ts for
test day

454

I took the SAT three times in high school. My first two attempts were filled with anxiety.

I didn't relax the week before.

I didn't get a good night's sleep.

I didn't eat well the night before or the morning of.

I didn't stay focused during the test.

I didn't remain calm when I encountered concepts I didn't recognize.

I did worry about SAT details that I hadn't reviewed.

I did worry that I might have forgotten a particular SAT strategy.

I did take stimulants—two energy drinks!

I did make the SAT a bigger deal than it was.

My first two attempts at the SAT were much more stressful than they needed to be.

When I took the SAT the third time, however, I was completely calm. My relaxed and focused state of mind during the test made all the difference. It was actually flooding the day of my exam, and when I got out of the car, I stepped directly into a pool of ice-cold water. Because I was wearing canvas shoes, the water immediately soaked my feet. I ran to the restroom and got rid of my socks, so I wouldn't make funny, squeaky noises when I walked. Too embarrassed to expose my bare feet during the SAT, I took the entire test while my feet were freezing in my wet shoes. But through it all, I remained calm.

If you think you're having a bad SAT morning, consider that you may score high anyway—if you keep your cool!

I wish you the best on your test day and hope that this guide has helped you with your SAT and college goals. (If you decide to take the SAT with ice-cold feet, be sure to let me know how it goes. Maybe that's the secret!)

---

## ◄ Did this book help?

Did this book help you improve your SAT score, get into the college of your choice, and win scholarships? Drop me a line at testimonials@2400expert.com . . . I'd love to hear about it!

# 9,204,375

students have taken the new official SAT test*

# 1,874

students have achieved a perfect SAT score of 2400*

# 1

of those 1,874 students has authored a full-length SAT prep book

## Shaan Patel

wasn't a good standardized-test taker in high school. He grew up in a small motel and attended urban public schools in disadvantaged neighborhoods. The first time he took a practice SAT, he scored 1760. Although the score was respectable, Shaan wasn't satisfied. In the summer of 2006, he adopted a no-nonsense approach to SAT preparation and mastered the effective strategies of the SAT elite. In his senior year, Shaan took the October 2006 SAT and achieved what less than .02% of high school students have: a perfect 2400.

Shaan's 2400 took his academic success to new heights: He gained admission to prestigious universities, secured over $230,000 in scholarships, and received several national awards, such as Presidential Scholar, *USA Today*'s All-USA High School Academic Team Honorable Mention, and National Merit Finalist. Shaan currently attends the Keck School of Medicine at USC and plans to become a physician.

Shaan wrote *SAT 2400 in Just 7 Steps* to help students across the nation achieve their SAT and college goals. He hopes this book will open the gates of elite SAT preparation to students from all backgrounds.

*Estimated through 2011.